Progress in
EXPERIMENTAL PERSONALITY RESEARCH

VOLUME 4

CONTRIBUTORS TO THIS VOLUME

WILLIAM E. BROEN, JR.

SEYMOUR EPSTEIN

HENRY L. MINTON

ROSS D. PARKE

K. EDWARD RENNER

LOWELL H. STORMS

RICHARD H. WALTERS

LEONARD WORELL

PROGRESS IN
Experimental
Personality Research

Edited by Brendan A. Maher

DEPARTMENT OF PSYCHOLOGY
BRANDEIS UNIVERSITY
WALTHAM, MASSACHUSETTS

VOLUME 4

1967

ACADEMIC PRESS   New York and London

ACADEMIC PRESS INC.
111 Fifth Avenue, New York, New York 10003

United Kingdom Edition published by
ACADEMIC PRESS INC. (LONDON) LTD.
Berkeley Square House, London W.1

LIBRARY OF CONGRESS CATALOG CARD NUMBER: 64-8034

Second Printing, 1972

PRINTED IN THE UNITED STATES OF AMERICA

CONTRIBUTORS

Numbers in parentheses indicate the pages on which the authors' contributions begin.

WILLIAM E. BROEN, JR. (269), *Department of Psychology, University of California, Los Angeles, California*

SEYMOUR EPSTEIN (1), *Department of Psychology, University of Massachusetts, Amherst, Massachusetts*

HENRY L. MINTON (229), *Department of Psychology, State University of New York, Albany, New York*[1]

ROSS D. PARKE (179), *Department of Psychology, University of Wisconsin, Madison, Wisconsin*

K. EDWARD RENNER (127), *Department of Psychology, University of Illinois, Urbana, Illinois*

LOWELL H. STORMS (269), *Neuropsychiatric Institute, University of California Center for the Health Sciences, Los Angeles, California*

RICHARD H. WALTERS (179), *Department of Psychology, University of Waterloo, Waterloo, Ontario*

LEONARD WORELL (91), *Department of Psychology, University of Kentucky, Lexington, Kentucky*

---

[1] Present Address: Department of Psychology Miami University, Oxford, Ohio.

PREFACE

Personality researchers have been pursuing problems in the psychology of conflict for well over half a century. Psychoanalytic psychology regarded the development of motivational conflicts and their methods of resolution as the prime determinants of personality development generally, as well as being the origin of the character and occurrence of psychopathology. Since Freud's first approaches, there have been many other systematic attempts to resolve the basic questions. Lewin applied the descriptive concepts of vector psychology, Miller applied the principles of neo-behavioristic learning theory, and more recently still we have seen approaches taking their models from economics and statistical treatments of decision-theory.

Whatever the concepts used, the fundamental questions are common to all systems. First, there is the matter of the general characteristics of motivational conflict. Do competing motives generate behavior with features that are to be found in all such conflicts, regardless of the specifics of the motives involved? Second come the questions of differences between people in their response to conflicts: Are these differences systematic and are they to be explained by reference to previous experience, differences in neurological balance, or what? Finally, there are the many questions that arise when we apply any particular set of principles derived from the study of conflict to specific behavioral patterns—for example, the interpretation of certain neurotic patterns as due to definite categories of motivational conflict.

In the fourth volume of this serial publication, we are able to present contributions that bear upon many of these matters. The first provides a comprehensive theoretical and empirical analysis of behavior in conflict and stress situations with wide-reaching implications for psychopathology and psychotherapy, as well as for motivational theory generally. The problem of the temporal integration of conflict is handled in the second paper—a problem with considerable significance for the long-standing question of the "neurotic paradox." Yet a third paper reports systematic work on the issue of individual differences, and, in particular, of the effects of prior exposure to conflict on tolerance for later exposure. In the fourth paper we see an excellent example of the fruitfulness of a behaviorally oriented model of conflict when applied to complex aspects of human behavior—in this case, schizophrenic psychopathology.

The rich range and variety of problems encountered by the personality psychologist is illustrated once again by the inclusion of two papers which contribute to the psychology of the need for power and the effects of punishment upon personality development in children.

Copenhagen, Denmark BRENDAN A. MAHER
August, 1967

CONTENTS

Toward a Unified Theory of Anxiety

SEYMOUR EPSTEIN

Some Ramifications of Exposure to Conflict

LEONARD WORELL

Temporal Integration: An Incentive Approach to Conflict-Resolution

K. EDWARD RENNER

The Influence of Punishment and Related Disciplinary Techniques on the Social Behavior of Children: Theory and Empirical Findings

RICHARD H. WALTERS AND ROSS D. PARKE

Power as a Personality Construct

HENRY L. MINTON

A Theory of Response Interference in Schizophrenia

WILLIAM E. BROEN, JR. AND LOWELL H. STORMS

CONTENTS OF PREVIOUS VOLUMES

TOWARD A UNIFIED THEORY OF ANXIETY[1]

Seymour Epstein

DEPARTMENT OF PSYCHOLOGY, UNIVERSITY OF MASSACHUSETTS,
AMHERST, MASSACHUSETTS.

[1]This paper, and the research reported in it, were supported by Grant MH 01293 from the National Institute of Mental Health, United States Public Health Service. The paper was written while the author was a visiting professor in the department of social relations at Harvard University.

1

I. Introduction

While all would agree that anxiety is the central concept in psychopathology, no one has produced a theory that reasonably well accounts for the
known facts about anxiety. Freud (1936), in his book *The Problem of Anxiety*,
states that despite a lifetime devoted to the problem, he has failed to solve the
riddle of anxiety. For him, the riddle was why anxiety and the defenses
against it should persist after circumstances have changed and the individual
knows that the original source of anxiety cannot reoccur. For Hoch (1950),
the central problem concerns the contradiction inherent in anxiety as both
an adaptive and destructive process. As a signal, it provides a useful warning
of danger, but it, in itself, can become more dangerous than the danger it
warns of. As Hoch aptly puts it, ". . . why should the alarm burn down the
house?" (p. 108). There is not even agreement as to what anxiety is. According to some, it is synonymous with fear. According to others, it is fear with
the object unknown. Some define anxiety by its physiological correlates,
while others insist that it must be defined as a subjective experience. There
are those who discuss the consequences of unconscious anxiety and those
who argue that unconscious anxiety is a contradiction in terms. Where a
distinction between anxiety and fear is made, there is disagreement as to
whether anxiety is primary and fear secondary, or whether it is the other
way around.

The theory of anxiety to be presented here has its roots in a series of
studies on sport parachuting that were originally concerned with the
measurement of conflict. In the course of these studies we could not help
but become increasingly interested in anxiety and how it is mastered under
normal circumstances. Our interest in anxiety was spurred by an unantici-

pated finding that was both remarkably reliable and general, and not readily accounted for by Western behavior theories. Later we learned that Pavlov had observed a similar phenomenon in dogs subjected to stress, and that his explanation closely corresponded to our own. The theory we shall describe attempts to provide a framework for integrating the known facts about anxiety with each other and with new ones that emerged from our research. It will be seen that an extension of the theory suggests the existence of a highly orderly psychophysiological system for modulating the intensity component of all stimulation.

The paper is divided into four main sections and a summary. One section reviews the empirical findings on parachuting and presents some theoretical formulations that are relatively close to the data. A second presents a general theory of anxiety, is more speculative, includes findings and observations by others, and attempts to refine the concepts of anxiety, fear, and arousal, which were used loosely in the preceding section. A third extends the theory to the mastery of the intensity component of stimulation in general, and argues for a psychophysiological system that provides the basis for the organism's expanding contact with its environment and involves a rudimentary form of learning. A fourth is concerned with speculations about the implications of the theory for a variety of problem areas in psychology, and includes suggestions for the kinds of experiments that remain to be done to test the theory.

II. The Investigation of Fear and Its Mastery in Sport Parachuting[2]

There are few situations better suited to the investigation of conflict and stress than sport parachuting for a novice jumper. Not only does parachuting provide an extreme degree of stress, but, more important, it allows for a degree of experimental control that is normally available only in the laboratory. Parachutists are trained by a relatively standardized procedure, which provides the experimenter with a range of cues that have a common meaning to his subjects and that are relatively uncontaminated by other life experiences. The experimenter can vary the intensity of stress by testing at different times in relation to an anticipated jump. Furthermore, it is possible to arrange the rate and time of jumping to meet the needs of the experimenter. Thus, order and sequence effects can be controlled by having some subjects tested first on the day of a jump and second on a control day, and others in reverse order. Finally, the effects of practice and mastery can readily be investigated by testing parachutists with different amounts of experience and testing the same parachutist at different points in training.

[2] All the research reported in this paper was carried out in collaboration with Dr. Walter D. Fenz, who is both a sport parachutist and a psychologist.

In all these respects, parachuting has considerable advantages over other real-life stress situations, such as natural disasters (Grosser, Wechsler, & Greenblatt, 1964), warfare (Bond, 1952; Grinker & Spiegel, 1945; Kardiner, 1941), surgery (Janis, 1958), criminal interrogation (Luria, 1932), and academic examinations (Luria, 1932).

A. REACTIONS TO CUE DIMENSIONS IN SPECIALLY DEVISED PROJECTIVE TESTS

1. The Model of Approach-Avoidance Conflict

Our early work on the measurement of conflict was influenced by Lewin's (1931, 1946) and Miller's (1948, 1959) models of approach-avoidance conflict and displacement. It was assumed that approach-avoidance conflict can be represented by the interaction of two gradients, one for approach and the other for avoidance, and that the gradient of avoidance as a function of goal-relevant cues is steeper than the gradient of approach. Unlike Miller, our gradients represented "drives," defined as directed forces, rather than overt responses or tendencies to produce overt responses. In this respect, our thinking was closer to Lewin's than Miller's, although it did not strictly coincide with Lewin's either. It was assumed that drives can be measured by either their directing or activating component. While Miller has been primarily concerned with predicting whether an organism will approach or avoid at different distances from a goal, we were equally concerned with measuring the individual's inner state, i.e., his level of tension. This raised the question of how to combine the inferred approach and avoidance gradients to obtain an estimate of overall arousal. One

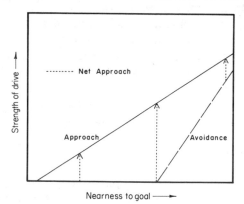

FIG. 1. Hypothetical gradients of approach and avoidance drives for a novice parachutist before a jump. The abscissa can represent either distance, time, or goal-relevant cues. The gradients are assumed to be monotonic functions and are represented as straight lines only for the sake of convenience.

strategy would be to simply consider the fear, or the avoidance gradient, and forget the other, but this seemed unwarranted since physiological correlates of tension and arousal are influenced by positive as well as negative incentives. The assumption was tentatively made that the gradients of arousal combine additively. Thus, from the very outset we were forced to distinguish between fear, as an avoidance motive, and the concept of arousal, as the combined nondirectional component of all motives.

Figure 1 presents hypothetical gradients of approach and avoidance for a novice parachutist. As the parachutist does, in fact, jump, the avoidance gradient is represented as below the approach gradient at the goal. The abscissa can represent either cues, distance, or time. Figure 2 presents the net directional tendency obtained by subtracting the avoidance gradient from the approach gradient. The curve is inverted V-shaped, as once avoidance enters the picture, it increasingly counteracts the influence of approach. Figure 3 presents net activation obtained by adding the avoidance and approach gradients. It can be seen that the curve is a monotonic positively accelerated function. That Figs. 2 and 3 have high face validity is immediately apparent upon observing the behavior of novice parachutists. Consistent with Figs. 1 and 2, most novice parachutists report that they were very eager to jump some time before the scheduled event, but once in the aircraft had second thoughts about going ahead and considered calling the jump off. Figure 3 is supported by observations of a rapid increase in tension and behavioral disorganization as the moment of the jump arrives.

In the first study aimed at testing the model of approach-avoidance conflict, novice parachutists and control subjects were tested with a specially devised word-association test containing four levels of relevance to parachuting (Epstein & Fenz, 1962). Out of curiosity, a number of anxiety words were included at the end of the test, where they could not influence

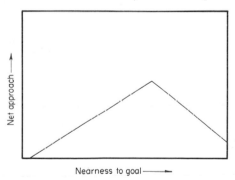

FIG. 2. Net approach increment as a function of the conflict between approach and avoidance drives for a novice jumper. This curve was obtained from Fig. 1 by subtracting the avoidance from the approach gradient.

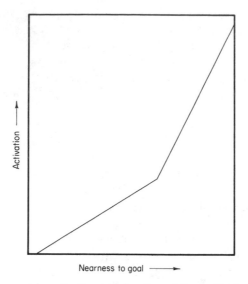

FIG. 3. Net increment in activation as a function of the conflict between approach and avoidance drives for a novice jumper. This curve was obtained from Fig. 1 by adding the approach and avoidance gradients.

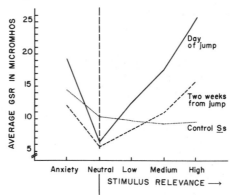

FIG. 4. Average GSR of novice parachutists and control subjects for a stimulus dimension and for anxiety words in a word-association test (from Epstein & Fenz, 1962).

the rest of the dimension. The results for GSR are presented in Fig. 4. Confirming prediction, parachutists on a control day produce a steeper GSR gradient than nonparachutists, and parachutists on the day of a jump produce the steepest gradient of all. The data are highly reliable. All 16 parachutists produced a gradient on a control day and all 16 produced a steeper gradient on the day of a jump. No control subject produced a gradient. In this study it was meaningless to evaluate the exact slope of the

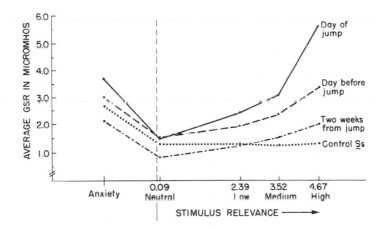

FIG. 5. Average GSR of novice parachutists and control subjects for anxiety words and a stimulus dimension scaled for equal-appearing intervals (from Fenz, 1964).

curve, apart from its being a monotonic increasing function, as the abscissa was not an equal interval scale. However, in a further study (Fenz, 1964) in which the units on the abscissa were scaled, the curve was found to be positively accelerated, as hypothesized (see Fig. 5).

While the results on GSR as a measure of activation were highly rewarding, the directional hypotheses, as measured by content of associations, fared less well. There was no support for the hypothesis that with increasing closeness to the jump, approach responses become stronger to remote cues and weaker to goal-relevant cues. It was observed in both the word-association test and in responses to a specially constructed TAT (Fenz & Epstein, 1962) that with increasing closeness to a jump, approach responses increased along the entire dimension, and what tendency there was, was for the increase to be greatest at the goal-relevant rather than remote end of the dimension, which was opposite to prediction. Findings such as this led us to conclude that it is necessary to distinguish behavioral approach-avoidance conflict from conflict between verbal expression and inhibition, i.e., repression conflict, as only the latter influences responses to projective techniques. Limited support for this view is presented later, and in greater detail elsewhere (Epstein, 1966).

2. The Expression and Inhibition of Fear in Novice Parachutists

In the study of the TAT referred to in the preceding paragraph, it was found that on the day of a jump there was a surprising increase in denial of fear of parachuting in stories told to a picture of a parachutist. An example of such a response is: "He is not afraid at all; just looks that way because of the wind that is blowing in his face. He will have a wonderful jump. It will be great, just great!" The subjects who denied fear on the picture of high relevance for parachuting showed an increase in fear responses to pictures unrelated to parachuting. Thus, if a conflict between expression and inhibition of fear is postulated, the subjects behaved according to the conflict model; that is, they showed an increase in fear responses to remote cues for parachuting and an increase in avoidance of fear to pictures directly suggestive of parachuting. Not only did this finding teach us an important lesson about the kinds of conflicts that projective techniques do and do not measure, but more important, it alerted us to a new kind of conflict which involved the expression and inhibition of fear.

The major battle that a novice parachutist must engage in if he is to gain proficiency and not seriously endanger himself is against his own fear. There appear to be three general procedures for controlling fear, namely (1) avoiding fear-producing cues in perception, thought, and overt response, (2) producing distracting responses, particularly ones whose content is incompatible with fear, and (3) emphasizing the positive motivation to jump and focusing upon cues that have adaptive significance for jumping. These processes combine in different ways to establish different defenses, among which we have evidence for the following: (1) selective perception and biased hypothesis formulation, (2) inhibition of anxiety-producing responses, including a failure to complete partial perceptions, (3) denial, (4) making responses incompatible with anxiety, (5) stimulus displacement, (6) drive displacement.

The preparation of the parachutist often includes direct training in selective perception and making responses incompatible with anxiety. The parachutist is instructed to look ahead and not down in order to avoid anxiety-provoking cues of height. When landing, he is cautioned to look at the horizon, as the sight of the ground rushing to meet him could cause him to raise his legs instead of using them to cushion the impact. He is told to concentrate on what he must do, i.e., to "think positively," so that there is no room left for worrying. Experienced jumpers frequently establish a light-hearted mood with ribald singing and joking, but the situation for the novice is too grim for this, and the contrast would simply emphasize his own opposite mood.

The set against perceiving anxiety-producing cues can be so great that even relatively strong and unambiguous stimuli may go unnoticed or be misperceived. A parachutist reported to us that he was surprised at how calm he was on the day of his first jump, until he looked down and saw his knees knocking together! In the study on word association previously referred to (Epstein & Fenz, 1962), parachutists on the day of a jump failed to perceive more than 20% of the anxiety words presented. They also showed a mild

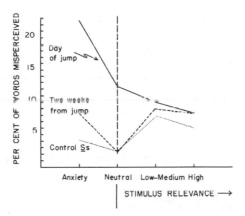

FIG. 6. Perceptual errors of novice parachutists and control subjects for anxiety words and words on a dimension of relevance for parachuting (from Epstein & Fenz, 1962).

deficit for neutral words, but no deficit for parachuting-relevant words (see Fig. 6). We believe that the results provide unequivocal evidence for perceptual defense, as the phenomenon came and went in the same subjects depending on the time of testing in relation to a jump. This is not to say that we believe that an unconscious recognition of the words took place and was followed by repression. That such is probably not the case was indicated by the observation that when an anxiety word was misperceived as a neutral word, no early GSR preceded the response, and the magnitude of the GSR corresponded to that for a neutral word. What, then was the mechanism for the perceptual defense? We suspect it involved an active set to avoid making hypotheses about anxiety cues. In like manner, we presume there was an active set to make hypotheses about parachute-relevant cues, resulting in *relative* perceptual sensitization to such cues. The influence of set effects was very likely increased by the general decrease in perceptual acuity brought about by the high level of arousal on the day of a jump (Fenz, 1964).

It was already noted in the study with the TAT (Fenz & Epstein, 1962) that on the day of a jump, novice parachutists exhibited denial of fear of parachuting and an increase in fear responses unrelated to parachuting. It is noteworthy that only the source of the fear was denied and not the fear itself. Such partial denial is sufficient to accomplish its purpose of reducing fear of parachuting, and does not require the ignoring of certain salient cues, such as the fear itself. Thus, it is seen that one way defenses work is that following a perception of potentially anxiety-provoking cues, the perceptual-interpretive process is directed to a less veridical and less anxiety-producing conclusion. While the preceding example can be referred to as stimulus displacement, another finding qualifies as drive displacement. Among a number of subjects who demonstrated an increase in denial of fear of parachuting in their TAT stories on the day of a jump, there occurred a corresponding increase in anger responses. It is as if, in the first case, the parachutist were to say, "It is not parachuting, but other things that I fear," and in the second, "What I feel is anger, not fear." The same explanation that was presented for stimulus displacement applies equally well to drive displacement. All drives have a common element of arousal. Once the arousal is interpreted as anger, this not only avoids responses that would increase fear, but substitutes an emotion that the subject can interpret as the very antithesis of fear.

The defenses just referred to, which required a diversion of the perceptual and interpretive process into channels that reduce anxiety, can be broken down for analytical purposes into two processes, although phenomenologically they are undoubtedly experienced as one. One process involves the inhibition of response tendencies, including interpretation and further perceptions that are highly veridical but anxiety producing, and the other the production of other responses that are less veridical, but less anxiety producing. Inhibition should be possible at any point in the chain, and inhibition can also occur without the production of substitutive responses. Thus, a person can simply recognize that he is thinking anxiety-provoking thoughts, and stop.

The foregoing defenses, whether consisting of biased perceptual hypotheses, rechanneling of already initiated response sequences, or the simple stopping of an ongoing response, all involve a component of inhibition. By inhibition we mean that a response disposition is prevented from expression by the occurrence of some other reaction, the removal of which results in the expression of the response tendency. There is considerable evidence that anxiety does not simply dissipate, but is actively inhibited. Such evidence is provided not only by the occurrence of stimulus and drive displacement, but more important, by the after-discharge of anxiety. Basowitz, Persky, Korchin, and Grinker (1955) report that army paratroopers showed an unexpected rise in fear some time after their stressful training period was over. We noted an upsurge in TAT anxiety responses two weeks after a jump as compared with two weeks before and the day of a jump (Fenz & Epstein, 1962). What is the mechanism by which inhibition takes place? If there were simply an avoidance of anxiety-producing perceptions and responses, it would not constitute inhibition, and should not result in displacement and after-discharge. It is necessary to postulate an active process that directs perceptual hypotheses and rechannels response tendencies so that both the perceptions and the response sequences take a different course than they normally would. Once the active inhibitory set is removed, the response sequences and perceptual sets that had been initiated but restrained are free to run off in their natural sequence. When the need for controlling anxiety in the parachuting situation is no longer present, the parachutist can stop directing his hypotheses along certain lines and making distracting, denying, diverting responses that are incompatible with fear. An after-discharge of fear then occurs as a result of the partial perceptions and initiated response-dispositions now becoming salient and capable of being followed through in terms of their obvious implications.

If there is one unifying thread for the defenses of the novice parachutists, it is that they tend to be extreme, or unmodulated. To the extent that the parachutist has not yet had the experiences to make him feel confident, he can reduce his fear only by relatively gross manipulations of his perceptions and thoughts. The greater the fear that must be controlled, the more extreme and compulsive the defenses must be. Given unmodulated defenses, once they fail, the parachutist is subjected to overwhelming anxiety. This was well illustrated by two young women novice jumpers, whose denial was so extreme that they appeared completely unconcerned and relaxed before their first jump until they boarded the aircraft. Their apparent composure was unnerving to the male jumpers, who were struggling to contain their fear. Upon boarding the aircraft, apparently denial was no longer possible, and the girls' only line of defense collapsed. One developed a coarse tremor and the other was seized with a paroxysm of vomiting. Both asked to be let out, and both gave up jumping. While this example demonstrates the breakdown of control in an all-or-none defense system, the next example demonstrates a problem caused by excessive control. The parachutist in question had taken up the sport to prove to himself that he could master any challenge. He progressed very rapidly. If he had any failing it was that, unlike other beginning parachutists, the direct manifestation of whose fear interfered with their performance, for him it was the compensatory reactions that made for difficulties. Instead of jumping up six inches, he would jump so high that he would have to be cautioned against hitting the aircraft. One day his main chute failed to open. He was observed to keep falling without attempting to activate his reserve chute until it was almost too late. Parachutists are instructed to wait 10 seconds before releasing their reserve chute in order to prevent them from panicking and releasing it so early that it tangles with a slightly delayed opening of the main chute. He later reported that he wanted to make sure that he waited the full 10 seconds, and so slowly counted to himself "chim-pan-zee-one, chim-pan-zee-two," etc. The degree to which the control was excessive was indicated by the degree to which he overestimated the 10 seconds, which was considerable and nearly fatal.

The two cases just described illustrate an important principle about the defenses of novice parachutists, namely, that they tend to have an all-or-none characteristic. It will be seen that with increasing experience, the all-or-none inhibitory system for the control of anxiety increasingly shifts to a modulated control system that is initiated by earlier and smaller increments of anxiety.

3. The Expression and Inhibition of Fear in Experienced Parachutists

Unlike the novice parachutist, who is manifestly tense and whose performance is disrupted by his high level of anxiety, the experienced parachutist gives the appearance of thoroughly enjoying the experience. He exhibits a level of dexterity that would not be possible under high levels of anxiety. He performs "delayed freefalls" during which he falls freely through space and executes difficult maneuvers, such as passing a baton or an egg to a fellow jumper, also in freefall. For the experienced skydiver, the descent once the parachute opens is anticlimactic. Movies of parachutists in freefall leave no doubt that the jumper is immensely enjoying himself. How has the change come about that converts the terrified novice into the experienced jumper? We originally thought that fear was simply extinguished as the result of successful experience; that is, that fear dissipated as the parachutist learned that his fears were unfounded. Our data forced us to revise this viewpoint.

Our most interesting finding was accidental. One day, one of the novice parachutists failed to keep his appointment. Dr. Fenz tested an experienced jumper in his place and, surprisingly, instead of producing a monotonic gradient of GSR as a function of the stimulus dimension, he produced an inverted V-shaped curve. We ran two more experienced parachutists, and they also produced inverted V-shaped curves. When the same subjects were tested on a control day, all produced monotonic gradients that could not be distinguished from those of novice parachutists. The results, as they were specific to the day of a jump, could not be explained by increasing

TABLE I

FORM OF GSR CURVES AS A FUNCTION OF EXPERIENCE

Level of experience	Monotonic gradient	Inverted V, peaking 1 step back	Inverted V, peaking 2 steps back	Total subjects
Group 1 (1 jump)	6	0	0	6
Group 2 (5–8 jumps)	3	2	1	6
Group 3 (25–50 jumps)	1	2	3	6
Group 4 (>100 jumps)	0	1	5	6

familiarity with the words, but suggested an active process of adaptation associated with preparation for the jump. We decided to study the phenomenon systematically. Table I summarizes the curve forms produced by four groups of parachutists with different amounts of experience. With increasing experience, the curve changes from a monotonic gradient to an inverted V-shaped curve, which peaks at increasingly remote points from the goal-relevant end of the dimension. All curves in Table I were produced on the morning of a jump. When testing was conducted after a jump or on a control day, monotonic gradients were invariably obtained. The one subject in the most experienced group whose peak turned out to be characteristic of less experienced subjects was as experienced as the others in his group, but was considered to be emotionally unstable, and was undergoing psychotherapy. The results thus suggest that the peaking does not indicate the effect of experience per se, but the degree of emotional control that has been acquired as a result of the experience.

As the results just described are based on cross-sectional data, it is possible that the form of the curves is the result of a personality factor associated with how much experience a parachutist is apt to acquire. The only way that it can be unequivocally established that the change in the peaking of the curves is a developmental phenomenon is to obtain longitudinal data. Figures 7, 8, and 9 present curves for three subjects, each tested at three levels of experience. The curves on the right are presented in "deviation scores" that adjust for mean reactivity and lability as established by reactions to neutral stimuli. It can be seen, in Fig. 7, that the three curves produced by a single subject reproduce the three curve forms found in the group data. In Fig. 8, the monotonic gradient is observed to flatten from the first to the second testing session, and peaks back two steps on the third testing. In Fig. 9, all curves are monotonic, and this subject at first

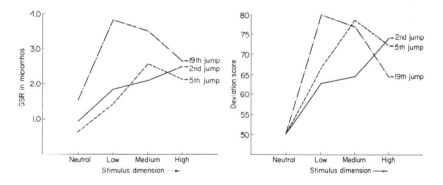

FIG. 7. Magnitude of GSR as a function of relevance of words to parachuting for subject 1 (from Epstein, 1962).

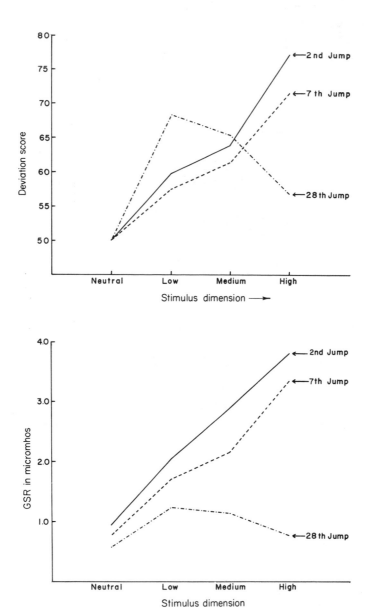

FIG. 8. Magnitude of GSR as a function of relevance of words to parachuting for subject 2 (from Epstein, 1962).

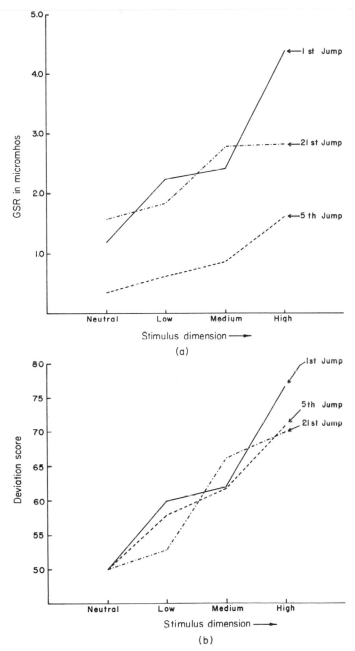

FIG. 9. Magnitude of GSR as a function of relevance of words to parachuting for subject 3 (from Epstein, 1962).

appears to provide an exception to the pattern illustrated by the group data and the other two subjects. However, a closer look reveals that he is simply developing at a slower rate. At the first testing, he produces his steepest gradient. The gradient flattens somewhat by the second testing. By the third testing, a budding inverted V-shaped curve can be detected, as the reaction to the highest point on the dimension is lower than at either of the other sessions, and the reaction to the next highest point on the dimension is higher than at either of the other sessions. Thus, the developmental pattern for all three parachutists is consistent with the findings from the cross-sectional data. That the inverted V-shaped curves are not simply a product of repeated testing is proven by the group data, which are all based on first testing sessions, and by the absence of such curves in novice subjects who were tested several times.

How is one to account for the unanticipated, yet orderly, development of inverted V-shaped curves with peaks that shift toward increasingly remote cues? The results cannot be attributed to increasing familiarity with the parachuting words, as the curve appears only on the day of a jump. On a control day, novice and experienced parachutists produce monotonic gradients that are indistinguishable from each other. It will be recalled that in the section on the measurement of conflict, approach-avoidance conflict was represented by the interaction of an inferred gradient of approach and an inferred steeper gradient of avoidance. The curve of net approach obtained by subtracting the avoidance from the approach gradient was inverted V-shaped. This curve represented direction of response, and would not appear to be appropriate for an analysis of a non-directional measure, such as GSR. That is, it would not, unless one were willing to assume that nondirectional activation, as measured by the GSR, is subject to inhibition, and that the gradient of such inhibition is steeper than the gradient of activation. In Fig. 10, it is assumed that with increasing and successful exposure to a source of stress, two developments take place, a heightening of a gradient of anxiety and the development of a gradient of inhibition that increases in height and becomes increasingly steeper than the gradient of anxiety. As a result, as anxiety mounts, it becomes inhibited at increasingly early points or, putting it otherwise, the peak of anxiety advances to earlier and earlier points on a dimension of cues relevant to the source of anxiety. It should be noted that the excitatory and inhibitory gradients are represented by similar formulas, which differ only in their exponents. (We are indebted to Alice H. Epstein for producing the curves and formulas for Figs. 10 and 19 according to our description.)

An alternate model that we considered and rejected assumed that rather than a steeper gradient of inhibition than of activation, there was a gradient of dissipation of activation, which became increasingly steeper than the

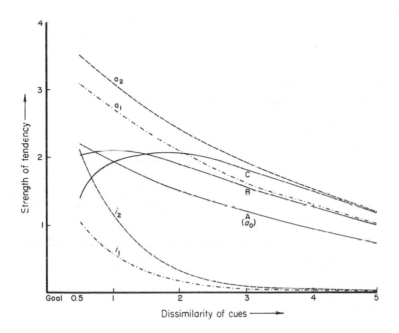

FIG. 10. Theoretical curves for the development of inverted V-shaped curves that peak increasingly earlier with experience. Curve A represents the initial generalization gradient of activation before inhibition has developed. The upper two broken-line curves, a_1 and a_2, represent successive levels in the buildup of conditioned activation. The lower two broken-line curves, i_1 and i_2, represent successive levels in the buildup of inhibition of activation (or of activation-producing responses). Curve B represents net activation as obtained by subtracting i_1 from a_1. Curve C represents net activation at a further level of development obtained by subtracting i_2 from a_2.

The curves are of the form ae^{-kx}. The curves for the three levels of conditioned tendency to experience activation, in order of increasing height, are described by the formulas $2.5e^{-.25x}$, $3.5e^{-.25x}$, and $4e^{-.25x}$. The curves for the two levels of inhibition, in order of increasing height, are described by the formulas $2e^{-1.25x}$ and $4e^{-1.25x}$ (from Epstein, 1962).

expanding gradient of activation. Such a model would assume that with repeated exposure to stress, anxiety both generalizes and dissipates, the latter occurring at a faster rate for cues at the upper end of the dimension. We favored the inhibitory model for a number of reasons. One was that it was apparent that novice parachutists actively attempted to inhibit anxiety, and it seemed not unreasonable to assume that the experienced jumpers were successful in accomplishing at an efficient and highly automatic level what the novices were attempting in a crude manner. Second, it was obvious that autonomic reactions could be inhibited, as exhibited by the inhibition of vomiting, crying, voiding, and even fainting until an appropriate time and place are available. Thus, runners and rowers often do not faint until just after crossing the finish line, and concentration camp victims have been reported to show a reduced incidence of fainting when fainting was punishable by death (Bettelheim, 1943). It is not necessary to assume a direct inhibition of anxiety or other autonomic reactions, although this possibility should not be ruled out, but only that responses that mediate anxiety can be inhibited. Included would be inner responses, such as thoughts, imagery, and perceptual hypotheses, as well as overt responses. Third, one of the implications of the inhibition as opposed to the dissipation of anxiety model is that the former, only, would predict that an individual who has been repeatedly exposed to stress would be particularly susceptible to breakdown once inhibitory controls have been taxed to their limit, which is supported by observations of men in combat (Bond, 1952; Grinker & Spiegel, 1945). Fourth, we have observed experienced parachutists become suddenly anxious when their routine was interfered with and when they did not have an opportunity to prepare themselves mentally for a forthcoming jump, as in the case of a jumper who fell asleep during the long ascent of the aircraft to a high altitude. He was awakened in more than sufficient time to prepare for the jump physically, but reported that he felt strangely anxious and unready to jump, and as a result made a poor jump from which he obtained no enjoyment. Finally, the inhibition model allows for a more parsimonious explanation of our total data, including evidence for an after-discharge of anxiety in experienced parachutists.

What are the implications of the change from a monotonic gradient to an inverted V-shaped curve whose peak advances to increasingly remote cues? We submit that it solves Hoch's (1950) paradox of anxiety as the alarm that burns down the house. The development of the inhibitory gradient provides the insulation that prevents the conflagration. As a result of the expanding gradient of anxiety and its inhibition, an increasingly early and efficient warning signal is provided at increasingly low levels of arousal until, if the process were not stabilized or reversed by perception of real danger, the anxiety would be displaced out of existence. Given a continued awareness of danger, the process stabilizes at some point less than complete displacement, but in arriving there has forced discrimination of relevant cues and the development of an ability to inhibit anxiety-producing responses at many levels, providing for a modulated system for the control of anxiety. It is proposed that this is the normal process by which anxiety is mastered.

A direct comparison of the defensive system of novice and experienced parachutists is of considerable interest. The novices utilized drastic defenses, including perceptual denial and distortion, to cope with high levels of anxiety. No such reactions were observed in the experienced jumpers. As a result of a double process of expansion of anxiety and inhibitory gradients with experience, the experienced parachutists developed a control system characterized by early warning signals at low levels of anxiety, as contrasted with the late signals and drastic defenses against high levels of anxiety used by the novices. Because of their more subtle nature, the defenses of the experienced parachutists are not as easily investigated as those of the novices. The experienced parachutists often deny that they experience any fear at all, although their polygraph responses to selected cues belie their words. It is not unreasonable to assume that the defenses of the experienced parachutists include habitual and less drastic versions of the defenses of the novices, including concentration upon the task at hand, making responses incompatible with anxiety, and the direct inhibition of needless worrying. The early warning signals of anxiety, in addition to stimulating defenses against an increase in anxiety, serve the useful function of countering the tendency of familiarity to breed contempt and unnecessary risk taking.

B. Ratings of Fear as a Function of an Approaching Jump

Informal observation of novice parachutists supports the conclusion that the gradient of avoidance is steeper than that of approach, as the eagerness exhibited some time before the scheduled event is seen to gradually give way to doubt and fear as the time of a jump approaches. The situation is less clear for experienced parachutists, who do not clearly manifest overt signs of fear at any time. To uncover the pattern of how their fear is distributed in time, a more systematic procedure than casual observation is necessary.

Thirty-three experienced parachutists, all of whom had made over 100 jumps, and thirty-three novice parachutists, none of whom had made more than 5 jumps, were asked to rate their fear and avoidance feelings at fourteen points in time before and after a jump. They were instructed to place a rating of 1 at the point in time at which their fear or feeling of avoidance was least and a rating of 10 at the point in time at which it was most. Having defined their range of subjective fear, they were told to make relative ratings of all the other points on the time dimension. Similar ratings were made for approach. The study is described in detail elsewhere (Epstein & Fenz, 1965), and only the most relevant aspects of it will be summarized here. In interpreting the findings it is important to recognize that comparisons cannot be made between absolute magnitude of fear for the two groups, as both are required to assign a value of 1 to their least and 10 to their greatest degree of fear, no matter what the absolute magnitude. Comparisons can only be made between the patterns of fear over time. If the only difference between the groups is magnitude of fear, they should produce identical curves in the distribution of their fear ratings.

In Fig. 11 it can be seen that the peak of avoidance of the novice

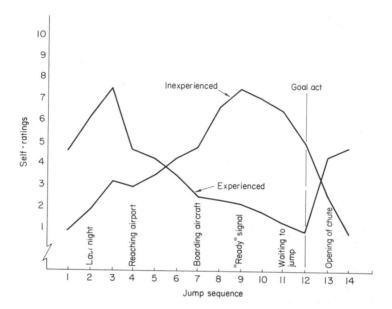

FIG. 11. Self-ratings of fear and avoidance of novice and experienced parachutists as a function of the sequence of events leading up to and following a jump (from Fenz & Epstein, 1967).

parachutists occurs at the "ready" signal. It is notewortny that maximum avoidance does not correspond to the period of falling before the chute opens, which is the point of maximum uncertainty and danger. Rather, maximum fear corresponds to a decision point, where the parachutist can either acknowledge that he is ready and proceed, or state that he is not ready, and delay the jump, or even call it off. The anxiety is adaptive in that it reaches its peak at a point where it can influence the outcome. Once the commitment is made, fear declines, but is still high at the moment of the jump.

Examination of the curve of the experienced parachutists reveals that avoidance rises from a week before the jump (point 1) to the morning of the jump (point 3), after which it declines over a prolonged period until it reaches its lowest point at the freefall (point 12). It then rises after landing. For the experienced parachutists the morning of a jump is a decision point, as it is then that they often decide whether or not they will jump that day. Often the decision is determined by observation of the weather. Once having decided to jump, there is no question but that an experienced jumper will, as he no longer has a major decision to make that he thinks he may regret. The curves for the experienced and novice parachutists are similar in that they both show a rise and fall before the jump. Their major difference is that the peak occurs at a much earlier point for the experienced than the novice parachutists, so that the period of decline of fear is considerably extended for the experienced parachutists.

The forward shift in the peak of self-rated fear with experience is consistent with the study of GSRs as a function of a cue dimension in a word-association test, with the self-ratings of fear replacing the GSR, and a time dimension in a real-life situation replacing the cue dimension. The explanation that was offered in the previous study can equally well be applied to the present data, namely, with experience two developments take place, an increase in the gradient of anxiety and the development of a gradient of inhibition of anxiety, the latter with increasingly steeper slope. An observation of particular interest in this respect is that an after-discharge of anxiety occurs only for the experienced parachutists (see Fig. 11), which supports the assumption that they inhibited over a more extended period. The one observation on which the present findings do not parallel the findings on the word-association test is that in the latter case the novice parachutists produced monotonic gradients on the day of a jump, whereas in the present case they show a slight falling off in avoidance ratings before the jump. This can be accounted for by the consideration that the word-association test is already removed from the goal act of jumping because the relevant cues are represented symbolically. There is no problem in explaining the downturn of the curve of self-rated fear for the novices before the jump, as it can be assumed that they have had some relevant experience, including 1 to 4 previous jumps, training, and related experiences elsewhere in controlling fear associated with height.

The experienced parachutists in the study just reported had made between 100 and 500 jumps. The question remains whether with more experience the peak of fear and avoidance would be displaced yet further. We have been able to obtain data on a few parachutists who have made over 1000 jumps. Such subjects are not easy to come by, and our sample is necessarily small. Moreover, a number of the subjects returned the forms with a covering note stating that they wanted to cooperate, but that jumping had become so routine that they did not experience any fear. Some returned the forms filled out for the approach ratings only, or checked the lowest avoidance rating for all points. We were able to obtain 6 usable records for approach ratings and 3 for avoidance ratings. Considering the very small number of cases for avoidance and the lack of uniformity among them, not even tentative conclusions can be arrived at for avoidance, other than that parachutists who have made over 1000 jumps tend to deny experiencing fear. The data for the approach ratings, while limited, are highly consistent. The combined curve for the 6 subjects forms an increasing monotonic gradient from a week before to the moment of a jump, with all 12 points, falling in line. If the tentative assumption can be made that approach reflects the opposite side of the coin of avoidance, then a subtle measure is provided for measuring avoidance. Such an assumption is supported by the finding in the previous study as curves of "inverse approach" and avoidance were almost identical for both groups. If an increase in avoidance can be inferred from a decrease in approach, then the parachutists who have made over 1000 jumps can be said to produce a monotonic decreasing gradient of avoidance from a week before the jump to the moment of the jump, without any intermediate peak. When the same procedure is followed for the groups in the previous study, they produce inverted V-shaped curves of inferred avoidance whose peaks coincide with the peaks of the self-ratings of avoidance. Thus, the results are consistent with the conclusion that with increasing experience up to over 1000 jumps, fear is increasingly displaced forward in time. In view of the small size of the sample and the indirect means of measuring avoidance, the conclusion for parachutists with over 1000 jumps must be considered highly tentative.

C. Physiological Arousal as a Function of an Approaching Jump

Studies of anxiety have sometimes investigated physiological indices of stress, arguing that subjective reports of fear are untrustworthy. Others have argued that anxiety is of necessity a subjective state, and that physiological measures cannot be used as a substitute for self-reports. Because of the orderliness of the findings on the ratings of fear, a unique opportunity was provided for comparing subjective ratings of fear with presumed physiological correlates. To this end, a study was conducted (Fenz & Epstein, 1967) in which physiological reactions of novice and experienced parachutists were monitored during a time period overlapping that on which the subjective ratings of fear had been obtained in the study reviewed earlier herein.

1. Reactions during Ascent in the Aircraft and after Landing

The sample consisted of 10 novice sport parachutists, none of whom had made more than 5 jumps, and 10 experienced parachutists, all of whom had made more than 100 jumps. A few additional jumpers were tested for special reasons, and are reported on separately. A transistorized battery-operated polygraph was used to obtain continuous recordings of heart rate, respiration rate, and skin resistance during ascent in the aircraft up to a point immediately before jumping, when it was necessary to disconnect the electrodes; and again shortly after landing; and on a control day. Following are the points at which readings were taken from the records: (1) a control day, when *S* did not intend to jump; (2) after reaching the airport on the day of a scheduled jump; (3) shortly before boarding the aircraft; (4) after boarding the aircraft, (5) at the beginning of taxiing; (6) at the end of taxiing; (7) at the beginning of engine warm-up before take-off; (8) at the end of engine warm-up; (9) during take-off; (10) after being air-borne; (11) at 1000 feet; (12) at midpoint altitude; (13) at final altitude during the jump-run; (14) shortly after landing. Inexperienced parachutists jumped at an altitude of 3000 feet, and experienced parachutists at an altitude of 15,000 feet. To investigate the effect of altitude upon the physiological measures, a few experienced parachutists also jumped at an altitude of 5200 feet, which was high enough for them to have a short delayed freefall.

The major findings are presented in Figs. 12, 13, and 14. The data on heart rate are presented with and without a correction for altitude, as it is the only measure that is known to show marked effects for the altitude in question. Skin conductance, respiration rate, and the corrected data

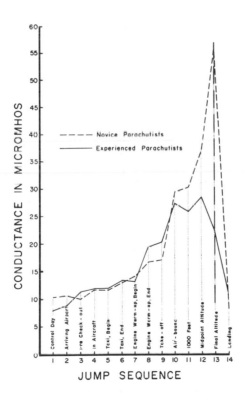

Fig. 12. Basal conductance of experienced and novice parachutists as a function of the sequence of events leading up to and following a jump (from Fenz & Epstein, 1967).

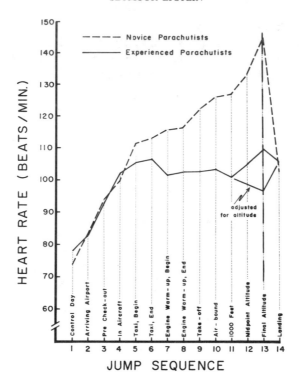

FIG. 13.   Heart rate of experienced and novice parachutists as a function of the sequence of events leading up to and following a jump (from Fenz & Epstein, 1967).

for heart rate all produce inverted V-shaped curves for the experienced parachutists and monotonic gradients for the novice parachutists. In all cases, there is a sharp decline after the jump for the novice jumpers. Two of the measures exhibit an after-discharge effect for the experienced parachutists. The findings for the corrected values of heart rate were confirmed by uncorrected data for the experienced parachutists who jumped at lower altitudes.

It will be recalled that the curve of subjective fear ratings for the experienced parachutists decreased from the morning of the jump to freefall. In order for the physiological data to produce corresponding results, it is necessary for the curves of the physiological reactions of the experienced parachutists to decline continuously from point 2 (arriving at the airport) to final altitude. This obviously does not occur. Rather, the physiological curves during this period reach a peak and then fall off, i.e., they are inverted V-shaped. The peak of the curve for self-rated fear for the experienced parachutists apparently occurs much earlier than the peak of any of the

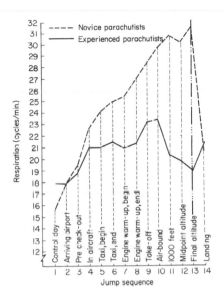

Fig. 14.   Respiration rate of experienced and novice parachutists as a function of the sequence of events leading up to and following a jump (from Fenz & Epstein, 1967).

physiological measures. Physiological activity of the novices increases monotonically up to the moment when the electrodes are disconnected. It will be recalled that fear ratings showed a drop after the ready signal. Since no physiological measures were taken after the ready signal, it is impossible to determine whether a downturn in the curve of the physiological measures would also have occurred. However, considering that the fear ratings peaked considerably earlier than the physiological measures for the experienced parachutists, it would not be surprising if the same were true for the novices, in which case the physiological measures would very likely not show a downturn at any time before the actual jump. This remains to be investigated in future work. No matter what the result, it cannot affect the conclusion that for both fear ratings and physiological arousal the experienced parachutists give evidence of earlier inhibition than the novices.

   The difference in the curves of the fear ratings and the measures of physiological arousal for the experienced parachutists indicates that these are two different variables, although both are governed by the same principles of gradually increasing response magnitude up to a point, followed by later inhibition. This raises the question of the nature of the inhibition. Both Wilder (1957) and Lacey (1956) note that compensatory physiological mechanisms keep the level of activity of a particular organ system within homeostatic limits. As the base level of certain physiological reactions increases, the increase in reactivity produced by an increment in stress decreases, and may even become negative. Such a process cannot be responsible for the inverted V-shaped curves in the present data, since the novices, not the experienced jumpers, reach the highest base levels of physiological activity. The inverted V-shaped curves for the physiological measures appear to be the result of a psychological inhibitory process in reaction to cues produced by the mounting physiological state, or by the external cues associated with the approaching jump, or both. It is possible that the experienced parachutist notices that he is breathing rapidly, that his heart is pounding, or that he simply feels a disquieting degree of tension, and reacts to this by directing his thoughts in a manner such as to reduce the tension. This process does not have to be conscious.

It is of some interest to compare Figs. 12, 13, and 14 to determine whether the different physiological measures reflect a unitary system of arousal and its inhibition or are independent. Turning first to the curves of the novice parachutists, it is observed that they differ in their rate of acceleration. Skin conductance is markedly positively accelerated, heart rate is slightly negatively accelerated, and respiration rate is more negatively accelerated. In the absence of equal units of measurement, the interpretation of the relative shapes of the curves, beyond noting that they are monotonic, can at best provide a hypothesis that the three measures are arranged in a hierarchy of susceptibility to inhibition. This hypothesis can be tested by examining the data of the experienced parachutists and, better yet, by noting the points at which the curves of the novice and experienced parachutists diverge. If the hypothesis is correct, the experienced parachutists should first produce a peak for breathing rate, next for heart rate, and last for skin conductance. Assuming that the after-discharge effect reflects degree of inhibition, skin conductance should demonstrate the least degree of after-discharge and breathing rate the most. The hypothesis is supported in most, but not all, instances. Deceleration is exhibited relatively early (point 5) for respiration and heart rate, and relatively late for skin conductance (point 11). However, while the actual peak for skin conductance occurs last (point 12), heart rate, corrected for altitude, peaks earlier (point 6) than respiration rate (point 10), rather than the reverse. Respiration rate and heart rate demonstrate an after-discharge effect after landing, whereas skin conductance does not, which is in support of hypothesis.

The foregoing test of the hypothesis by the data of the experienced parachutists is not nearly as important as a test based upon the points of divergence of the curves of the experienced and novice parachutists. The curves of the experienced parachutists taken by themselves show many reversals, suggesting that if the study were replicated, the exact point

TABLE II

INTRASUBJECT CORRELATIONS AMONG BASAL CONDUCTANCE, HEART RATE, AND
RESPIRATION RATE FOR 10 NOVICE AND 10 EXPERIENCED JUMPERS OVER
THE ENTIRE JUMP SEQUENCE (POINTS 1–14)

Variables correlated	Novice parachutists		Experienced parachutists	
	Mean *N* at .01	Range	Mean *N* at .01	Range
Basal conductance–Heart rate	+.18 0	−.46 to +.64	+.65 6	+.19 to +.91
Basal conductance–Respiration rate	+.15 0	−.51 to +.60	+.61 5	+.30 to +.83
Heart rate–Respiration rate	+.44 1	−.05 to +.66	+.75 8	+.34 to +.93

of maximum peaking might well shift. On the other hand, the data on the divergence of the curves are so orderly that once the curves intersect there is an uninterrupted increase in magnitude of divergence up to final altitude. In support of hypothesis, the curves of respiration rate diverge first (point 3), heart rate next (point 5), and skin conductance last (point 11). The overall findings support the hypothesis that while the three measures reflect a uniform principle, as indicated by their similar shapes, they also are somewhat independent and arranged in a hierarchy of susceptibility to inhibition.

2. Intraindividual Correlations among the Physiological Measures

It will be recalled that physiological measures were obtained for each of 10 experienced and 10 novice parachutists at 14 points in time. Thus, it was possible to obtain correlations for the physiological measures for each of the individuals for 14 paired scores. The data are summarized in Table II,

TABLE III

INTRASUBJECT CORRELATIONS AMONG BASAL CONDUCTANCE, HEART RATE, AND
RESPIRATION RATE FOR 10 NOVICE AND 10 EXPERIENCED JUMPERS
UNTIL AIRBOUND ONLY (POINTS 1–10)

Variables correlated	Novice parachutists		Experienced parachutists	
	Mean *N* at .01	Range	Mean *N* at .01	Range
Basal conductance–Heart rate	+.42 4	+.13 to +.72	+.56 5	+.05 to +.96
Basal conductance–Respiration rate	+.33 4	−.62 to +.76	+.46 4	−.01 to +.91
Heart rate–Respiration rate	+.53 5	−.09 to +.70	+.69 6	+.11 to +.96

which presents the range, mean, and number of positive, negative, and significant correlations for novice and experienced parachutists.

The correlations of the experienced jumpers run much higher than those of the novices. Nineteen of the 30 correlations of the experienced parachutists are significant, as compared to 1 out of 30 for the novices. The range of correlations for the novices varies from moderately negative to moderately positive, while the correlations of the experienced parachutists are all positive. For both groups, heart rate and respiration rate are more closely related to each other than either is to skin conductance.

What is one to make of the difference in the correlations of the novice and experienced parachutists? To test for the possibility that the high levels of arousal reached by the novices shortly before the jump might acount for the difference, correlations were computed for both groups using only data obtained from the first 10 points, thereby eliminating the extremely high values of the novices. In Table III it can be seen that when this is done, the correlations of the novices are similar to those of the experienced parachutists. The slightly higher correlations of the experienced jumpers can be attributed to the fact that even with the last 4 points eliminated, the novices reached higher arousal levels. The data for the novices as well as the experienced parachutists now reveal a closer relationship between heart rate and respiration rate than between either and skin conductance.

As to the question whether there exists a general factor of physiological arousal, two findings are relevant. One is that while the measures are positively related at the low to moderate levels of stress, they are unrelated at high levels of stress. A general factor of arousal at low levels of arousal gives way to independent variation at higher levels of arousal. The other is that two of the measures are more closely related to each other than to the third measure. It may tentatively be concluded that there is a general factor of arousal, that there are group factors, and that there are specific factors, and that the contribution of each is influenced by the overall degree of arousal. That the picture is yet more complicated is indicated by the widespread individual differences in the correlations. Correlations between heart rate and skin conductance were as low as $-.46$, and between respiration rate and skin conductance as low as $-.51$. There were no strong negative correlations between heart rate and respiration rate. The finding that the different physiological systems tended to respond in a similar manner to increasing stress up to a certain point and to go their own way under greater stress, coupled with the marked individual differences in degree of relationship among the physiological measures, has obvious implications for psychosomatic disorders.

3. Personality Type, Physiological Reactivity, and Performance

In order to investigate the relationship between personality type, physiological activity, and performance, three experienced parachutists were selected who appeared to differ widely in emotional control. They were rated on personality characteristics and on performance by two jumpmasters who knew them fairly well and had observed their jumping. Ratings were made on graphic rating scales and, in addition, thumbnail personality descriptions were obtained. Measures of basal conductance, heart rate, and respiration rate were obtained for the same 14 points reported in the group data. The results, plotted separately for each individual, are presented in Figs. 15, 16, and 17.

ST is an experienced parachutist who performs well in competition as well as in routine jumping. Both raters agree that he is highly competent, exhibits good control when jumping, and responds adequately to emerg-

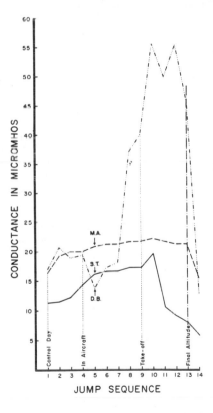

FIG. 15. Basal conductance of three experienced parachutists as a function of the sequence of events leading up to and following a jump (from Fenz & Epstein, 1967).

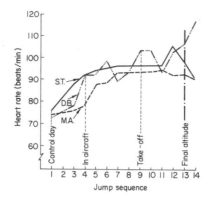

FIG. 16. Heart rate of three experienced parachutists as a function of the sequence of events leading up to and following a jump (from Fenz & Epstein, 1967).

encies. The only negative comment is that ST is slightly impulsive, as a general personality characteristic, but not in his jumping. The other judge rates him as emotionally stable. Both agree that he is average in general activity and "markedly consistent" in performance. Turning to the figures, ST produced inverted V-shaped curves on all three measures. For skin conductance, the downturn of the inverted V is particularly marked, so that the level at final altitude is lower than at any of the other points. The other two measures also reach relatively low levels at final altitude.

DB is less experienced than ST, but has made over 150 jumps, and on this basis would be expected to be highly competent. However, he is described by both judges as having a high activity level, exhibiting poor emotional control, and being below average in performance. On all three curves DB reaches higher levels of physiological arousal than the other two parachutists, and on all three measures his level of arousal is high at final altitude. It is noteworthy that his curves exhibit more variability than the others and have multiple peaks. His control system can thus be compared to a poor servomechanism, which overshoots the mark one moment and overcompensates the next.

The third parachutist, MA, is a woman. She is described as low in activity level, emotionally unreactive, slightly erratic, and average to below average in performance. One of the raters notes that she fails to respond adequately to emergencies. MA's curves of skin conductance and heart rate show the least degree of variability among the three jumpers. Consistent with her personality description, she is physiologically unreactive. The one exception is breathing rate, where she shows a marked decrease before final altitude.

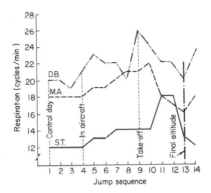

Fig. 17. Respiration rate of three experienced parachutists as a function of the sequence of events leading up to and following a jump (from Fenz & Epstein, 1967).

D. Summary and Conclusions

The finding of greatest interest in the investigations of sport parachuting was the development of inverted V-shaped curves as a function of experience. This curve form appeared in both longitudinal and cross-sectional studies of responses to cue dimensions in specially constructed projective tests. It also appeared in fear ratings as a function of a time dimension and in physiological reactions during ascent in the aircraft. The generality of the finding as well as its high degree of reliability suggests the existence of an extremely fundamental process. The form of the curve and the manner in which its peak is displaced toward increasingly remote cues was explained by a two-process theory of anxiety that assumed that with experience two developments take place, a heightening of a gradient of anxiety and the development of an inhibitory gradient with steeper slope. It was hypothesized that through this double process anxiety is mastered and turned to adaptive advantage, providing an early warning signal at a low level of arousal.

A comparison of the defenses of novice and experienced parachutists revealed that the novices use drastic defenses, tending toward the all-or-none variety, for controlling intense levels of anxiety, whereas the defenses of the experienced parachutists are modulated and involve early inhibitory reactions applied to low intensities of anxiety or arousal. Examination of the pattern of physiological responses of a poor experienced jumper revealed that he differed from the other experienced jumpers in that his physiological reactions during ascent in the aircraft were more labile and indicative of a poorly modulated control system for autonomic regulation.

Different functional relationships for physiological arousal and self-reported fear require that they be considered as distinctive concepts. While both were governed by similar principles of generalization and inhibition, rising fear and its inhibition considerably preceded rising physiological arousal and its inhibition.

The early peak of fear and the later peak of physiological arousal suggests a concept of defense in depth. The finding that the peaks for respiration rate and heart rate preceded the peak of basal skin conductance indicates that the concept of defense in depth is applicable among different physiological systems. Other investigators (Lacey, 1956; Wilder, 1957) have reported that at sufficiently high levels of arousal, homeostatic inhibitory regulators reverse the effect of increasing stimulation upon the activity level of certain physiological systems. The overall results point to a complex of psychological and physiological inhibitory reactions which provide an organized system of defense in depth and breadth for maintaining overall arousal within homeostatic limits. Within this system, fear and its inhibition provide an early line of defense; a later increase in physiological arousal and its psychologically mediated inhibition, a second line of defense; and reflexive, or physiologically mediated, inhibition, a third, and emergency, line of defense.

III. A General Theory of Anxiety

In the preceding section we presented findings from a series of studies on sport parachuting. Our most interesting results could not be predicted from established theories, and we were forced to develop our own theory to account for the data on parachuting. In the present section, corroboration is sought from other sources, the concepts of fear, anxiety, and arousal, which up to now have been used loosely, are defined, and the theory is expanded to include a general theory of anxiety and its control.

A. DIFFERENTIATION OF FEAR, ANXIETY, AND AROUSAL

Should a distinction be made between anxiety and fear, or are they simply two ways of talking about the same thing? Is anxiety a conscious, subjective state, or is it meaningful to speak of unconscious anxiety? Can anxiety be measured by physiological indices, or is physiological activity distinctive from anxiety? In short, what is anxiety, and how does it relate to fear and physiological arousal? We submit that the three terms, fear, anxiety, and arousal, are distinct but related concepts. Fear is a motivational concept, arousal refers to the nondirectional component of all motives, and anxiety lies somewhere in between.

1. Fear Defined as an Avoidance Motive

A motive has three characteristics: a state of heightened arousal, a tendency to approach or avoid, and a designated class of goal objects. A hungry animal is both aroused by and approaches food in preference to other objects. In like manner, a frightened animal is aroused by and makes avoidance responses in the presence of certain objects. Because avoidance reactions are readily conditioned to a wide variety of objects, we do not have a few major fear motives with special names, as we have for approach motives, such as sex, hunger, and thirst.

Fear is conditioned to situations that have produced rapid increases in arousal, such as pain. Given a situation in which an animal experiences bodily injury and pain, fear is highly adaptive in that it facilitates escape behavior. The arousal component of the heightened motive mobilizes the animal's resources, and increases the strength of its avoidance efforts (Canon, 1963). As fear generalizes and becomes increasingly anticipatory, its effectiveness as a defense against danger and high levels of arousal is increased. It is able to provide an early warning signal and, if unheeded, a gradual increase in arousal which serves to keep the organism at a distance from the source of danger.

Recognition that fear contains the three components that define all motives is useful in answering a number of questions. Let us consider the question whether fear can be unconscious. So far as the arousal component of a motive is concerned, it is a physiological state that either exists or does not exist. It cannot be unconscious in the sense that it ceases to exist at a manifest level but is active at other levels. Arousal can be influenced, it is true, by mediating responses that can be repressed and otherwise controlled, but it is they, and not the arousal, that become unconscious. The directive component of a motive and the class of goal objects to which it is directed can both be unconscious. In regard to the former, all that is necessary is for an individual to be unaware of certain approach or avoidance reactions that he exhibits in his behavior. He may even substitute one motive state for another, as illustrated by the parachutists who experienced anger instead of fear on the day of a jump. As to the goal objects of a motive becoming unconscious, this provides the most obvious example of all. Such cases are observed in vague feelings of fear of unknown origin, and in phobias, where the fear is displaced.

Viewing fear as a motive provides leads to the kinds of reactions that can increase or decrease fear. To eat as if hungry will tend to increase appetite, to behave as if brave will increase courage, and to behave as if frightened will increase fear. The assumption that relevant action influences motivation helps explain the finding of a decrease in self-reported fear by parachutists once they have passed a decision point. After the decision to jump, thought and action are directed toward approaching the goal, which is incompatible with fear as an avoidance motive. A second example, with some interesting sidelights, is provided by a report on the Israeli soldier during the Suez crisis. The item appeared in the *New York Times* a few years ago and, although I retained the clipping, I unfortunately do not have the date, and am unable to supply an exact reference. In interviews, the soldiers reported that their greatest fear occurred before the battle, during briefing. Upon advancing toward the enemy, they claimed fear abated. The observers, on the other hand, reported that the soldiers were more frightened, often to the point of disorganization, during battle than at any other point, and concluded that self-reports are not to be trusted. Our findings on parachutists throw light on the discrepancy. The soldiers were correct in reporting their avoidance motive of fear, and the observers were correct in reporting the cognitive disruption produced by high levels of arousal, which very likely was a composite of fear, the excitement of battle, and an extremely high state of vigilance. An alternate interpretation is that the arousal component increased and the directional component decreased, as only the latter could be repressed, which it was, because it was inconsistent with the approach behavior. As will be seen later, high levels of undirected arousal are assumed to have a special aversive quality, which is distinguishable from the directed state of fear. The two explanations just proffered are not incompatible, and differ only in the degree to which fear is held to contribute to total arousal. Had a signal to retreat been given, and the men fled in haste, from either viewpoint it would be predicted that they would describe this period as the one in which they experienced the greatest fear, as the behavior would be consistent with an avoidance motive.

2. Arousal as the Common Component of All Motivation and Stimulation

An increase in arousal, as objectively recorded by a polygraph, can be produced by a number of conditions that have nothing to do with fear or anxiety, such as surprise and pleasant excitement. Heart attacks are precipitated by good news as well as bad news, and visitors to seriously ill patients must exercise caution against exciting them. It is apparent that the organism can tolerate a limited intensity of arousal, no matter what its source.

Arousal is built into the organism as the reaction to any form of intense stimulation, such as a loud noise, physical injury, and acute proprioceptive stimulation as produced by falling. In this respect, arousal is different from fear, which is learned. This is not to say, of course, that arousal is not influenced by learning, as it is evident that for human adults most stimuli are highly arousing because of their acquired, or signal value, and not their absolute intensity. It is simply to note that stimulus intensity is the most fundamental source of arousal, and its effects are not necessarily dependent on learning. Evidence that general arousal is more fundamental than specific emotions is provided by the observation that a general state of excitement can be detected in infants long before specific emotions can be. In adults subjected to intense emotional arousal, the distinctive attributes of the different emotions become diffuse and merge with one another. Thus, extreme states of happiness and unhappiness often cannot be differentiated, both being attended by alternate weeping and laughter A similar running together of emotions is reported in states of intense fear, as witness the following description of a soldier in combat (White, 1956): "He can no longer inhibit the bodily signs of anxiety: perspiration, tremor, restlessness, fast-beating heart, quickened breathing, force themselves upon him. Thought and judgment deteriorate, actions are erratic and poorly controlled, new acts are started before the old ones are completed . . . . Scarcely aware of what he is doing, the panic-stricken person may rush wildly about, laughing, shouting, crying in rapid succession. These reactions sometimes lasted many days in soldiers exposed to prolonged fire. In some cases, a stuporous and comatose state follows the peak of panic" (pp. 207–208).

It is noteworthy that at very high levels of arousal there are often dramatic shifts from excessive excitation to excessive inhibition. Sargant (1957) provides the following example: "One man, for instance, had lain trembling in a ditch, half paralyzed with fear, when his company was ordered to attack. But as soon as his officer taunted him with: 'A girl would put up a better show,' he suddenly became wildly excited, shouted 'Come on boys!' leapt out of the trench to the attack, and then fainted. Other soldiers ran about shouting in panic, this phase being followed by a sudden dumbness. One man had fallen down paralyzed and speechless in a village street which was under bombardment; but when picked up by his comrades, suddenly began to shout and struggle" (p. 27). That extremely high levels of arousal are followed by extreme states of inhibition suggests the operation of an unmodulated emergency defense system.

It is postulated that the level of excitation or arousal, no less than blood sugar concentration and body temperature, must be kept within a homeostatic limit for the organism to survive. Because arousal is more fundamental than fear and anxiety, it is not surprising that it has been conceived of as "primary anxiety." Thus, Freud (1936) considered the "birth trauma," which is described as a state of stimulation beyond the infant's capacity to cope with, to be the prototype of all later anxiety. Unfortunately, he failed to develop the concept further, and remained content to leave it as a prototype for other forms of anxiety which he considered to be of greater significance. Fenichel (1945) explicitly distinguishes "primary anxiety," which he defines as stimulation beyond the organism's normal adaptive capacities, from signal anxiety. While signal anxiety is of primary importance for the psychoneurosis, primary anxiety is at the root of the traumatic neurosis, which is not dependent on the "meaning" of the stimulation: "... there are stimuli of such overwhelming intensity that they have a traumatic effect on anyone" (p. 117). Descriptions of the traumatic neurosis (Bond, 1952; Grinker & Spiegel, 1945; Kardiner, 1941) indicate that the following variables are important in its inception: (1) the intensity of stimulation; (2) the level of arousal preceding stimulation; (3) the rate of stimulus input; (4) the opportunity for motor discharge; (5) surprise. The first two variables are directly and cumulatively related to the total level of arousal reached. Motor discharge limits total arousal by providing for its dissipation. One wonders, however, if it is the motor discharge per se that is helpful, or whether it must be channeled into directed action. Very likely both contribute to reducing arousal. Rate of stimulus input and surprise, holding the other variables constant, cannot directly contribute to total stimulation, and must be explained by a consideration of the organism's mechanisms for coping with the intensity aspects of stimulation. This topic will be discussed later. For now, we can but state that inhibition is more efficient when it is gradually built up against small increments of stimulation than when it must be applied all at once for the first time, and that expectancies can be viewed as a form of selective inhibition that serves to modulate the effect of the intensity component of the expected stimulus, and makes the use of a blanket emergency form of inhibition unnecessary.

The theorist whose views on arousal most closely approach our own is Pavlov (1927, 1928, 1941). Pavlov hypothesized that there is an upper limit of total excitation that an organism can endure beyond which cortical damage occurs. As this limit is approached, protective, or "transmarginal," inhibition is invoked. Transmarginal inhibition is a key concept for Pavlov, and enters into almost all his explanations of maladaptive behavior, including experimental neurosis in animals and psychotic and psychoneurotic reactions in humans. Because of its special significance, Pavlov's theory will be presented in greater detail later.

So far, no attempt has been made to define arousal. At this point, we prefer to avoid a neurophysiological definition, and to consider arousal as a behavioral concept that is useful in accounting for reactions to variations in the intensity component of stimulation, and in taking into account the organism's apparent level of alertness, varying from relaxed sleep to emotional excitement (Woodworth & Schlosberg, 1954).

Up to now we have referred to arousal as though it were a unitary concept that could be measured by a single index. Certainly this is an oversimplification. Whether considering psychologically mediated inhibitory reactions at nonemergency levels of stress, as in our experienced parachutists, or reflexive homeostatic controls of intense arousal, it is apparent that different measures of physiological activity produce different results. To make matters more complicated, the relationships among the measures are known to vary from individual to individual and from situation to situation. Thus, given a situation of alert attention, heart rate declines while skin conductance rises (Lacey, Kagan, Lacey, & Moss, 1963). Under other conditions of stress both rise. Given meaningful functional differences between the physiological measures, it is pointless to attempt to reduce them to a common denominator of arousal through transformations or special methods of scoring, as some have attempted, although such attempts may succeed under restricted circumstances. Heart rate, unlike basal skin conductance, serves a vital function. It is thus not surprising that it is characterized by rapid self-regulatory shifts, such as deceleration following rapid acceleration, and vice versa. For measuring increases in autonomic arousal under conditions in which subjects serve as their own controls, we have uniformly found basal skin conductance to be our best measure. This is probably because it shows no reversal effects, but approaches an asymptote with increasing stress.

The picture is further complicated when one considers measures of arousal other than those of the autonomic nervous system. According to Pavlov, cortical inhibition following strong stimulation disinhibits the autonomic nervous system. A person in such a state would be judged low in arousal by the EEG, and high in arousal by measures of autonomic activity. In a study of the effects of severe sleep deprivation (Johnson, Slye, & Dement, 1965), it was noted that reactions to external stimulation all but disappeared, cortical activation, as measured by the EEG, was extremely low, and autonomic arousal extremely high. Depending on the measure taken, such a person would be described as either very high or very low in arousal. In this case, it is of interest that reactivity to external stimulation was low and autonomic arousal high, although under other circumstances they tend to be positively related.

Despite the complications just mentioned, it would be premature to reject the hypothesis that there is a general arousal system. In addition to subsystems of arousal, it is quite possible that there is an integrative system that responds to the total degree of afferent excitation directed toward the cortex, as has been postulated for the reticular activation system. In the meantime, the concept of a total quantity of stimulation against which the organism must defend itself appears to be useful at the behavioral level, and a rough index of it can be obtained by measures such as basal skin conductance. The arguments that have been and will be presented in this paper would not be materially affected if it turned out that there are only subsystems of arousal, as it is maintained that the same principles apply to all functionally organized systems of arousal and their inhibition. Certainly, in terms of evaluating present research findings, it is important to avoid accepting generalizations about "arousal" without considering the ways in which it was measured. This is particularly true in comparing studies that have used cortical activation, striated muscle tension, autonomic arousal, and indices of behavioral activity, as if they were all measuring the same thing.

3. Anxiety as Undirected Arousal following Perception of Danger

Having defined fear and arousal, the question remains whether there is a need for an additional concept, anxiety. Fear was defined as an avoidance motive and arousal as the nonspecific component of all motives. We believe that there is a particular qualitative state that corresponds to descriptions of anxiety and is neither fear nor arousal but shares some features of both. We define anxiety as a state of undirected arousal following perception of danger. Thus, anxiety differs from fear in that it is not channeled into specific avoidance behavior. It differs from arousal in that it is limited to arousal produced by the perception of danger. Anxiety might thus be called unconsummated fear, or arousal in search of becoming fear. An analogy will help clarify the distinctions between anxiety, arousal, and fear. Imagine a car moving along a road in the jungle. Suddenly the driver sees a herd of elephants advancing toward him. He turns the car around, races the motor, and flees as rapidly as he can. Fear corresponds to the perception of danger converted into the decision to flee and the motivation that sustains the flight. Now consider a situation in which the driver hears the hoof beats of the elephants but cannot determine the direction from which they are coming. He races the motor, but is unable to decide if he should go forward, backward, right, or left. The racing motor in the motionless car is analogous to anxiety. In human terms, the undecided driver with pounding heart is experiencing anxiety. Arousal corresponds to the speed of the motor, which could be the same for the car in motion and the stationary car with racing motor. It is assumed that the state of anxiety has a particularly aversive quality, which is adaptive in that it provides a strong incentive for arousal following the perception of danger to be directed into action.

In the foregoing example, the difference between decision and indecision was chosen as the dividing point between fear and anxiety. Once our anxious car was shifted into gear, the distribution of energy from anxiety to fear was already largely accomplished, although the car was not yet in motion. The decision to set the dividing point at the boundary between decision and indecision is somewhat arbitrary, and it perhaps would have been equally defensible to set it between decision and action. The difficulty in selecting a dividing point lies in the diffuse nature of the boundary between fear and anxiety. All that is clear is that at one extreme there is undirected arousal and at the other directed fear and flight. It is assumed that the quality of the affect following perception of danger shifts from anxiety to fear along a continuum, so that there exists a proportion of anxiety to fear in the mid ranges, rather than categorical states. A decision for action produces a major resolution of the undirected state, and thus provides a practical dividing point between fear and anxiety. However, a decision to engage in a specific course of action that cannot be carried out still contains elements of anxiety. The proportion of anxiety to fear is influenced by the degree of commitment to a course of action. A person in full flight who has no doubt that this constitutes the best course of action will experience only fear. A person in equally full flight who has doubts about whether he should run straight ahead, turn right or left, or hide, will experience anxiety as well as fear, the proportion of anxiety to fear being determined by the proportion of uncommitted to committed arousal. The perceived effectiveness of the action must be an important variable in determining the proportion of anxiety to fear, as it determines whether alternatives need be considered. High levels of threat are almost sure to raise questions about whether a chosen course of action is best, at least in the initial stages.

With the preceding analysis in mind, let us examine the specific kinds of conditions that can be expected to give rise to anxiety rather than fear. These should include all situations that do not permit directed activity for coping with the threat. Unconscious threat obviously provides such a situation, as do conditions where the source of danger cannot be located for external reasons. Examples include the harassment of troops by enemy shelling at unpredictable intervals, a person visiting a strange place where he does not know what to expect, and fear of the dark. Given a clearly perceived source of danger, anxiety can be produced by physical restraint that prevents action. An example of such a situation is a pilot pinned against the walls of an aircraft that is plummeting earthward. Conflict can produce anxiety, as the individual's own values constitute a restraining force against fear-instigated avoidance behavior that could remove him from the danger. Situations that involve a future element of threat that the individual cannot do anything about at the moment can be expected to produce anxiety. That such a state of anxiety is worse than immediate fear is attested to by reports of combat pilots who crash-dived their aircraft because they no longer could tolerate the anxiety produced by impending missions (Bond, 1952).

The assumed difference in affective quality between directed and un-directed arousal has widespread implications. It has already been noted that as undirected arousal mounts, because of its special aversive quality it provides an increasingly strong incentive for the organism to seek directed action, at least up to the point where extremely high levels of arousal may paralyze action. This can account for the development of fixations in organisms faced with insoluble problems, as any action, no matter how inappropriate, is less aversive than high levels of undirected arousal. It explains why people motivated by strong anxiety are highly suggestible and easily swayed by a leader or group to action that they normally would not consider. It accounts for the development of superstition, magic, and ritual in areas of stress for which there is no appropriate action, and for the readiness of patients to develop symptoms that substitute known for unknown fears.

The recognition that there are three related concepts, arousal, anxiety, and fear, permits a resolution of some problems that have evoked controversy among proponents of theoretical systems that recognize only two concepts, fear and anxiety. Some have argued that fear is more basic than anxiety, while others have maintained the reverse. The first view is supported by the observation that fear is learned in concrete situations and becomes converted into anxiety through repression. The second is supported by arguments that anxiety is an undifferentiated reaction that is observable in infants, while fear requires articulation of the source of threat. Support for the second view is also said to be provided by an analysis of the startle response in adults, which consists of a momentary diffuse reaction followed by a specific fear reaction (May, 1950). From our viewpoint, the nonspecific reaction of the infant and of the startled adult is a general arousal reaction that is more fundamental than both fear and anxiety. Anxiety develops out of an anticipation of high levels of arousal, and is immediately converted into fear as the arousal is channeled, in thought and deed, into specific avoidance behavior. Thus, under most circumstances, anxiety is not recognized as a separate, identifiable stage, but requires a blocking of the fear response before it is identified. In the sense that anxiety normally precedes fear for a fleeting moment, it can be considered more fundamental than fear. However, the picture is complicated by the consideration that the development of anxiety can follow fear, as when the feared object is repressed. The one thing that is clear is that nonspecific arousal, as a component of both fear and anxiety, is more fundamental than either.

B. The Generalization and Inhibition of Anxiety: A Two-Process Theory

The most interesting finding that emerged from the work on parachuting was the development of inverted V-shaped curves with experience. In order to account for the data, it was assumed that with successful experience two developments take place, a heightening and broadening of a gradient of anxiety, and the development of a gradient of inhibition, which becomes increasingly steeper than the gradient of anxiety. (Although anxiety, fear, and arousal were defined earlier as distinctive concepts, we shall also use the term anxiety, generically, to include all three. This is justified by the observation that the same principles apply to all three, and it would be unnecessarily cumbersome to refer to "anxiety, fear, and arousal" when their distinctive characteristics are not of concern.) We submit that these two developments are not restricted to parachuting, but have broad general significance for the mastery of anxiety. The heightening and broadening of the gradient of anxiety can be attributed to the increased classical conditioning of anxiety with repeated exposures to the same source of stress. It has the adaptive value that it automatically alerts the organism in advance of danger that normally would serve to keep the organism at a safe distance. Given a situation in which the source of threat must nevertheless be faced, and has been previously faced with successful outcome, it is assumed that inhibition allows the anxiety to be controlled. As the gradient of inhibition is steeper than that of anxiety, the advantage of the early warning signal is retained and the anxiety does not become excessive.

The double process of the expanding anxiety gradient and its inhibition is thus seen to be highly adaptive for the proactive mastery of stress and, as will be shown later, a related process is involved in the belated, or retroactive, mastery of stress. In both cases, mastery proceeds in small increments, but in one case it involves expanding the range of awareness of cues, whereas in the other it involves gradually approaching an area of stimulation that was once overwhelming and, in effect, decreasing the range of cues that are highly arousing. In proactive mastery, anxiety serves the constructive purpose of focusing attention upon significant cues and thereby requiring the person to deal with them. More specifically, the gradually expanding inhibitory gradient that causes the peak of anxiety to advance to increasingly remote cues serves to concentrate attention upon the cues that have not been mastered, and prevents energy from being wasted by concern with cues that have already been mastered. Anxiety and its inhibition are thus seen to be intimately connected with expanding awareness and the development of competence. This observation will be treated more extensively in a further section.

The remainder of the present section is devoted to an exploration of the generality of the two-process theory of mastery of anxiety. Four widely divergent sources of support for the theory are presented, including the proactive mastery of stress in combat flying, Pavlov's concepts of transmarginal inhibition and the paradoxical phase, the retroactive mastery of stress as exhibited in the repetition compulsion, and the retroactive mastery of stress as exhibited in acute grief.

1. The Proactive Mastery of Stress in Combat Flying

Bond (1952), a psychiatrist assigned to the Eighth Air Force in England during the second world war, noted that there were two processes that had to be considered in order to understand the reactions of flyers to combat. One is an expanding awareness of sources of danger, and the other an increasing ability to deal with danger. As the originally perceived sources of danger are mastered, the expanding gradient of anxiety forces attention to new sources. In stepwise fashion, the range of competence is expanded, but so is the range of cues capable of arousing anxiety, which places an increasing demand upon the forces of control.

In the following quotation from Bond, it would appear that he is referring to the same two processes that we postulated in our two-process theory of anxiety and its mastery:

> For practical purposes, danger is never treated as an entity but is divided into segments and each studied individually. Every dangerous event, as it comes up, is broken off and isolated to become the subject of rumination and repetitive conversation. Every possibility is explored, every potential outcome considered, and all defensive action carefully rehearsed. Once mastered, the event drops into the preconscious, and attention is then turned to a new one. The importance of this process may be inferred from the fact that the conversation of pilots is virtually limited to the hazards of the day....
>
> This mastery of a situation through the repetition of it, lies at the core of the toughening process that takes place in the ego, particularly during training and the early stages of combat. The process never ceases but becomes active with each new threat. Of particular importance is the timing of a trauma in relation to the toughening process. For instance, an event that may have a profound effect upon a cadet in his first flight will mean but little to a man in the basic phase and will scarcely be noticed by a seasoned flyer. This toughening process fulfills the function of pushing back the borders of the unknown, of replacing fantasy with reality, so that no longer is every event a blank screen on which inner fears are reflected but instead calls forth facts and certainties that limit the reflection and provide an outlet in the form of defensive action.
>
> At the same time that this process is taking place in a strengthening and protective way, there is a reverse trend. As a man learns the boundaries of a particular danger and devises methods to combat it, he also learns of new dangers that exist and new signs of them. Most men are at first protected by their inability to recognize danger and accordingly do not respond to it emotionally.... The lack of response on the part of the novice is often mistaken for courage (Bond, 1952, pp. 84–85).

Bond's statement, "Once mastered, the event drops into the preconscious and attention is then turned to a new one," would appear to correspond to the advancing inverted V-shaped curves observed in our parachutists.

2. Pavlov and the Paradoxical Phase

During the Leningrad flood, a number of Pavlov's dogs were trapped in their cages, and could only be rescued by dragging them under water. When tested for conditioned responses that they had previously demonstrated with great reliability, a number of the animals failed to show the expected responses. They gave the appearance of being inhibited and unresponsive. Pavlov deduced that the trauma had pushed them to their limit of tolerance for excitation and had triggered a massive defensive inhibitory reaction, which he referred to as "transmarginal inhibition." In the weeks immediately following the trauma, a peculiar and remarkably orderly sequence of changes was observed to take place before normal responding was eventually restored. Pavlov was later able to produce the effect in the laboratory by a number of conditions that induced a high state of excitation, such as intense stimulation, difficult discrimination, and rapid alternation between excitatory and inhibitory stimulation. The first stage following the general inhibitory state he called the "ultraparadoxical phase." This consisted of a complete reversal of the original gradient. The animal produced full responses to stimuli it had previously failed to respond to, and no responses to stimuli to which it had previously produced full responses. This was followed by a series of phases that he called "paradoxical," which consisted of maximum responses being produced at an intermediate point on the original dimension of stimulus strength, so that a series of inverted V-shaped curves was substituted for the original monotonic gradient. In successive phases, the peak of the curve advanced toward the end of the dimension containing the stronger stimuli. This was followed by an "equalization phase," in which all stimuli produced uniformly large responses. Following this, more paradoxical phases occurred, until the original gradient was restored. Each major phase lasted about a week, with the paradoxical phases on each side of the equalization phase considered separately. Repeated exposure to the same source of stress resulted in repetition of the cycle, each time more rapidly, until a point was reached beyond which the original gradient remained unaffected.

Figure 18 presents curves representing phases in the paradoxical sequence plotted from data on a single case provided by Pavlov (1927, pp. 271–272). The stimuli, in increasing order of original strength as determined by magnitude of conditioned response, were as follows: light (L); tactile stimulation at the rate of 24 per minute (T); a metronome (M); and a whistle (W). The original gradient of response strength is reproduced in

Fig. 18 as curve I. Pavlov describes the experiment as follows (the references in brackets are our own).

In between the different positive stimuli the differentiated tactile stimulus of 12 per minute was introduced, being applied during 30 seconds and then reinforced as usual. This seemingly small factor produced an extraordinary effect. On the day following this experiment and on the succeeding nine days all conditioned reflexes had disappeared excepting only for a very occasional small secretion [see Fig. 18, cycle II].... The first of these extremely peculiar changes is illustrated by the next experiment [see Fig. 18, cycle III]. The experiment shows exactly the reverse of what was observed during the normal state of the animal. The strong stimuli have either no effect or only a very small one;

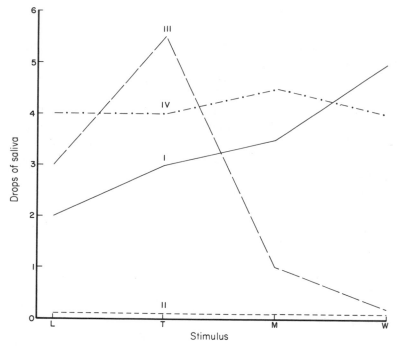

Fig. 18.   The sequence of phases, including the paradoxical phase, observed by Pavlov and attributed by him to the dissipation of transmarginal inhibition. The curves were plotted from data supplied by Pavlov on a single case (Pavlov, 1927, p. 271). Phase I corresponds to the original gradient, phase II to total inhibition, phase III to paradoxical responses, and phase IV to the stage of equivalence.

the weak stimuli have a greater effect than normal. All positive stimuli were, of course, reinforced. This state of the cortex we called the *paradoxical phase*. The paradoxical phase in this dog continued for fourteen days and was then succeeded by the following change: [see Fig. 18, cycle IV].... This was called the *phase of equalization*, since all the stimuli became equal in their effect. The phase of equalization lasted for seven days and was then succeeded by still another phase during which the effect of stimuli of medium strength was greatly increased, the effect of the strong stimulus was slightly diminished, while the weak stimulus had no effect. After seven days more, all the reflexes had returned to their normal value. In the succeeding experiments on the same problem, in order to be quite certain, we used different intensities of one of the positive stimuli. The results obtained were exactly comparable with the results of the previous experiments. It thus became obvious that the difference in the reaction to stimuli in all these different phases is determined by the relative strength of the stimuli (Pavlov, 1927, pp. 271–272).

Pavlov's explanation of the paradoxical phases was that they were produced by the dissipation of transmarginal inhibition. He assumed that as the inhibition lifts, it selectively releases from inhibition first stimulation of low potential excitation, and gradually stimuli of greater potential excitatory value. While he does not go beyond this analysis, it is evident that in order to account for the increase in magnitude of responses to weak stimuli it is necessary to assume that they were weak in the original gradient only because of inhibition, and were disinhibited by the transmarginal inhibition. The equalization stage can also be accounted for by disinhibition and the assumption that the original gradient was produced by selective inhibition of different stimuli associated with the same response. Following the assumption that the paradoxical phases were produced by a dissipation of transmarginal inhibition, Pavlov reasoned that an increase in inhibition would drive the cycle in the reverse direction. He was able to demonstrate this by the use of inhibitory drugs and by testing under conditions of drowsiness, which he considered to be a state of partial cortical inhibition.

Not only was Pavlov able to demonstrate prolonged paradoxical phases following high levels of excitation, but he was able to demonstrate similar effects for brief intervals with stimuli of relatively low intensity. Thus, the principle that inhibition becomes increasingly dominant over excitation as magnitude of stimulation increases applies to microcosmic as well as macrocosmic levels of organization of excitation and inhibition. Accordingly it is necessary to take into account inhibition produced by the total level of excitation even in relatively simple conditioning situations. Pavlov noted that there was a direct relationship between intensity of the conditioned stimulus and magnitude of the conditioned response only up to a point, after which further increases in the intensity of the conditioned stimulus produced inhibitory effects that reversed the relationship. He observed the same curvilinear relationship between food deprivation and magnitude of the conditioned response, and noted that motivation and stimulus intensity exert a combined influence upon inhibition. In the following quotation he comments on the combined effect of stimulus intensity and "excitability to food," or hunger.

If we start from the habitual sufficient feeding of the dog, during which the law of the relationship between the magnitude of the effect and the intensity of excitation manifests itself, and if we increase the animal's excitability to food, whether by decreasing the daily ration or by lengthening the interval between the last feeding and the beginning of the experiment, or merely by making the food more tasty, we shall surely observe very interesting modifications in the magnitude of the conditioned reflexes. The law of the dependence of the magnitude of the effect and the intensity of excitation becomes abruptly changed; now both strong and weak stimuli are comparable in their effects, or, what happens even more often, strong stimuli produce a smaller effect than the weak ones (the equivalent and paradoxical phases), the strong stimuli decreasing and the weak ones increasing their effects (equivalent and paradoxical phases on a high level) (Pavlov, 1941, p. 54).

The sequence of paradoxical phases following intense stimulation illustrated by Pavlov's dogs is similar to the sequence of inverted V-shaped curves that we observed in our parachutists, with two exceptions. One is that the parachutists did not exhibit a state of equivalence, and the other is that the direction of the cycle was reversed. This latter difference is readily accounted for as our results were attributed to increasing inhibition and Pavlov's to decreasing inhibition. When he experimentally increased inhibition, Pavlov's findings corresponded to ours. The state of equivalence in Pavlov's data and its absence in ours can be accounted for in either of two ways. One is that, given inverted V-shaped curves and some un-reliability of measurement, it is possible when plotting only four points to have them fall on both sides of the curve so that they show little variation. The other is that the stage of equivalence is the result of the disinhibition of a generalization gradient produced by differential inhibition. The gradual dissipation of transmarginal inhibition could conceivably contribute just the right amount of inhibition at some point to accomplish such disinhibition without adding further inhibitory effects of its own. This analysis applies to the Pavlovian situation, but not to parachuting, as only in the former case was dissipation of inhibition a factor. In support of the interpretation of disinhibition for Pavlov's data, the responses in the equalization phase are approximately full strength.

The advancing peak of the curves of the experienced parachutists was seen to be highly adaptive in preparing the parachutist for coping with stress about to be encountered. What adaptive significance, if any, can the posttraumatic paradoxical sequence have? We submit that it corresponds to the retroactive mastery of stress in much the same manner as the other corresponds to the proactive mastery of stress. In this respect, it is note-worthy that with repeated exposure to the same source of stress, the cycle of the paradoxical phase is shortened, until the organism is able to with-stand the original stress without deviating from its normal pattern. The mastery of stress, whether proactive or retroactive, appears to involve something akin to an innoculation with increasing increments of stress. In one case this serves to broaden the range of anxiety-provoking cues that can be dealt with effectively, and extends awareness and proficiency, while in the other the development is in the reverse direction, and reduces the range of cues that elicit high levels of arousal.

In order to account for the inverted V-shaped curves of experienced parachutists it was assumed that the gradient of inhibition of anxiety is steeper than the gradient of generalized anxiety. The same assumption accounts for the paradoxical phases observed by Pavlov, where inverted V-shaped curves were produced with peaks advancing in the opposite direction. The opposite direction of the changing peaks in Pavlov's data is explained by a reduction rather than an increase in inhibition, which is consistent with Pavlov's assumption that the phenomenon is due to the dissipation of transmarginal inhibition.

Pavlov's finding that the principles that determine the paradoxical phase hold for small as well as massive quantities of excitation and inhibition extends the applicability of the assumption that the gradient of inhibition is steeper than that of excitation beyond the area of anxiety, and suggests that it describes a general law for the modulation of excitation at many levels of organization, which we will refer to as the *law of excitatory modulation (LEM)*, and discuss in detail later.

3. The Belated Mastery of Stress: The Repetition Compulsion and Mourning

Freud was so impressed with the repetitive dreams of traumatized soldiers that it led him to revise his theory of dreaming. In *Beyond the Pleasure Principle* (1959), Freud conceded that not all dreams are motivated by wish-fulfillment, and introduced a new principle, the repetition compulsion. The repetition compulsion refers to a tendency for a trauma to be repeated. It occurs in the speech, thought, and imagery of adults, and in the play of children. Freud deduced that the repetition is an attempt by the organism to gain belated mastery of an experience that had overwhelmed it. According to Fenichel (1945), "The repetition dreams of the traumatic neurotic represent a regression to this primitive mode of mastery; by experiencing again and again what once had to be gone through in the trauma, the control may slowly be regained. It brings belated discharge and thus helps to get rid of tensions" (p. 120).

Fenichel also noted that control is gained because the repetition occurs actively rather than passively, and the individual is able to proceed at his own rate in dealing with increasing intensities of arousal. He describes the repetition compulsion in children as one of the principal ways in which anxiety generated by excessive stimulation from an unfamiliar world is mastered: "The ways by which the normal ego learns to overcome its early and still untamed anxiety is very characteristic. Whenever the organism is flooded with a very large quantity of excitation it attempts to get rid of it by subsequent active repetitions of the situation that induced the excessive excitation. At first the passive experiences that aroused anxiety are reproduced actively by the child in order to achieve a belated mastery. Later on, the child in his play not only dramatizes the exciting experiences of the past but he also anticipates what he expects to happen in the future" (pp. 44–45). In a summary statement on different forms of repetition compulsion, Fenichel notes, "This type of repetition is seen first and most clearly in children's games, where what was experienced passively before is repeated actively in an amount and at a time chosen by the ego. The same pattern occurs in repetitive dreams and symptoms of traumatic neurotics and in many similar little actions of normal persons who in thought, stories, or actions repeat upsetting experiences a number of times before these experiences are mastered" (p. 542).

From the foregoing, it is apparent that three main elements are credited with producing mastery of the trauma through repetition. These are (1) discharge of pent-up tension, (2) the substitution of an active for a passive experience, and (3) reexperiencing the trauma in small doses that the organism can manage. While the change from passive to active experience can account for the ameliorative effects of play and story telling, it is unable to account for repetitive dreams, a passive occurrence. We believe that the repetition in small doses is the most fundamental reaction. The repetition produces a desensitization, which is analogous to the habituation of a strong stimulus repeatedly presented. The desensitization can be attributed to the development of selective inhibition. Unlike Pavlov's concept of transmarginal inhibition, which referred to an emergency defense against overwhelming excitation by a blanket form of inhibition that interfered with normal functioning, the inhibitory reactions that develop gradually through repetition are assumed to be selective and to constitute "mastery" in the sense that they do not interfere with the organism's general level of functioning. It is possible that the repetition compulsion and the posttraumatic paradoxical phases described by Pavlov are the same phenomenon. The essential element common to both is that they involve a working back to the original trauma from reduced levels of intensity and displacement. While the experience of the displaced representations of the trauma is itself painful, it is nevertheless at a level that the organism can assimilate. The repetition compulsion can be viewed as a compromise, or net effect between excitatory and inhibitory gradients: "The ego's attitude toward the repetition is a very ambivalent one. The repetition is desired to relieve a painful tension; but because the repetition itself is also painful, the person is afraid of it and tends to avoid it. Usually, therefore, a compromise is sought: a repetition on a smaller scale or under more encouraging circumstances" (Fenichel, 1945, p. 543).

Although we have emphasized the passive aspects of the repetition compulsion, we do not mean to imply that active mastery is not important. It is noteworthy that the same pattern that occurs passively in dreams and in the conditioned reactions of Pavlov's dogs occurs actively in children's play, in the directed thoughts of adults, and in psychotherapy. Active and passive mastery are necessarily related; passive mastery sets limits for active mastery by determining the level of arousal that can be tolerated, and active mastery can facilitate or hinder passive mastery, depending on its pacing. Thus, the child in his play, and the psychotherapist with his client can regulate the rate and intensity of the traumatic cues that are dealt with. If the pacing is too rapid it will drive the reaction in the opposite direction of desensitization, and serve only to produce increased defensiveness. Normal mastery proceeds by working through anxiety in small doses; abnormal mastery by shutting out.

Like the repetition compulsion following traumatic stimulation, the "work of mourning" following severe loss provides an example of retroactive mastery of stress. Lindemann (1944) notes that the symptoms of acute grief include ". . . sensations of somatic distress occurring in waves lasting from twenty minutes to an hour at a time, a feeling of tightness in the throat, choking with shortness of breath, need for sighing, and an empty feeling in the abdomen, lack of muscular power, and an intense subjective distress described as tension or mental pain. The patient soon learns that these waves of discomfort can be precipitated by visits, by mentioning the deceased, and by receiving sympathy. There is a tendency to avoid the syndrome at any cost, to refuse visits lest they should precipitate the reaction, and to keep deliberately from thought all references to the deceased" (p. 141). Thus, as in the traumatic neurosis, cues that can be associated with the stressful event are disturbing and tend to be avoided. That the distress following loss produces a high level of arousal is revealed in the following statement: "The activity throughout the day of the severely bereaved person shows remarkable changes. There is no retardation of action and speech; quite to the contrary, there is a push of speech, especially when talking about the deceased. There is restlessness, inability to sit still, moving about in an aimless fashion, continually searching for something to do. There is, however, at the same time, a painful lack of capacity to initiate and maintain organized patterns of activity" (Lindemann, 1944, p. 142).

The normal mastery of severe loss requires emotional discharge in response to cues associated with the loss. The process must progress in small doses if it is not to be overwhelming and increase defensiveness. Abnormal defenses include a variety of reactions that are used to avoid the grief work, such as hostility to those who would encourage the process, or whose presence serves as a reminder, denial, withdrawal, avoidance of cues associated with the loss, and distraction. Symptoms produced by these defenses include conversion reactions, psychosomatic disorders, agitated depression, manic activity, and a syndrome consisting of a loss of spontaneity, emotional blunting, and an inability to become interested in anything. Lindemann describes such individuals as having an appearance that is "wooden and formal, with affectivity and conduct resembling schizophrenic pictures" (p. 145). In the course of avoiding the pain of their grief and holding their hostility in check, such persons appear to have developed a blanket type of inhibition against all emotion. Thus, the principle is again illustrated that abnormal defenses consist of an all-or-none defense system, whereas normal defenses consist of modulated inhibitory reactions that develop out of dealing with stress in small doses.

C. NORMAL AND ABNORMAL DEFENSES

It has been demonstrated that the successive inhibition of increasingly generalized anxiety serves to expand an individual's effectiveness in coping with threat and constitutes the normal process for the proactive mastery of stress. In like manner, the successive inhibition of increasingly less generalized anxiety allows the organism to undo the debilitating effects of overwhelming past threat and constitutes the normal process for the retroactive mastery of stress. From this viewpoint, abnormal defenses are any responses or response dispositions that interfere with the normal process of mastery.

It will be recalled that experienced parachutists exhibited a defense system in depth, consisting of an early line of defense based upon fear and its inhibition, followed by a later line of defense based upon increasing physiological arousal and its inhibition, psychologically mediated. Physiological homeostatic controls against yet higher levels of arousal constituted a third line of defense. Finally, Pavlov's concept of transmarginal inhibition would constitute a last, critical line of defense against excessive arousal. In the opposite direction, the most forward line of defenses are defenses against fear and anxiety, which themselves can be viewed as defenses against primary arousal. Defenses against fear and anxiety include various forms of denial and the usual psychoanalytic defense mechanisms. If such early defenses are too extensively employed, the later lines of defense are not given an opportunity to develop. Putting it otherwise, though denying reality, anxiety can be avoided, but only at the cost of not learning to deal with reality. As a result, the organism is left with a single line of defense between potentially anxiety-producing cues and the instigation of emergency biological defenses. This is what we have described as an all-or-none defense system. Does this mean that all defenses that involve denial are abnormal? The answer is no; the denial is not abnormal unless it is so complete as to completely short-circuit the normal process of mastery. The novice parachutist who initially denied the existence of anxiety-producing cues later became the experienced parachutist who had more effective ways of dealing with anxiety. It is important to recognize that defense mechanisms, including perceptual denial, can be used to a greater or lesser degree, and that a limited amount of denial or avoidance may be useful in permitting the individual to master certain aspects of a task which by themselves produce all the anxiety he can manage. Thus, "abnormal" defenses should not be judged so much by the specific quality of the defense as by whether they shut off the process of mastery, or simply help pace it. Of course, the more extreme the defense, the more likely it is to produce a complete shutting off.

As a consequence of the work of mastery, selective inhibitory controls are developed in depth. This produces a highly modulated control system as contrasted with an all-or-none control system of defense. As the modulated control system was developed through dealing with successive increments in anxiety, it is associated with a high degree of perceptual discrimination and the ability to inhibit anxiety-producing responses at a number of points along a range of anxiety-producing cues, including cues that are self-produced. Control can thereby be initiated early, so that the adaptive features of anxiety as a warning signal at a relatively low intensity of arousal can be retained. Moreover, should the defense fail at one point, it can be instituted at the next. The disadvantages of an all-or-none defense system are obvious. The individual with such a control system is exceedingly vulnerable, as once the defense breaks down he has no means of dealing with the threat. As noted in the section on acute grief, an individual with an all-or-none defense system is forced to constrict his environment, his thinking, and his emotions, lest he come upon cues or make responses that supply the opening wedge for destroying the defense. Finally, apart from the potential for being overwhelmed, there is the increased danger caused by the absence of an effective warning system. Grinker and Spiegel (1945) describe the "old sergeant syndrome," which consists of a disappearance of anxiety after prolonged combat. They report that they were not able to interview a single case, since such people did not last very long.

Turning to the question of the circumstances under which abnormal defenses are apt to develop, apart from biological differences and differential reinforcement, there is a general principle that deserves consideration.

Ultimately, all defenses are defenses against high levels of arousal. The higher the resting level of arousal, the more desperate is the need for defense against increases in arousal. As the level of arousal approaches the individual's upper limit of biological tolerance, it becomes impossible for him to invest the extra increment of arousal necessary to undertake the work of mastery; that is, labeling a source of threat momentarily increases the threat. Attempts to motivate an individual to do so can only strengthen the development of an all-or-none defense system. Not until an acute state of arousal has somewhat dissipated can the work of mastery begin, and even then pacing is important, as excessive increments in arousal will tend to reverse the process.

We have emphasized the importance of inhibition throughout, noting that abnormal defenses consist of undifferentiated or diffuse inhibitory control, and normal defenses of selective and modulated inhibitory control. As already indicated, it is necessary to distinguish between two kinds of psychologically mediated inhibition, namely, passive and active. The former is responsible for the desensitization that occurs as a consequence of repeated stimulation so long as the intensity of stimulation is not excessive. This kind of inhibition was assumed to be responsible for the paradoxical phase in Pavlov's dogs following trauma, and the repetitive dreams that occurred in the traumatic neurosis. Active inhibition was involved in the proactive mastery of stress in sport parachuting, where it was noted that parachutists learned to make responses that reduced their level of anxiety, and that with experience, the responses occurred earlier, thereby causing a continuous displacement and reduction in the peaks of the curves of fear and arousal. A similar process occurs in avoidance conditioning, which provides an interesting paradigm for the active mastery of fear (Solomon & Wynne, 1954).

In avoidance conditioning, an animal is presented with a cue, such as a buzzer, before receiving a shock. By making the appropriate response, such as pressing a lever, before the scheduled onset of the shock, the animal can avoid receiving the shock. The avoidance response is thus an experimental analogue of a defense mechanism invoked by signal anxiety. Early in the experiment, before the animal learns to make the avoidance response, anxiety is increasingly conditioned to the buzzer. As a result, a gradient of anxiety develops that increases from the onset of the buzzer to the time when the shock is delivered (Solomon & Wynne, 1954). Evidence for the gradient is provided by the animal's agitated behavior, including an increase in urination and defecation. When the animal first learns to make the avoidance response, it occurs late in the interval. With increasing experience, the avoidance response occurs earlier, until it almost immediately follows the onset of the buzzer. The explanation for the advancing response is that the sooner it occurs, the sooner it interrupts the mounting anxiety. The animal's behavior is consistent with such an interpretation, as after an early response it shows few signs of anxiety, while if the response is delayed, anxiety appears. As a consequence of the increasingly early avoidance responses, the peak of anxiety is displaced forward in time in much the same manner as for our experienced parachutists.

All that is necessary for adapting the avoidance model to the data for the parachutists or to a general model for the inhibitory control of anxiety in humans is to assume that humans make avoidance responses in thought and imagination in much the same manner as animals make overt avoidance responses. Although the cues to which anxiety was conditioned in the avoidance paradigm for the animal were external, the anxiety-producing cues for the human can be either internal or external. Thus, the experienced parachutist learns what he must think or not think to shut off the mounting anxiety produced by his own thoughts and images, as well as by external cues. With experience he, like the animal, can learn to make his avoidance responses earlier and with increasing efficiency. There is one important distinction between the human in the natural situation and the animal in the avoidance-conditioning experiment. For the animal, once the avoidance response is made, buzzer and shock are turned off completely. For the human in the real-life situation, it is necessary to maintain a continuous defense against thoughts and responses that can increase anxiety. Thus, the concept of active inhibition is meaningful only in the human situation. It is, of course not necessary for the avoidance responses to be conscious. Very likely, as they become habitual with experience, and require little effort, they become unconscious.

IV. Extension of the Theory of Mastery of Anxiety to a Theory for the Modulation of the Intensity Component of All Stimulation

It is proposed that the principles uncovered for the control of anxiety apply to a broad adaptive system for the modulation of the intensity component of all stimulation.

In the study of anxiety it was noted that the two-process theory that was formulated not only accounted for very different kinds of data from our own studies of parachuting, but also accounted for a wide range of phenomena reported by others, such as the peculiar, but highly orderly, sequence of paradoxical phases observed in Pavlov's dogs, the mastery of stress in combat flying, and the working-through process in the traumatic neurosis and acute grief. The wide range of applicability, as well as the remarkable reliability of relatively complex phenomena revealed in our own data, suggests the operation of a fundamental principle. That the phenomenon is even more general than the work on anxiety suggests is indicated by the observation that the same principles account for a variety of findings unrelated to anxiety in its usual sense. In this respect, it will be recalled that Pavlov observed the paradoxical phase at relatively low as well as at extreme levels of stimulation. Moreover, it will be shown that the parameters of the traumatic neurosis may well be identical with those of the startle reaction; that is, the principles that account for a momentary state of disorganization produced by relatively mild stimulation are the same as those that account for an enduring pathological state of disorganization produced by overwhelming stimulation.

It is our belief that there is a fundamental psychophysiological system by which the organism reacts to the intensity component of all stimulation, a system that constitutes a rudimentary form of learning. This system, which accounts for "intensity learning," brings the organism into efficient contact with its environment, and is more basic than, influences, and is in turn influenced by, cue learning, or conditioning.

The theory is presented in the form of a number of postulates. It is beyond the scope of this paper to defend the postulates as thoroughly as might be done. This will have to await a further publication. The reader who is interested in a more detailed presentation of relevant viewpoints and a more detailed review of pertinent studies is referred to the works of Berlyne (1960), Duffy (1962), Diamond, Balvin, and Diamond (1963), and Sokolov (1963).

The postulates are offered in the spirit of bold speculation, with the aim of determining how far the principles uncovered in the study of anxiety can be stretched to encompass other areas. If they extend as far as we have reason to hope they will, some astonishing integrating principles will emerge. If they do not, they will at least point the way to some basic experiments that need to be done, and were bypassed because they seemed mundane in comparison to problems involving more complex learning, such as conditioning within the paradigm of a paired CS and UCS.

A. POSTULATE 1. THERE IS A GRADIENT OF INCREASING EXCITATION AS A FUNCTION OF INCREASING STIMULUS INTENSITY

This postulate is perhaps self-evident. It merely recognizes that stronger stimuli transmit greater amounts of energy than weaker stimuli. The word excitation was chosen in preference to alternatives, such as arousal, because excitation is an inferred process that is not considered to exert a direct influence upon behavior; it is the net effect of excitation and inhibition at a particular level of organization that is presumed to influence behavior, including indices of arousal. Thus, postulates on excitation cannot be tested apart from postulates on inhibition.

It is necessary to qualify the postulate by restricting it to a range between a lower and upper limit, since below a threshold value it will not matter how much weaker a stimulus is, and above a point where all receptors are maximally aroused or where neural transmission has reached its capacity, increasing intensity of stimulation can make no difference.

B. POSTULATE 2. THERE IS A GRADIENT OF DECREASING EXCITATION AS A FUNCTION OF INCREASING TIME SINCE THE PRESENTATION OF A STIMULUS

This postulate simply refers to the declining effectiveness of a stimulus with the passage of time. While it may appear self-evident to the point of not being worth stating, this is no longer true when it is considered in conjunction with the corresponding postulate on inhibition. Limits are necessary to allow for refractory periods when time intervals are very short, and for the consideration that when the interval is great enough, further increases in time will no longer matter.

C. POSTULATE 3. THERE IS A GRADIENT OF INCREASING EXCITATION AS A FUNCTION OF NUMBER OF STIMULUS PRESENTATIONS WITHIN A FIXED TIME INTERVAL

This postulate assumes that excitatory tendencies within a restricted time interval are cumulative. It is not as self-evident as the previous ones, since cumulative effects are readily masked by the dissipation of excitation with time and by rapidly developing inhibitory effects with successive presentations of the same stimulus.

D. POSTULATE 4. THERE IS A GRADIENT OF INCREASING INHIBITION AS A FUNCTION OF INCREASING STIMULUS INTENSITY

The postulates on inhibition are not testable, except through their relationships with the postulates on excitation, which require further postulates on the nature of the interaction of the two. They are stated simply to make explicit the assumption that the organism must not only respond to stimulation, but must protect itself from excessive stimulation.

E. POSTULATE 5. THERE IS A GRADIENT OF DECREASING INHIBITION AS A FUNCTION OF INCREASING TIME SINCE THE PRESENTATION OF A STIMULUS

This postulate simply notes that just as excitation dissipates in time, so does inhibition.

F. POSTULATE 6. THERE IS A GRADIENT OF INCREASING INHIBITION
   AS A FUNCTION OF THE NUMBER OF STIMULUS PRESENTATIONS
   WITHIN A FIXED TIME INTERVAL

This postulate assumes that inhibition, like excitation, is cumulative. It is required to account for the organism's failure to experience traumatic levels of arousal from the cumulative effects of repeated mild levels of stimulation.

G. POSTULATE 7. THE GRADIENT OF INHIBITION AS A FUNCTION
   OF STIMULUS INTENSITY IS STEEPER THAN THE GRADIENT OF
   EXCITATION

If the gradient of inhibition is steeper than the gradient of excitation, then indices of net excitatory strength as a function of increasing stimulus intensity should first increase, and then reverse direction (see Fig. 19).

There are several sources of support for the deduction that the curve of net excitatory strength as a function of increasing intensity of stimulation is inverted V-shaped. One is Pavlov's (1941) observation that up to a point, the magnitude of the conditioned response is proportionate to the intensity of the CS, but with increasing intensity, the relationship is reversed. The higher the level of motivation, the earlier the point of reversal. A second source of support is Sokolov's (1963) finding that as stimulus intensity increases, orienting reflexes give way to defensive reflexes. A third line of evidence is provided by experiments on the effect of extraneous stimulation upon sensory thresholds. The overall evidence tends to support the conclusion that moderate levels of intensity of extraneous stimulation reduce sensory thresholds, whereas strong levels elevate thresholds (Berlyne, 1960; Diamond *et al.*, 1963; Duffy, 1962; Sokolov, 1963). A final source of evidence for inhibitory effects becoming increasingly dominant at high levels of stimulation is provided by the curve form of physiological activity as a function of increasing stimulation. According to Wilder (1957), at moderately high resting levels of physiological activity a small increment in stimulation may increase physiological activity, and a greater increment decrease it.

H. POSTULATE 8. THE GRADIENT OF INHIBITION AS A FUNCTION
   OF TIME SINCE THE PRESENTATION OF A STIMULUS IS STEEPER
   THAN THE GRADIENT OF EXCITATION

This postulate draws attention to the less stable nature of inhibition than excitation as a function of time. In Fig. 19, inhibition is represented as varying more sharply with time than excitation. The effect of time upon the gradients is represented in a manner corresponding to the effect of stimulus intensity. Thus, it is assumed that the residual net excitation following a strong stimulus after a lapse in time is comparable to that of a weaker stimulus more recently presented. Shortly after the presentation of a strong stimulus, inhibition is stronger than excitation, i.e., the net difference is in favor of inhibition. As time increases, excitation equals and then exceeds inhibition. Finally, both decay to zero. "Spontaneous recovery" corresponds to the period when inhibition falls below excitation. The time intervals that correspond to the dominance of inhibition over excitation and vice versa are influenced by stimulus intensity. For example, unless stimulus intensity were great enough to begin with, the gradients would not cross. The greater the intensity of the stimulus, the greater should be the magnitude of spontaneous recovery and the time lag for it to appear. The upper regions of the excitatory and inhibitory curves in Fig. 19 would apply only to levels of intense stimulation to begin with.

The postulate is supported by Sokolov's (1963) observation that following strong pain or sound stimulation there is an immediate defense reflex which, after a brief interval, is followed by an orienting reflex. A failure to take the time interval into account following the presentation of an extraneous stimulus may account for the contradictory results of different investigators on the effect of extraneous stimulation upon sensory thresholds (Berlyne, 1960; Duffy, 1962).

I. POSTULATE 9. THE GRADIENT OF INHIBITION AS A FUNCTION OF THE NUMBER OF STIMULUS PRESENTATIONS WITHIN A FIXED INTERVAL IS STEEPER THAN THE GRADIENT OF EXCITATION

The combined effect of gradients of inhibition and excitation leads to the prediction that given repeated stimulation with intensity held constant, indices of physiological arousal should first increase and then decrease when inhibition becomes dominant over excitation. Thus, the buildup of excitation and inhibition as a function of repeated stimulation is viewed as similar to the buildup of excitation and inhibition as a function of increasing intensity of stimulation, and is represented by the same curves (see Fig. 19). This is not to deny there are important differences between stimulating the organism with one large quantity of energy versus presenting the same total energy in smaller quantities distributed over time. From a consideration of the dissipation of excitation and inhibition over time alone, it is obvious that there must be a difference (see postulate 8). A prolonged single stimulus can be viewed as the equivalent of a number of stimuli of shorter duration.

Postulate 9 is supported by Sokolov's (1963) observation that with repeated presentation of a moderately strong stimulus, such as an electric shock, orienting reflexes give way to defensive reflexes. The greater the number of stimulations, the weaker the stimulus that is required to evoke a defensive reflex. The facilitation and deficit in sensory and motor responses

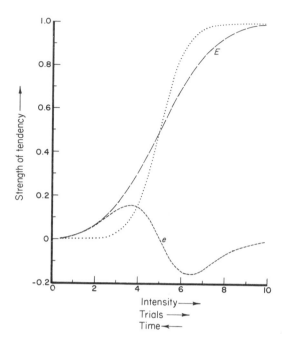

FIG. 19.   Theoretical curves of excitation (E), inhibition (I), and net excitation (e) as a function of stimulus intensity. The curve of inhibition is represented by the integral of the normal curve: $I = \int \phi(x)$; the curve of excitation by the formula $E = \int \phi(x/2)$. For both curves a constant of 5 has been added to the abscissa in order to have zero correspond to the origin rather than the midpoint of the intensity dimension. The curve of net excitation was obtained by subtracting inhibition from excitation.

On the basis of certain reasonable assumptions, sigmoidal curves appear to be more appropriate than linear functions. These assumptions are that the curves of excitation and inhibition are bounded by lower and upper asymptotes, the former having the value of zero and the latter corresponding to the maximum load that the nervous system can transmit. It follows that if inhibition is to increase more rapidly than, and overtake, excitation within the midrange of the dimension, and the curves begin and end at the same points, it is necessary for excitation to increase more rapidly than inhibition at the extremes of the dimension. As a result, the curve of net excitation completes a full cycle, rising to zero again after a negative, or inhibitory, phase. The full cycle requires that the entire dimension of stimulus intensity within a subsystem of excitation and inhibition be represented. It is presumed that under most experimental conditions only the first half of the dimension is included, so that linear representation of the inferred curves is normally adequate. Under such circumstances inverted V-shaped curves of net excitation are obtained regardless of whether the inferred curves of excitation and inhibition are represented by sigmoidal or linear functions. Given the full range of the dimension, net excitation is zero at both the lower and upper end. That a dynamic equilibrium is reached between the greater magnitudes of excitation and inhibition at the upper end of the dimension, rather than a smooth canceling out, is supported by the observation that at high levels of stress abrupt fluctuations occur between symptoms of extreme arousal and extreme inhibition (Sargant, 1957).

that correspond to orienting and defensive reflexes, respectively, can be predicted from Fig. 19, if it is assumed that facilitation corresponds to the portion of the curve where excitation exceeds inhibition, and deficit to the portion of the curve where inhibition exceeds excitation.

Data from our own laboratory (Epstein & Fenz, 1966) provide more direct confirmation of the postulate. Figure 20 presents the effects of nine presentations of a loud noise at 10-second intervals upon basal skin conductance. In accordance with the model, basal conductance rises at first, then falls.

Inhibition is very likely a direct function of the *rate* of increase of excitation. Given a rapid buildup of excitation, such as can be produced by the repetition of a moderately strong stimulus with a very brief inter-stimulus interval, inhibition must build up yet more rapidly in order to overtake excitation. As a result, with a rapid rate of stimulus input, so long as it is not overwhelming, there can only be a brief interval during which excitation exceeds inhibition. This explains why individuals are often able to perform effectively during a crisis with a surprising absence of anxiety, only to experience a prolonged after-discharge of anxiety later. Presumably, the initial perception of the crisis produced a rapid rise in excitation, which triggered a yet more rapid rise in inhibition. The situation is represented in Fig. 21, where the time period A–B, which immediately follows perception of the crisis and where excitation exceeds inhibition, is relatively brief. During the crisis, inhibition remains greater than excitation. After the crisis, both gradually fall off, with inhibition falling off more rapidly (postulate 8). As a result of the slow rate of decrease, the period during which excitation exceeds inhibition is much greater postcrisis (C–D) than precrisis (A–B). The differential rate of change in excitation for the two periods can be compared to the striking of a bell, where the energy is transmitted to the bell all at once, but dissipates gradually, as indicated in the prolonged reverberation.

The representation of the curves by the integral of the normal distribution has some interesting implications. It is consistent with a model of the nervous system as having neuronal threshold values that are normally distributed, with most neurons within a system having an intermediate threshold value, while a few have very low and a few very high threshold values. As a result, as stimulus intensity increases, the number of neurons whose threshold is exceeded corresponds to the integral of the normal curve. The reference to trials and time on the abscissa is for consideration in the discussion of later postulates.

It has come to our attention that Trehub (1954) arrived at a similar formulation. In an unpublished doctoral dissertation he noted that visual threshold varies with autonomic activity in a manner consistent with predictions derived from a theory of heteromodal stimulation which assumes that a negatively accelerated facilitative function interacts with an ogival inhibitory function, which is steeper in slope throughout most of the function.

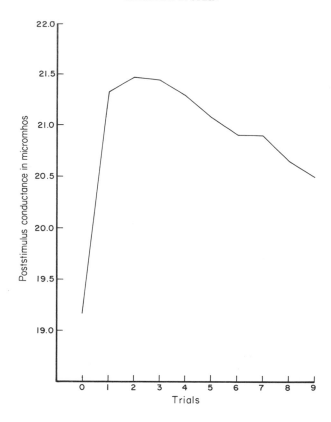

Fig. 20. Basal skin conductance as a function of the presentation of a loud noise at 10-second intervals over 9 trials (from Epstein & Fenz, 1966).

J. POSTULATE 10. EXCITATION FROM ALL SOURCES COMBINES INTO A TOTAL LEVEL OF EXCITATION; THE GRADIENT OF INHIBITION AS A FUNCTION OF TOTAL EXCITATION IS STEEPER THAN THE GRADIENT OF TOTAL EXCITATION

It is assumed that stimulation from many sources, internal and external, produces a total level of excitation against which the organism must defend itself. This is not to deny that there are subsystems of arousal and inhibition. The postulate assumes the existence of a phenomenon analogous to Pavlov's concept of transmarginal inhibition, at least in behavioral terms. It is consistent with Malmo's (1959) suggestion that Hull's (1943) concept of generalized drive can be viewed as the organism's state of total physiological activation, which can be estimated from physiological indices. Finally, the concept of total arousal is consistent with the observation that there are centers, such as the reticular activating center, that transmit and integrate

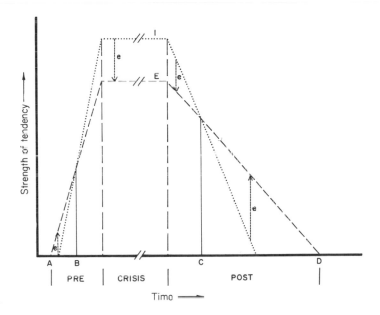

FIG. 21. Theoretical curves of excitation (*E*), inhibition (*I*), and net excitation (*e*) during and after a crisis. Period A–B corresponds to the brief period during which excitation exceeds inhibition upon initial perception of the crisis. Period B–C corresoponds to the prolonged period during and immediately after the crisis, when inhibition exceeds excitation. Period C–D corresponds to an after-discharge of anxiety, when excitation again exceeds inhibition.

the intensity component of various sources of stimulation, and constitute, at least in part, a relatively general activation system (Duffy, 1962; Lindsley, 1951; Malmo, 1959). That inhibition occurs in relationship to total stimulation, internal and external, and that the gradient of such inhibition is steeper than the gradient of excitation is supported by Pavlov's (1941) observation that the higher the level of motivation, the lower the intensity of a stimulus that will produce inhibitory effects. It is also supported by Pavlov's observation of paradoxical phases following intense levels of overall stimulation.

K. POSTULATE 11. INHIBITION IS ORGANIZED IN DEPTH AND BREADTH

As Diamond *et al.* (1963) convincingly point out, inhibition is not restricted to the operation of antagonistic muscles, which produce conflict and tension, but is represented at all functional levels of organization, peripheral and central, sensory and motor, microscopic and macroscopic. In short, inhibition is the very essence of control, and it is only its failure at an earlier level that produces conflict at the motor level. We are postulating that at all levels of organization, the gradient of inhibition is steeper than the gradient of the excitation that it inhibits, thereby providing a modulated control system of excitation.

Inhibition in depth was illustrated by the findings in our studies of experienced parachutists, where fear and its inhibition preceded a later increase in physiological arousal and its psychologically mediated inhibition. At yet higher levels of stress it is known that the activity of individual organs is regulated by homeostatic inhibitory controls, and finally, at extremely high levels of stress a more widespread inhibition appears to take place, which corresponds to Pavlov's concept of transmarginal inhibition. Inhibition in depth can also be viewed in terms of the sequence of reactions beginning with perception and terminating in an overt response. As indicated in the analysis of responses of parachutists, inhibition should be able to occur anywhere along this sequence.

Inhibition in breadth is illustrated by Pavlov's finding that the same principles of inhibition that account for paradoxical phases following traumatic stimulation apply to similar reactions produced by relatively mild levels of stimulation.

In seeking unifying principles underlying different functional levels of organization of excitation and inhibition, it is interesting to note that the parameters of the traumatic neurosis and the startle response appear to be the same, the two constituting a microcosm and a macrocosm of reactions to and defenses against excitation. As already noted, the critical variables for the inception of a traumatic neurosis are: (1) intensity of stimulation; (2) previous level of arousal; (3) rate of stimulus input; (4) surprise; and (5) opportunity for motor discharge. The first four are clearly critical for the startle response. It remains to be seen whether the fifth variable is also relevant. This can be determined by experiments in which the effects of a startling stimulus upon measures of physiological arousal are compared under conditions of free and restricted movement. As previously noted, initial level of arousal and intensity of stimulation directly contribute to total arousal, while motor discharge provides a means for reducing arousal. Expectancy, the reverse of surprise, functionally reduces the impact of the stimulus, undoubtedly through inhibition. The ability of the organism to tolerate a gradual increase in stimulus input, but not a sudden onslaught, can also be attributed to inhibition produced by expectancy. A simple but convincing test of the dampening effect of expectancy upon arousal is provided by unexpectedly shouting "boo" while monitoring polygraph reactions, as contrasted with the effect when the subject is told to expect the shout. The difference is consistent and dramatic. An inhibitory phenomenon must be postulated to account for the diminished reactivity produced by such expectancy, as the stimulus input is the same, and fatigue can be ruled out by reinstating the phenomenon so long as the reinstatement is not expected. In addition to expectancy, a second factor involved in the differential effect of slow and fast rates of stimulus input may be that inhibition is more efficient and of a different quality when it is built up gradually as the result of small increments in excitation than when it is evoked all at once by a sudden strong stimulus input. Gradual increases in small increments of stimulation somehow seem to provide an innoculation against being overwhelmed by a large final level.

It is interesting to compare the characteristics of three different levels of inhibition produced by different magnitudes of excitation. Consider a situation in which a stimulus of relatively mild to moderate intensity is presented repeatedly. On the first presentation it is apt to elicit a strong alerting reaction that, with repeated presentations, becomes smaller and smaller and produces a typical adaptation curve. Figure 22 presents GSRs elicited by a loud noise presented ten times. The experiment is the same

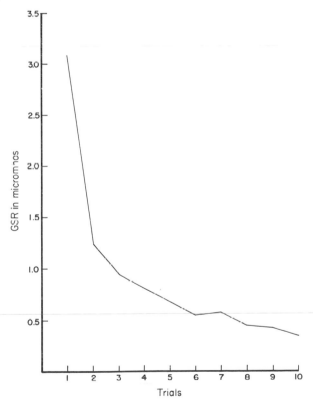

FIG. 22. Adaptation of the GSR as a function of the presentation of a loud noise at 10-second intervals over 10 trials (from Epstein & Fenz, 1966).

one from which the data in Fig. 20 were obtained, but whereas Fig. 20 presents basal conductance, a measure of the relatively stable level of tension of the subject, Fig. 22 presents the momentary deflections from baseline that constitute the GSR. How can adaptation such as represented in Fig. 22, be explained? As has already been suggested, adaptation can be interpreted as an inhibitory phenomenon. It can readily be shown that it does not depend on fatigue of the GSR, as it can be disinhibited by the presentation of an extraneous stimulus between adaptation trials. The inhibition that produces adaptation is adaptive and conservative, as it prevents the organism from wasting its energies upon stimuli that have no new information to impart. That it is highly selective is immediately demonstrated by introducing a small change into the situation, and noting that alerting reactions reappear at once. As reactivity to the adapted stimulus is reduced, the organism's attentional system is made free to respond to other stimuli. Now let us consider a more diffuse kind of inhibition that reduces contact with the environment. Given repeated presentations of a more intense stimulus, defensive reactions are finally, if not immediately, elicited, and raise thresholds in general (Sokolov, 1963). It is as if the organism, having been temporarily overstimulated, had to defend itself by shutting down stimulation from all sources. A similar, but more prolonged, form of inhibition was noted by Fenz (1964) in a study of the effects of stress produced by a forthcoming jump for a novice parachutist on the sensory threshold for a pure tone. Not only did a general rise in threshold occur on the day of a jump, but momentary applications of stimulation produced momentary rises in threshold roughly proportionate to the strength of the stimulation. At overwhelming levels of stimulation, as in the traumatic neurosis, a yet more diffuse ego-debilitating inhibition would be induced. The general principle can be stated that the greater the excitation that must be inhibited, the more inhibition shifts from a fine-tuned control system that increases the effectiveness of the organism's contact with the world to a diffuse blocking out of excitation that reduces contact.

As one last example of inhibition organized at different levels, and in this case one that could be classified either as an example of inhibition in depth or in breadth, let us reconsider Fig. 20. It is noteworthy that if the curve in Fig. 20 were extrapolated to the baseline, it would resemble a giant GSR. Analogous to the momentary rise and fall in arousal that follows the onset of a single stimulus and produces the GSR, there is a more prolonged rise and fall in a more stable system of arousal produced by the cumulative effect of repeated stimulation over time, which constitutes the curve of basal conductance in Fig. 20.[3] This more prolonged rise and fall leads to the speculation that inhibitory systems that control momentary sharp rises in

[3]This is admittedly highly speculative, and alternative explanations that do not require the concept of inhibition can undoubtedly account for the data. No doubt we will be wrong

arousal and those that control gradually mounting levels of arousal obey similar laws. The findings may correspond to a distinction made by Sokolov (1963) between "phasic" and tonic reactions, which Stenett (1957) aptly compares to the rise and fall of the waves superimposed upon the slow-moving tides. It is noteworthy that the rise and fall in the different organizational levels of excitation and inhibition correspond to what would be expected from the assumption that the gradient of inhibition is steeper than that of excitation.

We have but scratched the surface in considering the different levels of organization in which excitation is modulated by inhibition. For a more detailed account, with a consideration of the neurophysiological processes that are involved, the reader is referred to a thorough treatment of the concept of inhibition by Diamond *et al.* (1963).

L. Postulate 12. Stimuli of Low Primary Intensity Value Can Be Made Functionally Equivalent to Stimuli of High Primary Intensity Value through Learning and Conditioning

This postulate merely draws attention to the observation that through learning and conditioning a stimulus of low intensity can acquire signal value that can make it highly arousing. The word fire emitted at moderate intensity can be a far stronger stimulus than a neutral word shouted. The converse of the postulate is true within limits, as witness the functional reduction of stronger to weaker stimuli through adaptation.

M. Summary, and a Proposal for a General Law of Excitatory Modulation

It was assumed that there is a highly organized system for coping with the intensity component of stimulation at many levels of organization and that at all levels the gradient of inhibition is steeper than the gradient of excitation that it inhibits. A series of postulates were presented that related excitation and inhibition to stimulus intensity, time since stimulus presentation, and number and rate of stimulus inputs. Although in the statement of the postulates both gradients were related to external dimensions, an alternative approach is to relate only excitation to external dimensions and to relate inhibition to excitation. When this is done, the basic postulate for inhibition becomes so fundamental that it may qualify as a law, which we tentatively designate the law of excitatory modulation

in many particulars, but we believe that there is a point to seeing how much the theoretical approach that we have described may be able to explain. Further research will cut the theory down to size without our limiting it to begin with. It remains to be seen whether the postulates will stand, although some of the more speculative sources of support cited undoubtedly will not.

(LEM). While there is not much difference between the two alternatives, operationally, at this point, there is a theoretical advantage in parsimony favoring the LEM, and ultimately it may be possible to establish operational differences. The LEM, in simplified form, states that the gradient of inhibition is steeper than the gradient of excitation that it inhibits. Thus, as excitation within any system mounts, depending on its rate and absolute level, as well as the other parameters discussed under the postulates, it triggers an inhibitory reaction that mounts more rapidly, thereby providing the organism with a highly effective system for modulating excitation, which both protects the organism from being overwhelmed by excessive stimulation and allows it to deal with stimulation at efficient levels of intensity. The LEM, in more complete form, is represented by the curves in Fig. 19.

It was observed that the parameters of the traumatic neurosis are similar to those of the startle response, the two representing a microcosm and a macrocosm of reactivity to excessive stimulation. In considering different organizational levels of inhibition, it was noted that the same principles that account for defense against excitation at high levels of stimulation account for an increase in efficiency following stimulation of lesser intensity. Inhibition in the former case is diffuse, its purpose being to reduce stimulation from all sources, whereas in the latter case it is selective or fine tuned, and by reducing attention to uniformative cues increases attention to other cues.

V. Implications of the Theory for Different Problem Areas

The assumption that there is a highly complex and integrated system for reacting to the intensity component of stimulation, which serves not only to defend the organism against excessive stimulation, but to bring it into increasing and more efficient contact with its environment, has obviously important implications for a variety of problem areas in psychology.

In this section, we will speculate freely on what some of these implications are. We can but apologize for being less thorough than the data will allow, and point out that our purpose is not to present a definitive position on any of the problems we raise, but to indicate how the theory makes possible a new way of thinking about old problems, and suggests avenues for research.

A. Experimental Psychology

We have postulated the existence of a system of learning that is presumably more fundamental than conditioning. The two systems are considered to be supplementary, as conditioning is concerned with the cue component of stimulation and the other with the intensity component. That a crude form of learning is involved in reacting to the intensity component of stimulation is indicated by phenomena such as adaptation, where a stimulus is functionally reduced to a weaker one by being presented repeatedly. Adaptation must qualify as learning as it involves a change in performance with experience that cannot be attributed to maturation or fatigue. That it involves a form of inhibition can readily be demonstrated by its disinhibition. Assuming that the system for reacting to the intensity component of stimulation is more fundamental than conditioning, it follows that conditioning should be complicated by reactions to the intensity of the stimulus and by excitation contributed by all sources, including motivation. It should thus be helpful for the development of an adequate theory of conditioning to know more about management of the intensity component of stimulation. That "intensity learning" has seriously interfered with the process of conditioning is indicated by the conclusion of Stewart, Stern, Winokur, and Fredman (1961) that "...so far work on GSR conditioning has dealt with the adaptation and recovery of unconditioned responses rather than conditioning of responses" (p. 66). In our own investigations (Epstein & Burstein, 1966) of primary stimulus generalization of the conditioned GSR, we have been forced to conclude that, despite the importance attributed to the phenomenon by behavior theorists (Hull, 1950), neither we nor anyone else has been able to demonstrate decremental gradients of the GSR in individual human subjects, and the evidence for group data is, at best equivocal.

In order to demonstrate conditioning unconfounded with alerting reactions, Stewart et al. (1961) recommend the use of prolonged interstimulus intervals. The immediate reactions to the onset of a stimulus can then be discarded as alerting responses, and the delayed reactions accepted as the true conditioned responses. This approach has the obvious limitation that it restricts conditioning to delayed responses. An alternate solution is to use pseudo-conditioning control groups. This, too, has its problems since, unless one knows a great deal about the adaptation, recovery, and generalization of unconditioned stimuli and the influence of time relationships between stimuli, it is impossible to determine what a suitable pseudo-conditioning control group is. As an example, although backward conditioning has been used as a pseudo-conditioning control for forward conditioning, we simply do not know what complexities are introduced in the adaptation and recovery of unconditional responses when they are preceded by, as compared to followed by, an incidental stimulus. It may be necessary to develop an adequate psychology of the unconditioned response before we can hope to develop one of the conditioned response. Certainly, the psychology of the unconditioned response should be simpler, and what is learned from it should be theoretically useful to a theory of conditioning as well as in its own right.

It is noteworthy that behavior theorists have had little to say about the adaptation and spontaneous recovery of unconditioned responses, but have developed concepts such as reactive inhibition and its disinhibition to account for parallel phenomena in the conditioning paradigm. If explanations are found for similar phenomena in the absence of conditioning, they should have more than passing relevance to the conditioning situation. It is ironic, indeed, that behaviorists who have insisted that in order to understand complex processes, it is first necessary to understand simpler processes, may be caught in the web of their own logic, as their presumed fundamental unit of learning, conditioning of paired stimuli, appears to be not as fundamental as they assumed. What has been said about conditioning of the GSR applies to other autonomic responses as well, but is easier to illustrate with the GSR, which is a particularly sensitive indicator of orienting reflexes. It will be recalled that sensory acuity is influenced by stimulus intensity and that arousal itself can be inhibited at many levels. From this it follows that energetic effects determined by such variables as intensity of stimulation, rate of stimulation, time interval between stimuli, time interval between presentation of the stimulus and recording the response, and motivational state of the organism should singly, and in combination, exert an important influence on response magnitude.

As to the kinds of experiments that need to be done, the principles that were postulated should be put to experimental test. The most important assumption is that the gradient of inhibition, at all levels of organization, is steeper than the gradient of excitation. It remains to be established that the relationship of inhibition to excitation follows the same course for variations in excitation produced by stimulus intensity, decay time following stimulus presentation, and number of stimulus inputs within a unit of time. A question that needs to be investigated is whether, as proposed, the parameters of the impact of a stimulus, as measured by indices of physiological arousal, are stimulus intensity, prestimulus level of arousal, rate of stimulus input, surprise, and opportunity for motor discharge. A particularly interesting series of experiments would study phenomena paralleling those attributed to conditioning, but in the absence of conditioning in the sense of pairing a CS and UCS. In this respect, adaptation of an unconditioned response can be viewed as similar to extinction of a conditioned response, and spontaneous recovery and disinhibition are concepts that are equally applicable to conditioned and unconditioned responses.

Operationally, the testing phase for each of these phenomena is identical for conditioned and unconditioned responses. It has already been shown that a concept of central, not reactive, inhibition can account for adaptation and its disinhibition by demonstrating that response fatigue cannot explain adaptation. Why, then, should a different theoretical construct be necessary to account for the same phenomena in conditioning? Although phenomena such as the adaptation of unconditioned responses may appear to be self-evident and unworthy of experimental effort, this is hardly the case when one raises questions such as how adaptation of one response influences magnitude of response to related stimuli, i.e., generalization of adaptation, and how time relationships between stimuli influence rate of adaptation, spontaneous recovery, and magnitude of a disinhibited response. The difference between the effect of massed and spaced presentations of stimuli is of equal theoretical interest for conditioned and unconditioned responses. It would not be surprising if a variety of phenomena that have been attributed to conditioning can be demonstrated more simply and more reliably without conditioning. Conditioning, to some extent at least, involves making stimuli of a certain level of functional intensity, or attention-eliciting value, equivalent to other intensities, after which they must obey the laws of inhibition and excitation for their new intensity values, This must certainly complicate the operation of the laws relating to the cue value of the conditioned stimuli.

Research on unconditioned responses need not be restricted to an investigation of alerting reactions, which, it is postulated, constitute but one subsystem of a more general system for coping with the intensity component of stimulation. One series of studies that needs to be carried out would test the assumption that there is a system for dealing with the cumulative effects of stimulation from all sources. The unverified findings of Pavlov should be replicated, particularly in regard to paradoxical effects produced by strong stimulation at high levels of motivation. We need to know more about how different sources of arousal combine, such as arousal from internal and external stimulation, and arousal from aversive, pleasurable, and hedonically neutral excitation. When is there an additive and when a subtractive combination from different sources of stimulation? The entire field of what Freud referred to as mental economics, has yet to be brought into the laboratory.

B. DEVELOPMENTAL PSYCHOLOGY

The view that there is a psychophysiological system that provides the basis for the organism's most fundamental source of contact with stimuli from the outside world, and that involves a crude form of learning, more fundamental than cue learning, or conditioning, has obvious implications for developmental psychology.

It will be recalled that the two-process theory that was proposed accounted for the course of mastery of stress by experienced parachutists by assuming the development of a continuously expanding gradient of anxiety and a steeper gradient of inhibition of anxiety. The increasing gradient of anxiety automatically forced the parachutist to deal with an ever-increasing range of relevant cues, while the inhibitory gradient, an outgrowth of successful experience, served to keep the anxiety within limits. Applying the same model to the infant provides an explanation of how the infant, faced with strongly arousing stimulation and provided with successful experiences in coping with it, expands its range of awareness and competence. The question may be raised why the infant should be willing to face high levels of arousal in the first place. After all, the infant cannot be compared to the parachutist, who jumps despite his intense fear in order not to lose face or to prove to himself that he can face fear and overcome it. The answer is that the infant has no choice but to face certain sources of high arousal, whether produced by strong unfamiliar external stimuli or by his own untempered needs. As previously noted, mastery does not occur only through conscious effort, but is also acquired passively.

It is noteworthy that elements of the foregoing analysis correspond to Kierkegaard's view that it is necessary for the individual to pay the price of anxiety in order to expand his range of awareness and adequacy (May, 1950). According to Kierkegaard, facing anxiety is the very essence of normal adjustment, the only alternative being neurotic constriction. We believe that although the preceding analysis is very likely correct for the mastery of strong levels of arousal, it does not apply to expanding the range of awareness of cues associated with more limited stimulation.

Let us consider the role that adaptation may play in expanding the infant's range of awareness and competence. It will be recalled that adaptation was accounted for by assuming the development of excitatory and inhibitory gradients, the latter becoming increasingly steeper than the former. As the inhibitory gradient increasingly dominates the excitatory gradient, the net excitatory strength of the stimulus is reduced; that is, adaptation occurs. Phenomenologically, the stimulus loses its stimulating or attention-demanding value and becomes boring. How, then, can adaptation, a phenomenon that refers to a decrease in reactivity, account for an increase in the range of stimuli that are reacted to? There are two ways in which it can, one of which predicts a general increase in reactivity to other stimuli, and the other a selective increase. The general increase in reactivity to other stimuli requires the assumption that organisms are energy systems that are reactive to stimuli in the world about them. From this it follows that adaptation to one source of stimulation tends to increase attention and reactivity to other sources.

As so far described, one gains the picture of an organism responding randomly to any stimuli that happen to be present. However, even at the infant level, schemata and expectancies are quickly developed and determine which stimuli will or will not be attended to. Although conditioning provides part of the explanation of how such schemata emerge, we believe that an equally important part is played by what we have previously referred to as intensity learning. Let us begin with the hedonic theory of emotion of McClelland, Atkinson, Clark, and Lowell (1953), which provides a useful first step. According to McClelland, discrepancies from adaptation level, i.e., expectancy, up to a certain point are experienced as pleasurable, and beyond that as unpleasurable. Proceeding from the assumption that the organism must protect itself against high levels of arousal, we would add what we believe is an important modification, namely, that after a point, the higher the resting level of arousal, the smaller the increment in further arousal that will be experienced as pleasant. At sufficiently high levels of arousal, it is presumed that any increment is unpleasant. Thus, depending on its state of arousal, the infant will seek out stimulation of different degrees of arousal, or will avoid stimulation.

The foregoing explanation accounts for why an infant at a certain level of arousal will react to particular intensity values of stimulation in preference to others, but does not account for how schemata emerge, which are obviously more than a conglomeration of stimuli of similar arousal values. The question remains as to how, if at all, reactivity to one stimulus can selectively influence the development of reactivity to related stimuli in a manner such as to produce integrated and differentiated stimulus complexes. We submit that an orderly expansion of attention to and awareness of related stimuli is inherent in the process of generalization of habituation, and consists of two interrelated stages, the first consisting of mastery of the energy component of stimulation, and the second of becoming aware of the cue component. The explanation that follows will be seen to be similar in many respects to the one offered for the mastery of anxiety in sport-parachuting, where, it will be recalled, that as a result of experience, stimuli initially reacted to at high levels of arousal were reacted to at increasingly lower levels, and, in the process, the boundaries of reactivity and awareness were expanded.

Let us begin at a time in development at which an infant is unaware of the signal value of cues. It can nevertheless be depended upon to respond to the energy component of stimulation, i.e., it will react to bright lights, loud noises, and sufficiently strong tactual and olfactory stimulation. This is at least a beginning for bringing it into contact with the external environment. Now let us consider what happens if a stimulus is presented repeatedly, or is a stable part of its environment over a sufficient period. If the stimulus falls within an appropriate range of intensity, a remarkable phenomenon known as habituation, or adaptation, occurs. The stimulus initially elicits an alerting reaction, i.e., its intensity forces the organism to attend to it, and, with repeated exposure, the organism reacts with reduced increments in arousal, until it fails to respond altogether. What is remarkable is that somehow the same physical energy impinging upon the same sensory organs is reduced functionally to a weaker stimulus input. As noted previously, in view of evidence of disinhibition and lack of fatigue of the sensory and effector organs, it is difficult to see how the phenomenon can be explained by any mechanism other than centrally mediated inhibition.

During the process of habituation, the organism necessarily attends to the same stimulus a large number of times along a continuum of decreasing increments in arousal, which must include those levels most conducive to the efficient perceiving and registering of the stimulus. Putting it in other terms, habituation allows the organism "to get to know" the stimulus, so that a remarkable shift takes place: a stimulus that could only be responded to in terms of its energy component, is able to be responded to in terms of its cue component. In its most general terms, it might be said that the energy, or emotional, system of the organism provided the basis for establishing the first cognition.

Let us now turn to the phenomenon of generalization of habituation. Assume that stimulus A has been habituated. The inhibition responsible for the habituation generalizes to other stimuli, such as B, C, and D. It is also necessary to take into account the emergence of an excitatory gradient. While the inhibitory gradient was produced through reacting to the intensity component of the stimulus, the excitatory component is associated with the cue component. That cues can generate excitation independent of their signal value, or conditioning, is demonstrated by a familiar stimulus being attended to and reacted to when it is recognized among other stimuli, or when it provides a frame of reference which imparts arousal value to other stimuli that are related to, yet different from, it. It should be noted that while, for the purpose of simplification, the stimulus has been divided into excitatory and inhibitory components, the organism must respond to one total stimulus, the intensity component of which has cue properties, and the cue component of which has excitatory properties. The generalization gradients of excitation and inhibition are thus assumed to interact at the level of the total stimulus, and not to be independently associated with its components.

Fig. 23 presents a situation in which A has been inhibited beyond the minimal level of complete habituation. This is indicated by the inhibitory gradient being considerably higher than the excitatory gradient at point A. Now let us consider how the excitatory and inhibitory gradients generated by A influence reactivity to B, C, and D. In Fig. 23, it can be seen that B loses in net arousal value, C gains, and D remains unaffected. If the process were carried out further with A, or directly with B, C would lose, and

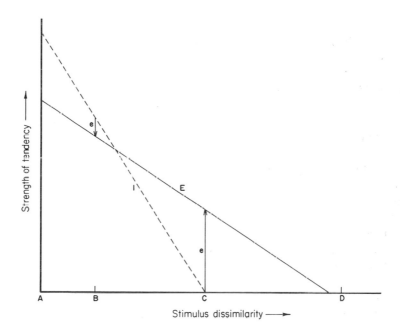

FIG. 23. Theoretical curves of excitation (E), inhibition (I), and net excitation (e) for the prediction of generalization effects of adaptation. Adaptation to A reduces the net excitatory strength of B, increases the net excitatory strength of C, and does not affect D.

D gain, in arousal value. The concept of a steeper gradient of inhibition than excitation thus predicts that with increasing familiarity with a stimulus, a highly orderly development takes place that produces a systematic increase in the excitatory value of related weak stimuli. This serves to foster, at nonthreatening levels of arousal, an expansion of awareness of stimulus complexes. Within the adult world, the same process of generalization of habituation can be observed in changing fashions in clothing, automobiles, and music. An innovation which at first is excessive, after repeated exposure, becomes dull, after which a further innovation becomes pleasantly arousing. After hemlines go up as far as they dare, they go down, and then up again. The process of habituation, and a gradual spread of increased reactivity to new sources of stimulation goes on endlessly, and, in so doing, forces stimulus dimensions to be well worked over, expanded, and differentiated. This model is supported by recently completed studies in our laboratory, where we found that following repeated exposure to a pure tone, the generalization gradient of reactivity to other tones was inverted U-shaped. It should be noted that in experiments in which the stimulus dimension is restricted, only a monotonic function would be observed.

Let us now consider the conditions that favor the normal development of mastery of strong stimulus inputs and the expansion of the horizons of awareness, and the conditions that interfere with this development. Assuming that at moderate to high levels of arousal, the increment in arousal that is experienced as pleasant is an inverse function of the resting level of arousal, it follows that infants at high resting levels of arousal should tend to avoid stimulation. As to the opposite situation, where arousal is very low, a not unreasonable hypothesis is that at relatively low to moderate levels of arousal the Weber fraction holds, that is, the effect of an increment in arousal is inversely proportionate to the resting level of arousal. Thus, given a low level of arousal to begin with, a constant increment in arousal is experienced as greater than given a moderate level of arousal to begin with. If the Weber fraction holds at low to moderate resting levels of arousal, and is superceded at high levels by the "law of defense," that is, the need of the organism to protect itself against excessive stimulation, it follows that the organism at moderate levels of arousal should be most apt to seek stimulation, develop expectancies, and therefore integrate experiences into schemata.

There is an obvious implication of the two-process theory of mastery of anxiety for child raising which provides a very different viewpoint from that which many interpret, or perhaps misinterpret, to be the psychoanalytic position. According to psychoanalytic theory, a secure childhood tends to provide for a frustration-tolerant adulthood. Freud, of course, believed that some frustration was necessary for normal development, and that abnormal fixations could be produced by excessive as well as insufficient gratification. Nevertheless, the emphasis in psychoanalytic theory, based upon observations of emotionally disturbed individuals, has been upon the damage caused by excessive frustration. Its influence upon parents and educators has all too often been to motivate them to attempt to reduce anxiety to a minimum. The viewpoint that emerges from the two-process theory of mastery of anxiety presented here is that the ability to tolerate stress is acquired, not through previous security, but through "innoculations" with increasing amounts of stress. More specifically, our theory suggests that a child who is to enter a world where he must deal with anger, frustration, and uncontrolled emotion should have some exposure to such experiences in the home, where they can be handled at levels that are not devastating, if he is not to be devastated when he experiences them in the outside world. Perhaps this is why frightening fairytales have had such remarkable survival value. It is probably because psychoanalysis has presented a convincing case for excessive stress in childhood producing permanent personality defects, that there has been a tendency to go to the opposite extreme and assume that maximum security in childhood produces maximum ego-strength in adulthood. An analysis of the normal mastery of anxiety leads us to conclude that this view is seriously in error.

As to research implications for developmental psychology, studies need to be done to investigate age effects on generalization of adaptation. Acquired expectancies should be an increasingly important variable with age. How many repetitions of a stimulus are necessary before a change produces a surprise effect, and how does this vary with age and arousal level? Experiments can be performed investigating excitatory and inhibitory processes by the operations discussed in the section on experimental psychology. This would include investigations of rate of adaptation and amount of spontaneous recovery and disinhibition as a function of variables such as age, stimulus intensity, and rate of stimulus input. Magnitude of physiological reaction and approach and avoidance reactions to different increments of primary stimulation should be investigated as a function of resting arousal level to determine whether the relationship is curvilinear, as proposed. Holding arousal level constant, how does age influence the relationship? The relationship of primary stimulus intensity to magnitude of physiological response, with age treated as a parameter, also bears investigation. Do more uniform gradients occur in the earliest years, before other factors intrude, or is even the simple correspondence between magnitude of the stimulus and magnitude of the response unstable at this time? The hypothesis should be tested that primary stimulus intensity is the predominant source of an increase in arousal in early infancy, but that expectancies play an increasing role with increasing age. Does this mean that a loud noise is more quickly adapted to by an older than a younger child, as the former has had more experience with loud noises, and has a better-developed system for establishing expectancies for later trials based upon experiences with earlier trials? While a few studies in this general area have been done, there is a need for organized research programs for investigating the emerging capacities of the child to deal with primary and acquired intensity values of stimulation. Such studies should yield important information on the nature of attention, the mastery of anxiety, and the development of an expanding world of reality.

C. Psychopathology, with an Emphasis upon Schizophrenia

The assumptions that the organism must maintain arousal within homeostatic limits, and that defenses against mounting arousal are more fundamental than defenses against fear and anxiety, have obvious implications for psychopathology. While it would be interesting to consider the implications of such concepts for a variety of pathological syndromes, this would carry us beyond the scope of the present paper. Instead, we shall provide a brief example of how an interpretation in terms of arousal and its control can be applied to a psychoneurotic disorder, hysteria, and a more detailed analysis of how it may be related to schizophrenia.

Hysterics are described as people who are emotionally labile, spontaneous, and relatively free of manifest anxiety. Repression is their major defense because, presumably, they are naive and unable to tolerate anxiety. An alternate explanation, which we believe better fits the facts, is that the emotional lability and spontaneity are consequences of a relative absence of the use of anxiety as an early warning signal or, putting it otherwise, of an absence of normal defensiveness. As a result, the hysteric is apt to experience unmodulated intense surges of arousal produced by his emotions or by strong external stimuli, which trigger emergency defenses of the all-or-none variety, including repression and hysterical symptoms. This accounts for why the traumatic neurosis, which is caused by overwhelming stimulation, is able to produce hysterical symptoms in individuals who do not fit the personality description of the hysteric. The hysteric's pattern of defense can be contrasted with that of the obsessive-compulsive who, by paying a constant price in the use of anxiety as an early warning signal for initiating defenses, is able to avoid strong surges of emotion and arousal. Hysterical symptoms can thus be viewed as emergency defenses elicited by high levels of arousal due to a lack of anxiety-induced defensiveness, whereas obsessive-compulsive symptoms are a direct consequence of anxiety-induced defensiveness.

Our theory of schizophrenia is a direct outgrowth of the two-process theory of mastery of anxiety. Having concluded that there is an upper limit of arousal that the organism can tolerate, and that a complex system exists that both protects the organism against high levels of arousal and brings it into increasingly efficient contact with the external world at modulated levels of arousal, it was only natural to wonder what would happen if this system failed to develop properly. This led to the hypothesis that a failure at such a fundamental level would lead to the most fundamental psychological disorder, namely, schizophrenia. At the time, we were not aware of other arousal theories of schizophrenia. Since then, we have learned that a number of such theories have been proposed from different viewpoints (see, for example, Broen & Storms, 1966[4]; Mednick, 1958; Pavlov, 1941; Venables, 1964). The major difference between our theory and other arousal theories stems from the fact that we began with a theory of anxiety and emerged with one on schizophrenia, whereas most of the others were tailor-made to account for data on schizophrenia. The other theories generally assume that the schizophrenic is overinhibited or underinhibited, depending on his diagnostic subgroup. According to our theory, excessive or insufficient

---

[4]See also final contribution in this volume (Editor).

inhibition per se is not the crucial characteristic. What is, is an inadequately modulated control system. Putting it otherwise, it is assumed that the schizophrenic has a crude all-or-none system of inhibitory controls, so that he is unable to vary his inner and overt reactions to correspond closely with the requirements of variations in internal and external stimulation. He thus tends to respond either too strongly or not enough, and may vary from one extreme to the other.

In the preceding section, it was concluded that the child who is kept at an exceptionally high or low level of arousal over prolonged periods will tend to avoid normal increments in stimulation. As a result, such a child will not learn to cope adequately with the intensity component of stimulation, and will tend to develop a crude defense system rather than a fine-tuned system for modulating stimulus inputs. It is instructive to compare the defenses of the schizophrenic and the neurotic in this respect. In the latter case, only cues that are associated with areas of unconscious conflict elicit all-or-none defenses. As a result, certain areas of experience are shut out, and the conflict remains encapsulated and incapable of resolution. Should a stimulus break through the defense, the neurotic is overwhelmed, and must rely on emergency defenses to reduce the excessive arousal, and therefore is unable to learn from the experience. With the schizophrenic, stimulation itself is defended against. What is walled off, then, is reality. What remains unlearned is the ability to cope with the intensity component of *all* stimulation, which is necessary for the development of a modulated control system for reducing initially excessive levels of arousal to levels that can be dealt with most efficiently.

The conditions that favor the development of an all-or-none defense system against the intensity component of stimulation can be assumed to be both biological and psychological. In regard to the former, individual differences in energy level must be important. The child who lacks sufficient energy as well as the child who is hyperreactive to stimulation are both more likely candidates for schizophrenia than the child who is normally reactive. In regard to the environmental conditions that favor schizophrenia, simple rejection may not be enough. So long as his physical needs are taken care of, it may be impossible to maintain the rejected child in a prolonged state of high arousal, as he can learn to avoid the source of stress selectively, that is, he can fail to form an attachment to the rejecting adult. This would predispose him to be psychopathic, not schizophrenic (Bender, 1950). Possibly the age at which rejection is experienced is critical here. As to maintaining a pathogenically low level of primary stimulation, this would be difficult, but not impossible, to accomplish outside of the laboratory. Thus, we suspect that a prolonged state of high arousal in infancy or early childhood provides one of the more likely routes to schizophrenia. An effective way to produce such a state would be to arouse expectancies and appetites repeatedly only to frustrate them. This could be accomplished by a mother-child relationship that is positive enough to have the child seek more of it and negative enough to leave strong needs unfulfilled. To maintain arousal at a sufficiently high pitch requires a delicate art of providing sufficient gratification at just the right moment so that the need is not abandoned. It is necessary to keep the carrot always in sight, making it available when interest flags, and removing it before the need is gratified. Such an art can readily be achieved without practice by an ambivalent mother who consciously means to love a child she unconsciously hates, and can neither reject it nor allow it to be happy.

Given the assumption that the basic defect in schizophrenia is an inadequately modulated inhibitory system for controlling excitation, a number of symptoms in schizophrenia are readily accounted for, including a tendency to over- and underrespond, poor contact with reality, anhedonia, poor impulse control, a defect in attention, cognitive deficit, and hallucinations.

That a tendency to over- or underrespond is an important symptom of schizophrenia is immediately apparent when one observes the behavior of catatonic patients. Such patients may'be in a state of excessive inhibition at one moment and agitated and assaultive the next. Some schizophrenics are withdrawn and unresponsive in general, whereas others are agitated and react intensely to stimuli that are unnoticed by normals. The inappropriate affect that is characteristic of schizophrenics is often exhibited in the form of a failure to react to what others would consider emotionally provoking stimuli, and of having emotional outbursts to relatively trivial events. Observations such as this led Pavlov (1941) to conclude that schizophrenic symptoms are manifestations of the paradoxical phase. From our viewpoint, a tendency to over- or underrespond directly follows from a failure to develop adequately modulated inhibitory controls. Given a crude inhibitory system, reactions have to be excessive or insufficient. It is thus not surprising that some schizophrenics appear to be generally overinhibited, others underinhibited, and others shift from one extreme to the other.

Poor contact with reality follows directly from the assumption that the schizophrenic, as a child, because of a prolonged state of high arousal, devoted his energy to learning to avoid rather than seek stimulation. This limited his range of experience. More important, he was unable to obtain practice in accomplishing the form of learning that is involved in modulating the intensity component of stimulation. Thus, he was forced to rely more and more on crude inhibitory controls for dealing with stimulus inputs. As a result, new stimuli had either to be experienced at excessive levels of arousal or shut out entirely.

Meehl (1962) includes anhedonia among the fundamental symptoms of schizophrenia: "Then there is a quasi-pathognomic sign emphasized by Rado (1956; Rado & Daniels, 1956) but largely ignored in psychologists' diagnostic usage, namely *anhedonia*—a marked, widespread, and refractory defect in pleasure capacity which, once you learn how to examine for it, is one of the most consistent and dramatic behavioral signs of the disease" (p. 829). In the preceding section it was noted that an increment in arousal up to a point is experienced as pleasant, and beyond that as unpleasant. It was further observed that as the resting level of arousal is increased, the increment that will elicit a pleasurable response shrinks until, at high enough levels of arousal, all stimulation is unpleasant. It follows that given a state of sufficiently high arousal, as was postulated during the childhood of the schizophrenic, there is little possibility for experiencing pleasurable stimulation. To the extent that this is true, it would appear that expanding contact with reality and happiness have a common source. Given the crystallization of defenses and avoidance reactions that developed from excessive states of arousal in childhood, an inability to enjoy stimulation could be expected to extend into adulthood, even if arousal levels were later stabilized.

A problem in impulse control is undoubtedly one of the most prevalent symptoms of schizophrenia. Schizophrenics tend to be either undercontrolled or overcontrolled, and the same schizophrenic may vary from one extreme to the other in a short period of time. There are no new assumptions required here, as what was said about the mastery of external stimulation requiring the development of modulated inhibitory controls is applicable to the mastery of internal stimulation. The schizophrenic is apt to have intense feelings or none at all; holding the intensity of the feeling constant, he is apt to violently express or completely suppress it. As a result of unmodulated impulses and their unmodulated expression, impulses are apt to be experienced as both uncomfortable and dangerous. It is therefore not surprising that many schizophrenics become emotionally flat and unreactive as a way of protecting themselves from impulses they cannot otherwise handle. Such a state of excessive control and loss of spontaneity is the one the patient has usually arrived at when he is judged ready for discharge from an institution. In a report on differences between Irish and Italian male schizophrenics, Opler (1957) noted that Irish schizophrenics are withdrawn and inhibited, and Italians explosive and subject to strong mood swings. It is noteworthy that although the manifest symptom picture is opposite, both syndromes support the generalization that schizophrenics are unable to exert modulated control over the experience and expression of their impulses.

It was previously noted that attention is mediated by the interaction of excitation and inhibition. In order to be attended to, a stimulus must arouse the organism to some degree, and at the same time arousal by other stimuli must be screened out. Given a crude all-or-none inhibitory system for reacting to stimulus inputs, it follows that the schizophrenic suffers from an attention defect. He may fail to attend to stimuli in general, which protects him from increasing arousal and depends upon a broad-gauged form of inhibition. Alternately, if he is less generally inhibited, he may fail in selectively focusing his attention on specific stimuli and screening out others, as this requires a fine-tuned inhibitory system, which he is lacking. As a result of an inability to focus attention on certain cues, he will tend to be influenced by all salient stimuli in his perceptual field at the moment, and will experience a state of disorganized and fleeting attention. This latter derivation follows from the assumption, made earlier, that all living organisms are responsive to stimulation, and to the extent that attention is reduced in one area it tends to be increased in others. From this it also follows that if attention is withdrawn from external stimulation it will automatically be increased to internal stimulation. This can account for the prevalence of delusions, hallucinations, and hypochondriacal symptoms in schizophrenia.

Cognitive deficit in schizophrenia can be derived from the defect in attention and, at a more fundamental level, from the inability to deal efficiently with the intensity component of stimulation, which is necessary for effective performance with regard to the cue component. The schizophrenic, in a sense, is too concerned with protecting himself from the arousal aspect of stimulation to attend adequately to cue aspects. It might be argued that, if this is so, lowering arousal level through drugs should permit the schizophrenic to perform in a normal manner. This is only partly true, as the schizophrenic may have developed habits of dealing with stimuli under conditions of high arousal that prevented him from learning to modulate excitation adequately, no matter what the level of resting arousal.

As to a theoretical program for testing the foregoing theory, experiments need to be done to investigate relatively simple reactions to the intensity component of stimulation, primary and acquired. The experiments described in the sections on experimental and developmental psychology are equally appropriate for investigating the inhibitory abilities of the schizophrenic. We need to find out the answers to the simplest of questions, such as whether the schizophrenic is able to demonstrate uniform gradients of physiological arousal as a function of increasing stimulus intensity comparable to normals. Do schizophrenics produce adaptation curves and exhibit spontaneous recovery and disinhibition in the same manner as normals? How does the schizophrenic react to stimulus dimensions composed of words of increasing emotional significance as compared to dimensions of primary stimulus intensity? Although some relevant experiments have been done from other points of view, research in this area has been relatively meager. Studies reported by Shakow (1963) on adaptation are of particular interest, as they lead to the conclusion that one of the few reliable findings in research on schizophrenia is that schizophrenics do not produce normal adaptation curves.

It is important to bear in mind, in testing the theory we have proposed, that it is not enough to compare group means, as other studies have generally done. We hypothesize that the fundamental defect in schizophrenia is neither excessive nor insufficient inhibition, but an inability to exhibit modulated control. If this is true, it can be expected that on almost any measure some schizophrenics will be found who produce greater responses than normals, others weaker responses, and yet others will not differ in mean response, since the individuals who overrespond will balance the ones who underrespond. It is predicted that the one thing that will characterize all schizophrenics is a failure to make their responses correspond closely to the varying energy requirements of repeated or varying stimulation. To evaluate this, it will be necessary to take into account individual deviations from expectancies. To use adaptation of the GSR to a repeated loud sound as an example, it is possible for a particular group of schizophrenics and normals to produce identical mean adaptation curves, with the curve of the normals adequately representing the individuals in the group, whereas that for the schizophrenics would be a conglomeration of responses produced by some subjects who give consistently strong responses, others who give consistently weak responses, and yet others who show marked fluctuations.

D. PSYCHOTHERAPY

There are two broad implications of the theoretical views that have been presented for psychotherapy. One follows from the distinction between anxiety and arousal, the other from the normal process of proactive and retroactive mastery of anxiety.

A failure to distinguish between repression in the service of reducing primary arousal and repression in the service of reducing guilt and anxiety can result in therapeutic mismanagement. Following the psychoanalytic model, it is frequently assumed that when a person exhibits avoidance behavior upon mention of a taboo drive, he has strong guilt feelings. Accordingly, the therapist is motivated to help the patient accept the drive and reduce what is presumed to be inappropriate guilt. When the patient resists the therapist's efforts, this is apt to reinforce the therapist in his conviction that his interpretation was correct. He fails to consider that the patient may have repressed the drive, not because of guilt, but because it was excessive, and could not be controlled otherwise. This view is consistent with Mowrer's (1950) conclusion that many neurotics suffer from an insufficiency of, rather than excessive, control. However, while Mowrer attributes the basic difficulty to an unwillingness to accept guilt and responsibility for socially unacceptable behavior, we believe that the difficulty iies not so much in a failure to accept guilt after the fact, as in an inability to control the drive before the fact, i.e., before it has been acted out or become disturbingly intense. The anxiety that is then experienced is the result of the strong arousal produced by the unfulfilled drive and the feelings of helplessness and inadequacy that follow the realization that the individual is a victim of his drives. Guilt also may contribute to anxiety, yet be denied. The refusal to acknowledge guilt and responsibility can be understood as a rationalization for the behavior once it has occurred, that is, since the individual cannot change his behavior, he may as well learn to live with it. The absence of guilt that Mowrer describes would seem to characterize the psychopath more than the neurotic. They differ in that the psychopath is presumably not motivated to change his behavior, whereas the neurotic cannot. Guilt, which can but serve as a motivator, cannot produce changes in behavior unless the means to do so are available, and for many neurotics this means the ability to modulate the intensity of their drives, so that they do not have to be either excessive or repressed. In fact, guilt can have a reverse effect upon behavior by adding to the person's feelings of helplessness and frustration, and thereby increasing the need to satisfy his drives. In summary, we believe that what most neurotics need to develop is control, not guilt.

Before considering the implications of the two-process theory of mastery of anxiety for teaching impulse control, it will be helpful to consider the implications of the theory for therapy where the retroactive mastery of anxiety is at issue. It will be recalled that the normal process of acquiring belated mastery, as exhibited in the traumatic neurosis, acute grief, and Pavlov's dogs, consisted of gradually working back toward the cues of the trauma by dealing with small, and increasingly less displaced, increments of stress. Abnormal resolution consisted of an all-or-none defense that short-circuited the normal process. It follows that it is necessary to break down such defenses before the working-through process can be attempted. We suspect that the treatment of acute grief, as described by Lindemann (1944), is more generally applicable than has been recognized. In order to expedite the working-through process, the therapist must be aware of the principles involved, so that he does not increase defensiveness by pushing the patient beyond his capacity to cope with the increased stimulation. He should attend to signs of biological arousal as a more reliable index of whether the pacing is correct than the verbal statements of the patient. By being aware of the need for desensitization, he can encourage the patient to go over material again and again, so long as it retains elements of anxiety, despite the patient's protests that he is adding nothing new. Recognizing the need for displacement, the therapist should be willing to treat the problem at a displaced level, and only gradually work toward a more direct confrontation.

It should be noted that the method just presented is not aimed at symptom removal, but at the mastery of a source of stress that has become encapsulated. Nevertheless, it has much in common with Wolpe's (1958) method of reciprocal inhibition, which involves the belated mastery of stress associated with symptom-specific stimulus dimensions. We believe that the theory presented here explains the success of Wolpe's procedure of desensitization, and why symptom substitution is not the problem that critics have predicted it would be. Wolpe's method requires a working through of anxiety to symptoms arranged along a hierarchy of increasing anxiety by progressing up the hierarchy through the desensitization of small increments of anxiety. By reducing anxiety to the symptoms, which are displaced representatives of the unconscious conflict or original source of stress, the entire anxiety gradient is lowered. Putting it otherwise, since the same generalization gradient that links symptoms to their source links the source to the symptoms, lowering anxiety to either should reduce anxiety to the other. Such a procedure is certainly psychodynamically different from symptom removal by hypnotic suggestion, which, by dissociating the symptom from the underlying conflict, encourages symptom substitution.

Wolpe's reciprocal inhibition is only one of many techniques for implementing the theory described here. The more general procedure would be to expedite the normal working-through process within the context of the psychotherapeutic interview. Unlike Wolpe, we do not believe that an extreme state of relaxation is required to master anxiety. It will be recalled that in the working-through process in grief and acute trauma, and in the paradoxical phases of Pavlov's dogs, the displaced representatives of the original stress were mastered at levels where anxiety was manageable, and not absent. The important consideration is that the conflict must be worked through at levels of anxiety that are not excessive, which must be gauged by the therapist through careful observation of signs of anxiety and physiological arousal. While the use of hierarchies of known sources of anxiety is a worthwhile adjunct to the general procedure described here, there is no reason for the hierarchies to be restricted to symptoms that the patient can directly report. An important innovation would be to use specially constructed projective tests, free associations, or diagnostic interviews, in conjunction with polygraph recording, to establish dimensions of anxiety-provoking cues in relation to areas of unconscious conflict. These then could be worked through by beginning with the displaced end of the dimension and gradually advancing toward a more direct confrontation with the conflict.

The model for the mastery of fear may well apply to the mastery of all other motives. If this is so, the effective control of an impulse requires that it be discriminated at various levels of intensity and that inhibition be learned over a considerable range of the dimension; that is, the individual must have experience in recognizing and controlling the impulse over a range of its intensity. As a result, the impulse can be inhibited early in its development. Once an impulse has reached great intensity, it may be impossible to control, as the high level of arousal associated with it interferes with higher-order functioning. Gaining experience in controlling impulses at many levels is important, as it provides security in the form that if control fails at one point, it can be instituted at the next. Moreover, unlike an inhibitory system which exists only at the inception of the impulse, it does not stifle the impulse, but allows it to be expressed at many levels of intensity without fear that it will get out of hand. What we are describing, of course, corresponds to a modulated control system as contrasted with an all-or-none system, which must either completely suppress the impulse or allow it unrestrained expression.

In order to teach impulse control, the therapist can actively help the patient recognize the drive at various levels of intensity, beginning with its most obvious manifestation that is unrecognized by the patient and proceeding to its more subtle forms of expression. As the impulse is most readily inhibited before it becomes intense, particular effort should be devoted to recognizing the antecedent cues and labeling the incipient reaction. As in the retroactive mastery of anxiety, by gradually extending this process, greater intensities of the drive can be brought under control. Although almost all therapists use to some extent procedures that embody the principles we are describing, we are advocating that they be practiced in a more orderly, detailed, and explicit manner than is usually the case. In fact, we would recommend that the patient be taught the principles and encouraged to practice them outside of the therapy hour. Many patients believe that they are the passive victims of their emotions, and are unaware how their thought processes, including their biased perceptual hypotheses, cause their drives to accelerate. They simply know that they are left with an unmanageable end-product. For some of these patients, discrimination training will be enough, as they already have adequate means for inhibiting the drive at low to moderate intensities once they recognize it. For others, it will be necessary to institute training in how *not* to make certain drive-accelerating responses, and how to make other responses that reduce the drive. We wish to emphasize that we are not describing a procedure for inhibiting the expression of a drive at the motor end once it has reached a high level of intensity, or for shutting it out entirely, but for modulating the experience of the drive itself, so that the individual has the freedom, once he recognizes a drive as inappropriate, to shut it off, if he so chooses.

VI. Summary

A theory of mastery of anxiety has been presented. The major assumptions of the theory are that with exposure to threat two developments take place, (1) a broadening, heightening, and steepening of a generalization gradient of anxiety, and (2) the development of an inhibitory gradient that becomes increasingly steeper than the anxiety gradient. The double process accounts for how, as a result of successful experience in facing a source of stress, anxiety provides an increasingly efficient warning system, producing earlier warning signals at reduced levels of arousal.

The theory was inductively arrived at from investigations of the mastery of fear in sport parachuting. From three different sources, namely, physiological reactions to a cue dimension of parachute-relevant words in a word-association test, subjective ratings of fear at different points in time before and after a jump, and physiological reactions before, during, and after ascent in the aircraft, the same finding emerged. Novice parachutists on the day of a jump produced steep monotonic gradients of fear and of physiological arousal as a function of a time or cue dimension, while experienced parachutists produced inverted V-shaped curves, the peak advancing toward the remote end of the dimension with increasing experience. Longitudinal testing of individuals verified group data. The results could not be explained away by increased familiarity with the cues, as the phenomenon occurred only preceding a jump. Given the diversity of situations that produced the same relationship, and the astonishing degree of reliability of the findings, it was concluded that a fundamental principle had been uncovered. It was later learned that similar phenomena had been observed by Pavlov in dogs subjected to stress, and by Bond in combat flyers.

Although measures of fear and physiological arousal followed the same general principles of generalization and inhibition, they were functionally distinctive, with the peak of self-rated fear of experienced parachutists occurring considerably before the peak of physiological arousal. This and other observations led to the conclusion that there is a defense system in depth for keeping overall levels of activation within homeostatic limits. It was observed that in addition to a system for controlling overall activation, there are subsystems of activation and its control, and that the assumption of a single overall system is not crucial for the theory, which can be applied equally well to the subsystems. The nature of the subsystems made it necessary to introduce a concept of inhibition in breadth as well as in depth.

The finding that physiological arousal and the subjective experience of fear produced different functional relationships led to an analysis of fear, anxiety, and arousal. It was concluded that fear is an avoidance motive, that arousal is the nonspecific excitatory component of all motives and reactions to stimulation, and that anxiety is a state of undirected arousal following the perception of danger. It was postulated that anxiety has a particularly noxious quality, which provides a strong incentive for it to be channeled into a motive, such as fear, that supports directed action. This has the adaptive advantage that it makes it increasingly likely that the organism will resort to some kind of directed action as crisis mounts, at least up to the point where stress may become so great as to paralyze action.

It was speculated that the system for maintaining high levels of arousal within homeostatic limits is part of a more general system for modulating the intensity component of all stimulation. A theory for this general system was proposed in the form of a set of postulates. Support for the generality of the theory was provided by the observation that the principles appear to apply to a wide variety of phenomena in and out of the laboratory, such as the repetition compulsion, the working through of acute grief, the after-discharge of anxiety, inverted U-shaped curves of physiological arousal as a function of repeated stimulation, the adaptation curve of the GSR, spontaneous recovery of adapted responses as a function of time and intensity of stimulation, the disinhibition of such responses, and the observation that the parameters of the traumatic neurosis and the startle response are very likely identical.

If it is true, as we suspect, that there is a single unifying assumption that underlies the functioning of all excitatory-inhibitory systems of organization, then it is of sufficient generality to qualify as a law. We proposed the law of excitatory modulation (LEM), which states that the gradient of inhibition as a function of increasing (or decreasing) excitation is steeper than the gradient of the excitation that it inhibits. This law describes the manner in which the intensity component of all stimulation, internal and external, is modulated, permitting the organism to work at efficient levels of arousal. As excitation mounts from any source, depending on its rate and intensity, as well as the organism's base level of arousal, it triggers inhibitory reactions that mount more rapidly, thereby reducing and even reversing the increase in excitation.

Implications of the theory were discussed for a number of different areas in psychology. For experimental psychology, it was noted that there is much to be gained by a psychology of the unconditioned stimulus, and that until this is accomplished it may be impossible to develop an adequate psychology of conditioning. For developmental psychology, we considered the implications of the system for coping with the intensity component of stimulation, primary and acquired. We speculated freely on how it might serve to bring the child into increasing contact with its environment. For schizophrenia, it was proposed that at sufficiently high and low levels of arousal the organism experiences further stimulation as noxious, and learns to protect itself from stimulation, thereby restricting its contact with the world. For psychotherapy, the importance of the distinction between fear and arousal was emphasized, and suggestions were made as to how the theory might be applied to the treatment of encapsulated areas of conflict and to the teaching of modulated impulse control, the absence of which was assumed to be a fundamental problem for many neurotics.

References

Basowitz, H., Persky, H., Korchin, S. J., & Grinker, R. R. *Anxiety and stress*. New York: McGraw-Hill, 1955.

Bender, Lauretta. Anxiety in disturbed children. In P. H. Hoch & J. Zubin (Eds.), *Anxiety*. New York: Grune & Stratton, 1950. Pp. 119–139.

Berlyne, D. E. *Conflict, arousal, and curiosity*. New York: McGraw-Hill, 1960.

Bettelheim, B. Individual and mass behavior in extreme situations. *J. abnorm. soc. Psychol.*, 1943, **38**, 417–452.

Bond, D. D. *The love and fear of flying*. New York: International Universities Press, 1952.

Broen, W. E., Jr., & Storms, L. H. Lawful disorganization: The process underlying a schizophrenic syndrome. *Psychol. Rev.*, 1966, **73**, 265–279.

Canon, W. B. *Bodily changes in pain, hunger, fear, and rage*. New York: Harper & Row, 1963.

Diamond, S., Balvin, R. S., & Diamond, Florence R. *Inhibition and choice, a neurobehavioral approach to problems of plasticity in behavior*. New York: Harper & Row, 1963.

Duffy, Elizabeth. *Activation and behavior*. New York: Wiley, 1962.

Epstein, S. The measurement of drive and conflict in humans: Theory and experiment. In M. R. Jones (Ed.), *Nebraska symposium on motivation: 1962*. Lincoln: Univer. of Nebraska Press, 1962. Pp. 281–321.

Epstein, S. Some theoretical considerations on the nature of ambiguity and the use of stimulus dimensions in projective techniques. *J. consult. Psychol.*, 1966, **30**, 183–192.

Epstein, S., & Burstein, K. A replication of Hovland's study of generalization to frequencies of tone. *J. exp. Psychol.*, 1966, **72**, 782–784.

Epstein, S., & Fenz, W. D. Theory and experiment on the measurement of approach-avoidance conflict. *J. abnorm. soc. Psychol.*, 1962, **64**, 97–112.

Epstein, S., & Fenz, W. D. Steepness of approach and avoidance gradients in humans as a function of experience: Theory and experiment. *J. exp. Psychol.*, 1965, **70**, 1–12.

Epstein, S., & Fenz, W. D. Adaptation of the GSR and basal conductance as a function of manifest anxiety. Unpublished mimeographed paper., 1966.

Fenichel, O. *The psychoanalytic theory of neurosis*. New York: Norton, 1945.

Fenz, W. D. Conflict and stress as related to physiological activation and sensory, perceptual and cognitive functioning. *Psychol. Monogr.*, 1964, **78**, No. 8 (Whole No. 585).

Fenz, W. D., & Epstein, S. Measurement of approach-avoidance conflict along a stimulus dimension by a thematic apperception test. *J. Pers.*, 1962, **30**, 613–632.

Fenz, W. D., & Epstein, S. Gradients of physiological arousal of experienced and novice parachutists as a function of an approaching jump. *Psychosom. Med.*, 1967, **29**, 33–51.

Freud, S. *The problem of anxiety*. New York: Norton, 1936.

Freud, S. *Beyond the pleasure principle*. New York: Bantam, 1959.

Grinker, R. R., & Spiegel, J. P. *Men under stress*. New York: McGraw-Hill, 1945.

Grosser, G. H., Wechsler, H., & Greenblatt, M. (Eds.). *The threat of impending disaster*. Cambridge, Mass.: M.I.T. Press, 1964.

Hoch, P. H. Biosocial aspects of anxiety. In P. H. Hoch & J. Zubin (Eds.), *Anxiety*. New York: Grune & Stratton, 1950. Pp. 105–116.

Hull, C. L. *Principles of behavior*. New York: Appleton-Century-Crofts, 1943.

Hull, C. L. A primary social science law. *Sci. Mon.*, 1950, **71**, 221–228.

Janis, I. L. *Psychological stress*. New York: Wiley, 1958.

Johnson, L. C., Slye, Elaine S., & Dement, W. Electroencephalographic and automatic activity during and after prolonged sleep deprivation. *Psychosom. Med.*, 1965, **27**, 415–423.

Kardiner, A. *The traumatic neuroses of war*. New York: Harper & Row (Hoeber), 1941.

Lacey, J. I. The evaluation of automatic responses: toward a general solution. *Ann. N. Y. Acad. Sci.*, 1956, **67**, 125–163.

Lacey, J. I., Kagan, J., Lacey, Beatrice C., & Moss, H. A. Situational determinants and behavioral correlates of autonomic response patterns. In P. H. Knapp (Ed.), *Expression of emotions in man*. New York: International Universities Press, 1963.

Lewin, K. Environmental forces. In C. Murchison (Ed.), *A handbook of child psychology*. (2nd ed.) Worcester, Mass.: Clark Univer. Press, 1931.

Lewin, K. Behavior and development as a function of the total situation. In L. Carmichael (Ed.), *Manual of child psychology*. New York: Wiley, 1946.

Lindemann, E. Symptomatology and management of acute grief. *Amer. J. Psychiat.*, 1944, **101**, 141–148.

Lindsley, D. B. Emotion. In S. S. Stevens (Ed.), *Handbook of experimental psychology*. New York: Wiley, 1951. Pp. 473–516.

Luria, R. *The nature of human conflicts*. New York: Liveright, 1932.

McClelland, D. C., Atkinson, J. W., Clark, R. A., & Lowell, E. A. *The achievement motive*. New York: Appleton-Century-Crofts, 1953.

Malmo, R. B. Activation: A neuropsychological dimension. *Psychol. Rev.*, 1959, **66**, 367–386.

May, R. *The meaning of anxiety*. New York: Ronald Press, 1950.

Mednick, S. A. A learning theory approach to research in schizophrenia. *Psychol. Bull.*, 1958, **55**, 316–327.

Meehl, P. E. Schizotaxia, schizotypy, schizophrenia. *Amer. Psychol.*, 1962, **17**, 827–838.

Miller, N. E. Theory and experiment relating psychoanalytic displacement to stimulus-response generalization. *J. abnorm. soc. Psychol.*, 1948, **43**, 155–178.

Miller, N. E. Liberalization of basic S-R concepts: Extensions to conflict behavior, motivation, and social learning. In S. Koch (Ed.), *Psychology: A study of a science*. Vol. 2. New York: McGraw-Hill, 1959.

Mowrer, O. H. Pain, punishment, guilt, and anxiety. In P. H. Hoch & J. Zubin (Eds.), *Anxiety*. New York: Grune & Stratton, 1950. Pp. 27–40.

Opler, M. K. Schizophrenia and culture *Sci. Amer.* 1957, **197**, 103–110.

Pavlov, I. P. *Conditioned reflexes*. (Transl. by G. V. Anrep) London: Oxford Univer. Press, 1927.

Pavlov, I. P. *Lectures on conditioned reflexes*. (Transl. by W. H. Gantt) New York: International Publishers, 1928.

Pavlov, I. P. *Conditioned reflexes and psychiatry*. (Transl. by W. H. Gantt) New York: International publishers, 1941.

Rado, S. *Psychoanalysis of behavior*. New York: Grune & Stratton, 1956.

Rado, S., & Daniels, G. *Changing concepts of psychoanalytic medicine*. New York: Grune & Stratton, 1956.

Sargant, W. *Battle for the mind*. Baltimore: Penguin, 1957.

Shakow, D. Psychological deficit in schizophrenia. *Behav. Sci.*, 1963, **8**, 275–305.

Sokolov, Y. N. *Perception and the conditioned reflex*. (Transl. by S. W. Waydenfeld) New York: Macmillan, 1963.

Solomon, R. L., & Wynne, L. C. Traumatic avoidance learning: The principles of anxiety conservation and partial irreversibility. *Psychol. Rev.*, 1954, **61**, 353–385.

Stenett, R. G. The relationship of alpha amplitude to the level of palmar conductance. *Electroencephalog. clin. Neurophysiol.*, 1957, **9**, 131–138.

Stewart, M. A., Stern, J. A., Winokur, G., & Fredman, S. An analysis of GSR conditioning. *Psychol. Rev.*, 1961, **68**, 60–67.

Trehub, A. A theory of sensory interaction: An experimental investigation of the relationship between autonomic activity and visual sensitivity. Unpublished doctoral dissertation. Boston University, 1954.

Venables, P. H. Input dysfunction in schizophrenia. In B. A. Maher (Ed.), *Progress in experimental personality research*. Vol. 1. New York: Academic Press, 1964. Pp. 1–47.

White, R. W. *The abnormal personality.* (2nd ed.) New York: Ronald Press, 1956.

Wilder, J. The law of initial value in neurology and psychiatry. *J. nerv. ment. Dis.*, 1957, **125**, 73–86.

Wolpe, J. *Psychotherapy by reciprocal inhibition.* Stanford, Calif.: Stanford Univer. Press, 1958.

Woodworth, R. S., & Schlosberg, H. *Experimental psychology.* New York: Holt, Rinehart & Winston, 1954.

SOME RAMIFICATIONS OF EXPOSURE TO CONFLICT[1]

Leonard Worell

DEPARTMENT OF PSYCHOLOGY, UNIVERSITY OF KENTUCKY,
LEXINGTON, KENTUCKY

I. Introduction and Definition

Although conflict occupies an important position in many systems of personality and therapy, the concept is not without ambiguity. A condition of conflict is said to exist when two or more incompatible response tendencies are simultaneously aroused (Berlyne, 1960; Brown & Farber, 1951; Miller, 1944; Worell, 1962). Special emphasis is placed on incompatibility, since it is assumed that as the degree of incompatibility is increased there is a concomitant augmentation in the magnitude of conflict. Unfortunately, this definition does not appear to be entirely adequate. The principal difficulty is that conflict is defined in terms of incompatibility between responses (tendencies) alone. In our view, this definition is insufficient because it ignores the *consequences* associated with these tendencies or dispositions. For example, we might have two responses that are physically

[1] Much of the work reported here was supported by USPHS Grants MH-04891 and MH-13432 from the National Institute of Mental Health.

incompatible, such as raising versus lowering one's hand, but this would not be regarded as conflictful if the consequence of one response were shock and of the other shock-avoidance. Recognition of the importance of this response-consequence relationship leads us to define conflict in terms of the degree of discriminability that exists between the *outcomes* of alternative potential choices. Accordingly, when a choice is between something a person likes and something he dislikes, outcome discriminability is high and level of conflict is low. In contrast, when the alternative choices are associated with outcomes that approximate one another in either desirability or uncertainty, discriminability is lowered and conflict is elevated. This statement of conflict corresponds in some essential respects to what has been termed the relative strength approach. The basic feature of the latter view is that the strength or degree of conflict varies with the *difference* in strength between competing tendencies, such that the more closely these tendencies approximate one another in strength, the greater the degree of conflict. Our definition departs from this by stressing the pivotal significance of outcome discriminability in relation to alternative behavior dispositions.

At least two objections may be raised to the discriminability of outcome definition. The first concerns the role of avoidance. It might be argued, for example, that an individual faced with what has been termed an avoidance-avoidance conflict is perfectly capable of discriminating between the alternatives and yet would be described as being in strong conflict. A moment's reflection, however, will indicate that this is an incomplete description of the situation. For one thing, if we used the most conventional measure of conflict; namely, reaction time, and we allowed the individual to do what is normally done; namely, leave the situation (field), we would find his reaction time in doing so short indeed. By this conflict criterion, then, an avoidance-avoidance condition constitutes low, not high, conflict. The situation is vastly changed and does become quite conflictful, however, by the simple expedient of compelling the individual to make a choice. This of course means that approach dispositions have been added to the situation and a transformation has been made into a more complex double approach-avoidance situation. Through this transformation the discriminability between the alternative outcomes has been markedly reduced, for the person must now determine the less aversive, or more positive, eventuality.

The second consideration is that the *absolute* strengths of dispositions may also contribute to the degree of conflict. Briefly stated, this position asserts that not only the degree of discriminability but also the amount of importance of outcomes are significant determiners of conflict strength. Although intuitively appealing, we will reserve a fuller examination of this often adopted assumption until a later section.

II. The Experimental Neurosis–Dissonance Paradox

Of the relatively few empirically based psychological models for conflict, those for so-called experimental neurosis and dissonance have not been given the comparative attention they deserve. This is especially apparent in the fact that sharply contrasting positions are found in these models regarding the *consequences* for behavior of prior exposure to different levels of conflict. Therefore, it seems worthwhile to review the major character of these formulations.

A. THE EXPERIMENTAL NEUROSIS MODEL

Although widely heralded in the 1930's as a breakthrough in the understanding of the development of abnormal phenomena, the psychology of the past 20 years has given fleeting attention at best to the domain of events embraced by the loose label experimental neurosis. It is not surprising, therefore, that many of the essential features of this domain were observed in what is now often referred to as a classic experiment by Shenger-Krestovnikova reported by Pavlov (1928). Since many of the facts are generally well known, it may be remarked briefly that an animal was confronted eventually with a very difficult discrimination between two stimuli, one of which was associated with reinforcement (reward) and the other with nonreinforcement. Escape from the situation was not readily possible since the animal was intractably restrained. Following relatively prolonged exposure to the stimuli, which posed demands for discrimination beyond the animal's capacity, a breakdown in both discrimination and "normal" adaptive behavior was observed. Of major importance from the standpoint of the impairment of discrimination was the observation that simpler discriminations were likewise disturbed. Thus, the effects of exposure to the strongly conflictful conditions appeared to generalize to prior discriminations that had been made with comparative ease. Apart from this direct conflict transfer effect, it was also noted that the animal developed a more generalized emotional disturbance characterized by muscle tremors and rage.

Subsequent investigators have both confirmed and extended these early observations. For example, in the matter of restraint, both Cook (1939) and Dworkin (1939) have presented evidence indicating that where the opportunity for escape from the difficult discrimination or strong conflict is available, the nonadaptive and generalized behaviors do not emerge. Therefore, forcing exposure to the conflict appears to be a critical ingredient. In addition, the results from Pavlov's laboratory strongly suggested that the discrimination need not involve punishment; rather, the mere presence of rewarding and nonrewarding outcomes was sufficient. Although a large number of studies have produced the typical behavioral effects using noxious stimulation as well under restraint (e.g., Anderson & Parmenter, 1941; Masserman, 1943; Lichtenstein, 1950; Liddell, 1956), equivalent effects were obtained by Dworkin (1939) through the simple presence or absence of reward. This would appear to be consonant with the common-sense expectation that strong discrimination conflict, albeit divorced from punishment, normally possesses an aversive character.

Finally, both the range and generality of behavioral effects have been elaborated. The varieties of behavioral outcomes have included (a) physiological changes, such as increased muscular rigidity, frequent micturition and defecation, heightened breathing and heart rates, and (b) psychological changes indicating hypersensitivity, immobility, stereotypy, and sexual and social disability (Liddell, 1944; Masserman & Pechtel, 1953). Moreover, although the generality of behavior alterations observed has frequently been limited to relatively restricted classes of stimuli, such as the experimental apparatus (Gantt, 1944) or the laboratory generally (Pavlov, 1928), they have occasionally been noted to be quite pervasive (Liddell, 1956). We may conclude that although the facts concerning both the diversity and generalization of behaviors resulting from exposure to difficult discriminations or strong conflict have a firm empirical footing; it is lamentable that a knowledge of the specific conditions governing either the appearance of particular patterns of behavior or the scope of generalization of these behaviors is so prominently lacking. For our present purposes, however, recognition of the operation of these generalization effects of strong discrimination conflict is most important.

B. THE DISSONANCE MODEL

With something like the heraldry generated for experimental neurosis, the relatively recent formulations of cognitive dissonance (Festinger, 1957, 1964) have betokened to many the possibility of encompassing hitherto intractable problems in the provinces of general psychology (Festinger, 1961; Lawrence & Festinger, 1962) and especially social psychology (Brown, 1962). Although phrased within the framework of cognitions and dissonance, it has become clear from recent work (Festinger, 1964) that dissonance is specifically meant to refer to a very definite phase of conflict resolution. In particular, dissonance embraces what occurs in the post-decisional conflict period. Thus, traditional conflict is seen as composing the preamble to a choice, whereas dissonance is concerned with the vicissitudes of the aftermath of choice.

At the most general level, the dissonance model proposes that an individual holds various "cognitions" or "knowledges" about the world and himself. Although these cognitions may enter into a variety of relationships with one another (such as predecisionally), the two most important are their degree of consonance or dissonance. Thus it is said that a condition of dissonance exists when cognition 1 is either the "obverse" of, or does not "imply" or "lead to," cognition 2. The reverse of these, of course, reveals the presence of consonance. Beyond this bare outline of cognitive contents, the central distinguishing feature of dissonance is that it is intolerable to the organism. Consequently, dissonance will motivate the individual to do whatever he can either to eliminate or reduce the inconsistency. It naturally follows that the stronger the dissonance, the more active and pronounced will be the push toward dissonance reduction.

Since dissonance-consonance is regarded as a postdecision conflict phenomenon, two important implications should be noted. The first is that to arrive at a condition of dissonance, the individual must somehow be put into a condition of conflict. Not only must he be exposed to a pair or more of conflicting cognitions, but he must also be brought to make a conflictful choice. Since the making of such a choice will normally be avoided, however, very special emphasis is placed on the extraction of a "commitment" through what has been most frequently designated as "forced compliance." Hence, in brief, the individual must in some way be compelled to do something that he does not wish to do.

The second point is that once the conflictful decisional act has been made, the machinery of dissonance reduction is brought into play. Since dissonance cannot be maintained, there are three major possible forms of its reduction: the committed-to alternative may be increased in attractiveness, the rejected alternative may be further berated, or both the fore going may occur simultaneously. Stated somewhat differently, dissonance strains toward consonance.

As is well known, the dissonance formulation has been more than modestly heuristic. Since our major purpose is to derive essential points of similarity and difference between the two models presented, we will not go into the burgeoning dissonance literature (save selectively at subsequent points). For an empirical affirmation of the position, however, one might consult Brehm and Cohen (1962); for a decidedly iconoclastic presentation, see Chapanis and Chapanis (1964).

C. THE PARADOX

While it seems evident that there exist a number of relatively minor differences between the experimental neurosis and dissonance models in terms of their preferences for certain language forms and contents and for comparatively simple versus complex experimental arrangements, it is abundantly clear that both approaches are fundamentally focused on the effects of responding to conflict. Moreover, in order to induce the organism to respond at all to the conflict alternatives, rather than to flee, adherents of both models have found it necessary to resort to some form of compulsion (e.g., physical restraint or social or economic pressure). Implicit, and frequently explicit, in the use of this strategem is the recognition that conflict is normally aversive. Despite this putative aversive quality, however, the prediction of the behavioral consequences of responding to conflict are diametrically opposed in the two models. The foundation of the dissonance model is that following a conflict choice immediate pressures are activated to "spread apart" the conflicting alternatives. Hence, postdecision conflict is not maintained. In sharp contrast, the empirical findings emanating from experimental neurosis research strongly suggest that choices made to difficult discrimination conflicts not only do not lead to a spreading apart of alternatives but also are associated with a disruption of response to weaker conflicts. Thus, postdecision conflict appears to be both maintained and generalized. Simply stated, then, the paradox is: How can responding to conflict simultaneously produce conflict reduction on the one hand and the persistence and generalization of the conflict on the other?

III. The Generalization of Conflict

A. A DEFICIENCY OF DISSONANCE

Among the strengths accorded the dissonance model is that it is at once simple and yet comprehensive in its explanatory power. The simplicity is deceptive, for if we were to take the model's major premise as a *sine qua non*, conflict would be a universally momentary state providing that a choice or commitment were made. This benign eventuality, however, is clearly dissonant with the observations made of human behavior in an impressive array of situations. As an illustration, consider Lifton's (1961) description of the effects of the elaborate "thought reform" procedures of the Chinese Communists against Westerners who had dedicated their lives to China but were still largely "committed " to Western democratic ideals. Lifton found that, following extremely severe conflict experiences and a reversed "public commitment," there occurred not conflict reduction but indecision between the merits of Communist and democratic ideology. Beyond this, it is not uncommon for clinical descriptions to contain statements indicating that *both* before and after a decision there is hesitancy, doubt, indecision, and so on. Against such a background and that gleaned from an examination of the findings of experimental neurosis, we began to doubt the generality of the dissonance formulation and to ask instead: Does responding to conflict exert an effect on response to subsequent conflict? In appraising this issue, we were first led to consider relatively simple conflict situations and then more complicated contexts.

B. RELATIVELY SIMPLE HUMAN DEMONSTRATIONS

1. The Methods of Conflict Induction

In our early efforts to find very simple means of inducing conflict among humans, we noted that historically conflict had been produced through one of two primary procedures, i.e., training or the posing of difficult discriminations (Worell, 1963). The first of these, training, has taken one of two variants: either different amounts or kinds of training are given to different stimuli or the same stimulus, as illustrated in the work of Sears and Hovland (1941), or the previous training of the person is used by having instructions elicit differential strengths of outcomes. This latter approach characterizes research within the dissonance model where subjects have been instructed (i.e., forced compliance) to say they will eat large or small amounts (varying outcomes) of a disliked vegetable (Brehm, 1959), or to agree that they will lie (Festinger & Carlsmith, 1959).

The second major variant of conflict induction has been that in which two or more stimuli, such as lights or tones, of varying similarity to one another are simultaneously or consecutively presented. Although the general method clearly arose from Pavlovian work, the rationale (Brown, 1942; Miller, 1944) for including difficult discrimination as a form of conflict is based on the empirical phenomenon of stimulus generalization. In this phenomenon, it has been repeatedly demonstrated that when an organism is trained to respond to a standard stimulus, the strength of response tends to follow a declining gradient as progressively dissimilar stimuli from the training stimulus are exposed. Thus, with reference to discrimination conflict, when an organism is simultaneously presented with two stimuli that are very much alike, greater conflict is aroused than when the confrontation is between two comparatively dissimilar stimuli. This occurs because the dispositions aroused by the more similar stimuli are more equivalent in strength (i.e., the relative value of outcomes associated with these dispositions are less discriminable from one another). It follows that stronger conflict arises from the greater generalization between the behavioral dispositions to the two more similar stimuli.

In comparing these two primary methods of producing conflict, there is nothing to indicate that they are fundamentally different. Thus, the traditionally accepted indices of conflict, such as vacillation, hesitancy, increased reaction time, and so on, have consistently been found with both procedures. Moreover, the blurring of any essential distinction becomes apparent when we observe that with lower organisms in the discrimination conflict setting different amounts or kinds of training are given to stimuli, whereas with humans instructions are very often used to induce a stronger behavioral disposition to one or another of the simultaneously presented stimuli. As an outgrowth of these considerations, we early elected to use the discrimination conflict paradigm in portions of our work with human, and usually adult, subjects.

2. The Empirical Outcomes

In all the work on conflict generalization, a three-stage paradigm has been employed (Worell, 1962). The first stage is designed to obtain base rates of responding to conflict and consists of a series of exposures to a predetermined level or degree of conflict. This is followed by an intermediate stage in which specific variations in the strength of conflict are introduced. Finally, the third stage permits the assessment of generalization effects by reintroducing subjects to the conditions encountered in the initial stage.

Using this paradigm and a brightness discrimination apparatus that permitted wide variations in the presented intensity of two simultaneously illuminated lights, a preliminary study was performed in which groups of college women were given training in responding to one of five levels (severities) of conflict following exposure by all to a weak conflict situation (Worell, 1962). Of the five groups, two were exposed to very strong conflict, two to intermediate levels of conflict, and the final group was given very weak conflict. The two most severe conflicts consisted of conditions where the two simultaneously presented lights were of equal measured intensity such that one group received two equally very bright lights and the other two equally very dim lights. Intermediate conflict was composed of either the presentation of a very bright and moderately bright pair or a moderately bright and very dim couplet. Finally, the very weak conflict condition comprised the simultaneous appearance of a very bright and a very dim illumination.

Our primary focus was on the effects of these conflict conditions on the subsequent resolution of weak conflict. In anticipating the results, two opposing theoretical formulations, designated the *competing response* and the *dynamogenic* positions, were considered. These proposals may be respectively subsumed into the long-standing distinction between associative, or learned, and nonassociative approaches.

a. The Competing Response Hypothesis. From the standpoint of the competing response view, it may be assumed that responding to different levels of conflict leads to the learning of differing conflict-specific responses. Thus, in the case of a person who has been repeatedly exposed to relatively strong conflicts over reasonably prolonged periods, it might be expected that he would acquire such responses as withholding a decision or competing dispositions to consider each alternative carefully. Following such acquisition, in new but similar situations the person may be expected to elicit those behaviors or dispositions that he has previously learned. Consequently, according to a competing response (or dispositional) view, the effects of prior exposure to conflict would be seen as having a limited generality—limited by the similarities between former and present situations. Through this reasoning, it was expected that persons who had previously been trained under strong conflict would be more retarded in resolving weak conflict than those who had previously experienced less severe conflict training conditions. Thus, strong conflict training would lead the individual to react to current weak conflict as though it were more conflictful than it had formerly been.

    b. The Dynamogenic Hypothesis. The dynamogenic view, in contrast, advances the proposition that conflict may generate motivational consequences. This proposal is similar in many respects to the dissonance one, so that the predictions stemming from both approaches are identical in relation to the postconflict performance of some, but not all, of our experimental groups. In any event, the general suggestion that conflict may entail tension-arousing or drive properties has frequently been made (Brown & Farber, 1951; Lewin, 1933; Luria, 1932; Miller, 1944, 1959; Miller & Stevenson, 1936). Beyond this, several studies designed to test this motivational hypothesis have been in accord in indicating that heightened force or vigor of response appears as the degree of conflict is increased (Castaneda & Worell, 1961; Finger, 1941; Worell & Castaneda, 1961b). These amplitude findings are congruent with the view that one consequence of conflict is an elevation of motivation, or drive, and that increasing degrees of conflict produce larger increments in drive.

    If conflict generates drive, it would be expected that the effects of conflict on performance in a contiguously presented task would materialize irrespective of the similarity between the conflict and subsequent situation. This is derived directly from the Hullian proposal that drive serves as an indiscriminate energizer of performance (Hull, 1943). More concretely, then, from a dynamogenic position it was anticipated that people who were formerly exposed to strong conflict would be more efficient (i.e., faster) in resolving weak conflict than those who had previously experienced weaker conflicts. In addition to basing this prediction on the conflict-drive formulation, we were also relying on the findings of an earlier study in which increased drive, as assessed by the Taylor Manifest Anxiety Scale, produced more efficient conflict resolution in the same weak conflict situation as used here (Worell & Castaneda, 1961b).

    Before going further, a few words may be said about the predictions

arising from the somewhat similar dissonance position. First, with regard
to our very strong conflict groups (i.e., where equally bright lights are
presented), it would be difficult for dissonance theory to make any prediction, since there is no possibility for a spreading-apart phenomenon
to occur between the indentical conflicting alternatives. Second, predictions could, however, conceivably be made for the intermediate and
weak conflict groups. It may be noted that in the intermediate groups one
of the two conflict alternatives during training is the *same* as one of the
two conflict alternatives in the subsequent weak conflict condition. Thus,
for example, for one intermediate group a very bright light constitutes one
alternative during training and the same very bright light is part of the
subsequent weak conflict, while for the other intermediate group a very dim
light appeared in training and the identical light occurred in the subsequent weak conflict. In each of these conditions, Ss were asked to choose
the brighter of the two simultaneously exposed lights.[2] Considering the
foregoing, if dissonance leads to either (a) an enhanced value of the chosen
alternative, i.e., the very bright light in the first intermediate conflict group;
or (b) a diminution in the value of the rejected alternative, i.e., the very
dim option in the second intermediate group, then by the generalization of
dissonance effects it might be expected that both intermediate conflict
groups would be more rapid in weak conflict resolution than a group
trained previously in weak conflict. Put somewhat differently, for one
intermediate group the very bright alternative should be strengthened,
whereas for the other intermediate group the very dim alternative would
be weakened; both of these conditions should produce more efficient
subsequent weak conflict resolution.

  c. The Findings. The basic findings for the three stages of the experiment are graphically depicted in Fig. 1. The most important among these,
together with their attendant implications, are worth considering briefly.
First, there is clear support for the view that the effects of conflict generalize
to other related but less conflictful situations. Thus, when an individual's
decision-making proficiency has been impaired by exposure to relatively
severe conflicts, he also demonstrates an impaired ability to resolve subsequent weaker related conflicts. This result tends to support the importance
of the *similarity* between the original conflict situation and a contemporary
one.

  The significance of similarity is further underlined when we compare
the foregoing finding with that obtained in earlier work by Worell and

[2]In the original study, half of each of the five groups was asked to choose the "brighter"
light while the remaining half selected the "dimmer" light. For simplicity of exposition, we
have described the reasoning for the "brighter" condition. However, the same reasoning is
applicable to the "dimmer" condition.

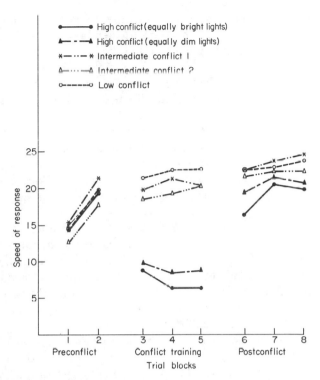

FIG. 1.   Response speeds over trials for the five conflict groups during preconflict, conflict training, and postconflict conditions. Each trial block represents the average performance on eight trials.

Castaneda (1961a), where the generalization of conflict effects was studied in relation to learning. In two experiments, high or low experimentally induced conflict occurred prior to the presentation of each pair of two verbal paired-associates tasks. Different degrees of conflict had been aroused by the simultaneous exposure of two lines of either equal or unequal length, while the paired-associates lists were composed of words with either high or low amounts of intralist competition. The findings showed no effect of the conflict conditions upon performance. Taken in conjunction with the present results, the absence of conflict-learning effects provides strong justification for a particular emphasis on the significance of the similarity between the instigating conflict situation and the subsequent conflict-performing one.

   Second, that conflicts do generalize is consistent with the competing response formulation; that they do not facilitate subsequent weak conflict performance does not support either the dynamogenic or dissonance positions. Although we have argued elsewhere (Worell, 1962) that a modified dynamogenic interpretation may have some credibility in relation to the present data, this will not be pursued further here. In addition, the dissonance prediction was not fulfilled in that the intermediate conflict groups did not show superior subsequent weak conflict resolution when compared to the weak conflict training group. We should be cautious, however, in seeing this as countermanding the dissonance view, since it could be maintained that the dissonance created in training for the intermediate group was relatively small (see the conflict training performances in Fig. 1) and that generalization of one component of a pair of dissonant alternatives has not been formally conceived as part of the system. Therefore, the most important element of our data here is the strong evidence that conflicts do generalize under some conditions, and this needs to be accounted for.

d. The Double Approach-Avoidance Hypothesis. Although the competing response formulation had been suggested earlier to handle the generalization of conflict effects, it has become clear that this formulation is too vague. The principal missing factor is a specification of the nature of the conflict conditions that produce such generalization effects. Our further analyses suggest a new model, both more detailed and more general in scope. This new model, broadly viewed, is a double approach-avoidance conflict conception. The general proposal is that conflict will generalize when the conflict is composed of double (or multiple) approach-avoidance alternatives. More specifically, the extent of conflict generalization depends on the degree of discriminability between the outcomes of the alternatives. Since in the simplest case of the double ApAv conflict each alternative has both positive and negative outcomes, the extremes of conflict generalization would be approached when the outcomes following from each alternative are increasingly more evenly balanced between the positive and negative eventualities. Thus, for example, consider the case where each alternative has been associated with equal probabilities for positive and negative outcomes. This is an essentially unresolvable, and hence maximally generalizable, conflict. Although a choice is made with a given outcome on one occasion, the history of the individual has been such that this *or* the opposite outcome will occur for the very same choice in the future. Moreover, exactly the same contingencies apply to the alternative choice. In this way, then, not only are conflicts maintained but they persist in their effects in new but related situations.

In applying this conception to the present study, we may view the very strong conflict conditions as generating double ApAv conflicts in which the outcomes of being right and wrong are equally distributed in relation to each choice. Since the outcomes are evenly balanced, there is continued uncertainty as to which alternative is to be preferred. The conflict cannot be effectively resolved because the balance is never shifted in favor of a given alternative experientially. Therefore, the conflicting dispositions are not only maintained but are "carried" into new situations that contain similar stimulus conditions.

An additional but related condition that contributes to the nonresolution of the double approach-avoidance conflict is a repetition of the conflict experience. When the conflict occurs not only once, but tends to be repeatedly experienced, each repetition serves as a reminder to the person that the conflict has not been resolved. One empirical effect of such conflict repetition may be noted in the performance of the very strong conflict groups (Fig. 1) where the speed of resolution declines with successive conflict (double ApAv) exposures during training. With the aid of this conflict index, then, we infer that strong double ApAv conflicts appear to be intensified through repeated encounters.

In sum, we may note that the double approach-avoidance conflict model appears promising in relation to conflict generalization. We will examine this model more closely in subsequent more complicated human situations, but first we will consider some additional important simple human demonstrations of the generalization of conflict.

e. Conflict Tolerance in a Minor Key. Since previous work showed pronounced effects of strong conflict on the effective handling of subsequent weaker conflicts, we became interested in the possible bidirectionality of conflict generalization. That is, if strong conflict leads to impaired weak conflict resolution, then exposure to weak conflict should have a facilitating effect on subsequent strong conflict performance. In terms of the double ApAv model presented earlier, the discrimination *weak* conflict situation presents a heavily unbalanced double ApAv condition such that one alternative is discriminably associated with a more favorable outcome (i.e., positive over negative). Since under these circumstances conflict resolution is facilitated, we would expect a transfer of this facilitation to a new related conflict situation, even though the new conflict is more intense. These considerations were put to test in an experiment where adult female *S*s were placed in either very strong or weak conflict during pretraining, and then were either continued at the same conflict level or switched to the opposite conflict intensity (Worell & Worell, 1964).[3] As shown in Fig. 2, performance in both strong and weak conflict situations is significantly influenced by the severity of previous conflict exposure. Specifically, people who have experienced weak conflict more readily resolve subsequently similar weak *and* strong conflict situations. Complementarily, as is evident,

[3] The original study included a third phase of postconflict; since the data for this phase paralleled those obtained for the conflict training phase, its presentation has been omitted.

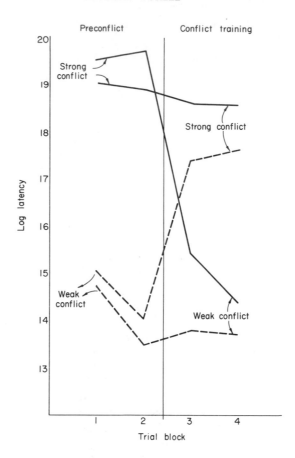

FIG. 2. Mean log latencies per trial block during the preconflict and conflict training stages. Each block comprises eight trials.

prior strong conflict exposure impairs the efficiency of decision making in *both* strong and weak conflict. In sum, previous experience with strong conflict is associated with responding to later related conflict situations as *though* they were more conflictful, whereas previous encounters with weak conflict lead to the reverse contingency.

   f. Conflict Generalization in Special Populations. Subsequent to the formulation and demonstration of the generalization of conflict phenomenon among comparatively normal and adult subjects, several provocative extensions of this work were carried out with more diverse populations. For example, Haruyo Hama (1965) has explored conflict generalization among classified schizophrenics, neurotics, and normals in Japan. In order to induce varying levels of conflict, a modified version of the Stroop Color-

Word Test was used wherein colored cards were presented that bore printed words that were either the same as, moderately similar to, or different from the depicted color. Thus, high conflict consisted of a printed color word that did not correspond to the card color, moderate conflict, words that suggested the color; and low conflict, words that corresponded to the actual color. Using the three-stage conflict generalization paradigm of weak conflict → conflict training → weak conflict, she found that both strong and moderate conflict training produced a significant retardation in post-conflict performance. An additional interesting aspect of these results was that both the neurotic and schizophrenic groups were more retarded in their response to the initial weak conflict situation than the normals, suggesting that the former groups entered the experimental situation with greater conflict.

Moving to another age range, Matsuyama (1965) examined the generalization of conflict using the brightness discrimination apparatus with children in grades 1, 3, and 5. It is interesting to note that the conflict generalization effect was found only among the children in grade 5; neither of the two younger age groups demonstrated significant generalization. Although these younger groups behaved in the initial weak conflict condition with greater apparent conflict (i.e., they were slower in resolving conflict) than the fifth graders and were therefore similar in their performances to the pathological groups in Hama's study, we suggest that the respective roles of both clinical and developmental factors on response to conflict and its generalization need further study.

C. More Complex Human Demonstrations

1. The Schill Study

Schill's work (1966) was primarily oriented toward demonstrating the generalization of conflict with personality-relevant materials. However, the study is also interesting in that it contains implications for the double approach-avoidance generalization model discussed earlier. In this respect, additionally, predictions stemming from this conception were compared with those arising from the dissonance model.

Employing the standard three-stage paradigm, Schill had his college subjects initially rate a list of personality traits in terms of how strongly they would approve or disapprove of the traits use by others in describing them or their personality. The ratings permitted the construction of personally meaningful conflicts by pairing varying valued traits and requiring the individual to select the particular trait by which he would most prefer to be described.

Five training groups were differentiated, three strong conflict and two weak conflict. These were:

(a) Approach-approach conflict (ApAp), where the two traits of each pair had been assigned the same rating of approval (i.e., either strong, moderate, or slight).

(b) Avoidance-avoidance conflict (AvAv), where trait pairs consisted of equal disapproval value.

(c) Double approach-avoidance conflict (DoApAv), in which two sets of traits were employed such that each set contained one approved and one disapproved characteristic. Further, each pair of these sets was so constructed that the members would be equal in net approval and disapproval strength.

(d) Weak conflict (WC2), which was composed of trait pairs containing one approved and one disapproved characteristic.

(e) Weak conflict (WC4), where, as in (c), two sets of traits were selected, but here one set contained two approved characteristics and its paired set contained two disapproved characteristics. This group served as a control for group (c).

Following an initial exposure to weak conflict and the foregoing conflict training conditions, all subjects were finally placed in a weak conflict condition again. The performances of the five groups during conflict training and postconflict are depicted in Fig. 3. Two principal aspects of Schill's results are worth expanding.

First, the right-hand portion of Fig. 3 clearly provides support for the generalization of conflict; all three strong conflict groups show significantly impaired conflict resolution. The findings at this more complex personality level parallel those obtained in the simpler brightness discrimination studies.

Second, these generalization effects accord closely with expectations that would be derived from the proposed double approach-avoidance conflict generalization model. It will be recalled that this model suggested that increasing conflict generalization would appear as the discriminability between the positive and negative valence of outcomes associated with choice alternatives became increasingly uncertain. Specifically, this means that double approach-avoidance conflicts will in general produce greater conflict generalization. Schill's data indicate that both the double approach-avoidance and avoidance-avoidance groups are more retarded in conflict resolution during the conflict training and postconflict stages than the remaining groups. Since Ss in the AvAv group were required to make a choice, thereby adding approach to the avoidance alternatives, we infer that this group was highly similar to the DoApAv conflict group. In sum, then, we may regard these data as providing relatively strong support for the

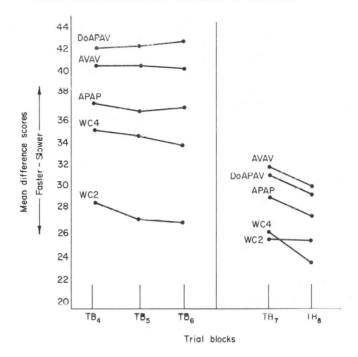

FIG. 3. The main difference scores for successive trial blocks (conflict training and postconflict) for the various conflict groups. (In all cases, each trial block was subtracted from the last trial block of pretraining—trials 11–15. A constant, 30.00, was added to each score; therefore, the smaller averages represent faster speeds.)

proposal that double approach-avoidance conflict underlies the generalization of conflict.

2. *Generalization Versus Dissonance*

In addition to the foregoing results, Schill obtained a rerating of the personality traits after the postconflict stage. This rerating permitted at least a rudimentary test to be made between the dissonance and conflict generalization models in accounting for preference changes. From a dissonance position it would be expected that following choice in a strongly conflictful (dissonant) situation, tension is produced for either the chosen alternative to become more preferred, the rejected one to be viewed less desirably, or both.

From the standpoint of conflict generalization, the prediction of preference change following a conflict choice is not as simple, particularly when only a single nonrepeated statement of preference is involved. In contrast to dissonance, the generalization model would expect a person who has experienced strong conflict to develop competing dispositions regarding the preferability of outcomes associated with each alternative despite the fact that a particular alternative was chosen. This would mean two things: (1) following strong conflict choice, the individual is expected to be in doubt about or question his selections and rejections, and (2) over *repeated* assessments of preference, he is likely to vacillate in his preference for both the selected and rejected alternatives. At the opposite pole, making choices in weak conflict should not produce hesitation and doubt, but rather should lead to a clearer or wider discrimination between the alternatives.

Evidence bearing on the importance of repeated assessments of preference may be found in a study by Worell (1964) in which interest was focused on experimentally modifying preferences for conflict. Following exposure to conflict, it was noted that the initial stated perference did not faithfully reflect subsequent stated preferences. Additional support for the repetition view may be gained from recent research by Festinger and Walster (1964) conducted, interestingly enough, within a dissonance framework. They used two groups who were first to rate and then choose between two hairstyles. One group was told before the rating that they would later be asked to choose between two particular hairstyles; they then rated the hairstyles and were confronted with the choice. This group, in effect, was exposed twice to the same conflict. The second group, in contrast, was not told anything about subsequently choosing between a given pair, but rather immediately rated the styles and then were confronted with a choice. Their findings indicated that significantly more subjects in the first group showed a lack of correspondence between the ratings and the choices. Thus, this group showed a reversal of preference, a phenomenon that they labeled "regret" and that we conceive of as conflict generalization.

Taken together, the foregoing results strongly point to the need for repeated assessments of preference following conflict exposure. Unfortunately, Schill's study did not include such repetition. However, a portion of his data on preferences is relevant to the assumption that conflict generalizes. Reference to Table I discloses the changes in preference that appeared for both selected and rejected alternatives in two strong conflict groups (i.e., approach-approach and avoidance-avoidance) as compared to the weak conflict (WC2) group. It may be noted that the greatest increase in preference for selected alternatives and the greatest decrease in preference for rejected alternatives occurred in the weak conflict group. These results are in accord with the conflict generalization proposal that suggests that after strong conflict there is more doubt about and less discrimination between the conflict alternatives as a function of the generalization of conflict effects.

TABLE I

ANALYSIS OF PREFERENCE CHANGES

	WC2	APAP	AVAV
Direction and magnitude of changes for 25 chosen alternatives (controlled for frequency of exposure)[a]			
Chi square:	+ 28	+ 7	− 1
A. Between WC2 and APAP 12.06 (*p* .001)			
B. Between WC2 and AVAV (Since AVAV yielded a negative value no χ^2 could be performed. However, since this difference is larger than that analyzed above, it is necessarily significant.)			
Direction and magnitude of changes for 21 rejected alternatives (controlled for frequency of exposure)[a]			
Chi square:	− 21	+ 4	− 9
A. Between WC2 and AVAV 4.80 (*p* .05)			
B. Between WC2 and APAP (Since APAP yielded a positive value, no χ^2 could be performed. However, since this difference is larger than that analyzed above, it should necessarily be more significant.)			

[a] A change toward the "approve" side equaled a plus, while a change toward the "disapprove" side equaled a minus total.

Magnitude depended upon the extent of change. Thus, a change from "slightly approve" to "moderately approve" equals a + 1, to "strongly approve" + 2, etc. On the other hand, a change from "moderately approve" to "slightly approve" equals − 1, etc. Scores shown in the table represent a composite of all + and − changes (From Schill, 1966).

IV. Intrapersonal Instability and Conflict

A. RELATIVELY SIMPLE HUMAN DEMONSTRATIONS

We have already briefly alluded to the possible relationship between conflict and variability of behavior. Our aim here is to explore this problem in more detail. Despite the widespread occurrence of variable or unstable behavior by individuals in response to both old and new situations, the problem has been largely ignored by careful researchers until recently (Fiske, 1961; Nowliss, 1965; Wessman & Ricks, 1966). As indicated in earlier work (Worell, 1963), our operating assumption is that the instability of an individual's behavior over time is a predictable event.

As conceived here, variability or instability in its simplest form refers to the difference in quality, magnitude, and so on between any two responses such that the greater this difference, the larger the variability. An important distinction between two types of variability has been made by Fiske and Rice (1955), who suggest that variable behavior may be seen as occurring in response to either changing environmental stimulation or constant and repeated stimulation. Our major emphasis has been on the latter. In this regard, we have asked such questions as how it comes about that some people show highly unstable time performances in a classical reaction time situation while others are relatively consistent, or that some shift their responses in a yes-no test given on successive occasions while others tend to reproduce their original performance.

Elsewhere we have proposed a conflict model to handle the problem of intrapersonal instability (Worell, 1963). In general, it was suggested that in any particular situation the unstable or variable individual is a relatively conflicted one, while the nonvariable person is relatively free of conflict. In order to show the application of conflict more clearly, let us look at both a relatively variable and a nonvariable person when they are exposed to the same stimulation on repeated occasions. It is assumed that any response that appears to any stimulus at any given time is the strongest response in that person's repertory. Taking now the behavior of a comparatively nonvariable individual under the same repeated stimulation, such a person is viewed as having either one or a few relatively strong dispositions in relation to the stimulus context. Although the situation may arouse some alternative and competing dispositions for this person, these are consistently weaker than the few or lone dominant one(s). In the language of conflict, this individual is relatively conflict-free.

In opposition, the comparatively variable individual is seen as one in whom the stimulus arouses two or more equally strong dispositions. Thus, on one occasion one disposition is stronger, whereas on others an alternative disposition assumes dominance. Moreover, it seems clear that (a) the more alternative dispositions that are aroused and (b) the nearer in equality of strength among these alternatives, the more variable the person's behavior would appear.

In order to test this conflict formulation of instability, three relatively simple experiments were performed (Worell, 1963). The following three issues were examined: (1) If the unstable individual is in greater conflict, then conflict situations of varying degrees of severity should be systematically associated with varying amounts of intraindividual instability. Thus, greater conflict should produce more unstable *intraindividual* behavior. (2) If the variable individual is more conflicted, such an individual should behave *as though* he were in greater conflict than a less variable person even when the objective situation does not appear to be a particularly conflictful one. This means that for a group of individuals exposed to the same stimulation, as for example a simple reaction-time stimulus, the more variable individuals as determined in that situation should respond as if the situation were conflict arousing (hence should show slower performance in simple RT). (3) Finally, drawing from the generalization of conflict work, it was expected that prior exposure to strong conflict would predispose an individual to show greater amounts of intraindividual instability in a newly encountered similar situation.

Using either a discrimination conflict or a simple reaction-time task, all three derivations were strongly supported. Thus, strong conflict produced greater intraindividual instability than weak conflict, the more unstable individuals in a situation respond to that situation as though it were more conflictful, and finally, there is a clear generalization of intraindividual variability from strong to weaker conflict situations.

B. MORE COMPLEX EXTENSIONS

1. Personality Conflict, Response Originality, and Recall

Moving to a more molar level, we became interested in applying the conflict-variability formulation to the relationship between personality conflict and several indices of variability (Worell & Worell, 1965). The initial problem was to construct a scale for assessing personality conflict that would be consistent with our conflict-variability theory. In several approaches (Dollard & Miller, 1950; Lewin, 1935), the concept of personality conflict is framed in terms of approach and avoidance tendencies. Our approach to assessing personality conflict was to treat it as a differential between the total strengths of approach and avoidant tendencies within a set of functionally related behaviors (or needs).[4] As avoidance increases to approximate the strength of approach, conflict increases concomitantly. Since we were not in possession of a scale to measure this differential directly, approach and avoidance were assessed separately and conflict was calculated in terms of a resulting ratio. Specifically, the strength of approach in two need areas was obtained from modified achievement and affiliation scales of the Edwards Personal Preference Schedule (Edwards, 1954), where the person indicates by forced choice which need-related behaviors he would most prefer to use. In contrast, the strength of avoidance in each need area was assumed to be reflected in the total number of changes, relative to need, that occur when the person is again asked to indicate by forced choice which behaviors he most frequently uses. Thus, the individual who states that he uses substantially fewer behaviors, more behaviors, or different behaviors in a need area than he would like to use is an individual in conflict. By changing his behavior choices so that they no longer correspond to his stated preferences, he is demonstrat-

[4] The concept of functionally related behaviors stems from Rotter's (1954) definition of psychological need as "the potentiality of occurrence of a group of functionally related behaviors in specified situations directed toward a group of functionally related reinforcements" (p. 115).

ing that competing dispositions are replacing the presumably preferred alternative. In comparison, the comparatively nonconflicted person tends to use the behaviors that he states he prefers, indicating that the preferred behaviors are dominant and not in conflict with other potential alternatives.

To illustrate this difference between relatively conflicted and non-conflicted individuals, the hypothetical strengths of n possible responses to a given stimulus are indicated on the ordinate of Fig. 4. It can be seen that the conflicted person may have several potential responses of similar strength, R_1–R_4, whereas the nonconflicted individual has one response, R_1, that is dominant over other possible responses.

This formulation was empirically studied in a word-association situation administered within a general achievement and academic approval context. Specifically, Ss were given a written list of 50 words from the list used by Russell and Jenkins (1954) to which they were required to supply three associations for each word. Upon completing the association portion, all Ss were given a second identical list of words to which they were requested to recall their own associations.

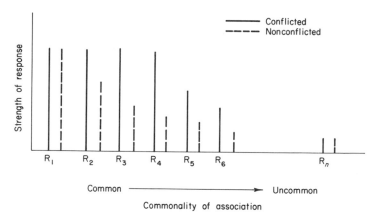

FIG. 4. Theoretical relationship between response strength and commonality of association for Responses R_1–R_n to a given stimulus.

Within this context, two dependent measures were selected that were expected to show differences between high and low conflict subjects according to our theoretical model. First, it was anticipated that when recall of previous associations is required, the conflicted person would reproduce fewer of these responses, since some of his initial associations are assumed to be in conflict with competing associations. Reference to Fig. 4 indicates that for those stimuli that arouse competing tendencies in the conflicted individual, any one of a number of potentially dominant responses may occur upon repetition of the situation. The conflicted person does not "forget" his earlier response, R_1, but simply replaces it with another of equal response strength, R_2, R_3, or R_4. The nonconflicted person, with only one dominant response R_1 will tend to give the same association R_1 to the repeated stimulus and thus will demonstrate higher "recall."

Second, a commonality (i.e., frequency of common associations) comparison of the initial word associations with those of a norm group (Russell and Jenkins, 1954) should reveal more uncommon or "original" responses for conflicted individuals. The first association is likely to be most common in terms of frequency for a given population. Therefore, a nonconflicted person with one dominant response R_1 is likely to give a common or frequent association. In contrast, Fig. 4 indicates that the conflicted individual may also give R_1, but he is equally likely to give R_2–R_4, since they are approximately as dominant for him as is R_1. It is clear then that the conflicted person is more likely to give associations that, although dominant for him, are atypical for the group.

The findings indicated clear support for the conflict-variability model. Strongly conflicted individuals demonstrated inferior recall of their own associations and also produced more original associations. Apart from affirming the conflict-variability proposal, the results on response originality appear relevant to the problem of creativity. Although nonconformity of response is not a necessary criterion of creativity, it is frequently used as such in tests to assess creativity (Barron, 1955; Wilson, Guilford, Cristensen, & Lewis, 1954). In the light of this, our data suggest that an important antecedent to producing original and potentially creative responses is personality conflict.

V. Conflict and Moral Training

In general, three principal components of a "moral" concept may be distinguished: (1) moral judgment, as expressed in verbal standards concerning what is right or wrong; (2) moral conduct, as measured by resistance to temptation in the absence of the punitive agent; and finally (3) in the event of transgression, the occurrence of confession, reparation, or self-critical responses that are taken to signify the internalization of a moral standard. Reviews of the empirical relationships among these three areas (Becker, 1964; Hoffman, 1963; Kohlberg, 1964) indicate that they do not covary sufficiently to justify the assumption of a unitary moral personality component such as superego or conscience.

The low interrelationships have led several investigators to the view that a given class of moral behaviors may be learned through exposure to fairly specific antecedent conditions (Aronfreed, 1963; Bandura & McDonald, 1963; Hill, 1960; Mischel & Gilligan, 1964). In seeking such antecedents, three broad variables have been stressed: positive reinforcement (Hill, 1960; Kagan, 1958; Sears, Rau, & Alpert, 1965), punishment (Aronfreed, 1964; Whiting & Child, 1953), and contiguity (Bandura, 1962; Mowrer, 1960); the last-mentioned variable may involve such events as model-child exposure. In the present account, we will use all three antecedents. Our specific aims are to explain the acquisition of a verbal moral standard by which behavior is guided and the actual behavior choices that accompany this verbal standard. But first it is necessary to describe the essential features of what may be termed the moral dilemma.

A basic defining property of the moral training situation is that the trainer (e.g., teacher or parent) is confronted with a trainee (e.g., student or child) who is strongly attracted to a goal that is disapproved of by the trainer. Within the confines of this situation, there are two types of trainers that may be distinguished. The first type may be characterized as one who is primarily oriented toward inducing inhibition of the approach to the attractive goal. A common solution for eliminating such behavior is punishment, real or promised. Considerable research on the use of punishment procedures with attractive goals has indicated that the resultant simple approach-avoidance conflict can be resolved by inhibition of response to the goal in the presence of the punitive agent. Moreover, by applying either severe punishment or delivering punishment at the onset of the approach response, the trainer may produce a generalized inhibition or resistance to temptation even in the absence of the training agent (Aronfreed & Reber, 1965, Solomon, 1960; Walters & Demkow, 1963).

While the orientation of the second type of training agent is also to inhibit approach to an attractive goal, he is desirous of inducing an approach to a formerly less attractive alternative as well. This type of training is focused on instilling what may be termed a sense of obligation such that the trainee not only learns what he ought not to do but also what he ought to do. To illustrate, consider the admonition of a mother to her child who has just eaten half of a candy bar: "Don't be selfish and eat all that candy yourself; you ought to share it with your brother." Here, eating the rest of the candy has a higher initial approach value than does giving it to someone else, while sharing has low initial approach and may be avoidant because it involves a loss of candy. The mother provides a verbal punishment, "don't" (true of the first type trainer also), but in addition she gives an immediate alternative that promises reward by reinstatement in her favor. At the same time, she provides verbal discriminative labels, *selfish* and *share*, that become an intrinsic part of the punishment-reward sequence and form the basis for later use as evaluative standards.

The moral dilemma thus resolves into a double approach-avoidance conflict, where approach to attractive goals is punished and approach to alternative unattractive goals is made rewarding. The training problem is one of reversing the original gradients, so that the initially attractive alternative becomes aversive (morally unacceptable) and the unattractive alternative gains in approach properties (morally good). When the person acquires a simultaneous avoidance and approach to two goals, we have produced the conditions that are required for the development of an evaluative standard. The internal and external cues leading to the choice of the punished (attractive) goal become conditioned not only to punishment and hence avoidance, but also to the alternative behavior leading to the rewarded goal. This formulation is consistent with findings that suggest that punishment is highly effective in producing response inhibition when an alternative rewarded response is provided (Solomon, 1960; Whiting & Mowrer, 1943). In both of these studies, however, the alternative goal (food) was intrinsically rewarding. In the present model, the rewarding value of the alternative is acquired in one or both of the following ways: (a) through association with the termination of punishment and (b) through direct reinforcement of the originally unattractive alternative.

In a preliminary test of this model, two groups of children were exposed to repeated choices between an attractive toy and an alternative unattractive object. One group of children was designated as a relatively pure punishment group; following a choice of the attractive object during training, the E said in a firm tone: "No, that's for older children." In contrast, the second group, which we labeled the punishment-alternative group, received the same verbal punishment for the attractive choices during training, but the E immediately pointed to the unattractive object and made a redirecting statement "You should have chosen the other one." Both groups were given five training trials during which different pairs of attractive and unattractive objects were presented for choice. Following training, both groups were exposed to a new attractive-unattractive pair. Here, however, before S made a choice, the E left the room on a pretext and S was alone with the pair of toys for 5 minutes. Upon E's return, S made his choice and was then asked a series of questions about the reason(s) for his choice.

On the basis of the double approach-avoidance moral training conception outlined earlier, the following three predictions were made. First, it was expected that the punishment-alternative group would more frequently select the unattractive alternative than the pure punishment group both during and after training. The detailed basis for this prediction is found in Fig. 5, where hypothetical gradients of approach and avoidance to the two goals X and Y are shown before and after training. Before training, the initial gradients for both the punishment (P) group and the punishment-alternative (PA) group are represented by the solid lines with an arbitrary

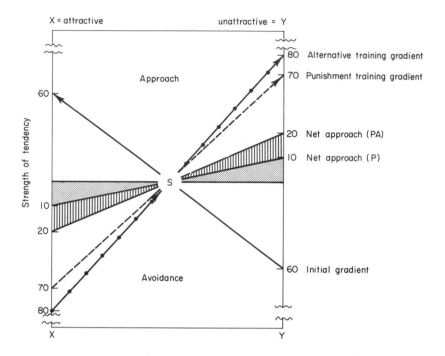

FIG. 5. Hypothetical gradients in the strength of dispositions to approach or avoid an attractive and an unattractive goal in a two-choice situation. Net tendencies are obtained by algebraic summation of approach and avoidance. Note that since the slopes of the gradients are not essential to the present formulation, they are depicted as equivalent.

approach value of 60 for the attractive toy X. Given a situation where the choice of Y results in a loss of X, the value of avoidance of the unattractive Y is assumed to be inversely equal to X, and hence also 60. The effects of training are represented by the broken lines. Here, for the P group, the avoidance value of the punished goal is set at 70 to indicate a final increment of avoidance over approach as a result of training. Using the former reasoning, the magnitude of avoidance to the punished attractive goal X produces an equal approach value to the unattractive choice; hence a value of 70. Consequently for the P group at the end of training, an algebraic summation of the particular approach-avoidance gradients for the two alternative goals results in a net approach of 10 to the originally unattractive goal Y and is matched by a comparable avoidance for the initially attractive goal X. These resultant values are depicted by the gray segments of Fig. 5.

For the PA group we have, in addition to the occurrence of the same punishment, a *contiguous* redirection of choice behavior. This contiguous redirection is expected to add an increment of approach value to the originally undesirable goal Y and is represented by the dotted lines in Fig. 5. The resultant net approach tendency is shown in the striped segment of the Y ordinate. In sum, the PA group should show a stronger tendency to select the formerly undesirable object.

A part from our interest in the actual behavior choices made by Ss in the presence of the training agent, we also expected that children in the punishment group would manifest a greater tendency to handle the objects, especially the attractive toy, when E was absent from the room than would children in the punishment alternative group. This would signify that the training conditions produced stronger resistance to temptation among children who were given punishment plus redirection. The principal basis for this prediction was an expected generalization of the effects of training. That is, since our conflict model predicted that greater inhibition of approach would be generated for the PA group in relation to the attractive object when the trainer was present, then by generalization the same relatively greater amount of inhibition should appear when the trainer was absent.

Finally, we anticipated that the punishment-alternative group would show a readier adoption of a verbal evaluative standard. This would be evident in the verbalizations of the children concerning the reasons for their choice following the final trial. Since the evaluative material for both groups consisted of E's verbalization "that's for older children," the adoption of a moral verbal standard would be reflected in statements by the child containing a direct reference to an age variable such as older, younger, big, or little. The rationale for this prediction was based on the relationship of the verbal rule ("that's for older children") to the differential strengths of double approach-avoidance conflict created in the two groups. Thus, for both groups, the introduction of the verbal rule *immediately* following punishment leads to the rule itself's becoming an integral part of the punishment procedure through temporal contiguity. The rule itself thus becomes punitive. For the punishment-alternative group, however, there is a difference in the abruptness with which the trainer's punitive verbalizations are terminated from that of the punishment group. For the PA children punishment is terminated both immediately and explicitly through E's redirection, thereby strengthening the likelihood of the use of the rule. In effect, a statement of the rule by the child serves as a cue or signal for the termination of punishment and the concomitant reinstatement of the trainer's approval. In contrast, there is no clear termination of punishment in the P group, so that the effectiveness of the stated rule as a signal is attenuated.

In brief review, a double approach-avoidance conflict conception of moral training proposes that a central component of "morality" is the relinquishment of initially attractive goals that are associated with social sanctions in favor of the adoption of less desirable goals that elicit social approval. Accordingly, it is expected that the acquisition of (a) unattractive choices, (b) resistance to temptation, and (c) verbal-evaluative standards will be facilitated by placing an individual in a temporally contiguous double approach-avoidance conflict in which approach to an attractive goal is repeatedly punished and approach to an unattractive alternative is associated with immediate termination of punishment as well as with reward.

The findings of our preliminary study provide some interesting contrasts. The data clearly indicated that the PA group made more selections of the unattractive object both during and after training. Moreover, this group also demonstrated a reliably greater tendency to evoke the trainer's verbal rule, thereby indicating the comparatively greater effectiveness of punishment-redirection in providing for the adoption of a verbal moral standard. In contrast, the groups showed no differential inclination in handling the objects when E was absent from the room. Hence, resistance to temptation was unaffected by the training conditions.

The data contain several interesting implications. The first is that within the context of a double approach-avoidance conflict, trainers who punish either physically or verbally but follow through with an immediate suggestion for an alternate behavior may provide for both the acquisition of the desired behavior and the evaluative verbalizations that represent moral standards. This points to the possibility that some of the observed differences in the relative effectiveness of physical versus verbal punitive methods (Allinsmith, 1960; Burton, Maccoby, & Allinsmith, 1961) may be due, at least in part, to how the punishment is terminated as well as to how it is administered. Parents who use verbal discipline are more likely to provide verbal alternatives in conjunction with admonition, and therefore may be conditioning both their verbal labels and the alternatives to the termination of their disapproval.

Second, apart from the utility of the double approach-avoidance conception in accounting for the more effective adoption or originally less desirable goals in the present study, the model is in accord with findings obtained in other areas. Most noteworthy, for example, is some recent experimental work on the reversal of sexual choices (Feldman, 1966). A number of studies concerned with the problem of inhibiting approach to males by male homosexuals found that producing a simple approach-avoidance conflict by means of aversive conditioning was ineffective in initiating approach to females (Freund, 1960). However, when punishment of approach to the attractive homosexual object was immediately followed by presentation of a female stimulus picture, increased preference for females in subsequent situations was obtained (Feldman &

MacCulloch, 1966). Of particular relevance to the present paradigm is the suggestion that contiguity of presentation of the initially unattractive alternative is an essential variable. Additional experimental support for this notion comes from several studies in which the aversive conditioning procedure is ineffective when the introduction of the unattractive alternative, a female picture, is delayed for several days (James, 1962). Although these studies were not specifically framed within a double approach-avoidance context, they do point to the significant contribution of contiguity and termination of punishment for the reversal of attractive and non-attractive choices.

Third, although our finding of a lack of correspondence between behavior in the presence and absence of the trainer is consistent with the previously described low interrelationships among indices of morality, it is also congruent with the observations that moral standards do not necessarily predict behavior when the cues for punishment are minimal (Hartshorne and May, 1928). In our study, punishment was delivered for a verbal choice only and was effective, either alone or when combined with redirection, in inhibiting verbal choice in the presence of the punitive agent. However, this effect did not generalize when two important variables were changed; from verbal choice to motor response and from the punitive agent's presence to his absence. We may infer from this that general injunctions from parents and society concerning good or bad attributes of behavioral alternatives may be very effectively acquired by a child, but they will not necessarily be used when the situational gradients of approach or avoidance are substantially altered. Thus, we find additional endorsement for the view that moral behavior is not a unitary process but rather will vary with changes in both training conditions and situational contingencies.

Finally, we would like to note that a conflict approach to moral training contains many testable consequences in terms of the systematic variation of a number of distinct parameters, both singly and in combination, such as the amount of punishment and reward, the degree of attractiveness and aversiveness of goals, the effects of degrees of contiguity between the approach-avoidance conflicts, and so on.

VI. The Problem of Conflict Intensity

In our introductory remarks, a definition of conflict was offered in terms of the discriminability of outcomes associated with competing response dispositions. It was noted that this conception resembles what has been labeled the relative strength view of conflict, whereby the intensity of the (induced) experienced conflict increases as the disparity between the competing dispositions is diminished. In addition to the contribution to conflict of the relative strengths, several theoretical positions explicitly make room for an absolute strength consideration as well (Brown & Farber, 1951; Berlyne, 1960; Spence, 1956; Yates, 1962). According to this view, it is assumed that a choice between two stimuli of mild intensity or valence is more easily made than a choice between two stimuli of high intensity or valence. In fact, the "intuitive" appeal of this notion has been so strong that the contribution of absolute strength to conflict strength is widely accepted despite the fact that the empirical evidence for it is either lacking or equivocal.

Consider the alternatives. The relative strength view poses the query: Is it more conflictful to make a choice between $1.00 on the one hand and $.90 on the other, than it is to choose between $1.00 and $.25? The evidence that the degree of conflict increases as the competing choices approach equality is strongly positive (Barker, 1942; Bilodeau, 1950; Brown, 1942; Cartwright, 1941; Casteneda & Worell, 1961; Korman, 1960; Schill, 1966; Worell, 1962; Worell & Casteneda, 1961; Worell & Hill, 1962), although Andreas (1958) and Broadhurst (1957) were unable to obtain confirmatory data. In contrast, the absolute strength position asks the question: Is it more conflictful to make a preemptive choice between two $1000 bills than it is to decide between two $1.00 bills? Contrary to the relative strength findings, the issue of whether conflict is an increasing function of absolute strength when the competing dispositions are approximately equal has produced widely discrepant results. Thus, Andreas (1958) found that increasing the absolute strengths led to significantly greater motor conflict, but Barker (1942), Bilodeau (1950), Casteneda and Worell (1961), Maher Weisstein, and Sylva (1964), Sears and Hovland (1941), Schill (1966) and Worell (1962) obtained no significant effects, while Berlyne (1957) found the contradictory effect of significantly delayed performance with weaker intensities of conflict. As a consequence, it would be fair to say that the status of the absolute strength assumption is at best equivocal.

In view of our highly positive results with several conflict-inducing situations in support of the relative strength view, the opportunity to examine the absolute strength hypothesis under similar conditions was tempting. We now have data from two separate studies, using different methods of conflict induction and dissimilar stimulus materials, that provide no evidence in support of the absolute strength position. Rather, the sole reliable determinant of conflict intensity was the relative strengths of the competing dispositions.

Using the brightness discrimination situation described earlier, 30 male volunteers were exposed to 16 trials of insoluble conflict where the intensity of illumination in both windows was the same. Thus, the intensity of the approach tendencies was equated across subjects. Differential strengths of avoidance were introduced by administering high, intermediate, or low levels of electric shock on trials 1, 5, 9, and 13. Shock intensity levels were predetermined for each individual in terms of his upper and lower tolerance limits, and S was told that he would be shocked for "wrong" choices. Analysis of the objective differences in shock intensity for the three groups indicated that they were receiving significantly different magnitudes of shock intensity. In this manner, there were both objective and subjective differences among the three groups in terms of the absolute strengths of avoidance to the two lights. Two dependent measures of conflict were used, decision time and number of position shifts in choice (variability). Neither measure provided significant differences among the three avoidance groups. Despite the fact that the high group was making decisions under periodic punishment at the upper tolerance level and the low group was responding under a barely noticeable pain level, no measurable differences in degree of conflict appeared.

A second study used a modified version of the conflict-inducing technique employed by Schill (1966). S was presented with a 19-category rating sheet moving from strongly disapprove to strongly approve. By placing in any one category all the adjectives that he judged to be equal in acceptability, S provided a pool of stimulus words that were subjectively scaled for approach, avoidance, or neutrality. Sets of two words were presented in the apparatus window and S pushed a telegraph key under his choice. Each S faced the task of choosing between 15 pairs of his own subjectively rated words. The findings again were nonsignificant; increasing the absolute strengths of neither approach-approach nor avoidance-avoidance conflicts produced reliable effects on the latency of choice behavior. We are therefore led to conclude that, despite its commonsense appeal, the absolute strength hypothesis has yet to acquire an empirical foundation.

VII. Summary and Implications

For the past several centuries the simple idea of conflict has led a remarkable life; it has managed to invade virtually every significant sector of thought about the organic universe. Consider the conceptions that have stood out concerning the living process in recent history: at the organismic level, Darwin proposed that interorganism conflict was at the root of the evolution of species; at the intrapersonal level, Freud contended that the individual had to come to some sort of terms with conflicting intrapsychic events; at the economic level, Marx advocated that the individual in society needed to understand a new dialectic, that of conflict between classes; and at the general societal level, Toynbee suggested that the rise and fall of civilizations rested on a recognition of the response made to conflict in terms of challenge and response. Against such a background we may well view contemporary empirical psychology's contribution to a furtherance of understanding of conflict as somewhat sparse. We have therefore been interested in bringing attention to several issues concerning the operation of conflict and, perhaps more importantly, raising questions for further consideration. In this respect, we have proposed that the examination of complex conflicts, such as multiple approach-avoidance ones, has been relatively neglected; that the conditions leading to the persistence of conflicts as opposed to their resolution, as in moral training, is not sufficiently understood; and that more consideration should be given to the effects of both repeated exposures to conflict and repeated encounters with situations as an aftermath of such exposures.

References

Allinsmith, W. The learning of moral standards. In D. R. Miller & G. E. Swanson (Eds.), *Inner conflict and defense*. New York: Holt, Rinehart & Winston, 1960, Pp. 141–176.

Anderson, O. D., & Parmenter, R. A long-term study of the experimental neurosis in the sheep and in the dog. *Psychosom. Med. Monogr.*, 1941, **2**, Nos. 3 & 4.

Andreas, B. G. Motor conflict behavior as a function of motivation and amount of training. *J. exp. Psychol.*, 1958, **55**, 173-178.

Aronfreed, J. The effects of experimental socialization paradigms upon two moral responses to transgression. *J. abnorm. soc. Psychol.*, 1963, **66**, 437–448.

Aronfreed, J. The origin of self-criticism. *Psychol. Rev.*, 1964, **71**, 193–218.

Aronfreed, J., & Reber, A. Internalized behavioral suppression and the timing of social punishment. *J. Pers. soc. Psychol.*, 1965, **1**, 3–16.

Bandura, A. Social learning through imitation. In M. R. Jones (Ed.), *Nebraska symposium on motivation*. Lincoln, Nebr.: Univer. Nebraska Press, 1962. Pp. 211–268.

Bandura, A., & McDonald, F. Influence of social reinforcement and the behavior of models in shaping children's moral judgements. *J. abnorm. soc. Psychol.*, 1963, **67**, 274–281.

Barker, R. G. An experimental study of the resolution of conflict by children; time elapsing and amount of vicarious trial-and-error behavior occurring. In Q. McNemar & M. A. Merrill (Eds.), *Studies in personality*. New York: McGraw-Hill, 1942.

Barron, F. The disposition toward originality. *J. abnorm. soc. Psychol.*, 1955, **51**, 478–485.

Becker, W. Consequences of different kinds of parental discipline. In M. L. Hoffman & L. W. Hoffman (Eds.), *Review of child development research*. Vol. I. New York: Russell Sage Foundation, 1964. Pp. 169–208.

Berlyne, D. E. Conflict and choice time. *Brit. J. Psychol.*, 1957, **48**, 106–118.

Berlyne, D. E. *Conflict, arousal, and curiosity*. New York: McGraw-Hill, 1960.

Bilodeau, Ina McD. Conflict behavior as a function of the strengths of competing response tendencies. Unpublished doctoral dissertation, Univer. of Iowa, 1950.

Brehm, J. W. Increasing cognitive dissonance by a *fait accompli*. *J. abnorm. soc. Psychol.*, 1959, **58**, 379–382.

Brehm, J. W., & Cohen, A. R. *Explorations in cognitive dissonance*. New York: Wiley, 1962.

Broadhurst, P. L. Emotionality and the Yerkes-Dodson law. *J. exp. Psychol.*, 1957, **54**, 345–352.

Brown, J. S. Factors determining conflict reactions in difficult discriminations. *J. exp. Psychol.*, 1942, **31**, 272–292.

Brown, J. S., & Farber, I. E. Emotions conceptualized as intervening variables with suggestions toward a theory of frustration. *Psychol. Bull.*, 1951, **38**, 465–495.

Brown, R. Models of attitude change. In *New directions in psychology*. New York: Holt, Rinehart & Winston, 1962.

Burton, R. V., Maccoby, E., & Allinsmith, W. Antecedents of resistance to temptation in four-year-old children. *Child Develpm.*, 1961, **32**, 689–710.

Cartwright, D. Relation of decision time to the categories of response. *Amer. J. Psychol.*, 1941, **54**, 174–193.

Casteneda, A., & Worell, L. Differential relation of latency and response vigor to stimulus similarity in brightness discrimination. *J. exp. Psychol.*, 1961, **61**, 309–314.

Chapanis, N. P., & Chapanis, A. Cognitive dissonance: Five years later. *Psychol. Bull.*, 1964, **61**, 1–22.

Cook, S. W. The production of "experimental neurosis" in the white rat. *Psychosom. Med.*, 1939, **1**, 293–308.

Dollard, J., & Miller, N. *Personality and psychotherapy*. New York: McGraw-Hill, 1950.

Dworkin, S. Conditioning neuroses in dog and cat. *Psychosom. Med.*, 1939, **1**, 388–396.

Edwards, A. L. *Edwards personal preference schedule*. New York: Psychological Corp., 1954.

Feldman, M. P. Aversion therapy for sexual deviations: A critical review. *Psychol. Bull.*, 1966, **65**, 65–79.

Feldman, M. P., & MacCulloch, M. J. The application of anticipatory avoidance learning to the treatment of homosexuality. I. Theory, technique and preliminary results. *Behav. Res. Ther.*, 1966, **2**, 165–183.

Festinger, L. *A theory of cognitive dissonance*. Evanston, Ill.: Row, Peterson, 1957.

Festinger, L. The psychological effects of insufficient rewards. *Amer. Psychol.*, 1961, **16**, 1–11.

Festinger, L. (Ed.), *Conflict, decision and dissonance*. Stanford, Calif.: Stanford Univer. Press, 1964.

Festinger, L., & Carlsmith, J. M. Cognitive consequences of forced compliance. *J. abnorm. soc. Psychol.*, 1959, **58**, 203–210.

Festinger, L., & Walster, Elaine. Post-decision regret and decision reversal. In L. Festinger (Ed.), *Conflict, decision and dissonance*. Stanford, Calif.: Stanford Univer. Press, 1964.

Finger, F. W. Quantitative studies of "conflict": I. Variations in latency and strength of the rat's response in a discrimination jumping situation. *J. comp. Psychol.*, 1941, **31**, 97–127.

Fiske, D. W. The inherent variability of behavior. In D. W. Fiske and S. R. Maddi (Eds.), *Functions of varied experience*. Homewood, Ill.: Dorsey, 1961. Pp. 326–354.

Fiske, D. W., & Rice, Laura. Intra-individual response variability. *Psychol. Bull.*, 1955, **52**, 217–250.

Freund, K. Some problems in the treatment of homosexuality. In H. J. Eysenck (Ed.), *Behavior therapy and the neuroses*. London: Pergamon, 1960. Pp. 312–326.

Gantt, W. H. Experimental basis for neurotic behavior. *Psychosom. Med. Monogr.*, 1944, **3**, Nos. 3 & 4.

Hama, Haruyo. The effect of prior exposure to conflict in post-conflict performance. *Japan. J. Psychol.*, 1965, **36**, 1–9.

Hartshorne, H., & May, M. A. *Studies in the nature of character*: Vol. I., *Studies in deceit*. New York: MacMillan, 1928.

Hill, W. Learning theory and the acquisition of values. *Psychol. Rev.*, 1960, **67**, 317–331.

Hoffman, M. L. Child-rearing practices and moral development: Generalizations from empirical research. *Child Develpm.*, 1963, **34**, 295–318.

Hull, C. L. *Principles of behavior*. New York: Appleton-Century-Crofts, 1943.

James, B. Case of homosexuality treated by aversion therapy. *Brit. med. J.*, 1962, **1**, 768–770.

Kagan, J. The concept of identification. *Psychol. Rev.*, 1958, **65**, 296–305.

Kohlberg, L. Moral Development. In M. L. Hoffman & L. W. Hoffman (Eds.), *Review of child development research*. Vol. I. New York: Russell Sage Foundation, 1964. Pp. 383–431.

Korman, M. Ego strength and conflict discrimination: An experimental construct validation of the ego strength scale. *J. consult. Psychol.*, 1960, **24**, 294–298.

Lawrence, D. H., & Festinger, L. *Deterrents and reinforcement.* Stanford, Calif.: Stanford Univer. Press, 1962.

Lewin, K. Environmental forces. In C. Murchison (Ed.), *Handbook of child psychology.* Worcester, Mass.: Clark Univer. Press, 1933.

Lewin, K. *A dynamic theory of personality.* New York: McGraw-Hill, 1935.

Lichtenstein, P. E. Studies of anxiety: I. The production of a feeding inhibition in dogs. *J. comp. physiol. Psychol.*, 1950, **43**, 16–29.

Liddell, H. S. Conditioned reflex method and experimental neurosis. In J. McV. Hunt (Ed.), *Personality and the behavior disorders.* Vol. I. New York: Ronald Press, 1944.

Liddell, H. S. *Emotional hazards in animals and man.* Springfield, Ill.: Charles C. Thomas, 1956.

Lifton, R. J. *Thought reform and the psychology of totalism.* New York: Norton, 1961.

Luria, A. R. *The nature of human conflicts.* New York: Liveright, 1932.

Maher, B. A., Weisstein, N., & Sylva, K. The determinants of oscillation points in a temporal decision conflict. *Psychon. Sci.*, 1964, **1**, 13–14.

Masserman, J. H. *Behavior and neurosis.* Chicago: Univer. of Chicago Press, 1943.

Masserman, J. H., & Pechtel, C. Conflict engendered neurotic and psychotic behavior in monkeys. *J. nerv. ment. Dis.*, 1953, **118**, 408–411.

Matsuyama, Y. Effects of stimulus context and development on discrimination conflict. *Japan. J. Psychol.*, 1965, **36**, 248–252.

Miller, N. E. Experimental studies of conflict. In J. McV. Hunt (Ed.), *Personality and the behavior disorders.* Vol. I. New York: Ronald Press, 1944.

Miller, N. E. Liberalization of basic S-R concepts: Extensions to conflict behavior, motivation and social learning. In S. Koch (Ed.), *Psychology: A study of a science.* Vol. 2. New York: McGraw-Hill, 1959.

Miller, N. E., & Stevenson, S. S. Agitated behavior of rats during experimental extinction and a curve of spontaneous recovery. *J. comp. Psychol.*, 1936, **21**, 205–231.

Mischel, W., & Gilligan, C. Delay of gratification, motivation for the prohibited gratification, and response to temptation. *J. abnorm. soc. Psychol.*, 1964, **69**, 411–417.

Mowrer, O. H. *Learning theory and behavior.* Vol. 1. New York: Wiley, 1960.

Nowlis, V. Research with the Mood Adjective Checklist. In S. S. Tomkins & C. E. Izard (Eds.), *Affect, cognition and personality.* New York: Springer, 1965.

Pavlov, I. P. *Lectures on conditoned reflexes.* (transl. W. H. Gantt) New York: International Publishers, 1928.

Rotter, J. B. *Social learning and clinical psychology.* Englewood Cliffs, N. J.: Prentice-Hall, 1954.

Russell, W. A., & Jenkins, J. J. The complete Minnesota norms for responses to 100 words from the Kent-Rosanoff Word Association Test. *USN Office Naval Res. tech. Rep.*, 1954, Contract No. N8, Rep. No. 11.

Schill, T. The effects of type and strength of induced conflict on conflict generalization and later preference for conflict stimuli. *J. Pers.*, 1966, **34**, 35–54.

Sears, R. R., & Hovland, C. I. Experiments on motor conflict: II. Determination of mode of resolution by comparative strengths of conflicting responses. *J. exp. Psychol.*, 1941, **28**, 280–286.

Sears, R. R., Rau, L., & Alpert, R. *Identification and child rearing.* Stanford, Calif.: Stanford Univer. Press, 1965.

Solomon, R. L. Personal communication in O. H. Mowrer *Learning theory and the symbolic processes.* New York: Wiley, 1960, Pp. 399–406.

Spence, K. W. *Behavior theory and conditioning*. New Haven, Conn.: Yale Univer. Press, 1956.

Walters, R. H., & Demkow, L. Timing of punishment as a determinant of response inhibition. *Child develpm.*, 1963, **34**, 207–214.

Wessman, A. E., & Ricks, D. F. *Mood and personality*. New York: Holt, Rinehart & Winston, 1966.

Whiting, J. W. M., & Child, I. L. *Child training and personality*. New Haven, Conn.: Yale Univer. Press, 1953.

Whiting, J. W. M., & Mowrer, O. H. Habit progression and regression - a laboratory investigation of some factors relevant to human socialization. *J. comp. physiol. Psychol.*, 1943, **36**, 229–253.

Wilson, R. C., Guilford, J. P., Cristensen, P. R., & Lewis, D. J. A factor-analytic study of creative-thinking abilities. *Psychometrika*, 1954, **19**, 279–311.

Worell, Judith, & Worell, L. Personality conflict, originality of response and recall. *J. consult. Psychol.*, 1965, **29**, 55–62.

Worell, L. Response to conflict as determined by prior exposure to conflict. *J. abnorm. soc. Psychol.*, 1962, **64**, 438–445.

Worell, L. Intraindividual instability and conflict. *J. abnorm. soc. Psychol.*, 1963, **66**, 480–488.

Worell, L. The preference for conflict: Some paradoxical reinforcement effects. *J. Pers.*, 1964, **32**, 32–44.

Worell, L., & Castaneda, A. Individual differences in conflict resolution and the ease of learning. *Amer. Psychologist*, 1961, **16**, 400. (a)

Worell, L., & Castaneda, A. Response to conflict as a function of response-defined anxiety. *J. Pers.*, 1961, **29**, 10–29. (b)

Worell, L., & Hill, L. Ego strength and anxiety in discrimination conflict resolution. *J. consult. Psychol.*, 1962, **26**, 311–316.

Worell, L., & Worell, Judith, Generalization of conflict and conflict tolerance. *Psychol. Rep.*, 1964, **14**, 203–215.

Yates, A. J. *Frustration and conflict*. New York: Wiley, 1962.

TEMPORAL INTEGRATION: AN INCENTIVE APPROACH TO CONFLICT RESOLUTION[1]

K. Edward Renner

DEPARTMENT OF PSYCHOLOGY, UNIVERSITY OF ILLINOIS,
URBANA, ILLINOIS

I. Introduction

This chapter will review empirical research and provide a theoretical treatment of the process of temporal integration. Specifically, we will be concerned with how an organism resolves equivocal situations when it must make a choice between several alternatives when each of these alternatives has several consequences. Some of the consequences may be desirable and others aversive to the individual; some may occur immediately after the choice, others some time after the choice, and finally, the outcomes may

[1] Much of the experimental work reported herein and the preparation of this paper were facilitated by Grant MH 11633 from the National Institute of Mental Health, United States Public Health Service. In addition, the studies by Renner and Murphy (1966) and Renner and Specht (1967) were carried out while both Murphy and Specht were NSF summer research participants at the University of Illinois.

or may not be recognized by the organism as contingent upon its choice. Thus, we will be concerned with a process that is assumed to be an integral part of our daily living; namely, of deciding what to do, evaluating the consequences produced by our actions, and using this information to make future decisions. As such, the work borders on aspects of conflict resolution and conflict theory. We will also be concerned with how adequate a particular decision is, and in this sense the work approaches the areas of adjustment and psychopathology. However, the principal aim of the chapter is to provide a theoretical treatment of the process of temporal integration. This will be done using concepts of incentive motivation that have developed largely from the animal laboratory. The empirical research reported here is basic research on problems of incentive motivation. Although much of the chapter will focus on concepts of motivation, using the language of general experimental psychology, it will also deal with personality processes by illustrating how human behavior and adjustment may be conceptualized within such a theoretical framework of motivation.

A. TEMPORAL INTEGRATION AND PERSONALITY

The first requirement is to specify the problem area in greater detail. This is most easily done by referring to several aspects of human behavior that have concerned personality theorists. After the nature of the problem is clear in its general sense, we will translate it into an empirical and then a theoretical framework.

1. Naturalistic Observations

Our everyday experiences offer ample illustrations of temporal integration and the important role this process plays in our behavior. Daily we are faced with numerous decisions that require weighing in some form the immediate and long-term outcomes of the alternatives available. For example, we may go to the movies for an evening of fun but at a monetary loss, or we may retain the money with its promise of future rewards but lose the enjoyment of that movie. At a fundamental level, society continually confronts us with choices that involve decisions of the same kind. For instance, consider the situation of a potential high school dropout who may either stay in school and do what is now a boring and perhaps a failure-ridden task with the delayed promise of a reasonably well-paying job and steady employment. Or, he has the alternative of leaving school and gaining the immediate relief of escape from unpleasant intellectual tasks and personal restraints that go with staying in school, but with the possible delayed outcome of low earning power, later unemployment, and the deprivation of material possessions that a higher income could have provided. The decision to drop out may be facilitated by the immediate reward of money and temporary purchasing power provided by a presently available unskilled job, although of long-range ultimate disadvantage. How are such decisions made? What determines whether we go to the movies or stay home, or whether we drop out of school or stay in school? In some decisions it seems clear that the long-term consequences of an action may not be at all effective and the choice may be determined primarily by the immediate consequences. It is not clear, for example, that the possibility of later unemployment resulting from dropping out of school is a particularly effective consideration relative to, say, the temporary purchasing power from a presently available job. For now, the point to be made is simply that our daily lives involve numerous occasions when we must decide between equivocal situations. A theoretical account of the process whereby we resolve such decisions is the purpose of the present paper. We will seek to provide a quantitative approach to this process through concepts of incentive motivation, using general theoretical terms that also may be extended to human behavior. We will be explicit about the implications of our research and our theoretical formulation for viewing personality processes.

More generally, we can ask what determines how choices are made, how the separate effects of the outcomes are combined into a net effect, and how this in turn influences future behavior. This future influence may be seen from a habit viewpoint as increasing or decreasing the likelihood of the occurrence of that same response under similar external stimulus conditions, or, from a motivational viewpoint, as providing information about the location of certain outcomes that will be approached or avoided as either desirable or aversive. We will deal with both habit and motivational considerations as elements governing temporal integration (decision making), with the emphasis on motivation.

2. As Individual Differences

The concepts of temporal integration also may be related to traditional types of personality dynamics. For example, the capacity to forego immediate gratification for more important but delayed outcomes has been assumed to result from specific kinds of previous socialization conditions (usually early ones) and to represent one of the highest forms of personality development or integration, such as level of ego strength or maturity. The capacity to delay gratification has been put into expectancy terms by Mischel (1966), who has shown that the development of the capacity for a preference for larger-delayed over immediate-smaller rewards occurs as a function of a long list of antecedent socializing conditions. A correlational strategy applied to the problem of temporal integration would seek to find correlates

of resolving equivocal situations in one way or another; such an approach
to personality theory is based on the assumption that similar characteristics
will have common antecedent conditions. Although the present chapter will
take a view incompatible with the correlational approach, the example does
illustrate that organisms engage in behavior resulting in deferred outcomes
and that this capacity is important in a variety of theoretical and empirical
viewpoints for describing and understanding personality functioning. We
have called this the process of temporal integration and will present a
general theoretical treatment of the process.

B. TEMPORAL INTEGRATION AND PSYCHOPATHOLOGY

Equating the process of temporal integration with personality constructs
and individual differences, such as integrated behavior and maturity, implies
that a person with a "healthy" personality is able to make effective use of
remote outcomes in order to govern his behavior. It follows that an "un-
healthy" personality represents either a disruption of the capacity to delay
gratification or at least an ineffective system of weighing the long- and
short-term consequences. For example, psychopaths have been described
as seeking immediate gratification and disregarding long-term consequences
because in their socialization history they lacked those experiences that
are assumed necessary to develop the capacity for deferring gratification
(McCord & McCord, 1964). It appears that psychopaths have steeper
temporal gradients of fear arousal than normal persons (Hare, 1965),
lending support to the concept that the long-term aversive consequences of
an act play a small role and that immediate gratification may play a large
role in directing their behavior. Extremely poor people have been described
as lacking a sense of time and of living a day-to-day existence in which there
is no concern over the future and where the satisfaction of immediate needs
predominates over all other considerations (Mowrer, 1960, p. 380). Finally,
the behavior of patients has been described as "stupid" (Dollard & Miller,
1950), "paradoxical" (Mowrer & Ullman, 1945), or "masochistic" (Cameron, 1963, pp. 670–671), as if, for them, the consequences of their actions
either had not been heeded, were ignored, or became opposite in value
(i.e., pleasure in pain).

The use of such terms as stupid, paradoxical, or masochistic to describe
the apparently self-defeating behavior of patients reflects the difficulty we
have in reconciling these behaviors with psychological theories on the
known effects of reward and punishment. We expect an organism to select
the most rewarding or least punishing alternative, and his apparent failure
to do so has resulted in numerous attempts to show that the behavior does
not in fact violate the law of effect. One such example was the suggestion
(Mowrer & Ullman, 1945) that because the effectiveness of a reward declines

when it is delayed (a relationship known as the temporal gradient of reward), a delayed outcome may be reduced in effectiveness and a small immediate reward be more effective than a larger but remote punishment. This explanation and the demonstration experiment of Mowrer and Ullman provided an analogue of "nonintegrative" behavior but did not specify the process whereby multiple outcomes are combined nor, as Dollard and Miller note (1950, p. 187), did it deal with the situation in which punishment is immediate and reward delayed.

The tendency has been to seek an experimental analogue of a particular kind of behavior and to suggest that it may provide an illustration of particular types of symptoms. A contrasting alternative is to seek a general theory of how equivocal situations are resolved. This is the strategy employed in the work on temporal integration, with a resulting specification of the necessary conditions to obtain a nonintegrative solution.

C. SPECIFICATIONS OF THE PROBLEM

The introduction is now sufficient to permit us to specify in psychological terms the nature of the problem and the direction we feel a solution should take. The first requirement is to single out the factors that determine the utility or value of a consequence for the organism independent of the behavior in question. It should then be possible to specify in advance the conditions under which a given outcome will be desirable (reinforcing) or aversive (punishing) to the organism, and to show that it is this net outcome that determines the direction of behavior, i.e., the choices that the organism makes. Specifically, the organism's preferences (motivations) should reflect what is either more desirable or less aversive, as defined independently of the choice itself.

Presumably, there is an accounting system whereby the numerous outcomes of a particular behavior are integrated into a net value; it is this value that defines the utility of the outcome. An action may always be viewed as involving both reward and punishment, for the act of selecting response A over response B precludes obtaining the advantages of B at that moment. At the very least, the selection of A over B is a choice between A plus non-B versus B plus non-A, a positive and negative component in both cases. Such a multiple approach-avoidance conflict is always involved in a choice between goals where some measure of privation of one goal is implied in the choice of the other. Most choices have even more complex outcomes, and the outcomes themselves are usually distributed over a time interval after the response, with only some of them more or less clearly associated with the choice. An understanding of how such temporally distributed outcomes are combined into their net utility should enable us to determine why a particular choice was made. Stated simply, choices involve the process of temporal integration in the sense that what is desirable or aversive represents the net subjective value of the outcomes with respect to the alternatives available. Presumably, those factors that determine utility should provide, in addition, a theory of conflict resolution and a description of how complex decisions are made.

In defining independently the values of rewards and punishments that are to be combined into a net value we are proposing to scale, or quantify in a relative way, the value of both positive and negative outcomes. In addition, we are proposing that the general theoretical system must specify the variables that modify the value of a particular reward or punishment, and how they do so. Thus, the same reward or punishment may have different values on different occasions or in different circumstances. It is in these two senses that we are proposing a relative approach to incentive: (1) The value of particular rewards and punishments are to be scaled relative to each other, and (2) the value of a particular reward or punishment is relative because it depends on many other factors, which may be specified and quantified within the theoretical approach.

D. PLAN OF THE PAPER

The paper will first review our own experimental work. To do this it will be necessary to consider several methodological problems and to describe the apparatus. We will then review the relevant empirical findings that will provide the basic data necessary to arrive at the general theoretical treatment of the process of temporal integration in the following section. At this point we will review the related work of other investigations, which will provide the body of literature within which we wish our results to be subsumed. We will then relate our findings and our theoretical approach to other theoretical positions, such as theories of personality processes, psychopathology, and conflict theory. We will conclude by summarizing what we see as the generalizations and implications of the work to date.

II. Experimental Approach to the Problem of Temporal Integration

In this section we will summarize work that has been carried out in our laboratory, first at the University of Pennsylvania and later at the University of Illinois. Much of these data are recent and have not yet appeared in the literature. Discussion of the particular theoretical interpretations that we wish to make of these results will be postponed until the next section, when our own findings will be incorporated into a more general review of the literature to provide a general theoretical treatment of the process of temporal integration.

A. Assumptions

As a starting point we have assumed that changes in performance in a learning task reflect the value or utility of that particular outcome for the subject. Consider the specific example of a temporal gradient of reinforcement (reinforcement is used in a general sense to refer to either a reward or a punishment) that describes the declining effectiveness of a reward or a punishment for establishing a response. This means simply that a delayed reward is less efficient than an immediate reward. We have suggested that this progressive loss in effectiveness as the time interval between the response and the reinforcement increases will also provide a quantitative estimate of the utility of that particular reward or punishment to the S. That is, it will index the worth or value of the outcome.

It should be noted at the outset that a temporal gradient is just an arbitrary way of plotting performance data. It is usually done after a set number of trials and it illustrates, for example, that after 100 trials Ss with immediate reward are performing better than Ss with delayed reward. If the E did something that would increase the speed of acquisition or the performance level at all delay intervals, such as run the S under a higher level of deprivation (e.g., Renner, 1963), then this would be raising the height of the temporal gradient. However, if an experimental manipulation facilitated performance under delayed but not under immediate reinforcement conditions (Renner, 1963), we would say that the slope of the temporal gradient had been modified. These two examples illustrate the kinds of changes in performance that also are assumed to reflect changes in the utility. In other words, we have assumed that performance data will provide an index of the utility and that those factors that change the height or the slope of the temporal gradient of reinforcement should also influence in a similar fashion the utility (relative desirability or aversiveness) of the outcome for that subject. It has been our working hypothesis that in a situation where there is more than one outcome the value of each may be described by its own temporal gradient.

B. Procedure and Apparatus

To test the usefulness of these assumptions we needed to develop an apparatus that would allow us to obtain performance data for both rewards and punishments in a comparable learning situation for both immediate and delayed conditions. The apparatus also had to be suitable for independently determining the utility of either outcome to the organism. Utility was determined by using a preference technique that required the S to balance the values of various shock–food combinations against the alternative of nonshock–nonfood. Therefore, we needed an apparatus that could serve both learning and preference purposes. If the performance data are to reflect the relative utility of an outcome for a particular set of circum-stances, it is critical that the utility be independently demonstrated or verified, but it must be in the same situation and under similar conditions if the performance-determined values are to be expected to hold.

A sketch of the apparatus is shown in Fig. 1; it is a choice box with a start section located in the center with a delay-shock chamber on either side and a goal-escape box at both ends. The S is placed in the start box and both

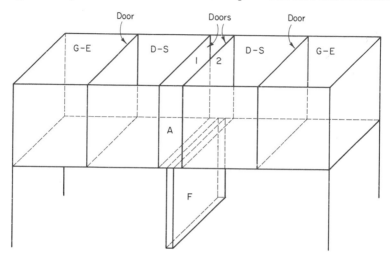

FIG. 1. Three-dimensional drawing of the choice apparatus. The area of the start box A is defined by two vertical-rising overhead-storing guillotine doors, 1 and 2. The response is forced by panel F, which lifts from below the grid floor to divide the apparatus in half. On either side of the start box are chambers D-S, which serve either as delay chambers or shock boxes. The end compartments GE serve as goal boxes or escape chambers (reproduced from Renner, 1964a, with permission of the publisher).

start box doors (labeled doors 1 and 2) are raised, giving the S a choice to the right or left side. After the S makes its response, a center door (labeled F), which stores under the apparatus, is raised, dividing the apparatus in half and confining the S to the side of its choice. Thus, the start box no longer exists as a separate section after the start of a trial, leaving four separate permanent compartments 8 inches square. The chambers on either side of the start box may be used to delay the S or to shock it after any pre-determined interval. The goal boxes at either end can be used to provide a food reward after any predetermined delay interval or to allow the S to escape from the shock chamber. There is a grid floor in the apparatus and each section can be individually electrified. The essential features of the apparatus include motor-operated doors that permit all events to be auto-matically timed and controlled. There are interchangeable side panels, which allow the interior color of any section of the apparatus to be made white, black, striped, or gray. At both ends of the apparatus are automatic pellet dispensers, which deliver the food at the rate of two pellets per second, triggered by the S's entering the goal box. The apparatus has the flexibility of allowing the E to obtain choice data between two aversive outcomes without enticing the response with a food reward or forcing the response with an additional aversive stimulus. It has been our practice to use both free and forced trials so as to equate the experience of the S with both sides of the apparatus. This can be done for a free trial by raising both start box doors and for a forced trial by raising only one of the doors. If the S fails to respond after 15 seconds, the center door is raised, gently forcing the animal to step into either the left or the right half of the box. It is seldom necessary to force a response.

The use of the apparatus can be best illustrated by describing the way a learning experiment would be carried out for both reward and punishment, which would yield comparable temporal gradients of reward and punishment (see Renner, 1964a, 1966a). For example, it is possible to let one side of the apparatus result in either an immediate or delayed reward (or punishment) and to let the other side result in nonreward (or nonshock). Thus in the punishment study the S must learn to choose the nonshock side so as to avoid the shock or, in the reward experiment, to choose the food side so as to avoid nonreward. In a similar fashion the apparatus can be used to study the relative utility of some combination of shock and food. Non-shock–nonfood can be allowed to occur on one side of the apparatus, and on the other side the S can be given some combination of shock and food. The nonshock–nonfood provides a common field (see Irwin, 1961) that permits an inference as to whether a particular shock–food combination is desirable or aversive to one group of Ss relative to the preference of another group. Thus, the same apparatus can be used for both learning and preference experiments. The theoretical assumptions and use of the apparatus can be clarified by considering several simple illustrative experiments that were among the first conducted in the series. They are reported at the outset here because of their simplicity and as an introduction to the procedures used, not necessarily for their theoretical implications. The subsequent studies build on this first work and, along with it, provide the substantive material for the theoretical position to be developed.

C. ANIMAL RESEARCH ON TEMPORAL INTEGRATION

1. Intensity of Deprivation

a. Some Illustrative Experiments. The first step was to obtain comparable temporal gradients of reward and punishment using the choice apparatus and to show that the height and slope of the temporal gradients could be modified (Renner, 1964a). In these experiments it was demonstrated that an increase in deprivation level raised the height of the temporal gradient of reward and an increase in shock intensity raised the height of the temporal gradient of punishment. These data are shown in Fig. 2. In the reward

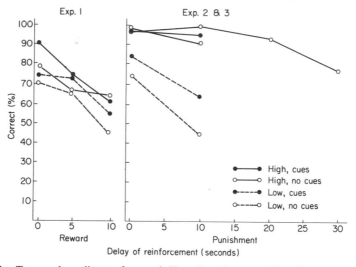

FIG. 2. Temporal gradients of reward (Exp. 1) and temporal gradients of punishment (Exp. 2 & 3). High drive was 23 hours of food deprivation or 0.8 ma of shock; low drive was 2 hours of food deprivation or 0.13 ma of shock. For the cue groups a light was present after the response was made in the delay and goal boxes on either the rewarded or punished side (reproduced from Renner, 1964a, with permission of the publisher).

study Ss were given a choice between a food reward on one side of the apparatus and nonfood on the other side, with outcomes occurring either 0, 5, or 10 seconds after the choice. In the punishment studies shock was present on one side, after delay intervals ranging from 0 to 30 seconds for different groups, and nonshock on the other side of the apparatus. The experiment was run under two intensities of shock and two levels of food deprivation. Figure 2 shows the percentage of correct responses at the end of the acquisition trials.

If these performance differences also reflect the relative utility of a reward and a punishment at those particular drive levels and delay intervals, it should be possible to demonstrate this by selecting an immediate shock, which would be more negative than a food reward was positive for Ss under a weak hunger drive when the food was delayed for a few seconds after the shock, as is illustrated in Fig. 3B. However, if increasing the strength of the hunger drive raises the temporal gradient and increases the utility of the food reward, then for more deprived Ss the same delayed food should

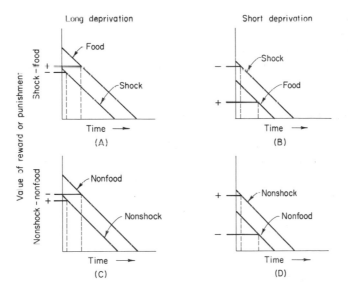

FIG. 3. Schema of a temporal gradient of punishment and temporal gradients of reward obtained after either long or short deprivation periods. When the temporal gradient of reward is elevated relative to the temporal gradient of punishment, there is a net positive value of reinforcement on the shock–food side (A), but a net negative value for the choice to nonshock–nonfood side (C). When these relative strengths are reversed through a lowering of the temporal gradient of reward, the net utility is reversed and nonshock–nonfood (D) should be preferred over shock–food (B). Adapted from Renner (1964a) with permission of the publisher.

outweigh the immediate shock and their combined value should be positive, as illustrated in Fig. 3A. The opposite utilities should hold for the nonshock–nonfood side of the apparatus, which should be positive for the Ss deprived for a short period of time (Fig. 3D) but negative for the Ss deprived for a long period of time (Fig. 3C).

The particular gradients used in Fig. 3 are schematic figures illustrating the empirical relationships obtained in Fig. 2; namely, after an arbitrary number of trials, immediately reinforced Ss perform better than those that received delay of reinforcement. However, Fig. 3 deviates from the typical presentation (as in Fig. 2) of temporal gradients by labeling the ordinate as the *value* of the reinforcement rather than as the percentage correct. This relabeling of the ordinate illustrates how we wish to use performance data to provide an index of the *relative* utility of those particular outcomes at that level of training. We have assumed that an increase in deprivation raises the height of the temporal gradient of reward and increases the utility of a food reward. In a preference study, these expected results were obtained (Renner, 1964a, Experiment 4) with a shock–food combination being defined as positive in value by deprived Ss, but negative by Ss that were less deprived.

Thus, in a relatively simple situation, a direct relationship was demonstrated between the temporal gradients of reinforcement obtained in a learning situation and in a preference task that obtained independent evidence on whether a given shock–food combination was desirable or aversive.

b. *Insulin-Produced Deprivation.* A preliminary experiment that provided a similar kind of demonstration was recently completed by Michael Murphy (Renner & Murphy, 1966). In this experiment, all animals were held at their pre-experimental body weight by weighing each S daily and adjusting the amount of food given just after its daily runs. The experimental Ss were given an injection of insulin 20 minutes before they were scheduled to run and the control Ss were given an injection of saline. If the effect of insulin is similar to the effect of increasing the level of deprivation, i.e., increasing the height of the temporal gradient by making the food more desirable, then we would expect that in a learning situation the insulin Ss would acquire a position response faster than the control Ss. If this performance difference represents a differential value of the incentive, it should also be possible to select values of shock and food such that the insulin Ss would prefer a shock–food combination over nonshock–nonfood, but that the control Ss would prefer nonshock–nonfood over the same shock–food combination. It should be noted that in this experiment the Ss were fed enough each day to maintain them, in an absolute sense, in a nondeprived state.

The results of Murphy's experiments are shown in Fig. 4; it may be seen that the trend of the data is in perfect accordance with the previous deprivation data (Renner, 1964a). In the learning experiment the Ss were delayed for 5 seconds and were given a choice between nonreward on one side of the apparatus and reward on the other side. It may be seen in the left-hand side of Fig. 4 that under 5-second delay of reward the insulin Ss tended ($p < .10$) to acquire the response at a faster rate than did the control Ss. The preference data shown in the right-hand side of the figure illustrate that when other Ss are given a choice between a shock–food combination on one side of the apparatus and nonshock–nonfood on the other side, insulin Ss preferred the shock–food side, whereas the control Ss preferred the nonshock–nonfood side. The same analysis as was made for the previous deprivation experiment can be made here. We see that in one case a shock–food combination is desirable, but in the other case it is aversive. It is desirable for those Ss that are either deprived (Renner, 1964a) or injected with insulin and it is aversive for those that are nondeprived (Renner, 1964a) or that have had an injection of saline. An injection of insulin or an increase in deprivation level operates in such a way as to change the utility or desirableness of a food reward for the S. These units of utility also may be reflected

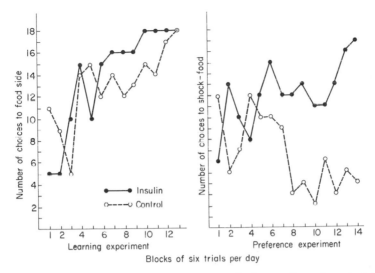

Fig. 4. Left: number of correct responses made by insulin and control Ss with 5-second delay of reward; right: number of responses made to the shock-food side by the insulin and the control Ss (from Renner and Murphy, 1966).

in performance data, suggesting that such differences in performance data may be conceptualized in motivational terms, and that such performance data may provide a quantitative way to index the relative utility of the particular outcomes in that particular situation.[2]

These two experiments, although comparatively simple and straightforward, illustrate the basic assumptions that are being made and the way the apparatus makes it possible both to obtain performance data and then to determine utility by using a preference procedure for the same set of experimental conditions.

2. Amount of Reward and Length of Delay

Davenport (1962) has generated indifference points between various amounts of reward and lengths of delay. In closely related work, Logan (1965a,b) has varied both amount of reward and length of delay in order to arrive at a quantitative index of the relative incentive value of various amounts of reward given after varying lengths of delay. Davenport's and Logan's work demonstrates that an increasingly larger amount of reward is necessary to offset longer delays of reward. Logan has suggested that delay and amount combine additively, each contributing some part to the

[2] Since this paper was written an attempt to replicate these findings on the effect of insulin was not successful, although there were only minor modifications in procedure between the two studies. The failure to replicate raises some question about the reliability of insulin as a manipulator of the incentive value of food (hunger) apart from its effect on blood sugar level.

total incentive value of an outcome. He has been interested in scaling the incentive values of such outcomes relative to each other.

The approach taken by Logan and Davenport is consistent with the type of analysis presented here. Specifically, we expect that larger amounts of reward would be more desirable than smaller amounts and therefore that the S would endure stronger intensities of shock in order to obtain them, but that the longer the delay interval, the less desirability (i.e., less utility) the reward would have to the organism. The work done in our own laboratory on amount of reward and length of delay has not yet been published. It consists of a series of five completed experiments; the basic findings from two of them will be summarized here.

In one experiment the Ss were given the task of learning a simple position response. One side of the apparatus produced food reward and the other side nothing. Some Ss received a one-pellet reward and others received ten pellets. The performance of the two groups is illustrated in Fig. 5. It

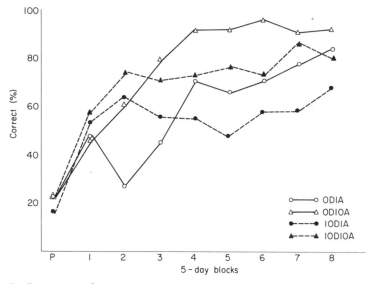

FIG. 5. Percentage of correct responses to the food side of the apparatus over trials by immediate and delay-of-reward groups receiving either a one-pellet or a ten-pellet reward. (D, delay; A, amount). Two trials per day were given (from Renner, 1966d).

may be seen that the large-amount (10-pellet) Ss made more correct responses than the small-amount Ss under both immediate and delay-of-reward conditions. Thus, increasing the amount of reward has increased the height of the temporal gradient of reward. It has been noted previously that a temporal gradient is but an arbitrary way to plot performance data. It may be seen from the acquisition data presented that the groups are converging at near-perfect performance; if sufficient trials were given, all Ss presumably after some number of trials would approach 100%. Over a sizeable number of trials, however, there are clear performance differences due to both delay and amount of reward. The main effects of both these conditions are statistically reliable. We contend that these performance differences reflect motivational factors stemming from the relative utility of the food reward under those particular amount or delay conditions. If an animal must wait 10 seconds for its reward, that reward is less desirable and has less utility than if it is given immediately. However, regardless of the length of delay, if the animal is given one pellet, this reward has less utility than ten pellets. Notice that our procedure does not require that ten-pellet Ss have experience with one pellet or that one-pellet Ss have experience with ten pellets, or that 0-second-delay Ss have experience with 10-second-delay or 10-second-delay Ss have experience with 0-second-delay. We are not depending on a contrast effect, but are rather arguing that the reward itself has differential value, i.e., utility, to the S and that this utility can be used to understand both choice behavior and performance. If this is the case, we should be able to observe these assumed differences in utility by using the preference techniques already described.

   In the preference work, values of deprivation and shock intensity were selected so that an immediate one-pellet reward offset an immediate punishment; that is, a 1-second-delayed shock–food combination was preferred over nonshock–nonfood. This outcome is illustrated in Fig. 6 by the preference of group 1D1A for the shock–food side. But if delay of reward reduces incentive value, then with a sufficiently long delay the same combination takes on a negative value (just as the temporal gradient of reward declines with time) and nonshock–nonfood should be preferred over an immediate-shock–delayed-food reward of one pellet. Group 30D1A received this treatment with the delay interval set at 30 seconds and, as may be seen in Fig. 6, preferred the nonshock–nonfood side. Since amount of reward is assumed to increase the utility, a larger amount, such as ten pellets, given after the 30-second delay, should increase the utility of the outcome and the preference data should show a greater percentage of choices to the shock–food side. These results may be seen in Fig. 6 for group 30D10A. All the differences mentioned are highly significant. Thus, a consistency has been demonstrated between performance in a learning task and an independent determination of utility in a different experimental task. It may be noted in Fig. 6 that a fourth group (30D1A No Shock) receiving no shock but one pellet after 30 seconds delay was indifferent between the food and nonfood sides, suggesting that one pellet of food reward delayed 30 seconds is about equivalent to nothing in its utility to the S. This observation is identical with the findings of Logan and Davenport, demonstrating that in

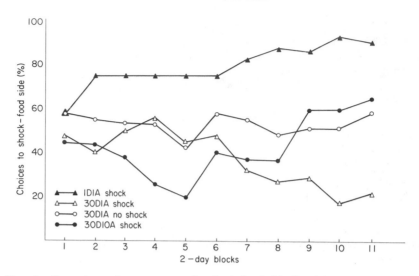

FIG. 6. Percentage of responses to the shock–food side (D, delay; A, amount) over blocks of 2 days of two free and two forced trials per day by the four experimental groups (from Renner, 1966d).

a very different situation with different experimental procedures, tasks, and apparatus, similar results are obtained on the value of one pellet.

3. Slope of the Temporal Gradients and Relative Utility

We now turn to a series of experiments that support the assumptions, but through a slightly different procedural approach. This approach was initiated by the observation (Renner, 1964a) that under strong intensities of shock the slope of the temporal gradient of punishment appears to be flatter than a comparable temporal gradient of reward obtained under 23 hours of food deprivation. This led to the prediction that if a relatively strong shock and sufficiently long delay intervals were used, a temporal gradient of punishment that was relatively flat could be obtained, and that, by adjusting the level of deprivation and amount of food reward, a temporal gradient of reward that was steeper and would intersect with the temporal gradient of punishment could be obtained. It was demonstrated that such temporal gradients, i.e., the temporal gradient of reward steeper than the temporal gradient of punishment (Renner, 1966a), could be established. These are comparable gradients and were established in the choice box using procedures similar to those reported earlier herein (Renner, 1964a). The data are illustrated in Fig. 7, where the upper panels show the acquisition data and, in the bottom panels, these data have been transformed into reciprocals in order to put them in the form of typical temporal gradients. It may be seen that when a reward is immediate, the Ss learn faster than

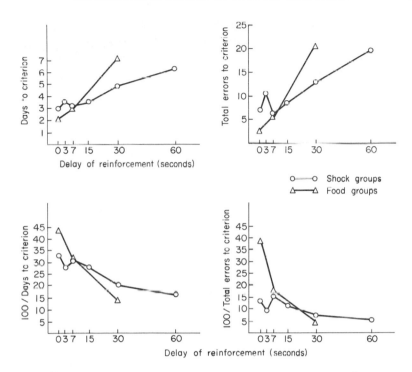

FIG. 7. Top: mean number of days to criterion and mean number of total errors to criterion as a function of delay of reward (left) and delay of punishment (right). Bottom: reciprocal of these values plotted to provide temporal gradients. Adapted from Renner (1966a) and reproduced with permission of the publisher.

when the punishment is immediate. If the same reward and the same punishment are sufficiently delayed, however, Ss will learn faster with the punishment than with the reward.

If this relative difference illustrated by the gradients also reflects the relative utilities of the two outcomes, then by selecting values from the range where the two types of temporal gradients will intersect, an immediate shock–food combination should be positive in net utility; yet the same shock–food combination should be negative in net value when delayed beyond the point where the two types of temporal gradients intersect. Under these conditions rats preferred an immediate shock–food combination over the same shock–food combination when it was delayed (Renner, 1966a) and this result was replicated (Renner, 1966e). Animals run in a Skinner box (Renner, 1966a) showed a preference for a bar that would deliver an immediate shock–food combination over a bar that delivered a delayed shock–food combination.

In a second set of experiments (Renner, 1966e), rats showed a greater preference for an immediate shock–food combination over nonshock–nonfood relative to a second group of animals, which showed a greater preference for nonshock–nonfood over the same shock–food combination when it was delayed. These data are illustrated in Fig. 8. These findings

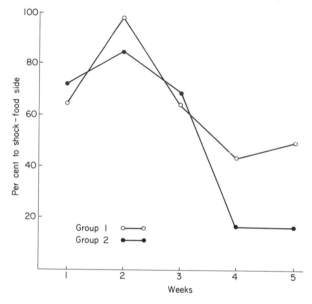

FIG. 8. Preference of subjects for shock–food versus nonshock–nonfood. Group 1 received 1-second delayed, and group 2, 30-second delayed, shock–food. Adapted from Renner (1966e) and reproduced with permission of the publisher.

were also replicated, as illustrated in Fig. 9, but with the added control of Ss (group 3) that had the occurrence of the delayed shock–food combination signaled by a light cue. These Ss still preferred nonshock–nonfood over the signaled delayed shock–food combination. The signal was introduced to give the subjects an opportunity to make whatever preparatory responses might be necessary in order to be as ready for the shock as the Ss in group 1, which received it immediately after the choice. This signal group was a control to exclude the alternative explanation that the delayed presentation of a shock resulted in the shock's becoming more aversive because the S could not prepare for it.

However, an objection may still be raised about the preference experiments. It can be argued that because the one shock is delayed, it is more aversive, even if signaled, because of the fear or dread of waiting, and that animals would prefer the immediate combination and find it more desirable simply because any preshock delay interval is itself aversive. The control provided by the cue in the one preference experiment (Renner, 1966e) is not

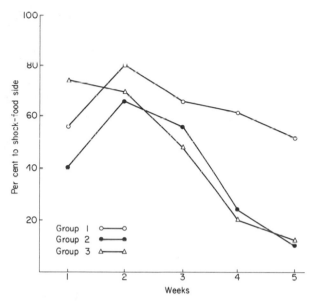

FIG. 9. Preference of Ss for shock–food versus nonshock–nonfood. Group 1 received 1-second delayed shock–food; group 2 received unsignaled, and group 3 signaled, 30-second delayed shock-food. Adapted from Renner (1966e) and reproduced with permission of the publisher.

decisive since there is no independent evidence that the cue was discriminated or that it was effective in allowing for preparatory responses, or that it reduced preshock dread. In order to consider this problem of the relative aversiveness of delayed versus immediate shock, an experiment was conducted by Laura Specht (Renner & Specht, 1967). In her study Ss were divided into two principal groups. One group was given a choice between an immediate shock–food combination on one side of the apparatus, and on the other side the same shock–food combination was given after a 30-second delay interval. If the results of the previous experiments were to be replicated, this group should prefer the immediate over the delayed shock–food side. A second group of Ss was given a choice between an immediate punishment on one side of the apparatus, and on the other side the same punishment delayed 30 seconds. We know from our learning experiments (Renner, 1964a, 1966a) that a 30-second delayed punishment is somewhat less effective in establishing a response than an immediate punishment. If a gradient notion is to hold with respect to utility, namely, that an immediate punishment is more aversive than a delayed punishment, we should expect these Ss to prefer delayed punishment over immediate punishment. The experiment included a third group that during the first stage of the experiment was run identically to shock-only Ss, but during the second stage of the experiment was run identically to the shock–food group; thus, we would expect this third group to show an initial preference for the delayed-shock side but, once food was introduced and a choice between a delayed or immediate shock–food combination resulted, to shift their preference to the immediate side. The data for this experiment are shown in Fig. 10, where it may be seen that in every respect the expectations were supported with all the differences significant at least at the $p < .05$ level.

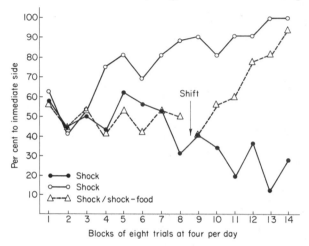

FIG. 10. Percentage of responses to the immediate versus the delayed side. Group 1 received shock only; group 2 received a shock–food combination; group 3 received shock only during the first stage of the experiment but shock–food during the second stage of the experiment. From Renner and Specht (1967).

In summary, this series of experiments has demonstrated that if conditions are arranged so that the temporal gradient of reward is steeper than the temporal gradient of punishment, then, under these conditions, an immediate shock–food combination is desirable in utility but the same shock–food combination when delayed beyond the point of intersection is negative in net value. The desirability of a food reward declines over a delay interval faster than does the aversiveness of a punishment, just as there is a similar relative difference in their effectiveness for establishing a response.

The data illustrate another important point: The gradients are to be conceptualized as highly flexible and not fixed in either relative slope or height. Many factors will change the height or the slope of the temporal gradient of reward or the temporal gradient of punishment, which is one way to plot performance differences in a learning situation. The gradient, however, will provide an index of the relative utility (desirableness or aversiveness) of that same reward or punishment when assessed in a comparable preference situation. The preference procedure provides a technique for determining the utility of that particular outcome for the subject. In addition, the data illustrate a relative approach to the definition of desirability and aversiveness. Thus, a given outcome is not necessarily a reward or a punishment for, as we have demonstrated, we can independently specify the conditions under which a given outcome, the same shock–food combination, may be either positive or negative in net utility for similar Ss.

4. Early Experience and Conflict Resolution

A final illustration comes from work on the effect of early experience with deprivation on the process of temporal integration. Adult rats that have been starved as infants will define a shock–food combination as positive in value by preferring it over nonshock–nonfood, but other adult Ss under the same level of deprivation will define the same combination as negative in net value (Renner, 1966b, Experiment 2), demonstrating again that the same outcome may be either positive or negative in net value. This particular experiment lacked independent evidence that the early deprivation modified the utility of the food reinforcement, although such a conclusion could be argued on the basis of other experimental results (e.g., Hunt, 1941). In addition, it was shown that early experience with delay of reward (Renner, 1966b, Experiment 1) facilitated the capacity of rats for dealing with a conflict situation requiring temporal integration. These two studies provided suggestive beginnings toward a specification of "psychological" influences (past experiences) that can be shown to influence utility systematically and, as a consequence, to influence the way in which complex outcomes are experienced as being either desirable or aversive.

These data were sufficiently encouraging for us to have completed two more experiments dealing with the effects of early deprivation. As has been noted, the original study lacked a demonstration that rats deprived as infants would as adults learn a response faster under delay of reward. The logic of our position would hold that Ss that are deprived as infants should, as adults, when run under the same adult level of deprivation as control Ss, learn a position response significantly faster. These results were in fact obtained, as is illustrated in the left-hand panel of Fig. 11.

After both groups of Ss reached asymptotic performance (100% correct choices), a shock was introduced on the food side. This shock drove the control Ss away from the food-reward side, but the early food-deprived animals continued to go to the shock–food side, demonstrating that for them the food had greater utility than it had for the control Ss. These data, in an even more striking and conclusive fashion, replicate and extend the previous findings (Renner, 1966b, Experiment 2). The data in Fig. 11 were obtained after the Ss became adults and similar in body weight to the controls; both groups were maintained on 1 hour of free feeding per day so that the absolute

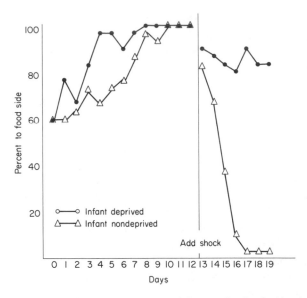

FIG. 11 Percentage of free responses as adults to the food side during the first stage of the experiment and to the shock–food side during the second stage of the experiment by rats that had been food-deprived as infants and others that had not been food-deprived as infants under 1 hour of free feeding per day. From Renner (1967).

level of deprivation as adults was identical for the experimental and the control Ss.

Another experiment provided an additional replication and extension of the same basic findings. It was conducted in order to control for the effects of order and to demonstrate that the preference by the early food-deprived Ss for shock–food in the previous experiment did not depend on a stronger habit developed in the learning stage. In the previous results (Renner, 1966b, Experiment 2) and those just reported, the preference stage was second, following an initial experimental phase. In this replication preference trials were given first and the data are shown in the left panel of Fig. 12. It can be seen that Ss that were deprived as infants preferred the shock–food combination, whereas the Ss nondeprived as infants preferred nothing over the same shock–food combination. All Ss were on 1 hour free feeding per day. In order to demonstrate that this preference was determined by the relative utility of the food for that particular S and not by some kind of peculiar response fixation or habit, all Ss were shifted from 1 hour to $21\frac{1}{2}$ hours of free feeding per day. According to the previously published findings (Renner, 1964a), the effect of lowering the level of deprivation should be to decrease the utility of the food reward and therefore one would expect the early food-deprived Ss to shift to the nonshock–nonfood side. In the second stage of

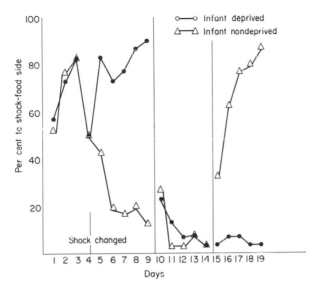

FIG. 12. Percentage of responses to the shock–food side by the early food-deprived and early food–nondeprived groups. During stage 1 (left) all Ss were on 1 hour of free feeding per day. During stage 2 (center) Ss were on $21\frac{3}{4}$ hours of free feeding per day. During stage 3 (right) early food-deprived Ss were on $21\frac{3}{4}$ hours of free feeding per day and early food-nondeprived Ss on 15 minutes of free feeding per day. From Renner (1967).

this experiment both groups preferred the nonshock–nonfood side. It should be noted that as soon as the deprivation level was shifted, the experimental animals, the early food-deprived Ss, immediately shifted their response to the nonshock–nonfood side. It took no additional trials or practice in the apparatus; the shift from 23 hours of deprivation to $2\frac{1}{4}$ hours of deprivation alone was sufficient to result immediately in the Ss' rejecting as aversive a shock–food combination that on the preceding experimental day they had defined as desirable.

During stage 3, early food-deprived Ss were maintained on $21\frac{3}{4}$ hours of free feeding per day in order to demonstrate that the shift to the nonshock–nonfood side was stable and enduring. On the other hand, during stage 3, the control Ss were shifted to 15 minutes of free feeding per day. These Ss had received a total of 84 trials by this stage in the experiment and had been consistently going on their free trials to the nonshock–nonfood side. If, in accordance with the previous findings (Renner, 1964a), increasing the deprivation level increases the utility of the food reward, then these control Ss should shift their preference to the shock–food side. This shift occurred almost immediately, presumably reflecting the accumulation of deprivation as the Ss progressively lost more body weight on successive days of the more severe deprivation procedure. The latter study again demonstrates that it is the utility or the relative desirability of the food reward that determines the choice. For the control Ss a shock–food combination that had been aversive now became a desirable combination and had a net positive utility for them. They quickly shifted their choice response as soon as the new level of deprivation was imposed. It apparently made no difference that they had a long series of training in which their preferred response was to the nonshock–nonfood side. Their choice was not a response that was controlled or elicited by the external stimuli in the start box, but rather, we would argue, that the S had learned information about the consequences of the alternative acts and its choice response depended on the S's current needs and its knowledge of what was where. When the S's internal motivational state was altered so as to change the utility of the outcomes, its choices immediately changed.

In both these recent food-deprivation experiments it should be noted that the experimental and the control Ss were identical in weight as adults. The early deprivation experience consisted of alternate periods of feeding and deprivation sometimes extending up to alternating blocks of 48 hours each, but marked by inconsistency. After the infant stage of deprivation the Ss were allowed to become full-grown adults before the adult experience was introduced.

D. Concluding Comments

No attempt was made to provide an exhaustive coverage of the studies conducted in our laboratory. The data presented here represent the highlights of our empirical results using four different experimental strategies in an effort to deal with the problem of temporal integration. We purposely have omitted here the methodological details of the experiments, as many of these have been published and reports of our own recent results are in some stage of preparation and should become available in the literature. These data are the body of facts that must be dealt with theoretically and that will provide the basis for a general theoretical treatment of the process of temporal integration. In the next section we will draw on these data and the published work of others to provide this theoretical treatment.

III. Toward a Theoretical Treatment of the Process

Our aim has been to incorporate our findings into the context of general psychology. This section will provide our initial theoretical integration of this work. Our primary concern for a general theoretical treatment of the problem reflects a conviction that "personality" cannot be viewed as a topic separate from general psychology, and that the concepts and language we use to deal with phenomena of interest to the personologist should relate closely to information from general experimental psychology. In our efforts

to do this, our thinking has been guided by our data and the kind of phenomena we wished to deal with. These guidelines have led us to take some
fairly specific stands on issues of learning theory. In fact, our efforts toward
a general theoretical treatment of the process of temporal integration have
resulted in direct concern with a number of theoretical issues of learning
theory. We make no claim that our empirical results and the theoretical
position is personality research as such, except through our convictions that
"personality" and general psychology cannot and should not be separated,
and that the kind of theoretical position taken here has particular relevance
to problems usually linked with the study of personality.

A. HEIGHT AND SLOPE OF TEMPORAL GRADIENTS AND RELATIVE UTILITY

The suggested approach to the process of temporal integration requires
a theoretical treatment of delay of reinforcement that will account for the
ways in which the height and slope of the temporal gradients of reinforcement
may be modified and that will also be applicable to the preference data. A
further desirable, but not necessary, component is a single set of concepts
that will apply to both reward and punishment; although this presents some
difficulties, an effort will be made to render the apparent differences in
empirical results consistent. The temporal gradient of reward will be discussed first, followed by an analysis of the temporal gradient of punishment
and ending with a synthesis of the two with respect to the process of temporal
integration.

1. Temporal Gradient of Reward

As has already been noted in a recent review of the delay of reinforcement
literature (Renner, 1964b) drive level (hours of deprivation) and delay seem
to combine additively, assuming response speed is a linear estimate of
response tendencies. The same conclusion seems to apply to choice data
(Renner, 1964a) as well, using accuracy measures as an estimate of response
tendency. In addition, work by Logan (1960, 1965a,b) and by Davenport
(1962), as well as the data collected in our own laboratory, suggests that
amount of reward and delay combine additively in both runway and choice
tasks. The height of the temporal gradient of reward (speed or level of
performance at any particular delay value) has been assumed to be controlled by incentive motivation conditions (Logan, 1960) resulting from the size
of reward or length of deprivation. For example, Logan (1965a) concluded
that "... decisions by rats involving simultaneous differences in delay and
amount of reward can be described by an additive combination of the
estimated relative incentive values of these factors" (p. 12).

It is possible to be more explicit about the mechanisms underlying the decremental effects of delay by assuming that extinction (nonreward) is the limiting case of delay of reward and, theoretically, to treat delay of reward as similar to nonreward (Spence, 1960). Renner (1964b) has suggested that the available literature can be handled by frustration theory although the primary test of this concept, delay-produced resistance to extinction, has not obtained uniformly positive results, but these tests have not always occurred under entirely appropriate conditions (for a partial review of the literature, see Renner, 1964b). Assuming that delay of reward produces frustration and results in competing reactions produced by conditioned avoidance, the height of the temporal gradient should be lowered under delay conditions. Apart from the motivational considerations, the delay interval itself provides an opportunity for irrelevant responses which presumably makes the acquisition of the correct response more difficult the longer the delay, independent of the frustration. Evidence for the aversive motivational properties of delay-produced frustration comes from a depression of performance early in delay-of-reward training that is absent for Ss receiving immediate reward (Ludvigson, Caul, Korn, & McHose, 1964; Renner, 1963), the facilitation of responses on nondelayed trials during partial delay of reward (Renner, 1966c), and postdelay performance (Holder, Marx, Holder, & Collier, 1957). The bulk of evidence points toward utilizing such a motivational concept to explain why a delayed reward loses some of its "desirableness," i.e., has reduced utility, as observed in the preference experiments on temporal integration. In short, the effect of delay may be seen as reducing the acquired incentive value of the reward (Logan, 1965a,b) and both the gradient and its height may be seen as reflecting this incentive value.

At an asymptotic level, associative factors should be absent; that is, all Ss should have learned about the reinforcement (e.g., where it is in a choice experiment) and performance should reflect motivational factors, although at these levels choice measures have a ceiling that may obscure some differences. Recall that in our work we have used essentially asymptotic levels to infer utility and have ignored the rate of acquisition. There is evidence that with continued training, perhaps reflecting an adaptation to frustration, the performance decrement under delay will diminish (Ludvigson et al., 1964) and under some conditions will reach the level of immediate reward (e.g., Ferster & Hammer, 1965), and finally there is suggestive evidence that performance may even exceed the level achieved under immediate reward using a speed measure (Renner, 1966c), similar to the Goodrich (1959) acquisition effect with partial reinforcement. Although this last suggestion has yet to be verified, it is becoming clear there is need for a stage of training conceptualization, for as long as the delay interval is within the capacity of the organism, given the particular situation, a choice response, for example, eventually can be acquired with sufficient training and the competing negative affective component may be adapted out.

A final empirical observation is that distinctive cues are utilized more under delay than with immediate (Renner, 1963, 1964a) or with partial reward (Renner, 1966c), which results in a flattening of the temporal gradient. In addition, a historical review of the literature (Renner, 1964b) shows progressively steeper temporal gradients as investigators eliminated external cues, ending with Grice's (1948) extremely steep gradient and Spence's (1947) suggestion that there may be no primary temporal gradient at all. Delay apparently permits the utilization of distinctive cues that can acquire conditioned secondary reinforcement power or, in our terms, have incentive motivational properties for the organism. This has been demonstrated by the capacity of a delay-interval cue on the reward side of a position response to increase the frequency of a new response that will provide the cue, but to inhibit the response if it removes the cue; if the delay-interval cue is on the nonreward side, however, it will inhibit a response that provides the cue and reinforce a response that removes the cue (Renner, 1966a). Thus, distinctive cues may be seen as influencing the slope rather than the height of the temporal gradient because of a delay × cue interaction (Renner, 1963, 1964a,b). The consequences of delay-produced cue utilization, with respect to the effects of frustration and competing avoidance reactions, has not been systematically treated; the use of cues appears, however, to be unique to the delay of reward situation and a less important factor in other nonreward situations (e.g., partial reward, Renner, 1966c).

2. Temporal Gradient of Punishment

There is considerable evidence for a temporal gradient of punishment similar to what exists for reward (see e.g., Church, 1963; Renner, 1964b; Solomon, 1964, for reviews of the literature). Recently this has been documented even more clearly for both animals (e.g., Renner, 1964a, 1966a; Baron, 1965) and human Ss (e.g., Banks & Vogel-Sprott, 1965; Walters, 1964).

The height of the temporal gradient of punishment can be elevated by increasing shock intensity (Renner, 1964a). With mild shock intensities the slope of the temporal gradient of punishment is similar to that obtained with food reward (Renner, 1964a); however, when the shock intensity is increased, temporal gradients obtained with reward are steeper than the similar gradient obtained with punishment. Under the higher shock intensity freezing occurs (Renner, 1964a) and the Ss receiving delay of punishment orient toward the goal (escape) door and no competing responses occur, which, presumably, also allows better cue utilization. A similar flattening of the temporal gradient of reward has been obtained by Carlton (1954), as reported in Spence (1956), by restricting competing responses. A final similarity with the reward literature is that a distinctive delay-interval cue associated with punishment will establish a new response that removes the cue, and will inhibit a response that produces the cue; but if the same cue is associated with the delay interval before nonpunishment, it will establish a response that produces the cue but will inhibit a response that removes the cue (Renner, 1966a). These data, like the reward data, support the acquired motivational effect of external cues, in the sense that they will reward or punish new responses and, following Mowrer (1960), with respect to punishment, represent "dread" and "relief" components. We may assume that these are learned incentive-motivational components, similar to the "hope" and "disappointment" of reward, which define the relative aversiveness and desirability of outcomes when they are assessed in a preference situation, such as used in the study of temporal integration. At present, our theoretical orientation is to view the temporal gradient of punishment as reflecting various incentive factors, based on mechanisms resembling those used for reward.

However, there is also evidence that is apparently contradictory to the assumption that the temporal gradient of punishment reflects the relative incentive value of an immediate versus a delayed punishment. We have argued that in situations where a temporal gradient is obtained, an immediate punishment should be more aversive than a delayed punishment. Recent data on this question indicate, however, that when a punishment is delayed it may instead be more, rather than less, aversive, as demonstrated by a preference for immediate over delayed punishment by both rats (Knapp, Kause, & Perkins, 1959) and people (Cook & Barnes, 1964; D'Amato & Gumenik, 1960) and by the preference of rats for an inescapable and unavoidable shock to be signaled rather than unsignaled (e.g., Lockard, 1963; Perkins, Seymann, Levis, & Spencer, 1966) and for people to prefer information over no information about an uncertain but unavoidable outcome (Lanzetta & Driscoll, 1966). However, Perkins, Levis, and Seymann (1963) report they have had difficulty replicating Perkins' earlier work (Knapp et al., 1959) showing a preference for immediate over delayed punishment by rats, and contradictory results were obtained in a Ph. D. dissertation by Wilson (1965), a student of Perkins, and by Laura Specht as reported in this paper. Thus, it appears as if both preferences can be obtained, depending on the specific experimental conditions. From our analysis of the problem and the conditions that yield one or the other preference, we have concluded, as did Wilson (1965), that numerous cues are required to obtain a preference for immediate over delayed punishment. These cues serve to render the situation so the S is choosing between two clearly inescapable and unavoidable outcomes. Such conditions clearly hold for the human experiments because instructions permit the delayed punishment or uncertain outcome to be clearly labeled as contingent and unavoidable; this is saying that after sufficient opportunity to learn (or after being told) that a punishment is inescapable and unavoidable it is more aversive in value than an immediate punishment when assessed in a preference situation. However, in a learning situation a gradient is clearly obtained (see e.g., Church, 1963; Renner, 1964b). We will suggest that the preference and the learning data do not require, at this time at least, the use of a different set of principles than needs to be proposed for reward, nor does it contradict the work on temporal integration.

If, as the S waits, a "dread" component operates, this should elevate the gradient, resulting in the dread plus shock being more aversive than shock alone, and immediate punishment should be preferred over delayed punishment. However, such preference should occur only if there were many cues and few competing responses, and after sufficient training had been given to offset the loss of effectiveness (value) of the punishment due to the passage of time. Thus, as long as delay has sufficient subtractive effect on the negative incentive value of the delayed punishment a temporal gradient will occur. A temporal gradient is always plotted after an arbitrary number of trials, and usually immediate-reinforcement Ss are performing better than Ss receiving delayed reinforcement. But this need not be the case, for after sufficient training the effects of delay may be overcome by a sufficient dread component. Yet if the punishment were delayed long enough, sufficiently long, for example, for it to be impossible to associate the punishment with the choice, then effectively the choice would be between immediate shock and nothing (i.e., the inescapable, unavoidable aspect would be lost), and an easy choice would result for the delayed side, again reflecting a gradient effect. These considerations illustrate the importance of considering the stage of training. Better performance at some stage of training with delay than with immediate reinforcement would result in an "inverted" delay of reinforcement gradient. Such a gradient is implied by a preference for immediate over delayed punishment, which may be observed under the special conditions just described, if the parallel is to be maintained between preference and performance measures.

3. Stage of Training and "Inverted" Temporal Gradients

One implication of a stage of training consideration is that there would be an initial preference away from immediate shock (but the Perkins data are equivocal on this point; Knapp et al., 1959, Experiment 1), and that the preference would not occur until relatively late in training, which was the case, requiring a total of 288 trials. Presumably it is first necessary for the S to learn that shock was inescapable and unavoidable, and for the decremental effects of delay to be overcome by the acquired incentive value of the highly distinctive cues. In a learning situation, this should result in eventual better asymptotic performance by a delay-of-punishment (or reward) group than is achieved by an immediate group, provided distinctive cues are available. Evidence for this kind of partial reinforcement crossover effect on acquisition of a response established with delayed punishment, similar to the Goodrich effect (1959) with partial reward, has not been demonstrated, although some evidence exists for delay-of-reward training (Renner, 1966c), at least under partial delay with a distinctive cue and perhaps with constant delay of reward. Thus, after a sufficient number of trials, there may be an increase in the desirableness of the reward, following Festinger (1961), or it could be phrased as conditioned approach to the cues of frustration, after Amsel (1958). Either of these theories could explain why delay of reward during acquisition may result in greater resistance to extinction. However, using choice data, a ceiling effect may not permit the increased desirableness of a delayed reward (and the increased aversiveness of a delayed punishment) to manifest itself after cues and sufficient training have offset the decremental effects of the delay interval itself. It seems clear, in any case, as Ludvigson *et al.* (1964) have noted, that "... delay can no longer be considered a unitary factor in behavior, but that several processes—some of which may change with learning—will have to be postulated" (p. 411). Further evidence for the parallel between reward and punishment comes from the observation of greater resistance to extinction of an escape response following partial delay versus immediate reinforcement of a conditioned stimulus to shock (Crum, Brown, & Bitterman, 1951, Experiment 1), and the persistence to continuous punishment following intermittent punishment during training of an instrumental approach response (Banks, 1966).

Thus, there are sufficient grounds to assume that the motivational variables and underlying processes are similar for both reward and punishment. What is important, however, is the stage of training, which apparently is achieved at very different rates because of the nature of the rewards and punishments usually used. For example, the role of competing responses (see Spence, 1956) for disrupting performance under delay of reward appears to be absent during delay of punishment due to freezing (Renner, 1964a). It follows that if the competing responses were restricted, or if activity during the delay were made instrumental, the relative slopes of the gradients could be reversed from what has been reported to date (e.g., Renner, 1964a, 1966a, e). With human *S*s (e.g., Cook & Barnes, 1964; D'Amato & Gumenik, 1960) the preferences for immediate over delayed punishment were observed under conditions where instructions would bring to asymptote the relative aversiveness of the outcomes and thus result in a choice for the immediate outcome; however, when the greater aversiveness must emerge from repeated experience with the consequences, a gradient has been obtained (e.g., Banks & Vogel-Sprott, 1965) and a delayed punishment is clearly less aversive than immediate punishment when assessed in a preference situation, as shown by Specht's data obtained in our laboratory. One can easily arrange to have the situation difficult enough so that delayed, or infrequent, but always contingent, outcomes are hard to detect and therefore do have a gradient effect (see e.g., Jenkins & Ward, 1965; Markowitz & Renner, 1966). This proposed similarity between reward and punishment indicates that motivational variables responsible for relative desire and aversion in a preference situation (e.g., temporal integration) also manifest themselves in learning data, and may be directly related to the stage of acquisition from which the incentive information must be acquired by the S.

4. Pure Motivational versus Habit-Confounded Experiments

It should be noted that the work reported on temporal integration to a certain extent confounds an acquisition and a motivational problem. The gradients were derived in the same apparatus as was used for the study of utility by the preference procedure. This was a deliberate strategy to insure that the resulting gradients, from which inferences regarding the relative desirableness or aversiveness were to be made, would be appropriate for the situation in which the relative value was to be assessed. The Ss were run in the learning situation until reasonably stable differences emerged. Other Ss were run in the preference situation in which they had to acquire information about the desirableness or aversiveness of the outcome as they went along, and after an approximately equivalent number of trials, stable preferences emerged that reflected the same information as was contained in the learning data. The variables that influenced the learning data acted in an equivalent fashion during preference testing on relative incentive value. Such a situation seems to provide a close approximation to the human real-life situations, where the incentive values that are seen as directing choices must emerge in a context of experience and where delay, as well as other variables, such as infrequency (see Jenkins & Ward, 1965), acts to obscure their effectiveness (i.e., their relative incentive value). Thus incentive learning must take place, and the choices and performance of an organism should reflect the relative stage of this incentive acquisition.

None of the work to date can be presented as an example of a "pure" motivational case, which, although of theoretical interest, is more difficult to implement and perhaps of less direct relevance to the natural situation. However, the implications of the theory are quite direct; if relative desire were tested after a delay-produced partial-reinforcement effect on acquisition had emerged, then, for example, a shock and delayed-food combination presumably could be found that was positive in net value, whereas the same shock in combination with immediate food should be negative in net value. Presumably, when a delayed punishment becomes more aversive (because of the negative value of the "dread" component relative to the effects of delay) or a delayed reward becomes more desirable (because of the relative value of the "hope" element relative to the effects of delay), it should be reflected in preference data bearing on utility, such as are used to describe the process of temporal integration.

B. MISCELLANEOUS PROBLEMS AND ISSUES

1. On Nonreward and Nonpunishment

An implicit assumption has been made that the nonoccurrence of an event is opposite in sign but equal in relative value to the occurrence of the event. Therefore, if A is greater than B (e.g., a reward outweighs punishment and is desirable in net value), then non-A should be greater than non-B (e.g., nonreward is negative and outweighs the positive value of nonpunishment, leaving the net outcome as negative). The power of this kind of theorizing is reflected in the recent use made by Mowrer (1960) of the concepts of relief and fear, and hope and disappointment; by the extension of frustration theory to choice situations and the active effects of nonreward (e.g., Amsel, 1962; Amsel & Ward, 1965); and by the aversiveness of time-out from positive reinforcement (Leitenberg, 1965). The two-process theories of punishment (e.g., Mowrer, 1947), referred to as the avoidance hypothesis by Church (1963), offer further testimony to the value of assuming a rewarding (relief) effect of nonpunishment.

Naturalistic observation further confirms the importance of a loss of a desirable consequence or the escape from a painful consequence as a relevant contingent outcome for influencing human choices and decisions. By emphasizing the choice aspects of all responses (where not responding is seen as an alternative having the consequence of the nonoccurrence of the contingent outcomes), behavior may be viewed as a series of choices that reflect the relative (or expected) desirability or aversiveness of the available outcomes. To date we have assumed that the nonoccurrence of an event contributes as much as the occurrence of the event, but opposite in sign (especially in Renner, 1964a). The usefulness of this assumption remains to be determined.

2. On Drive Discrimination

The present approach to temporal integration is related to and has implications for the problem of drive discrimination (for a review see Webb, 1955). In fact, our results provide an alternative way to conceptualize the problem and, in so doing, illustrate the advantages of the type of concepts that have been proposed.

Drive discrimination, in one form or another, acts as a central core in many of our theories and concepts about personality. For example, we expect an organism to be able to tell the difference between hunger and thirst, or happiness and sadness, and between levels of the same drive, i.e., degree of fear, hunger, or need for affiliation, and so on. Yet the experimental demonstrations of the organism's capacity to detect the stimulus aspects of drive states has not been particularly impressive and with humans may depend on situational stimuli (Schachter & Singer, 1962). In general, qualitatively different states can be discriminated, if pronounced enough in their levels, but discrimination between different levels of the same drive has been difficult to show empirically except when the difference is large and one of the values is near zero (see Webb, 1955). However, our theories require a much finer level of discrimination; for example, we explain why an animal stops part way to the goal in an approach-avoidance conflict by assuming that it becomes more fearful, and notices it, as it proceeds a few inches down the runway. Extensions to personality theory are even more dependent on such discrimination. Clearly, if an organism is to make such fine discriminations, we should be able to demonstrate them easily in the laboratory; if they cannot be demonstrated, then perhaps drive discrimination is not occurring at all and other explanations must be found, for example, that the Ss learn to run a set distance and stop (Elder, Noblin, & Maher, 1961).

However, our analysis of the situation is that previous work has asked the wrong question of the organism to solve these problems. Typically the problem has been approached by trying to demonstrate that a S can learn to go to the left when 10 hours hungry, but to the right when 20 hours hungry (see Webb, 1955) This approach assumes that distinctive internal drive stimuli are to become connected to specific responses—a highly cumbersome way for an individual to be constructed. But the question can be restated using utility concepts; for example, we have assumed a given reward to have greater utility (be more desirable) the greater the level of deprivation. If it is this kind of discrimination that is taking place, a more appropriate procedure is to show that a food reward has differential utility, depending on the level of deprivation, and that the organism can make relatively fine discriminations.

Our data bear on both these problems. The basic work on level of deprivation (Renner, 1964a), the replications (Renner, 1966b, Experiment 1), and the recent infant food-deprivation data reported in this chapter provide evidence of the differential utility of a food reward under different deprivation states. These findings are largely between groups; different Ss were used to define the utility of the outcomes under the different levels of deprivation. Evidence on the role of the discrimination comes from the infant food-deprivation data reported herein and illustrated in

Fig. 12. Recall that in this study all Ss were run under 1 hour of free feeding per day during the first stage, but were shifted to $21\frac{1}{2}$ hours free feeding per day during the second stage. The infant food-deprived Ss immediately switched from a preference for the shock–food side to the nonshock–nonfood side as soon as the drive level was shifted. This was true of all ten Ss on the first day. It made no difference that 54 trials had preceded the switch; what was desirable yesterday became aversive today for those Ss. They did not need to sample the situation under the new drive level; in our terms, they had learned what was where, and when the internal drive state was modified (which changed the utility of the outcome) the choice shifted. In Irwin's (1961, 1966) terms, the Ss had developed expectancies, which were demonstrated by the reversal of the preferred side when the preference relation was reversed. In addition, the latencies provided an illustration of differential free responses occurring in the presence of the different drive states; the relative speed of the choice switched from a faster response to the shock–food than to the nonshock–nonfood side during the first stage to the opposite relationship during the second stage. This analysis requires viewing different speeds as different responses (see e.g., Logan, 1966). The latency and choice data provide clear evidence of the S's monitoring its internal state and preferences among expected outcomes. From our point of view the most important consideration is that clear results are obtained when the problem is approached from an incentive viewpoint and the right question is asked of the organism—for example, How much is the food worth?—rather than as a discrimination problem.

This discussion of drive discrimination emphasizes one of the central theoretical points of this chapter, namely, that what the Ss are learning is information about the outcomes. This information, which may be seen as an awareness of what leads to what; that is, what may be expected to occur given one choice or another, determines the direction of behavior. Responses are not elicited by stimuli but are selected on the basis of expected outcomes; the stimuli serve to label the situation for the S, but the incentive values themselves will determine the choice, and the choice will change when incentive values are changed. Once the questions are asked in incentive terms—for example, Is the shock–food combination desirable or aversive?—evidence can be obtained illustrating the sensitivity of the decision-making process to the current needs of the organism.

C. INCENTIVE THEORY AND UTILITY

1. A Quantitative Scale of Incentive

This approach to the process of temporal integration makes it possible to talk about how much goodness is equal to how much badness, based on the temporal gradients and, in so doing, to relate this utility to acquisition factors; it also enables us to describe these gradients in terms of general behavior theory. For example, by deriving temporal gradients of reward and punishment in the same apparatus it was possible for the relative amounts of learning to provide an index, at least roughly, of the relative desirableness or aversiveness of an outcome, with a complex consequence being the simple sum of the separate values (Renner, 1964a, 1966a, e). By pitting $(+)$ avoidance and $(-)$ privation against $(-)$ punishment and $(+)$ reward and by varying the reward value, the punishment value, and the delay, it should be possible to approximate in terms of utility the underlying temporal gradients of reinforcement. It may be that a gradient notion is too restrictive and that performance differences are not sensitive enough or are too simple and a more quantitative approach to relative desire and aversion is needed (e.g., Logan, 1965a,b). To date, however, we have encountered no negative evidence or inconsistencies between our learning and preference data.

In terms of a general approach to reinforcement theory the emphasis is to avoid an a priori definition of reinforcement, or of a class of reinforcers, for an event may be either aversive or desirable, depending on the level of other variables and on situational factors, e.g., external cues available, opportunity for competing responses, and so on. The factors controlling the reinforcement value of an event become the relevant consideration, which will then allow for an explanation of the motivational fact of preference. Using an alternative approach, Premack (1965) has described preference in terms of reinforcement value; although based on different assumptions, there is a close parallel between Premack's work and the work on temporal integration, aimed at providing an independent specification of reinforcement value.

2. On Relative Incentive Value

The preceding discussion of reinforcement value raises the issue of relative incentive value. Such an approach excludes a definition of a class of rewards and a class of punishments, or of a given reward or punishment, as having a given reinforcing "power." An outcome may be either desirable or aversive, and may be more or less so in different circumstances and conditions, or for different Ss. Such a relative system is not a hopeless morass of chaos, for it is lawful relativity. A quantitative system of relative incentive value specifies the conditions under which utility may be changed or modified. At a theoretical level, our problem is then to explain how the organism scales this relative utility as it goes about the business of experiencing the outcomes of its behavior. In human terms, a dollar for services rendered may be either good or bad, and more or less so. Presumably, we learn where a dollar may be obtained, just as the rats learned where a food reward is located, but whether we choose to collect it depends on its value, which is a highly relative matter, depending on the organism, the time, the place, and the alternatives available. We must build our theories to describe what this relative utility is a function of. It requires that we view "learning" not as stimulus–overt-response connections that arc strengthened by reinforcers, but rather as the acquisition by the S of information about the location of outcomes and their relative value in a variety of circumstances. We have referred to this as incentive learning and see response selection as being determined on the basis of the organism's relative state (of expectancy) of desire and aversion (Irwin, 1966) toward the outcomes. Performance differences are seen as reflecting these same expectancies about the outcome of an act and the relative strength of the preferences for one set of consequences over another. This results in viewing performance differences, including differences in speed, as different responses (see e.g., Logan, 1966).

We have used the phrase "relative incentive value" in still another sense, not to be confused with the foregoing discussion. Here we are suggesting that using performance tasks we can arrive at an estimate of the relative value of, say, a reward with respect to, say, a punishment. Thus, although we do not have a yardstick of units of desire and aversion, these can in fact be defined relative to each other. We have chosen to do this kind of relative scaling by contrasting comparable measures of performance in the same situation, and then using this situation to assess utility. Logan (1965a, b) has gone directly to this scaling task by utilizing a series of measures to achieve a mathematical solution to the problem.

3. Habit and Motivational Views of Response Consistencies

Our particular position seemed to be dictated by both our empirical findings and the kind of problem, in the larger perspective, with which we wished to deal. Our approach fits into a motivational framework, and habit is given a relatively minor role. The important kind of learning that takes place is incentive learning, i.e., what is where, and performance and decisions are controlled by the utility or value of these outcomes.

However, before considering the relationships of our approach with other topics, each with its own theoretical focus, such as personality theory, psychopathology, and conflict theory, one additional general consideration should be taken up. In our experiments we used a free- and forced-trial procedure, thus forcing the S to sample the contingent outcomes. Yet, once a preference had been decided, e.g., preference for the immediate over delayed shock-food, side (e.g., Renner, 1966b, e), we could have "tricked" the subject. If we gave it all free-choice trials, it would now be "free" to select its preferred side all the time and to avoid the less desirable side all the time. However, if we now turned off the current on the delayed side (nonpreferred), the organism would be behaving in a "stupid" fashion by selecting the shock–food side over food alone. But it would have had no opportunity to learn about the altered outcomes and thus could not be expected to alter its responses, although if the S were given this new set of outcomes in a new preference situation, it would certainly prefer food alone over shock–food. The point is, when a set of outcomes is outside the response variation of the organism, the latter cannot possibly adjust its behavior, nor can the behavior itself (the response consistency) provide information on the relative utility of, for example, the new outcomes of food versus shock–food. In other words, the *persistence* of a response does not demonstrate that it is (or would be) preferred over some alternative. In this connection, a "habit" may appear to be controlling behavior; that is, where previous incentive learning has resulted in a consistent choice being made in a given stimulus situation, it is "reinforced" by the outcome, since its value relative to the alternative act has already been acquired. In this sense the habit is reinforced, but not strengthened in an S-R sense; rather, the outcome expectation is confirmed and the necessity for response variation excluded. Thus, we have a consistent response, but the persistence per se does not establish that the outcome is more desirable than other alternatives outside the range of response variation.

It was necessary to make this rather obvious point in order to anticipate our treatment of psychopathology and response persistence in the next section, and for the sake of completeness of specifying the limited range of response consistency that is to be seen as habit.

IV. Relationship to Other Theoretical Problems

A. TEMPORAL INTEGRATION AND PERSONALITY THEORY

We introduced the problem of temporal integration at the start of this paper by using an illustration of a high school dropout suggested by Irwin (1963). Although our analysis differs from his, the illustration seems particularly useful as an example, and having presented our empirical data and theoretical interpretations, we will return to this example to make some comments about personality per se.

1. Nonevents

We have argued, in essence, that all responses are choices and that a system dealing with the motivational fact of choice is a general approach to (or theory of) behavior. An implicit assumption of such an approach is that the organism is faced with a never-ending series of choices between competing alternatives. In the simplest case, the alternative to shock–food, i.e., nonshock–nonfood, was described as opposite in sign and value to shock–food (Renner, 1964a). The usefulness of such an assumption seems warranted with respect to decisions made by people where the loss of a desired reward or the avoidance of an unpleasant task is a relevant consideration, although some nonevents may contribute little, as when the high school dropout faces nonemployment but avoids at once the aversive school situation. If the nonevent is not important, then, in an identical fashion, the event, future employment advantages, also should have little positive value for keeping the person in school and in inhibiting dropping out. However, to date the only support for this assumption has been the observation that a cue for nonreward acquires negative value (Renner, 1966a). There is a need to make an explicit attempt to deal with what Mowrer has called disappointment and hope, and relief and fear (Mowrer, 1960).

When we start to discuss the *content* of such decisions we find ourselves very quickly dealing with personality processes that broaden into psychopathology. After all, are not some decisions (ways of resolving a conflict) inherently better than others, and therefore more adaptative, or healthier, or indicative of more ego strength? It is widely accepted that it would be better for the student to stay in school, and indeed we have national efforts to combat high school dropouts. But what are we to combat? What part of the human carburetor needs to be adjusted so that it runs more smoothly from society's point of view?

Our orientation toward such issues is to emphasize that the choices themselves are not more or less "good," except from the external viewpoint of society at large. The choices are to be viewed as highly predictable and lawful events that follow from the relative utilities of the expected outcomes. Personality is but an abstraction defining a particular content area to which we wish to apply our psychology. We should not try to find classes of people, such as those with weak ego strength, or with adjustment or maladjustment, but seek instead, ways to apply psychological principles to the specific content of our interest. Our approach implies at least continuity between normal and what we call neurotic behavior in the sense that the same general principles (e.g., the process of temporal integration) are assumed to apply. Dropping out of school (choosing future unemployment) is not maladjustment of processes within the person (although it may be "maladjusted" from some external criterion), but a chosen act to be treated as any other act—an event to be treated as a motivational phenomenon within psychological theory. An additional illustration and a discussion of several specific issues should clarify our position.

2. An Illustration

The term neurotic paradox is used to refer to the fact that patients seem to persist in responses that lead to punitive external consequences. We have assumed that whether or not a reward and punishment will have a net positive or negative effect will depend on the separate delay-of-reinforcement gradients generated for both the reward and the punishment. Since their relative height or slope may vary over a wide range, it is possible for an immediate punishment to be offset by a delayed reward, or vice versa. By considering separately the temporal gradients of the particular rewards and punishments present in the situation, we can specify the conditions under which an outcome will be experienced as desirable or aversive. As a direct parallel to the first conflict experiment (Renner, 1964a), it is possible to understand why any condition in which there is an unusually strong motivation may result in a "maladaptive response," as seen from an external frame of reference.

For example, an individual with an unusually strong fear of social rebuff, acquired either over his life history or as a function of the immediate situation, and a more or less normal desire for social interaction, is "predisposed" to form an "abnormal" fixation. A response that satisfies his desire for social interaction, even if it is immediately rewarding, may be overweighed by the punishment from, or fear of, social rebuff; therefore, any positive social approach response would be inhibited. If the response is one that reduces or eliminates his fear of social rebuff, however, such as an isolation or withdrawal response, the positive value of anxiety reduction (nonpunishment) will result in a stronger rewarding effect than the negative utility of the punishment resulting from lack of social interaction, even if the punishment is immediate. The final effect should be an avoidance of the social choice and the selection and persistence of an isolation choice. Although a punished response is selected, that choice is no more paradoxical than was the preference of deprived rats for immediate shock plus delayed food (Renner, 1964a), or than the relative choice of rats for immediate shock–food over nonshock–nonfood but nonshock–nonfood over delayed shock–food (Renner, 1966a, e), once the independent operations of the separate temporal gradients, which define the relative utility of the outcomes, are considered. After incentive learning has occurred and a decision is made, as in the foregoing example, the response should persist, for every isolation response is, in its net effect, relatively desirable with respect to the expected outcome of the alternative act. Once this learning has occurred and the decision has been made, the opportunity to acquire information about any change in the external environment is effectively absent, since the new contingent consequences are outside the range of response variation of the organism and thus adaptation is excluded as a possibility. In this context we will consider more specifically the question of response selection and persistence.

The temporal interval is only one important determinant that must be considered in conjunction with the temporal gradients (the height and slope of the gradients being determined by drive, expected amount of reinforcement, cues, and a host of other variables), before it is possible to determine the net effect of a particular reward or punishment. The height and slope of the temporal gradients of reinforcement of the underlying conflicting incentives are thus crucial, for what may seem like a "stupid" response of social isolation and its consequent unhappiness, from an external point of view, should be more desirable or less aversive in terms of utility for the organism than any of the possible alternative responses.

The necessary condition for our approach to be useful is that this relative utility be a lawful event that can be specified apart from the specific choice in question. Thus, in the work reported, on temporal integration for example, the same shock–food combination can be either positive or negative, depending on whether the S is hungry (Renner, 1964a), or whether a combined outcome is immediate or delayed (Renner, 1966a, e), or whether the S has been starved as an infant (Renner, 1966b). The outcomes themselves do not have an absolute value that defines what is "integrative" or not. The choices are lawful in terms of the value of the outcome when this value, or utility, is defined independently of the preference.

3. Comment on Self-Defeating Behavior

An attempt to provide an approach to the process of temporal integration with specific reference to personality functioning requires that a distinction be made between the acquisition and the persistence of a response. Previous work has provided illustrations in which a rewarded response (e.g., Mowrer & Ullman, 1945) or an escape response (e.g., Brown, Martin, & Morrow, 1964; Brown, Anderson, & Weiss, 1965) that originally was adaptive and was acquired in accordance with theoretical expectations is not inhibited or given up (i.e., shows persistence) when the contingent outcomes are changed. These findings have been used as an experimental analogue of what is presumed to be operating in some cases of human maladaptive behavior, but, apart from whether or not this analogy is accurate, the results have posed a theoretical problem in accounting for the persistence. The problem of self-defeating behavior, however, can be rephrased in terms of incentive and habit learning in order to consider, more generally, the problems of acquisition and persistence. In a study such as that of Mowrer and Ullman (1945) the results bear directly on the persistence of an act rather than on the motivational properties of the organism;

in contrast, our theories of personality and psychopathology tend to focus on motivational disturbances that lead to the selection of, preference for, and finally, persistence in, self-defeating behaviors. Incentive and habit learning can be two somewhat different, although closely related questions.

a. *Acquisition.* For example, in the Mowrer and Ullman (1945) experiment, rats were trained to approach food and thus acquired an adaptive and useful response. The Ss failed to relinquish that response only when it was later made less functional than an alternative response. It is important to note that this alternative response was outside the response variation of the established and the explicitly trained response, making it impossible for the S to evaluate the consequences of an alternative response. This will be generally true of any free-response situation. The net effect on the established response was most likely still rewarding, and thus the old response was maintained, for as Mowrer and Ullman note, a stronger shock would inhibit eating completely; that is, the net effect would be aversive. In this respect, the Mowrer and Ullman experiment is primarily an example of fixation or failure in growth and development. The problem of the selection and persistence of a symptom (i.e., a preference for the self-defeating choice), in its own right, was not demonstrated; what was demonstrated was the failure to adopt a better or more mature and "integrated" response. However, the eating response should not be given up unless the net outcome of the food–shock was negative, in which case the previously selected choice would be altered.

b. *Response Selection and Persistence.* Thus, a response may persist after some period of training when the contingent outcomes are modified so as to make the established response more aversive than some alternative, but as long as the alternative is outside the range of response variation, or outside the range of factors that change response variations, adjustment cannot occur (e.g., Mowrer & Ullman, 1945; Brown *et al.*, 1964, 1965). This form of response persistence does not deal with the motivational preferences of the organism, although apparently the theoretical aim is to do so, for as Brown (1965) has noted, since the S runs, the run-shock-escape sequence must be preferred over not running, by the behavioral criterion necessary to define what is desirable or aversive. Thus, Brown's (1965) comments show a preference for using motivational principles, although the free-response procedure of the experiments referred to (Brown *et al.*, 1964, 1965) demonstrates only the persistence of a response (habit) based on old expectancies and not an independent demonstration that the running response is actually more desirable than not running. The purer motivational question can be asked by specifying the conditions under which a response may be selected and finally persisted in because it is in fact more desirable or less aversive than the alternatives available (see e.g., Renner, 1964a, 1966a,b, Experiment 2; e). Thus, a response may persist because it is in fact subjectively the most economical choice for the organism. We can analyze Brown's (Brown *et al.*, 1964, 1965) experiments in this light. Staying in the start box without shock certainly would be less aversive than the punished instrumental response (an escape response during acquisition) if assessed in a preference situation.

What is at stake in the Brown experiments is the failure of punishing the running response to provide the rats with information on the change of contingent outcomes in comparison with a nonpunished control group. For the control group, however, the change is more distinct and presumably more discriminable. The importance of discriminating the change in conditions so that the punishment is effective is apparently an important and necessary consideration for permitting not running to appear as an alternative and for punishment to be more effective than nonpunishment (Seward, King, Chow, & Shiflett, 1965). The point here, however, is not a critique of the Brown experiments, but the value of separating the motivational question on net rewarding or punishing value and the habit question (persistence) in the search for the underlying mechanisms needed for a theoretical account of so-called self-defeating behavior. It is necessary to specify the motivational mechanisms independent of the behavior in question. A complete analysis of a free-response situation requires a treatment of motivational as well as "habit" (in our sense of the term) factors.

c. Motivation and Habit. Presumably, a variety of contingent outcomes can be arranged so that the organism will fixate or show a failure of growth and development, i.e., a failure to discriminate that a set of outcomes has been modified. This aspect, however, has been overemphasized as an analogy of self-defeating behavior, resulting in relative underemphasis of the motivational properties of the organism that may lead to both the selection and persistence of a response. The work on temporal integration, for example, approaches the problem by asking first a motivational question; that is, how the direction of choice behavior is determined by incentive learning (utility), with the term motivation (desire and aversion) being defined by the choices themselves using a free-trial–forced-trial procedure where all the alternatives are sampled by the *S*. Both the acquisition of incentive information, as reflected in choice, and of habit, as reflected in the persistence of a preferred (reinforced) response, appear to be important for understanding self-defeating behavior, with the fundamental question being the one phrased in terms of motivation.

The motivational question (incentive learning) can account for the initial selection of a response and for its maintenance in preference to the available alternatives, as well as for the failure to sample new alternatives.

In addition, the motivational approach, as it has been applied to the process of temporal integration, provides an independent specification of utility, apart from the choices, permitting a quantification of relative incentive value so that the same set of consequences may be seen as either rewarding or punishing (desirable or aversive) without having to make reference to the particular choice behavior in question. Viewed in this light, terms such as paradoxical, stupid, or masochistic are somewhat inappropriate. It is possible to define the process in terms of utility, thus allowing each organism to behave in an economical fashion and permitting both motivational and persistence (habit) factors to play a part.

B. TEMPORAL INTEGRATION AND CONFLICT THEORY

The emphasis on a decision-making process in situations where a choice must be made between alternative acts with equivocal outcomes brings the present work on temporal integration close to the area of conflict theory, and as such, our work needs to be related to Miller's (1959) approach-avoidance model.

1. Comparison with Miller's Approach-Avoidance Model[3]

We have previously noted (Renner, 1966a) that the Miller (1959) model deals with the strength of a tendency to make a response as a function of distance from the goal. As this model, based on spatial distance, has been extended to human behavior, "distance" has been used in a very general sense to refer to time or stimulus dissimilarity, as well as other dimensions. On the other hand, our work on temporal integration has dealt with temporal gradients that define the declining effectiveness (and assumed value) of a reinforcement as a function of delay after the response. The Miller model is concerned with response strength as a function of nearness to a goal that is about to be presented, unlike our work, which deals with the value of an outcome that has been presented in the past. In other words, the Miller model is an analytic analysis of a conflict situation, and ours is oriented toward the decision-making process and the principles of conflict resolution.

The Miller approach-avoidance model deals with response strength at some specified level of training. For example, he deduces from his postulates that increasing the number of reinforced training trials should cause the S to go nearer the goal, or that increasing the number of reinforced avoidance trials should cause the S to remain farther away from the goal (Miller, 1959, p. 208). Thus, the ordinate of the conflict gradients, strength of tendency to approach or avoid (Miller, 1959), refers to a tendency to respond or the

[3]The author is indebted to Judson Brown for helping to clarify for him the difference between the approach-avoidance model and the work on temporal integration by providing critical comments on an earlier unpublished work comparing the two approaches.

response strength of a particular habit. This may be contrasted with our gradients and conflict studies, which determine the incentive value of particular outcomes (not responses) at their asymptotic level.

In short, there are fundamental differences in terms of the empirical data, the theoretical problem being considered, and the type of theoretical assumptions being made. There is no reason at this point why our findings and the Miller model need be seen as necessarily related to each other, except in the general theoretical sense that both are concerned with conflict. Confusion and apparent similarity may arise from the use, in different senses, of similar terms.

2. Temporal Conflicts

Confusion is most likely with respect to the extension of the Miller model to the dimension of time, which Brown (1957) has labeled a temporal conflict. In this situation an organism is both rewarded and punished at some particular time if it responds. The approach and avoidance gradients in this example refer to the tendency of the S to make that response as a function of temporal distance from the time at which the reinforcement would be given if a response were made. A direct extension of the spatial distance model would lead to the prediction that many minutes away from reinforcement there would be some positive response tendency, but a few minutes before reinforcement there would be a negative response tendency, thus reflecting steeper avoidance than approach.

As a contrast, recall our finding that the temporal gradient of reward was steeper than the temporal gradient of punishment, and our subsequent demonstration that an immediate shock–food combination was desirable, but the same shock–food was aversive when delayed. Our work demonstrates the value of the outcome, and as such, it is a relatively pure motivational statement about the incentive value of the outcome to the organism; as we have argued, it is a way to study the decision-making process. The Brown extension of the approach-avoidance model is a relatively pure response-tendency statement about a habit at a given level of training and as such is an analytic study of a conflict. As noted earlier, this is a relative emphasis, for our experiments are not completely free from a response tendency, nor is the approach-avoidance model free from incentive factors.

Therefore, our work is *not* an extension of Miller's approach-avoidance model to the time dimension. The differences in empirical findings (relative slopes) are simply not comparable and do not constitute conflicting data. To the extent that there is contradiction it is at a comparatively abstract level, where we are concerned with how to interpret the empirical findings, what theoretical terms to use, how the concept of a goal gradient is to be applied, the relative importance of incentive and habit learning, and similar issues. Such a theoretical analysis of conflict theory and temporal integration goes beyond the scope of this paper, and probably is premature in terms of the available empirical data, but is certainly of high priority for future consideration.

3. On Learned Drives

One more contrast with conflict theory will be useful in order to put the work on temporal integration into perspective. Miller (1959) has noted that the avoidance gradient may be steeper because it is dependent on external cues, whereas the approach gradient is dependent on an internal state of the *S*, which has distinctive properties (recall our earlier treatment of the drive discrimination problem). However, as Maher (1964) has pointed out, in most social situations, to which the model has been freely generalized, both drives are usually learned and thus there would be parallel gradients and the organism would either approach all the way or avoid altogether. To handle this problem, Maher (1964) proposed an equilibrium state if the stronger of the two competing response tendencies mediates behavior only when its absolute momentary strength exceeds that of the weaker by an amount that is a constant fraction of the weaker (p. 289). In situations where the avoidance gradient is parallel but higher than the approach gradient, the subject should avoid the goal when some distance from it but be attracted to the goal when closer to it. In a situation in which the organism was free, however, it would never move toward, and thus never get closer to, the goal. This prediction, Maher notes, "... could only be tested empirically by compelling the animal into the goal region, or by using a temporal conflict situation" (p. 290).

The analysis by Maher illustrates the emphasis on the strength of some particular response (*response tendency*) that is to be made. Such considerations may be contrasted with our question of what an outcome is worth, i.e., its utility to the *S* when, for example, he may have the outcome immediately or must wait for it. We have suggested that this utility governs the choice an organism makes to approach or avoid a goal or incentive region. We have placed the burden of our approach on the assumption that incentive learning is of critical importance. In fact, the concern with *learned drives* suggests that generalizations made about human behavior are meant to include motivational characteristics or dispositions the *S* carries with him that govern his choices (decisions). We would view this as dispositions about the relative preference for some outcomes over others, in terms of which the *S* adjusts his response choices, rather than a tendency to make a particular response.

The Maher (1964) paper suggesting parallel response-tendency gradients with learned drives can be used to illustrate a final point about our incentive gradients. In the work on temporal integration it has been shown that the slope and height of the temporal gradients of both reward and punishment can be manipulated independently. The same factors responsible for determining the height and slope of the two types of gradient also influence utility, as was demonstrated in the preference situations. Thus, in a situation where both drives are learned there is the greatest possibility for the relative heights and slopes to be determined by the specific learning experiences. The possibility exists for either the temporal gradient of approach or the gradient of avoidance to be steeper. Given this situation, then in terms of utility as assessed in temporal integration, either an immediate or a delayed reward–punishment combination could be either desirable or aversive, depending on the factors controlling the relative strengths of the two gradients. The work on temporal integration has progressed under the assumption that the most fruitful approach to this type of problem is to specify those conditions that determine the relative slope of the temporal gradient of reward and the temporal gradient of punishment, and as a final step, independently to show that these gradients may operate in the same situation and that utility is dependent on these underlying gradients. Thus, when values are selected so that the temporal gradient of reward is steeper than the temporal gradient of punishment, a distant goal region should be aversive and thus avoided, but the same goal region when temporally close should be preferred and approached. The opposite should hold if the relative slope of the temporal gradients were reversed.

The approach to the process of temporal integration illustrates the value of focusing on those factors that determine or control the relative slope and height of the gradients rather than assuming fixed functions, as is done when one infers that the response-tendency gradients of a particular response accurately reflect an enduring motivational state, which is what is done when the Miller model is broadly extended to human behavior. In summary, the approach-avoidance model is analytic with respect to a conflict, whereas temporal integration is analytic with respect to the decision-making (conflict-resolution) process.

V. Generalizations and Implications for Personality

The work reported is basic research and may be considered as personality research only to the extent that these theoretical concepts will be of particular use to understand problems of human behavior. From our viewpoint, we are studying motivational phenomena and basic theoretical issues that have some bearing on the kinds of behavior ordinarily encompassed by the term personality. However, we have not yet attempted to apply our procedures to studying these processes directly in human behavior, and it would be unwise to make sweeping generalizations at this point. In short, we have not been interested in providing an analogue of neurotic behavior and in assuming that those specific conditions underlie parallel kinds of clinical phenomena. For example, we could arrange conditions so that a delayed negative outcome contributes little value to the net effect and show that a S will persist in selecting this given response. But this proves nothing about neurotic behavior. Rather, the more important aspect of the present experimental work is the illustration of concepts and experimental strategies that may be employed for attempting to cope with integrative and noninte-grative behavior.

We need to avoid thinking in concrete terms. There has been a tendency within personality research to assume that a particular type of behavior reflects a particular trait or disposition. This probably accounts, in part, for the excessive use of correlational techniques. Consider the example of a person who shows a great deal of capacity to delay gratification and work for very remote outcomes in the face of difficult external circumstances. Usually such a person is described as having courage, conviction, and per-severance, in general terms that reflect certain structural or dynamic aspects of the personality showing strength of character and adjustment. However, consider the same basic situation where a patient pursues some goal with the same perseverance; we then describe him as fixated, regressed, neurotic, self-defeating, or even masochistic. The correlational approach has been, then, to find what differential experiences have accounted for a different personality structure. It is not surprising that such approaches have not been particularly successful. From our point of view, there are innumerable consequences that have an acquired incentive value for the organism, and innumerable situations and circumstances that modify the relative utility of one outcome or another. Many writers have assumed continuity between normal and abnormal by stressing that the same basic processes underlie both; but they have looked at content (dispositions and traits) to find this similarity, rather than concentrating research efforts on specifying psycho-logical processes. With respect to the area called personality we would argue for attempting to apply general principles of behavior. As an illustra-tion, the process of temporal integration provides a specification of the mechanisms whereby decisions are made. It provides an account of the ways in which utility may be modified. It does not claim, for example, that because a shock–food combination is selected, the organism must have been deprived as an infant, for that is but one way to modify the utility of a food reward.

Notice that this approach makes no claim that there is a single way that one type of preference develops, or that it is based on the same type of experiences, e.g., lack of affection during infancy. What we have suggested is that outcomes have their incentive values modified for any number of reasons, but in a lawful way. Diagnosis in dealing with an individual case requires that we find out for that individual what he has acquired. The implication is to treat personality on the theoretical level by specifying those conditions that control utility, and at the applied level to be concerned with information and techniques for controlling the acquisition, extinction, and modification of utility. It requires the application of principles of general psychology rather than the treatment of personality as a uniform collection of characteristics that can somehow be useful apart from general psychological principles. The topic of personality is human behavior, and we must deal with it in terms of behavioral laws that govern the acquisition of this content, but not in terms of invented abstractions describing a uniform content from which we expect to be able to predict behavior. We wish to avoid the assumption that similar preferences (the value of an incentive relative to some other outcome) have common antecedent factors and will result in similar behavior in new situations. The unique content for each individual and the relative incentive values of the competing alternatives for him must be considered in predicting future response choices. Thus, with respect to the content of personality, we have argued that it should be treated as an idiographic issue, but that the content is acquired in accordance with nomothetic principles, i.e., general behavioral laws. The important principles that are uniform across people are concerned with incentive learning, not with response dispositions or content descriptions. A useful content description of personality should be possible only by developing suitable techniques for the idiographic study of behavior, with the content being a description of that person's motivational structure (previous incentive learning).

References

Amsel, A. The role of frustrative nonreward in noncontinuous reward situations. *Psychol. Bull.*, 1958, **55**, 102–119.

Amsel, A. Frustrative nonreward in partial reinforcement and discrimination learning: Some recent history and a theoretical extension. *Psychol. Rev.*, 1962, **69**, 306–328.

Amsel, A., & Ward, J. S. Frustration and persistence: Resistance to discrimination following prior experience with the discriminanda. *Psychol. Monogr.*, 1965, **79**, No. 4 (Whole No. 597).

Banks, R. K. Persistence to continuous punishment following intermittent punishment training. *J. exp. Psychol.*, 1966, **71**, 373–377.

Banks, R. K., & Vogel-Sprott, M. Effect of delayed punishment on an immediately rewarded response in humans. *J. exp. Psychol.*, 1965, **70**, 357–359.

Baron, A. Delayed punishment of a runway response. *J. comp. physiol., Psychol.*, 1965, **60**, 131–134.

Brown, J. S. Principles of intrapersonal conflict. *J. Conflict Resolution*, 1957, **1**, 135–154.

Brown, J. S. A behavioral analysis of masochism. *J. exp. Res. Pers.*, 1965, **1**, 65–70.

Brown, J. S., Martin, R. C., & Morrow, M. W. Self-punitive behavior in the rat: Facilitative effects of punishment on resistance to extinction. *J. comp. physiol. Psychol.*, 1964, **57**, 127–133.

Brown, J. S., Anderson, D. C., & Weiss, Carol G. Self-punitive behavior under conditions of massed practice. *J. comp. physiol. Psychol.*, 1965, **60**, 451–453.

Cameron, N. *Personality development and psychopathology.* Boston: Houghton Mifflin, 1963.

Carlton, P. L. Response strength as a function of delay of reward and physical confinement. Unpublished master's thesis, Univer. of Iowa, 1954.

Church, R. M. The varied effects of punishment on behavior. *Psychol. Rev.*, 1963, **70**, 369–402.

Cook, J. O., & Barnes, L. W. Choice of delay of inevitable shock. *J. abnorm. soc. Psychol.*, 1964, **68**, 669–672.

Crum, Janet, Brown, W. L., & Bitterman, M. E. The effect of partial and delayed reinforcement on resistance to extinction. *Amer. J. Psychol.*, 1951, **64**, 228–237.

D'Amato, M. R., & Gumenik, W. E. Some effects of immediate versus randomly delayed shock on an instrumental response and cognitive processes. *J. abnorm. soc. Psychol.*, 1960, **60**, 64–67.

Davenport, J. The interaction of magnitude and delay of reinforcement in spatial discrimination. *J. comp. physiol. Psychol.*, 1962, **55**, 267–273.

Dollard, J., & Miller, N. E. *Personality and psychotherapy.* New York: McGraw-Hill, 1950.

Elder, T., Noblin, C. D., & Maher, B. A. The extinction of fear as a function of distance versus dissimilarity from the original conflict situation. *J. abnorm. soc. Psychol.*, 1961, **63**, 530–533.

Ferster, C. B., & Hammer, C. Variables determining the effects of delay in reinforcement. *J. exp. Analysis Behav.*, 1965, **8**, 243–254.

Festinger, L. The psychological effects of insufficient rewards. *Amer. Psychologist*, 1961, **16**, 1–11.

Goodrich, K. P. Performance in different segments of an instrumental response chain as a function of reinforcement schedule. *J. exp. Psychol.*, 1959, **57**, 57–63.

Grice, G. R. The relation of secondary reinforcement to delayed reward in visual discrimination learning. *J. exp. Psychol.*, 1948, **38**, 1–16.

Hare, R. D. Temporal gradient of fear arousal in psychopaths. *J. abnorm. Psychol.*, 1965, **70**, 442–445.

Holder, W., Marx, M., Holder, Elaine, & Collier, G. Response strength as a function of delay of reward in a runway. *J. exp. Psychol.*, 1957, **53**, 316–323.

Hunt, J. McV. The effects of infant feeding-frustration upon adult hoarding in the albino rat. *J. abnorm. soc. Psychol.*, 1941, **36**, 338–360.

Irwin, F. W. On desire, aversion, and the affective zero. *Psychol. Rev.*, 1961, **68**, 293–300.

Irwin, F. W. Unchosen acts. In G. B. Watson (Ed.), *No room at the bottom.* Washington, D. C.: National Education Association, 1963.

Irwin, F. W. Criteria of expectancy. *Psychol. Rev.*, 1966, **73**, 327–334.

Jenkins, H. M., & Ward, W. C. Judgment of contingency between responses and outcomes. *Psychol. Monogr.*, 1965, **79**, No. 1 (Whole No. 594).

Knapp, R. K., Kause, R. H., & Perkins, C. C. Immediate *vs.* delayed shock in T-maze performance. *J. exp. Psychol.*, 1959, **58**, 357–362.

Lanzetta, J. T., & Driscoll, J. M. Preference for information about an uncertain but unavoidable outcome. *J. Pers. soc. Psychol.*, 1966, **3**, 96–102.

Leitenberg, H. Is time-out from positive reinforcement an aversive event? *Psychol. Bull.*, 1965, **64**, 428–441.

Lockard, Joan. Choice of warning signal or no warning signal in an unavoidable shock situation. *J. comp. physiol. Psychol.*, 1963, **56**, 526–530.

Logan, F. A. *Incentive*. New Haven, Conn.: Yale Univer. Press, 1960.

Logan, F. A. Decision making by rats: Delay versus amount of reward. *J. comp. physiol. Psychol.*, 1965, **59**, 1–12. (a)

Logan, F. A. Decision making by rats: Uncertain outcome choices. *J. comp. physiol. Psychol.*, 1965, **59**, 246–251. (b)

Logan, F. A. Continuously negatively correlated amount of reinforcement. *J. comp. physiol. Psychol.*, 1966, **62**, 31–34.

Ludvigson, H. W., Caul, W. F., Korn, J. H., & McHose, J. H. Development and attenuation of delay-engendered avoidance behavior. *J. exp. Psychol.*, 1964, **67**, 405–411.

McCord, W., & McCord, Joan. *The psychopath: An essay on the criminal mind*. Princeton, N. J.: Van Nostrand, 1964.

Maher, B. A. The application of the approach-avoidance conflict model to social behavior. *J. Conflict Resolution*, 1964, **8**, 287–291.

Markowitz, Nancy, & Renner, K. E. Feedback and the delay-retention effect. *J. exp. Psychol.*, 1966, **72**, 452–455.

Miller, N. E. Liberalization of basic S-R concepts: Extensions to conflict behavior, motivation and social learning. In S. Koch (Ed.), *Psychology: A study of a science*. Vol. 2. New York: McGraw-Hill, 1959.

Mischel, W. Theory and research on the antecedents of self-imposed delay of reward. In B. A. Maher (Ed.), *Progress in experimental personality research*. Vol. 3. New York: Academic Press, 1966.

Mowrer, O. H. On the dual nature of learning: A reinterpretation of "conditioning" and "problem-solving." *Harvard educ. Rev.*, 1947, **17**, 102–148.

Mowrer, O. H. *Learning theory and behavior*. New York: Wiley, 1960.

Mowrer, O. H., & Ullman, A. D. Time as a determinant of integrative learning. *Psychol. Rev.*, 1945, **52**, 61–90.

Perkins, C. C., Levis, D. J., & Seymann, R. Preference for signal-shock versus shock-signal. *Psychol. Rep.*, 1963, **13**, 735–738.

Perkins, C. C., Seymann, R. G., Levis, D. J., & Spencer, H. R. Factors affecting preference for signal-shock over shock-signal. *J. exp. Psychol.*, 1966, **72**, 190–196.

Premack, D. Reinforcement theory. In D. Levine (Ed.), *Nebraska symposium on motivation*. Lincoln, Nebr.: Univer. of Nebraska Press, 1965. Pp. 123–180.

Renner, K. E. The effect of drive level and availability of goal box cues on the temporal gradient of reinforcement. *J. comp. physiol. Psychol.*, 1963, **56**, 101–104.

Renner, K. E. Conflict resolution and the process of temporal integration. *Psychol. Rep.*, 1964, **15**, 423–438. Monogr. Suppl. 15–2. (a)

Renner, K. E. Delay of reinforcement: A historical review. *Psychol. Bull.*, 1964, **61**, 341–361. (b)

Renner, K. E. Temporal integration: The relative value of rewards and punishments as a function of their temporal distance from the response. *J. exp. Psychol.*, 1966, **71**, 902–907. (a)

Renner, K. E. Temporal integration: The effect of early experience. *J. exp. Res. Pers.*, 1966, **1**, 201–210. (b)

Renner, K. E. Delay of reinforcement: Cue utilization and the frustration effect. *Psychol. Rep.*, 1966, **19**, 167–171. (c)

Renner, K. E. Temporal integration: Amount of reward and the relative utility of immediate and delayed outcomes. Unpublished manuscript, Univer. of Illinois, 1966. (d)

Renner, K. E. Temporal integration: The relative utility of immediate versus delayed reward and punishment. *J. exp. Psychol.*, 1966, **72**, 901–903. (e)

Renner, K. E. Temporal integration: Modification of the incentive value of a food reward by early experience with deprivation. *J. exp. Psychol.*, 1967, in press.

Renner, K. E. & Murphy, M. Unpublished data, Univer. of Illinois, 1966.

Renner, K. E., & Specht, Laura. The relative desirability or aversiveness of immediate and delayed shock and food. *J. exp. Psychol.*, 1967, in press.

Schachter, S., & Singer, J. E. Cognitive, social, and physiological determinants of emotional state. *Psychol. Rev.*, 1962, **69**, 379–399.

Seward, J. P., King, R. M., Chow, T., & Shiflett, S. C. Persistence of punished escape responses. *J. comp. physiol. Psychol.*, 1965, **60**, 265–268.

Solomon, R. L. Punishment. *Amer. Psychologist*, 1964, **19**, 239–253.

Spence, K. W. The role of secondary reinforcement in delayed reward learning. *Psychol. Rev.*, 1947, **54**, 1–8.

Spence, K. W. *Behavior theory and conditioning.* New Haven, Conn.: Yale Univer. Press, 1956.

Spence, K. W. *Behavior theory and learning.* Englewood Cliffs, N. J.: Prentice-Hall, 1960.

Walters, R. H. Delay of reinforcement gradients in children's learning. *Psychonom. Sci.*, 1964, **1**, 307–308.

Wilson, M. E. The role of generalization and delay in nonintegrative learning. Unpublished doctoral dissertation, Emory Univer., 1965.

Webb, W. B. Drive stimuli as cues. *Psychol. Rep.*, 1955, **1**, 287–298.

THE INFLUENCE OF PUNISHMENT AND RELATED DISCIPLINARY TECHNIQUES ON THE SOCIAL BEHAVIOR OF CHILDREN: THEORY AND EMPIRICAL FINDINGS[1]

Richard H. Walters and Ross D. Parke

DEPARTMENT OF PSYCHOLOGY, UNIVERSITY OF WATERLOO, WATERLOO ONTARIO, AND
DEPARTMENT OF PSYCHOLOGY, UNIVERSITY OF WISCONSIN, MADISON, WISCONSIN

I. Introduction

In the child-training literature, the term punishment is used to refer to a wide range of disciplinary procedures, such as confiscation of privileges,

[1] Research grants to the senior author, extending over several years, have facilitated a number of investigations that led to the preparation of this paper. Acknowledgments of support of this kind are due to the National Research Council of Canada (Grant APT-94), the Ontario Mental Health Foundation (Grant 42), and the Defence Research Board of Canada (Grant 9401-24). Current grant numbers are given. During the past few months grants from the National Institutes of Health, United States Health Service, to R. H. Walters (Grant HD01456-02) and to R. D. Parke (Grant MH11979-01) have considerably accelerated the preparation of this paper.

withholding of rewards, isolation, nagging, scolding, and ridicule, as well as the infliction of physical pain. These procedures may involve in varying degrees the presentation of aversive stimuli, in the form of physical or verbal punishments, the withholding or withdrawal of positive reinforcers, or the mere nonresponsiveness of the socialization agent (Bandura & Walters, 1963b). In employing such disciplinary techniques, the socialization agent ordinarily focuses on reducing the strength, or the probability of occurrence, of socially disapproved responses, rather than on the eliciting of prosocial behavior. While there is every reason to believe, on the basis of laboratory studies, that the operations involved in the various disciplinary procedures do not usually produce identical effects, to some extent and under some conditions all may result in increased social conformity.

The main purpose of this paper is to offer an analysis, in social-learning terms, of some of the more frequently used techniques of discipline and to assess from available data their effectiveness for modifying children's behavior. Much of the relevant information comes from field studies, since for practical and ethical reasons, laboratory-experimental studies in which children have served as subjects have employed only the more attenuated forms of discipline. Nevertheless, since it is often difficult to determine whether a covariation between two classes of events observed in field studies does, in fact, reflect a cause–effect relationship, considerable attention has been given to outcomes of laboratory investigations. As far as possible, conclusions are based on data obtained from child or adolescent subjects, although clarification has sometimes been possible only by reference to research on animals and human adults. With a few exceptions, accounts of behavior therapy procedures (*e.g.*, Eysenck, 1960; Ullmann & Krasner, 1965) have been omitted from this review.

II. Physical Punishment

Theories of punishment have leaned heavily on the outcomes of laboratory studies with animals in which an aversive physical stimulus immediately follows, or accompanies, a specified response of the S (Church, 1963; Solomon, 1964). The available research strongly suggests that physical punishment may have diverse effects and that these effects are dependent on such parameters as the intensity, timing, and frequency of punishment, the strength and nature of the punished response, the relationship between the agent and recipient of punishment, and the consistency with which punishment is administered.

No investigator has utilized pain-producing physical stimuli in traditional laboratory-experimental studies with children, although the use of electric shock for modifying the behavior of two autistic children has been reported by Lövaas, Schaeffer, and Simmons (1965b).[2] The *S*s were administered painful shock through a grid on the floor of an experimental room or through electrodes placed on their buttocks. Over a lengthy series of sessions, Lövaas *et al.* demonstrated that shock suppressed self-stimulatory and tantrum behavior, that social responses could be established and maintained by means of shock termination, and that stimuli associated with shock, for example, "No," could acquire secondary negative reinforcing properties.

In laboratory studies of normal children, the nearest approximations to the traditional physical-punishment variable, electric shock, are probably the loud, unpleasant sounds employed by a number of experimental child psychologists (*e.g.*, Aronfreed & Leff, 1963; Karsh & Williams, 1964; Penney & Lupton, 1961; Walters & Demkow, 1963) and the bitter liquid (citrus acid) recently used in a punishment study by Fried and Banks (Fried, 1965; Fried & Banks 1965). While these stimuli undoubtedly have an aversive effect, they cannot strictly be classed as physically painful. This statement is probably also true of the loud sound employed by Watson and Rayner (1920) for inducing a phobia in a year-old infant. Nevertheless, there are good reasons for believing that studies using aversive auditory, visual, gustatory, or olfactory stimuli can throw considerable light on the manner in which physical punishment influences the behavior of children.

In the first place, much of the physical punishment administered by parents does not derive its effects from its physically painful quality. Physical punishment is not, generally speaking, a preferred technique of discipline among North American parents and very often takes the form of only a gentle tap on the hand or buttocks or some other equally mild form of physical contact (Sears, Maccoby, & Levin, 1957). Indeed, whatever efficacy parentally administered physical punishment has, even in its more intense forms, may in many instances derive from the fact that it is perceived by the child as signifying a threat of withdrawal of affection. For this reason, in a real-life situation physical punishment usually has some components that are more analogous to withdrawal-of-reward operations in the laboratory situation than to the operation of presenting a painful stimulus.

Moreover, the view, widely held in the child-training literature, that the effectiveness of most, if not all, disciplinary procedures derives from events that are associated with physical pain during the first year of life

---

[2]Since the original draft of this paper was prepared, a study of child *S*s by Nelson, Reid, and Travers (1965), in which painful electric shock was used as a punisher, has come to the authors' attention. The data yielded by the study suggested that shock had primarily an informational function similar to that of a 20-db tone. The overall results are, however, difficult to evaluate and are not directly related to the control of social behavior.

is almost certainly mistaken (Walters & Parke, 1965). The human infant responds with distress reactions to a wide variety of intense, sudden, but nonpainful, stimuli, including noises. It is therefore gratuitous to suppose that nonpainful physical interventions cannot in their own right generate the fear and subsequent anxiety that are generally accepted as essential for the maintenance of self-control (Kessen & Mandler, 1961). One is forced, of course, to question the assumption that parental responses that actually inflict physical suffering on a child can be regarded as lying on the same continuum as physical punishment that is no more painful than experiences that children regularly encounter in social interactions, for example, in play with other children. This assumption is, in fact, made in field studies that employ graduated scales, ranging from a point indicating mild non-painful slaps to one indicating severe beatings, and use linear-correlation techniques to assess the relationship between parental use of physical punishment and selected aspects of children's behavior. The validity of the assumption can, of course, be indirectly tested by providing laboratory demonstrations that the effects of nonpainful aversive stimuli on the behavior of children are essentially analogous to those produced when adults or subhuman organisms are administered painful electric shocks. If only for this reason, the use of loud noises as punishing stimuli in laboratory studies is thoroughly justifiable.

Moreover, the use of noise as an analogue to physical punishment in social situations readily permits investigations of certain parameters, for example, intensity, which seem to be important for understanding the manner in which punishment may change behavior. While experimental studies leave no doubt that in a number of traditional laboratory situations the presentation of nonpainful aversive stimulation leads to the modification of children's behavior in the manner desired by the experimenter (*e.g.*, Castaneda, 1956; Penney & Kirwin, 1965; Penney & Lupton, 1961; Penney & McCann, 1962), they provide meager information concerning the effects of varying such factors as the intensity, timing, frequency, or consistency of punishment and the context in which punishment occurs.

A. INTENSITY

Much of the evidence concerning the influence of intensity of punishment on children's behavior has been gleaned from field studies and case-history material. For example, in several studies in which data have been secured through questionnaires or parent interviews, parents have been rated or classified in respect to their punitiveness or to the severity of their child-training procedures. Although a high rating on scales of this type is usually secured only by parents who use relatively frequent and rather severe physical punishment, the majority of the points of the scales are defined in terms of the use or omission of disciplinary techniques other than physical punishment.

A second type of scale attempts to assess the extent to which a parent specifically employs physical punishment as a technique of discipline. However, ratings on this type of scale are invariably determined by both the frequency and the intensity of parental punishment without consideration of the possibility that variations in frequency and intensity are capable of producing very different effects. An example is provided by the ten-point scale for measuring maternal punitiveness devised by Sears, Whiting, Nowlis, and Sears (1953, p. 170). The defining points are as follows:

> 8. Frequent spanking; constant scolding; long separation; continued deprivations; repeated isolation with scolding; crossly directive in guiding behavior; punishes as a characteristic way of handling obscenity, destructiveness, attacks, quarreling, etc.
> 5. Has spanked occasionally; uses a little separation; expresses irritation about destructiveness; scolds usually when too much fussing; reasons when not upset herself.
> 2. Never spanks; usually reasons, irritated occasionally but tries not to show it; ignores physical attacks, or jokes; handles discipline by diversion or reason.

Global scales of this kind are quite evidently incapable of revealing unambiguous relationships between variations in intensity of physical punishment and aspects of child behavior. In spite of the contaminated nature of both types of scales, interview studies have nevertheless yielded some suggestive findings concerning the effects of parental use of severe physical punishment on children's behavior, particularly aggression.

Sears et al. (1953) interviewed mothers of nursery-school children and observed the behavior of the children in the school situation. They found a positive correlation between ratings of maternal punitiveness, mainly based on the parent's responses to aggression in the home, and the activity level of boys, and a negative relationship between the same parent variable and the activity level of girls. The study also yielded a slight, though probably nonsignificant, positive relationship between the maternal-punitiveness measure and the frequency of aggressive acts for both boys and girls when ratings of aggression were adjusted for the children's general-activity levels. The effects of maternal punitiveness on children's dependency were also investigated. When adjustments were made for activity level, children whose mothers were moderately punitive displayed less dependency in school than those whose mothers were rated high or low in punitiveness. Since the punitiveness scale takes little account of the mother's handling of dependency, the latter finding is especially difficult to interpret.

In a later study, based on data secured from interviews with mothers of kindergarten children, Sears et al. (1957, pp. 262–263) reported that mothers who made frequent use of physical punishment and who punished aggression severely were likely to have aggressive children, but the specific data on which this statement is based is not provided by the authors. The amount of aggression shown by the Ss was positively correlated with both maternal punitiveness and maternal use of physical punishment, but the relationships were relatively small when the influence of other correlated variables was partialed out. A follow-up study (Sears, 1961) yielded only small and mostly nonsignificant relationships between maternal punitiveness for aggression in the first five years of the children's lives and the children's antisocial aggression, assessed from a questionnaire, seven years later; there were, however, some indications that maternal punitiveness in early years reduced antisocial aggression and increased prosocial aggression by the time the children were twelve.

Sears *et al.* (1957) found a significant positive correlation between maternal punitiveness for dependency and the amount of dependency shown by children. However, there were very few instances in which a mother used overt punishment for dependency behavior, and the investigators consequently rated jointly the mother's irritation with, and her punishment for, dependency. The positive correlation therefore elucidates very little the problem of the relationship between intensity of physical punishment and the incidence of the punished behavior.

Eron and his associates (Eron, Banta, Walder, & Laulicht, 1961; Eron, Walder, Toigo, & Lefkowitz, 1963, Lefkowitz, Walder, & Eron, 1963) obtained ratings of the aggression of children, using sociometric techniques, and ratings of selected parental child-training practices by means of highly structured interviews. Scores on the parental scale were based on parents' answers to questions asking how they would respond to specific acts of aggression. High punishment in the home was consistently associated with high aggression in school, a finding that held up for both maternal and paternal punishment and for the aggression of boys and girls (Eron *et al.*, 1963). Children's mean aggression scores increased as the number of physical-punishment items chosen by the parents increased, a finding suggesting that parental use of physical punishment is an important determinant of aggression outside the home, especially since the use of nonphysical punishment was unrelated to aggression. Further evidence that parents who use severe methods of discipline, including severe physical punishment, tend to have hostile, unfriendly children is provided by Peck (1958), who employed factor-analytic methods to analyze the data from an interview study of adolescents and their families, and by Becker and his associates (Becker, Peterson, Hellmer, Shoemaker, & Quay, 1962).

Several investigations have involved comparisons of the child-training practices of parents of highly aggressive children with those of parents of nonaggressive children. Glueck and Glueck (1950) found that parents of delinquent boys made greater use of physical punishment than parents of nondelinquent boys. Bandura and Walters (1959) reported no difference between parents of aggressive and parents of nonaggressive adolescent boys in respect to punitiveness for aggression expressed against themselves, against siblings, or against peers; however, they found that the parents of the aggressive boys often resorted to quite severe physical punishment. Bandura (1960) compared the child-training practices of parents of aggressive and inhibited preadolescent boys. He found that parents of aggressive boys were more punitive for aggression that was expressed toward themselves than were parents of inhibited boys, but that the two groups of parents did not differ in respect to punitiveness for aggression toward siblings or peers. The mothers of the aggressive Ss made greater use of physical punishment than the mothers of the inhibited Ss, but the two groups of fathers did not differ in this respect.

The foregoing findings suggest that parental punitiveness, especially when it involves the frequent use of physical punishment for aggression, is an antecedent of aggressive behavior in children. However, they do not necessarily contradict the well-established laboratory finding that frequent and severe punishment will decrease the probability of the response with which it is correlated and may entirely suppress this response for a long period of time (Church, 1963; Solomon, 1964). While parents of aggressive children tend to punish aggression directed toward themselves (Bandura, 1960; Eron et al., 1963), they tend at the same time to encourage and reward aggression that is expressed outside the home (Bandura, 1960; Bandura & Walters, 1959). These parents, seem, in fact, to engage in discrimination training, which results in their children's demonstrating relatively little physical aggression inside the home but a great deal of aggression elsewhere (Bandura, 1960; Bandura & Walters, 1959; Sears et al., 1957). Moreover, aggressive parents may serve as aggressive models for their children (Bandura & Walters, 1963a,b; Sears et al., 1957).

Generally speaking, parents do not employ severe physical punishment except for aggression and flagrant disobedience. It is therefore not surprising that field studies provide little evidence concerning the effects of intensity of physical punishment on specific classes of responses other than aggression. In fact, studies that have investigated the effects of parental punitiveness on dependency and sexual behavior (e.g., Bandura, 1960; Bandura and Walters, 1959; Sears et al., 1957) have yielded few significant relationships between punitiveness and the frequency of the punished behavior, and those reported are far from consistent. In the case of sex behavior, of course, there is the additional difficulty of obtaining reliable information concerning the sexual activities of children. Thus, it is necessary to turn to laboratory studies for information concerning the effects of intensity of physical punishment on social behavior other than aggression. These studies have all utilized measures of resistance to deviation as the dependent variables.

Aronfreed and Leff (1963), using 6- and 7-year-old boys, investigated the effects of two levels of punishments on response inhibition in a temptation situation that followed punishment training. The children were first given ten discrimination trials involving a choice between two toys roughly comparable in attractiveness but differing along certain stimulus dimensions. For half the Ss, the discrimination was easy; for the remaining Ss, the discrimination was more difficult. The punishment consisted of verbal disapproval ("No"), deprivation of candy, and a noise; the intensity and quality of the noise was varied in order to modify the noxiousness of the stimulation. Half the Ss were presented with a 52-db sound from a door buzzer for making the "wrong" choice; the remaining Ss were punished with a 74-db noise from a burglar-alarm buzzer. Following training, each child was left alone with a pair of toys, including an attractive toy that was similar in some respects to the toys that were associated with punishment during training. Provided that the discrimination task, whereby the children presumably learned not to respond to objects having certain characteristics, was relatively simple, response inhibition was more frequently observed among Ss who had received high-intensity punishment than among those for whom the intensity of punishment had been low. However, when the discrimination task was difficult, "transgression" was more frequent among Ss under the high-intensity punishment condition than among the Ss who were administered the milder punishment. Aronfreed and Leff argue that the complex discrimination, combined with high-intensity punishment, created a level of anxiety too high for adaptive learning to occur.

Parke and Walters (1967) investigated the effects of differing levels of intensity of punishment in a series of three studies, all involving manipulations of at least one other variable. All three experiments involved a training procedure similar to that used by Aronfreed and Leff. Six- to 8-year-old boys were given a series of trials, on each of which they were required to choose one of a pair of toys; some toys, they were previously told, were for another boy. Whenever a S either commenced to reach for, or touched, a "forbidden" toy, he received a combination of physical and verbal punishment. Following training, the child was left alone for a 15-minute period in a room in which the punishment-associated toys were displayed. The number of times each S touched the toys, the latency of his first deviation, and the duration of his deviation were recorded by an observer seated behind a one-way-vision screen.

In the first of the studies, two levels of prior interaction between the agent and recipient of punishment and two levels of timing (early versus late punishment), as well as two levels of intensity, were employed. High-intensity punishment consisted of a verbal rebuke combined with a 96-db tone; the tone was reduced to 65 db for the low-intensity condition. Subjects who had received high-intensity punishment deviated less quickly, less often, and for shorter periods of time than did children who had been punished mildly. There were no interactions among the experimental variables. The second study involved the same two levels of intensity as were employed in the first, but altered the circumstances of timing. Although the findings for intensity were in the same direction as in the first study, they failed to reach significance. In the third study, noises, rather than tones, were used to ensure a heightened degree of noxiousness under both the low- and high-intensity conditions. Again, a factorial design, involving two levels of timing, was employed. A significant interaction between intensity and timing was obtained. When punishment was administered early in the punished response sequence, Ss under the low-intensity condition deviated more frequently and longer than those under the high-intensity condition; when punishment was administered late in the sequence, high-intensity punishment resulted in less inhibition than low-intensity punishment.

In spite of some discrepancies, the overall findings from field and laboratory studies generally support the expectation that high-intensity physical punishment in most circumstances more effectively inhibits the punished behavior than does punishment that is less intense. This is true even for the data on aggression, since severe punishment for aggression in the home, characteristic of the child-training practices of parents of aggressive children, is associated with a relatively low incidence of aggression within the home on the part of these children in comparison to the frequent aggression that they display elsewhere. However, there may be some conditions under which low-intensity physical punishment is more effective for inhibiting undesirable social responses than is punishment that is more intense.

For example, in the third of the studies reported by Parke and Walters, the low-intensity–late-punishment procedure had a considerable inhibitory effect. A possible explanation is that the low-intensity stimulus had primarily a cue, rather than an aversive, function and served largely to focus the child's attention on the association between the accompanying verbal rebuke and the act of holding the toy, thus providing the child with a clear cognition that he was engaging in a disapproved activity. A mild physical punishment, then, can serve as a fairly precise signal that an activity is disapproved. Under such circumstances, inhibition may be established and maintained not because of any intrinsic fear-arousing property of the punishing stimulus, but because it signals the agent's disapproval. The anticipated outcome of this disapproval will, of course, depend on the prior experiences of the recipient of punishment and could range from more severe physical punishment to loss of the agent's approval or attention.

A major problem with the laboratory investigations utilizing sound as a punishing stimulus is that they have set no "anchor" point around which the intensity of the sound can be varied. On the other hand, in studies utilizing electric shock with adult subjects an approximate threshold of discomfort has sometimes been determined, and the shock levels have then been adjusted in either direction. Possibly, some such determination should be made in the case of noise before intensity levels are selected. Moreover, it is evident that parametric studies involving systematic manipulations of noise level are required in order to identify orderly relationships between the intensity of the stimulus and characteristics of children's behavior. One may suspect that these relationships would be very similar to those found in animal studies in which electric shock served as the noxious stimulus (Solomon, 1964).

B. TIMING

In social situations punishment is often delayed. In some homes the father is the usual agent of punishment, and consequently deviations that occur when he is absent from the home may not be punished until he returns. The threat, "Wait until your father comes home," can elicit an aversive emotional reaction in the child as a result of this threat's having led to punishment on previous occasions. This emotional response may be reinstated whenever some interim event is an adequate stimulus either for the recall of the threat or for an anticipation of the father's return. As a result of his emotionally aroused state, the child may be strongly motivated to engage in prosocial activities, particularly if he has learned that punishment may sometimes be avoided or reduced by behavior of this kind. In fact, the father's return may specifically stimulate the child to display patterns of behavior for which he has previously been rewarded. A similar situation may arise when a child has committed an as yet undetected disapproved or prohibited act and anticipates detection by a parent. Although most parents to a greater or lesser extent reinstate symbolically the disapproved act, under such conditions the prosocial behavior, as well as the symbolized deviation, becomes associated with the punishment (Bandura and Walters, 1963b).

The effectiveness of delayed punishment is probably dependent in part on the completeness with which the deviation is symbolically reinstated. The usual parental statement, "I am going to punish you for X" (or an equally general and terse preamble to punishment), is unlikely to be an adequate means of reinstating the component features of the deviant act especially for younger children. One may suspect that if a parent were able to describe the deviation in detail or to demonstrate the deviant behavior in front of the child before administering the punishment (neither of which he is likely to be able to do), some of the disadvantages of delay might be overcome. Even so, many of the stimulus components, for example, the kinesthetic, tactual, and perceptual feedback experienced by the child when carrying out the deviant act would be absent during the period immediately preceding punishment. Probably, the only completely effective means of counteracting the disadvantages of delay is to force the child to re-enact the deviation before administering the punishment, a course of action that may be neither practical nor beneficial to the parent–child relationship.

A deviant response sequence ordinarily consists of a series of component instrumental acts and a goal response. Punishment that is administered immediately following the goal response is delayed in respect to the instrumental acts; consequently, variations in the timing of punishment within the deviant response sequence may be conceptualized as a special case of delay of reward. Mowrer (1960a,b) has provided a theoretical basis for predicting the effects of timing of punishment. According to Mowrer, each component of a response sequence provides sensory feedback in the form of response-produced kinesthetic and proprioceptive cues. Punishment may be administered at any point during the sequence of responses and result in a relatively direct association of a fear-motivated avoidance response with the response-produced cues occurring at the temporal locus of punishment. If the punishment is administered at the initiation of the deviant response sequence, the maximal degree of fear is attached to the cues produced by the instrumental acts involved in initiating the sequence. In this case, subsequent initiation of the sequence will arouse anxiety that activates incompatible avoidance responses, which are reinforced by anxiety reduction if they are sufficiently strong to forestall the deviant behavior. In contrast, punishment occurring only when a transgression has been completed attaches maximal anxiety to stimuli associated with the goal response or to the immediately subsequent responses and less strong anxiety to stimuli associated with the instrumental acts. Under these circumstances, the deviation is more likely to be initiated on future occasions than when punishment is associated with instrumental acts occurring early in the response sequence. Once an act has been initiated, secondary positive reinforcers associated with the instrumental behavior involved in the commission of the sequence may serve to maintain and facilitate it and thus to some degree to counteract the inhibitory effect of punishment (Walters & Demkow, 1963). Moreover, once a transgression is completed, response inhibition cannot serve to forestall or mitigate punishment (Aronfreed & Reber, 1965). Consequently, response inhibition should be more effectively achieved by punishment that is delivered early in the deviant response sequence than by punishment that is delivered only when the sequence is completed.

Mowrer's account undoubtedly overemphasizes the role of kinesthetic-proprioceptive feedback and that of the emotion of fear, and under-emphasizes the part played by perceptual-cognitive factors that are associated with the functioning of the distance receptors. Visual and auditory cues accompanying the commission of a deviant act can become as closely associated with the experience of punishment as kinesthetic-proprioceptive feedback; since such cues tend to be far more distinct and readily discriminable, they probably play a more important part in the maintenance of behavioral control. This consideration does not, however, vitiate the argument leading to the timing-of-punishment hypothesis.

The only interview study that has investigated the effects of parental delay or timing of punishment brought negative results (Burton, Maccoby, & Allinsmith, 1961). In the interview, mothers of nursery-school children were asked: "Suppose you wanted him to learn not to play with something—like the TV set or matches. If you saw that he was tempted to touch it, would you stop him before he touched it or wait to see if he really played with it and *then* correct him?" (p. 703). Answers to the question were rated on a five-point scale, ranging from stopping the child before he touched the object (rated 1) to permitting him to touch and then telling him not to touch it any more (rated 5). These ratings were related to indices of the child's resistance to temptation in a laboratory cheating situation. Contrary to expectation, children of mothers with low ratings were more resistant to temptation than were children of mothers with ratings that were high. However, as Burton *et al.* point out, the question was probably not sufficiently precise to yield information crucial to the timing-of-punishment hypothesis.

Laboratory studies of delay of punishment beyond the completion of a goal response have all dealt with rather simple instrumental tasks, and the delay intervals have been relatively small. Moreover, very few delay-of-punishment studies have been carried out with human Ss. Walters (1964a) found a delay-of-punishment gradient over intervals of 0, 10, and 30 seconds when children were punished for errors in a lever-pressing task by the presentation of a loud noise combined with the loss of a token. Gradients of punishment for adult Ss were reported in two studies by Banks and Vogel-Sprott for intervals up to 2 minutes. Again, the task involved a lever-pressing response. In the first of their studies, Banks and Vogel-Sprott (1965) demonstrated decreasing efficiency of learning over delay intervals of 0, 30, 60, and 120 seconds. There was a marked drop in efficiency from the 0-second to the 30-second condition, but the decline over the remaining intervals was relatively small. The second study (Vogel-Sprott & Banks,

1965) again yielded a significant loss of efficiency resulting from a 30-second delay interval.

Other relevant studies have been concerned with the relative effectiveness of punishment delivered at the initiation of an act and punishment delivered after a goal response is made. The prototype of this kind of study was carried out by Black, Solomon, and Whiting (cited by Mowrer, 1960b). These investigators found that pups who had been trained to avoid eating horsemeat by tapping them on the nose as they approached the tabooed food showed more "resistance to temptation" when deprived of food and offered no alternative nutriment than did pups who had been punished only after commencing to eat the tabooed food.

Walters and Demkow (1963), using boys and girls as Ss, investigated the effects of early and late punishment on resistance to deviation and reported some support for the hypothesized superiority of early punishment. Children in the early-punishment group were interrupted by a loud, unpleasant buzzer while commencing to reach for a toy, whereas late-punishment Ss were interrupted immediately upon touching a toy. A subsequent testing session, in which the Ss were observed while alone with the forbidden toys, suggested that early punishment had been somewhat more effective than late punishment in producing response inhibition. However, the difference between Ss under the two timing-of-punishment conditions was small and was significant only for boys.

In the first of their studies simultaneously investigating the effects of timing and intensity of punishment on response inhibition, Parke and Walters (1967) used two timing-of-punishment conditions. On the punishment-training trials, half the boys were punished with a combination of a verbal rebuke and a sound just as they reached out to take the more attractive of a pair of toys; the remaining boys were permitted to hold the chosen toy for a brief period before punishment was administered. This study failed to yield significant differences between early-punished and late-punished Ss on the response-inhibition test. Failure to obtain the expected timing-of-punishment effects within the context of a relatively complex experimental design may have been largely due to methodological factors.

In the first place, Ss received punishment only on those trials on which they chose the more attractive toy, and consequently the number of punishments they received was not under experimental control. To remedy this defect, in the second and third studies equally attractive toys were utilized during training, and punishments were administered on trials 1, 3, 4, 6, and 9, no matter which toy the S chose. Only the punished toys were available to the S during the testing session.

Secondly, precise timing of individual punishments was difficult to achieve under the early-punishment condition. Consequently, for the second and third studies equipment was devised to overcome this problem. At the commencement of each trial, Ss were required to place the hand used in choosing the toy on a small wooden platform, located behind a plexiglass barrier. The pressure of the S's hand on the platform closed a microswitch that controlled two red lights on the E's side of the barrier. When the S commenced to make his choice, he released the microswitch, thus lighting up the red lights. Under the early-punishment condition, the E delivered the punishment as soon as the lights signaled that the S's hand was beginning to move. Since the S had to raise his hand over the barrier before making his choice, the apparatus ensured that early-punished Ss were, in fact, punished very early in the course of the approach response. Under these conditions, the expected timing-of-punishment effect was obtained but the intensity effect was considerably attenuated.

The third study, which utilized the same equipment for the control of early timing, yielded a significant interaction effect involving timing and intensity of punishment. High-intensity early punishment produced considerably greater response inhibition than either high-intensity late punishment or low-intensity early punishment; on the other hand, late-punished Ss under the low-intensity condition showed almost as marked response inhibition as the early-punished–low-intensity Ss. A possible explanation of the inhibitory effect of the low-intensity late punishment has already been offered. It might be argued, however, that the low-intensity early punishment should have resulted in a clear association between reaching for a forbidden toy and the verbal rebuke, "No," and therefore should have been as effective as low-intensity late punishment for producing response inhibition. It was, however, apparent to the E and the observers who recorded the data that the early interruption of the child's reaching response was highly disconcerting and seemed to arouse an emotional reaction similar to, if not as strong as, that evoked by the high-intensity noise. The inhibitory effect of punishment under this condition, as well as under the high-intensity conditions, may thus be largely attributable to emotional factors, whereas the inhibitory effect of the low-intensity–late-punishment procedure may be attributable, for the most part, to cognitive factors.

The foregoing interpretation assumes that two sets of factors can play an important role in the acquisition and maintenance of self-control. While fear of punishment has undoubtedly an important deterrent effect, *anticipation* of punishment, with little accompanying fear, may on many occasions guarantee social compliance (Walters, 1966). In other words, behavior that is interpretable as resistance to deviation may be instigated by a contemporary set of stimulus components, some of which are emotional ("fear," "anticipatory guilt") and others that are cognitive. Perhaps the stimulus complex always includes some components of both kinds; nevertheless, the influence of cognitive cues may often predominate. The role of cognitive factors is further discussed in a subsequent section on the inhibitory role of reasoning.[3]

C. FREQUENCY

Field studies have yielded no precise data concerning the influence of the frequency of physical punishment on children's social behavior. On account of the kind of measures they employ, these studies have failed to disentangle the effects of frequency, intensity, and consistency, and the findings that have relevance were presented in the discussion of intensity.

The frequency of physical punishment has not as yet been systematically varied in any laboratory study with children. A *post-hoc* analysis of data secured by Parke and Walters (1967) in an extension of the first of the three studies already described suggested, however, that its influence should not be overlooked. After completion of the study as planned, Parke and Walters tested the remainder of the children in the school grades from which the original sample had been drawn until all available children had been employed as *S*s. Children under each of the experimental conditions were then divided into two groups, those receiving less than four punishments and those receiving four or more punishments. An analysis of variance of the data yielded no significant main effect for the frequency variable; on the other hand, there were several significant interaction effects, involving frequency, intensity, timing, and the agent–recipient relationship.

[3]Compelling evidence concerning the efficacy of cognitive structuring for inducing response inhibition was secured by Cheyne and Walters (1967). Grade 1 boys were assigned to one of four punishment-training conditions involving variations of intensity and timing of punishment similar to those employed by Parke and Walters (1967), except that the high-intensity and low-intensity noises were unaccompanied by a verbal rebuke. Other Grade 1 boys were assigned to a high-cognitive-structure condition under which punishment consisted of both a low-intensity noise and a verbal rebuke that were presented either early or late in the deviant response sequence. In addition, the low-cognitive-structure and high-cognitive-structure procedures differed in respect to the initial instructions given to the subjects; subjects under the latter condition were provided with reasons why they should not deviate while those under the former conditions were not. The provision of high cognitive structure was very effective for inducing response inhibition. Under the low-cognitive-structure condition, both the intensity and timing variables yielded the expected effects, but the effect of timing was essentially reversed when cognitive structure was high. The two least deviant groups of subjects were those who received high-intensity punishment early under the low-cognitive structure condition and those who received low-intensity punishment late under the high cognitive-structure condition. Telemetered heart-rate data suggested that inhibition among the former subjects was primarily maintained by emotional responses to punishment; in contrast, the latter group of subjects displayed little emotional responsiveness. The data thus indicate that self-control may be maintained through emotional responses to anticipated punishment ("fear") or through a clear understanding that a prohibition should not be violated; in the latter case, one may speak of cognitive, as opposed to emotional, control.

These interactions, although not readily interpretable, indicate the necessity of controlling for frequency of punishment whenever this variable is not itself under investigation.

D. NATURE OF THE RELATIONSHIP BETWEEN THE AGENT AND THE RECIPIENT OF PUNISHMENT

Bandura and Walters (1963b, p. 189) have argued that any disciplinary act may involve, in varying degrees, at least two operations, the presentation of a negative reinforcer and the withdrawal of positive reinforcement. If physical punishment achieves its effect partly because it signifies withdrawal of approval, acceptance, or affection, it should be a more effective means of controlling behavior when there is a close affectional tie between the agent and recipient of punishment than when the relationship between agent and recipient is relatively impersonal.

Sears *et al.* (1957) provided some evidence in favor of this proposition. Mothers who were rated as warm and affectionate and made relatively frequent use of physical punishment were likely to say that they found spanking to be an effective means of discipline. In contrast, cold, hostile mothers who made equally frequent use of physical punishment were more likely to report that spanking was ineffective. Moreover, according to mothers, spanking was more likely to be effective if it was administered by the warmer of the two parents. In contrast, data from a questionnaire study by LeVine (1961) suggested that the use of physical punishment by warm, affectionate mothers was less effective as a means of producing resistance to deviation in girls than its use by mothers who were cold.

Parke and Walters (1967) varied the nature of the relationship between the agent and recipient of punishment in interaction periods before punishment was administered. Forty boys experienced two 10-minute periods of positive interaction with the *E* on two successive days. Attractive constructional materials were provided for the *S*s, and as they played with them, the *E* provided encouragement and help and warmly expressed approval of their efforts. A second group of forty boys played, in two 10-minute sessions, with relatively unattractive materials while the *E* sat in the room without interacting with the children. An equal number of *S*s from each interaction condition was assigned to one of four punishment conditions, involving two levels of intensity and two levels of timing. Regardless of punishment conditions, children who had experienced positive interaction with the agent of punishment showed significantly greater resistance to deviation than *S*s who had had only impersonal contact.

The study by Parke and Walters represents the only attempt to demonstrate in a controlled laboratory situation the influence of the relationship between the agent and recipient of punishment on the effectiveness of punishment for producing response inhibition in children. However, evidence consistent with this finding was obtained by Freedman (1958), who reported that pups who had received "indulgence" training were more likely to refrain from executing a punished act in the absence of the experimenter than were pups who had been reared under conditions of severe discipline.

The few available findings thus support the hypothesis (Bandura & Walters, 1963b) that the inhibitory effect of physical punishment may be often primarily due to its capacity for serving as a dramatic signal of the displeasure of the agent, particularly if the agent has previously been a source of rewarding experiences, and only secondarily, if at all, to its pain-producing quality.

III. Verbal Punishment

Child-training practices involving verbal punishment were divided into scolding-nagging and ridicule by Bandura and Walters (1959), who found that fathers of aggressive boys were more likely to use nagging and scolding in disciplining their children than were fathers of nonaggressive boys. According to the boys' reports, these fathers were also more likely to make relatively frequent use of ridicule. Similar results were obtained in Bandura's study of aggressive and nonaggressive preadolescent boys. This study also yielded a parallel difference between mothers in respect to verbal punishment, excluding ridicule. That aggressive boys tend to be more verbally aggressive toward both adults and peers suggests that the parents of these boys were serving as aggressive models (Bandura, 1960; Bandura & Walters, 1959).

The word "wrong" has been employed as a punishing stimulus in a large number of experimental studies involving traditional learning tasks, for example, in many tests of Thorndike's (1932, 1935) later theories concerning the role of punishment in learning. There is some indication that "wrong" may have both informational and drive properties and thus facilitate learning (Brackbill & O'Hara, 1958; Meyer & Offenbach, 1962; Meyer & Seidman, 1960, 1961). Generally speaking, however, the studies in question have little bearing on the role of punishment as a disciplinary technique and will not be further discussed.

A study by Patterson (1965) of changes in children's choice behavior provides an exception to the preceding statement. Mothers and fathers of grade school children were required to punish their children with mild verbal rebukes for making the "wrong" response in a two-choice situation; the alternative response was left unrewarded. This procedure was more effective for changing the Ss' preferences than a combination of reward and nonreward used in previous studies by Patterson and his co-workers

(Patterson & Anderson, 1964; Patterson, Littman, & Hinsey, 1964).

There have been very few laboratory studies of the effect of verbal disapproval on the social behavior of children. Hollenberg and Sperry (1951) gave four sessions of doll play to two groups of nursery-school children. For control-group children, the E took a permissive role, customary in doll-play situations, and a steady increase in the Ss' aggressive responses, presumably attributable to weakening of inhibitions, was recorded. Children in the experimental group were rebuked for aggressive behavior in the second of the four sessions; the aggressive responses of these Ss were no more frequent in the second than in the first session and decreased in frequency in the third session. The inhibitory effect of punishment was, however, short-lived, since by the fourth session the difference between the experimental and control groups had largely disappeared.

In a training session, Nelsen (1960) approved the dependency behavior of one group of children and mildly rebuked children in a second group for dependency responses. In a subsequent social-interaction situation, the verbally punished Ss showed significantly less dependency behavior than the Ss whose dependency responses had met with approval.

A close parallel to disciplinary tactics that parents employ in everyday life is provided by experimental operations in which verbal rebuke precedes the withdrawal of a positive reinforcer or serves to deny a child access to an attractive object (*e.g.*, Robinson & Robinson, 1961; Setterington & Walters, 1964). Some studies of this type, in which an analogue of physical punishment was also included, were described in the previous section. The remainder of the present section will concentrate on studies that have investigated the effects of varying the severity and timing of verbal disapproval and rebuke.

A. Severity

Aronfreed and Leff (1963), in addition to utilizing two levels of noise, varied the loudness with which a verbal rebuke was administered. Under the low-intensity condition a relatively low sound was combined with a soft "No"; under the high-intensity condition a stern "No" accompanied a loud sound. Thus, the findings of Aronfreed and Leff may be as much due to the variation of the severity of verbal punishment as the variation in the loudness of the sound.

The remaining relevant studies have been conducted within the framework of dissonance theory (Festinger, 1957) and have manipulated the severity of threat. Aronson and Carlsmith (1963) had kindergarten children evaluate the attractiveness of several toys, using a paired-comparison procedure. The Ss were left alone with the toys for a 10-minute period after being threatened with punishment for playing with one of the most attractive of the toys. Each S was tested twice, once under a mild-threat and once under a severe-threat condition. The mild threat resulted in the greater devaluation of the toy when the test for attractiveness was re-administered after the period during which the S was alone with the toys. Similar findings were reported by Turner and Wright (1965).

Freedman (1965) prohibited children from playing with a highly attractive toy, using either a high or a low threat of punishment. Children who resisted playing with the toy were tested again after several weeks and were given an opportunity to play with the toy after the prohibition had been removed. Children who resisted temptation under mild threat were less likely to play with the toy during the second session than were Ss who had experienced the severe threat.

The results of these studies of severity of threat are difficult to interpret since, in addition to the severity, the content of the threat was varied. For example, Aronson and Carlsmith, under the severe-threat condition, threatened the Ss with both withdrawal of the attractive toys and ridicule. Under the mild-threat condition, the S was merely told that the E would be annoyed. Thus the mild-severe conditions that were utilized do not fall on a straightforward quantitative continuum. Moreover, only the data for Ss who resisted deviation during the period that they were alone with the toys were used in the analyses (Freedman, 1965). Nevertheless, these studies indicate that mild threat is more likely than severe threat to result in devaluation of an attractive, but forbidden, object [an outcome that should strengthen resistance to deviation (Bandura & Walters, 1963b)] and in long-term respect for a prohibition. Thus, the data seemingly contradict those obtained in studies in which punishment is actually administered.

This discrepancy may be attributed to the part played by cognitive factors in the maintenance of self-control. If a child is strongly attracted to a goal object that he cannot readily attain by socially acceptable means and has already learned to guide his behavior by the *general rule* that he should not violate prohibitions set by adults, he may devaluate the goal object as a means of maintaining self-control. On the other hand, if the punishment anticipated for the violation is sufficiently severe to produce fear-motivated inhibition, a change in his values is unlikely to occur (Bandura & Walters, 1963b). If, at a later time, threat of punishment is removed, a cue is provided that the formerly disapproved activity is now permissible and that untoward consequences to the agent are unlikely to ensue. Under these circumstances, a child's behavior should be guided by the extent to which he *now* evaluates the formerly prohibited activity. Consequently, a child who has previously devaluated a goal object in order to facilitate his observance of a prohibition should be less likely to display the formerly prohibited behavior than one who still places a high value on the goal object.

B. TIMING

Aronfreed and Reber (1965), in the first of the timing-of-punishment studies carried out under Aronfreed's direction, used a verbal rebuke without an accompanying noise as the punishing stimulus. Boys in one training condition were punished as soon as they commenced to reach out for an attractive toy; boys in the other condition were permitted to pick up an attractive toy and hold it for a brief period before punishment was administered. In the subsequent testing period, the Ss were left alone with an additional pair of toys. After a few minutes, the E returned and noted whether or not the attractive toy had been handled in his absence. The early-punished Ss deviated less frequently than the late-punished Ss, whose behavior in the testing situation differed little from that of a nonpunished control group.

Aronfreed (1965) has recently reported a series of parametric extensions of the basic study. After ten training trials involving punishment for choice of an attractive toy, the S was taken to another table and left alone for a 10-minute period with a highly attractive and a very unattractive toy. The latency of the S's response to the attractive toy was recorded by means of a microswitch. Four temporal positions of punishment were investigated. Under one condition, the S was punished as soon as he reached for an attractive toy; under a second condition, he was permitted to pick up the attractive toy and was punished at the apex of the lifting movement; under the third condition, the E counted 6 seconds after apex before administering punishment; under the fourth condition, 6 seconds following lift to apex were allowed to elapse, the S was then asked to describe the toy, and punishment was administered only after the description was given. The latency of deviation steadily decreased as the time between the initiation of the punished act and the administration of punishment increased; in fact, highly reliable differences between each of the adjacent points on the timing-of-punishment continuum were secured. Aronfreed reported that timing-of-punishment effects held for both boys and girls with both male and female experimenters.

Walters, Parke, and Cane (1965), using the punishment-training procedure of Aronfreed and Reber, investigated simultaneously the effects of timing of punishment and of the observation of consequences of responses of a film-mediated deviant model on the resistance to deviation of 6- to 7-year-old boys. Following one of two conditions of training involving early and late punishment, the Ss were either shown films depicting a boy who played with prohibited toys with varying consequences to himself or were assigned to a no-film condition. The combined data for all film conditions indicated that early-punished Ss deviated less quickly, less often, and for shorter periods of time than late-punished Ss; moreover, differences between early-punished and late-punished Ss were also apparent under the no-film control condition.

In the studies by Parke and Walters (1967), a sound of varying loudness was used as the major punishing stimulus. Since, however, the experimenter said "No" as he activated the sound generator, the timing of a verbal punishment was also manipulated. These studies, reviewed in the previous section, did not yield as consistent timing effects as the timing-of-punishment studies in which only a verbal punishment was employed.

The partial discrepancy between the findings from the two sets of studies may be due to minor variations in experimental procedures, particularly in the choice of the points of the punished response sequence at which punishment was administered. Parke and Walters attempted, over their three studies, to deliver the early punishment at an increasingly early point in the deviant response sequence. In the third study, it is possible that the early delivery of an intense punishment had a generalized inhibitory effect on the child's behavior, including the response that was punished, whereas the early delivery of a milder punishment, while somewhat disturbing, neither produced strong generalized inhibition nor clearly indicated to the child what he should not do. Although no exact data bearing on this question are available, it may be tentatively suggested that a punishment that is not sufficiently aversive to have a generalized inhibitory effect is ineffective for producing response inhibition unless the response for which it is delivered is far enough advanced for the recipient to recognize the precise nature of the act for which he is receiving punishment.

IV. Withholding and Withdrawal of Rewards

A. DEPRIVATION OF MATERIAL REWARDS

In contrast to physical punishment, deprivation of material rewards, such as treasured possessions and privileges, primarily involves the operation of withdrawing positive reinforcers. Its nearest analogues in experimental studies with children are studies of punishment in which candies, coins, or toys are taken away for wrong responses, and studies of frustration in which rewards previously dispensed for a response are withdrawn. Since deprivation of privileges sometimes involves thwarting or blocking an activity, as when a child is kept at home and thus prevented from playing with other children, the outcomes of frustration studies in which an activity is blocked or prevented may also throw some light on the probable effects of deprivation as a disciplinary technique.

The available evidence suggests that withholding and withdrawal of privileges, like the presentation of a noxious stimulus, have a variety of effects, depending on such factors as the relationship between the agent and recipient of punishment, the completeness with which a privilege is withdrawn, the timing of withholding or withdrawal, and perhaps most of all on whether or not dispensing or reinstatement is explicitly made contingent on the child's conforming to parental demands. Unfortunately, there have been very few studies in which these variables have been deliberately manipulated.

Data from field studies suggest that frequent use of deprivation of privileges by parents is associated with aggression in children. Bandura and Walters (1959) found that parents of aggressive boys made considerably more use of deprivation of privileges than did parents of nonaggressive boys; moreover, frequent use of this disciplinary technique was associated with a rejecting, punitive attitude on the part of the parent and with the use of physical punishment as a preferred disciplinary technique. In a subsequent study, Bandura (1960) reported that parents of aggressive boys made greater use of deprivation of privileges than did parents of inhibited boys. These findings do not necessarily indicate a simple cause–effect relationship between the parental disciplinary technique and the children's aggression. In fact, the parents of the aggressive boys frequently used deprivation in attempts to control their son's aggressive, defiant behavior. Nevertheless, there are grounds for believing that, under some conditions, deprivation of rewarding experiences can be an antecedent of aggression.

Laboratory studies (e.g., Haner & Brown, 1955; Holton, 1961; Longstreth, 1960; Olds, 1953; Penney, 1960; Screven, 1954) provide evidence that deprivation or withholding of material rewards can elicit effortful, vigorous responses from children and that the greater the frustration, the more vigorous will be the response. Since, according to the high-magnitude theory of aggression (Bandura & Walters, 1963b; Walters, 1964b; Walters & Brown, 1964), vigorous responses are more likely than weaker responses to be classified as aggressive, the outcomes of these studies are consistent with findings from field studies that report a relationship between parental deprivation of material rewards and childhood aggression.

Moreover, while responses to frustration depend on the prior social-learning experiences of the person who is frustrated (Bandura, 1962b; Bandura & Walters, 1963a,b; Davitz, 1952; Walters & Brown, 1963), deprivations may often serve as necessary, though not sufficient, conditions for the eliciting of antisocial patterns of behavior. Thus, the use of deprivation by parents of boys who have already developed aggressive orientations is likely to evoke further aggressive responses.

The study by Haner and Brown (1955) indicated that the vigor of response to frustration is greater if the frustrated agent is near to the goal than if the goal is more distant. Moreover, Holton (1961) and Penney (1960) both demonstrated that an increase in vigor will not occur unless the frustrated response is well established. These findings suggest that reactions of an intense nature are most likely to occur if deprivations take the form of interrupting a pleasurable activity that is already in progress or denying a privilege that has been granted on many previous occasions.

In some laboratory studies of frustration, children have been deprived, by a single action of the E, of a pleasurable object or activity. Davitz (1952) and Walters and Brown (1963) interrupted children's viewing of a movie sequence as it was about to reach its climax and at the same time took away candy that had earlier been given to the children. Davitz reported that responses to frustration were a function of prior training; boys who had been trained to give cooperative responses in interactions with one another responded cooperatively following frustration, whereas Ss previously trained to give aggressive responses in physical-contact games responded in an aggressive manner, Walters and Brown found no differences between frustrated and nonfrustrated boys in the extent to which they subsequently expressed aggression in physical-contact games; both the frustrated and nonfrustrated Ss were similarly influenced by prior aggression training. Analogously, Zipse (1965) exposed children to either an aggressive film model or a neutral film and then deprived half the Ss under each film condition of a promised candy. Deprivation had no effect on the amount of aggression shown by the children in a subsequent free-play situation; in contrast, exposure to an aggressive model produced a marked rise in free-play aggression.

In other studies, attractive objects have been removed over a series of trials. For example, Weingold and Webster (1964) trained pairs of children to make a cooperative sequence of lever-pushing responses. Following the acquisition period, in which candies were used as reinforcers, under a nonreward condition one member of each pair ceased to be rewarded for the cooperative response, while under a withdrawal-of-reward condition one member of each pair lost candies. The candies were not actually dispensed or removed, but the number of candies lost or won was registered on counters; thus, the procedure was analogous to that used in experiments in which tokens, subsequently exchangeable for toys, are employed as positive reinforcers. Weingold and Webster found that withdrawal significantly decreased the response-sequence rate for pairs of Ss, but that simple nonreward did not lower this rate over a 15-minute period.

Baer (1961, 1962b) trained children to press a bar for peanuts. On a subsequent session, the Ss watched a sequence of movie cartoons as they sat beside the bar. For Ss under a withdrawal-of-reward condition, the movie sequence was interrupted each time they pressed the bar. In comparison to simple nonreward, interruption of the movie depressed the rate of bar pressing and lowered the number of responses to extinction. In further

sessions, in which no peanuts were given, nonrewarded Ss showed considerable spontaneous recovery of the bar-pressing response, whereas the
responses of the punished Ss were completely suppressed. Baer (1960)
also demonstrated the development of escape and avoidance responses in
children, using the movie-interruption technique. In addition, this technique
was used to control thumb-sucking in a 5-year-old boy (Baer, 1962a);
contingent withdrawal and reinstatement of movie viewing considerably
weakened the thumb-sucking response, but noncontingent withdrawal
and re-presentation did not appreciably affect thumb-sucking behavior.

Birnbrauer, Wolf, Kidder, and Tague (1965) investigated the effects of
withdrawal and reinstatement of rewards on the performance of retarded
children in a programmed instruction class. The children had been accus-
tomed to receive both verbal approval and check marks for correct responses, with the check marks serving as tokens that were later exchangeable
for toys. During the experimental period, the tokens were withheld for
at least 21 days and then reinstated, and records were kept of the number
of items completed by each S, the percentage of errors made, and the
occurrence of disruptive behavior. There were marked individual differences among the children in response to the experimental procedure.
Ten pupils showed a decline in performance, while the performance of
the remaining five Ss remained unchanged. Four of the ten pupils whose
performance declined also showed an increase in disruptive behavior
while tokens were withheld. When the tokens were reinstated, the ten
adversely affected Ss returned to their initial levels of performance. The
data presented by Birnbrauer et al. are especially valuable because they
were secured in the context of a real-life social situation.

One source of individual differences among children in response to
withdrawal of reward may be the varying nature of the relationship between
the agent and recipient of punishment. However, the only direct evidence
that is available does not support this hypothesis. Aronfreed, Cutlick, and
Fagen (1963) assigned grade-school boys to four experimental conditions,
involving two levels of nurturance and two levels of cognitive structure,
a variable that is probably a facet of reasoning (Bandura & Walters, 1963b).
All Ss were punished for an act of aggression by the loss of Tootsie Rolls on
each of a series of ten trials. On an ensuing test trial designed to elicit self-
critical responses, the E made it appear that the S had committed the
destructive act of breaking a toy. During the training trials, the E maintained
a warm, nurturant attitude toward half the Ss; with the remaining Ss, his
attitude was formal and aloof. Aronfreed et al. reported that children under
the two nurturance conditions did not differ in the extent to which they
gave self-critical responses. A parallel finding was secured in a subsequent
investigation of conditions under which self-critical responses are learned
(Aronfreed, 1964).

These negative findings may be due to an inadequate nurturance manipulation since the experimenter–child interactions were confined to a single brief training period (Bandura & Walters, 1963b). In studies involving more extended experimenter–child interactions (Bandura & Huston, 1961; Mischel & Grusec, 1966; Parke & Walters, 1967), children who experienced prior nurturance from the experimenter showed more imitation of experimenter responses, more frequent self-critical reactions, and greater resistance to deviation than children with whom the experimenter interacted in an impersonal manner.

B. WITHDRAWAL OF LOVE

In the first part of this section, parental practices involving the withdrawal or withholding of material rewards and their laboratory analogues were described and discussed. In real-life situations the efficacy of these practices is undoubtedly due, at least in part, to the child's perception of the loss of material rewards as symbolizing the loss, or threat of loss, of parental love and affection.

Sears et al. (1957) list a variety of forms that withdrawal or withholding of love may take; these include refusing attention, accusing the child of hurting the parents' feelings, shutting him off from contact with the family (isolation), and other devices to indicate that the parent's affection is conditional on the child's conforming to parental demands. Laboratory analogues of such forms of discipline include withholding or withdrawal of affectional interaction and brief isolation.

Under the influence of the Freudian theory of anaclitic identification (Freud, 1925), many developmental psychologists have assumed that anxiety about possible loss of parental love is the major contributing factor to the child's adoption and "internalization" of parental values and standards. As a consequence, a distinction has been made between love-oriented and nonlove-oriented disciplinary techniques (e.g., Whiting, 1954; Whiting & Child, 1953), with parental threat of loss of love serving as the prototype of love-oriented techniques. It has been assumed that this technique, above all others, is related to the development of guilt for failure to meet parental standards of conduct. Data from field studies do not, however, consistently support this assumption.

Sears et al. (1957) found that mothers' use of love-oriented techniques of discipline was positively related to indices of conscience development in children, provided that the mothers were warm and affectionate toward their children so that the children had something to lose. Aronfreed (1961), on the basis of interview data, classified mothers according to their preferred disciplinary practices. The children of mothers who used "induction" techniques, which included withdrawal of love and reasoning, gave more "internalized responses to transgression" to a projective story-completion test than did children who predominantly used nonlove-oriented techniques. In contrast, Hoffman and Salzstein (1960) failed to find consistent evidence that parental withdrawal of love was related to the incidence of guilt responses given by children to projective tests.

In their comparisons of child-training practices of aggressive and non-aggressive boys, Bandura and Walters (Bandura, 1960; Bandura & Walters, 1959) found no difference between parents of relatively guilt-free aggressive boys and parents of relatively high-guilt nonaggressive boys in respect to the use of withdrawal of love as a disciplinary technique. Moreover, correlational data from the first of these studies indicated that parents who made relatively frequent use of withdrawal of love tended to have children who were hostile to their parents and openly aggressive to their teachers and peers.

In a laboratory study explicitly designed to test the hypothesis that the withdrawal of affectional demonstrativeness motivates children to acquire responses that elicit adult approval, Hartup (1958) compared the performance of two groups of children on simple cognitive tasks, using adult approval as the reinforcer. A female E interacted continuously for a 10-minute period with one group of Ss, who were affectionately encouraged, supported, and rewarded as they played with toys. The second group of Ss was treated in a similar manner for 5 minutes, then demonstrations of affection were withdrawn for the remaining 5 minutes of play. Girls and highly dependent boys under the withdrawal-of-nurturance condition performed more efficiently on the cognitive tasks than did girls and highly dependent boys under the continuous nurturance condition, but results in the opposite direction were obtained for low-dependent boys. Complex cross-sex effects have been found in other nurturance-withdrawal experiments in which the sex of the E and the sex of the S have been varied (Burton, Allinsmith, & Maccoby, 1966; Rosenblith, 1959, 1961). It appears that, under some conditions, nurturance-withdrawal stimulates achievement-oriented behavior likely to elicit approval, but that the increased motivation may lead to the breaking of prohibitions when deviation facilitates achievement (Burton et al., 1961, 1966). The available data do not permit a convincing theoretical interpretation of the cross-sex effects.[4]

In somewhat related studies, the behavior of children following a period of reduced social contact was compared with that of children who had interacted for a comparable period with an adult or with peers. Gewirtz

[4]Parke (1967) has recently presented additional evidence concerning the effects of nurturance and nurturance withdrawal on resistance to deviation in children. Boys and girls experienced either continuous nurturance or nurturance followed by nurturance withdrawal before being placed in a resistance-to-deviation test similar to that used by Walters, Parke,

(1954) reported more seeking of attention among children for whom adult contact was minimal during an easel-painting task than among children for whom adult contact was readily available. Gewirtz and Baer (1958a, b) found that a brief period of isolation from adult contact increased children's responsiveness to adult social reinforcement; on the other hand, Hartup and Himeno (1959) reported that preschool children who had been isolated were subsequently more aggressive in a doll-play situation than were children who had experienced adult contact. Walters and Karal (1960) argued that for young children isolation was probably an emotionally arousing experience that led to more intense responding, but that the behavior subsequently exhibited depended on the nature of the stimulus conditions and the relative strength of the component responses in the habit hierarchies associated with these conditions. This hypothesis seemed capable of reconciling the findings of Hartup and Himeno with those of Gewirtz and Baer since aggressive responses are likely to predominate in preschool children's doll play (Levin & Wardwell, 1962) but are unlikely to occur in a two-choice discrimination task.

In a study designed to test the arousal hypothesis, Walters and Ray utilized a condition that may be regarded as a close analogue to real-life punitive isolation. Following this condition, which was calculated to make isolated children fearful of the experimental procedures, the susceptibility to social influence of the "isolated-anxious" children was reflected in very rapid discrimination learning when the E's approval was used as the reinforcer. Subsequent studies by Lewis, Walters, and their associates (Dorwart, Ezerman, Lewis, & Rosenhan, 1965; Lewis, 1965; Lewis & Richman, 1964; Walters, Marshall & Shooter, 1960; Walters & Parke, 1964c) also suggest that isolation experienced in an unpleasant, threatening social context makes children more susceptible to adult social influence.

In the preceding discussion of withdrawal of material rewards, it was noted that this procedure eventually leads to a decrease in the incidence of the responses for which reward has been withdrawn. A similar decrease occurs when nonmaterial rewards, such as attention, are withdrawn or withheld over a series of trials. The studies in question differ from the withdrawal-of-nurturance and isolation studies in that they employ a straightforward extinction procedure. Although a temporary increase in the frequency or strength of the nonrewarded responses may occur when reinforcement is initially discontinued, these responses gradually decrease in strength if attention is systematically withheld.

and Cane (1965). It was made explicit through instructions that reinstatement of attention was contingent on S's conforming to E's prohibition. Children in the withdrawal condition deviated less frequently than children in the continuous nurturance group. The nurturance-withdrawal operation affected girls more than boys and children paired with a same-sexed E rather than opposite-sexed E.

The effects of contingent withdrawal of attention is evident in a study by Brackbill (1958), who first established smiling responses in infants by means of demonstrations of interest and affection. After smiling responses were well established, Brackbill withdrew the positive reinforcers by remaining totally unresponsive when the infants smiled. This extinction period was characterized not only by a decline in the incidence of smiling responses but also by the occurrence of infant "protest" behavior, such as increased crying and restlessness and attempts to avoid looking at the experimenter. This study, as well as Baer's (1960, 1961, 1962a, b) studies of the effects of withdrawal of material rewards, indicates that in some circumstances withdrawal of reward may have similar behavioral effects to the presentation of physical or verbal punishment. Further evidence of these effects are provided in a number of demonstrations of behavior therapy with children (e.g., Ayllon & Michael, 1959; Lövaas, Freitag, Gold, & Kassorla, 1965a; Williams, 1959).

It is evident from Brackbill's study and from others reviewed in this section that withdrawal of previously dispensed rewards may sometimes have an aversive effect while at other times it appears to lead to increased striving to obtain the reward that has been withdrawn. Thus, while under some circumstances aversive stimulation and withdrawal or withholding of positive reinforcers may have very different effects (Bandura & Walters, 1963b), under other circumstances their effects are apparently similar. Unfortunately, the differentiating characteristics of these sets of circumstances have not yet been clearly identified. This problem has very recently been noted, though in a more restricted context, by Leitenberg (1965).

The effectiveness of an extinction procedure can be considerably enhanced if a response incompatible with the nonrewarded response is concurrently rewarded. In fact, Brown and Elliott (1965) have successfully utilized a combination of nonreward of aggression and reinforcement of responses incompatible with aggression for reducing the rate of emission of aggressive responses in nursery-school children. A similar combination of procedures has been successfully employed by behavior therapists for modifying various classes of behavior of both adults and children (Bandura, 1961; Eysenck, 1960; Krasner & Ullmann, 1965; Ullmann & Krasner, 1965).

At this point in the continuum of procedures ranging from simple nonreward to the confiscation of valued possessions, the operations may no longer by considered as punitive. This is true also of the various techniques that have been classified as instances of reasoning. Since, however, reasoning is frequently used, both alone and in combination with punitive techniques of discipline, to inhibit socially undesirable behavior, its inhibitory role is discussed in the next section of the paper.

V. The Inhibitory Role of Reasoning

Various parental disciplinary maneuvers have been regarded as cases of reasoning. These include descriptions of untoward consequences that the child's behavior may have for others, the provision of examples of socially acceptable behavior that are incompatible with undesirable responses, explicit instructions on how to behave in specific situations, and explanations of motives for placing restraints on a child's behavior (Bandura & Walters, 1963b, p. 195).

Field studies have consistently yielded positive relationships between parental use of reasoning as a preferred technique of discipline and non-aggressive, conforming behavior among children. Sears *et al.* (1957) reported a positive correlation between maternal use of reasoning and the development of conscience in children. Bandura and Walters (1959) found that parents of nonaggressive boys made considerably more use of reasoning than parents of antisocial aggressive boys; moreover, within both their samples parental use of reasoning was consistently correlated with the extent to which the boys displayed guilt about aggression. Similarly, Glueck and Glueck (1950) found that parents of delinquent boys made relatively little use of reasoning in comparison to parents of nondelinquent boys. There was some indication in Bandura's field study (1960) that parents of aggressive boys were less likely to favor reasoning as a means of discipline than were parents of inhibited boys. Finally, use of reasoning was one of a number of "induction techniques" that Aronfreed (1961) found to be related to the development of guilt.

In contrast to the findings just presented, Burton *et al.* (1961) reported that children whose mothers made frequent use of reasoning tended to have children whose resistance to cheating was low. However, there is evidence that parental use of reasoning is positively related to the level of children's achievement standards (V. J. Crandall, 1963); since the testing situation used by Burton *et al.* was one in which children with high-achievement standards might be strongly tempted to cheat, their finding may not be as contradictory as it first seems. Both achievement and moral behavior involve the regulation of actions by a rule or standard, violation of which can lead to the emotional reaction that is commonly identified as guilt. The conflict produced by many cheating situations is therefore accompanied for children with high-achievement standards by anticipated alternative outcomes, each of which is associated with anticipation of guilt. This dilemma is not present in situations that permit an anticipated outcome that is not associated with prior guilt experiences.

A variety of laboratory studies have a bearing on the efficacy of reasoning as an inhibitory technique. These studies have involved variations in the extent to which children are provided with reasons for not deviating or with cues that serve to inform them of the probable nature of consequences of deviant acts.

A. PROVISION OF VERBAL INSTRUCTIONS

Aronfreed *et al.* (1963) employed two conditions of "cognitive structure" in a study of the learning of self-critical responses. One group of children was given explicit instructions to be careful and gentle during punishment-training trials, which have previously been described. These Ss gave a greater number of self-critical responses on the test trial, in which they appeared to have behaved in a destructive manner, than did Ss for whom the clarifying instructions were omitted. Similar results were obtained in a subsequent study (Aronfreed, 1963).

Aronfreed (1965) also demonstrated the effectiveness of reasoning, especially when combined with withdrawal of reward, for producing resistance to deviation in a transgression situation similar to that used in the timing-of-punishment study conducted by Aronfreed and Reber (1965). Children under a late-punishment condition were told that their behavior was age inappropriate after they had picked up a prohibited toy and were immediately afterwards punished by the withdrawal of a Tootsie Roll. Other Ss, under the same late-punishment condition, were provided with the same reason for not deviating 10–12 seconds after the Tootsie Roll had been withdrawn. Both groups showed more resistance to deviation than children who had experienced similarly timed punishment but who were not notified that their behavior was age-inappropriate. Reasoning immediately associated with the withdrawal of candy was more effective for inhibiting transgression responses than was reasoning supplied after the candy had been withdrawn.

Moreover, in further extensions of this study, the experimenter informed some Ss, at the same time as they were deprived of a Tootsie Roll, that they should not have *wanted* to *pick up* the prohibited toy; other Ss were told that they should not have *wanted* to *tell* about the toy, an act that had not yet occurred; while a third group of Ss was permitted to tell about the toy and were then punished. Focusing on intentions further increased the children's resistance to deviation provided that the verbal representation of the intention preceded the execution of the act to which this representation referred. Thus, the effectiveness of reasoning procedures for producing response inhibition was a function of both the procedures' content and their timing.

Aronfreed argues that both punishment and anxiety must be closely associated with verbal mediators if the latter are to be an effective means of producing response inhibition. Similarly, he argues elsewhere (Aronfreed, 1964) that the acquisition of self-critical responses is highly dependent on the association of these responses with anxiety reduction. Although

Aronfreed's interpretations of his experimental findings may be questioned, his studies leave no doubt of the importance of verbal mediation in the socialization process.

B. PROVISION OF SOCIAL MODELS

In reasoning with children, parents frequently provide them with examples of how they should or should not behave by referring to the actions of family members, acquaintances, friends, historical figures, and the fictitious characters of storybooks, movies, and TV shows and expressing approval or disapproval or citing the favorable or adverse consequences of the model's behavior. Laboratory studies in which children are shown a model punished for socially disapproved behavior have indicated that observation of adverse consequences to the model reduces the probability of the observer's exhibiting the deviant behavior.

Bandura, Ross, and Ross (1963) exposed nursery-school children to films that depicted an adult model employing considerable physical and verbal aggression in order to amass the possessions of another adult. Under a model-rewarded condition, the aggressor successfully appropriated these possessions and rewarded himself for doing so; under a model-punished condition, the aggressor received severe punishment for his behavior. Two control conditions were included. In one of these conditions, Ss were not exposed to models; Ss in the second control group saw the two adult models engaged in vigorous but nonaggressive play. In a subsequent testing situation, Ss in the model-punished condition exhibited significantly less aggression than did Ss who saw the aggressive model rewarded and did not differ significantly from control Ss who had not been provided with an aggressive model. In a subsequent study, Bandura (1965) utilized three film sequences in a further study of the influence of consequences to a model on children's aggressive behavior. The major portion of the film, which depicted an adult model's behaving in an aggressive manner toward an inflated rubber doll, was shown to all three groups. For two of three groups of children, consequences to the aggressor were depicted. Children who saw the model punished for aggression showed less aggressive behavior in a subsequent testing situation than did Ss who saw the model rewarded or neither rewarded nor punished.

In three studies, Walters and his associates (Walters, Leat, & Mezei, 1963; Walters & Parke, 1964b; Walters, Parke, & Cane, 1965) investigated the influence of observed consequences to a child model who broke a prohibition on the subsequent resistance to deviation of child observers. The results of these studies are consistent with those reported by Bandura and his collaborators. Children who saw the model punished for deviation broke a similar prohibition less readily, less often, and for shorter periods of time than did Ss who saw the model rewarded or suffer no adverse consequence. Although differences between Ss under the model-punished condition and Ss under the no-film condition were not entirely consistent, generally speaking, the former children showed a greater amount of response inhibition.

Studies of the influence of observed consequences to a deviant model clearly indicate that the observation of a punished model may deter the observers from exhibiting imitative deviant behavior. However, they indicate also that children may acquire some of the deviant responses displayed by the punished model and exhibit these on some subsequent occasion when punishment is not anticipated. It is therefore possible that parents who rely heavily on the use of negative models as a disciplinary measure run the risk of teaching their children to behave in socially disapproved ways. On the other hand, there is no evidence to suggest that the learning of deviant responses will result in the performance of these responses unless the anticipation of their punishment is subsequently dispelled (Walters, 1966).

An early study by Chittenden (1942) very effectively indicates how discrimination training, involving a combination of reasoning procedures, may inhibit aggressive behavior. A group of highly aggressive preschool children were trained to behave nonaggressively by exposing them to a series of "plays" in each of which dolls, representing preschool children, depicted both an aggressive and a nonaggressive resolution of a conflict situation. After each pair of alternative solutions had been demonstrated, the experimenter and the child together discussed and appraised the outcome in terms of its appropriateness and its effects on the protagonists. In comparison to a control group, the Ss who received training showed a decreasing tendency to select aggressive solutions to test problems that were interspersed among the training sessions. Moreover, comparisons of Ss under training and equally aggressive untrained Ss made before the former Ss were trained, immediately after training was completed, and again a month later indicated that the training had been successful in inhibiting aggressive behavior.

Although not specifically structured to investigate the manner in which consequences to a social model may influence the behavior of child observers, Chittenden's study is highly relevant to this issue. Moreover, because of the experimenter–child interactions during and after each play, it provides a closer analogue to a real-life situation in which a parent reasons with a child than do the more recent studies of the effects of observing rewarding and punishing consequences to social models.

In spite of the widespread recognition by agents of social control of the possibility of modifying behavior in social situations through the provision of real-life or symbolic models whose acts are rewarded or punished, psychologists have until recently taken little or no account in theoretical discussions of imitative behavior of the observation of the consequences of responses of social models. Mowrer (1960b, p. 115) described a form of imitative learning, which he labeled "empathetic." One person, A, provides the model and experiences a reinforcement; B, the observer "both experiences some of the sensory consequences of A's behavior as A experiences it and also intuits A's satisfactions (or dissatisfactions)." Imitation of film-mediated aggression, which has been the subject of a number of studies, may illustrate this process. The observer sees the film model, for example, inflict pain on others and notes the model's verbal and gestural expressions of satisfaction. As a result, he imitates the pain-producing behavior in the expectation that the behavior will bring satisfaction to him also. Mowrer's explanation of "higher-order vicarious learning," as he calls this process, seems to imply that the response-correlated stimuli of the model's behavior can arouse in the observer an expectation that he too will experience analogous response-correlated stimuli for acting in a similar manner to the model.

Mowrer's description of empathetic learning, like his explanation of delay-of-punishment effects, seems to place too much weight on the role of response-correlated stimuli, in the form of interoceptive feedback, and too little on the role of perceptual-cognitive factors. Once a person has learned the social significance of reward and punishment, observation of the social consequences of others' activities can provide him with cues of how he should or should not act in a given social situation if he is to maximize rewards and minimize punishments. In other words, observation of consequences to others may serve as a source of information that guides the behavior of observers even when they experience little or no vicarious affect.

Bandura and Walters (1963b) identified three possible effects of exposure to social models. They suggested, in the first place, that an observer may acquire responses that did not previously exist in his repertory, a process that apparently occurs on the basis of contiguity principles (Bandura, 1965, 1966; Bandura & Walters, 1963b); second, that inhibitions may be strengthened or weakened through observation of the model's behavior and the consequences it incurs; and third, that there may be a pure eliciting effect, that is, that behavior that has not been previously inhibited by punishment may be "released" through observation of a model. An interpretation of observed consequences to others as potential guides for the behavior of others suggests, however, that the effects that Bandura and Walters classified as inhibitory and disinhibitory can often be explained in terms of the association of cognitive-perceptual cues and the observer's responses and without any reference to the strengthening or weakening of fear. If this interpretation is entirely valid, it is not often possible to distinguish between disinhibitory and eliciting effects. In either case, presentation of the model evokes a response in the observer that would not have occurred in the model's absence, and the association between the stimulus situation and the imitative behavior is thereby strengthened. Although its validity may be doubted, this interpretation nevertheless merits serious consideration. It implies that any emotional response that the observer makes results from a *prior* association of this response with the fractional anticipatory imitative responses made by the observer, and not from an association of fear with the cues provided by the model. The function of emotional arousal, under such circumstances, may be twofold. In the first place, it may alter perceptual thresholds, facilitate or restrict the utilization of cues, and modify the breadth of learning (Bruner, Matter, & Papanek, 1955; Easterbrook, 1959; Kausler & Trapp, 1960). Second, it may change the stimulus situation through the modification of the observer's internal cues and thus elicit responses that are compatible or incompatible with the reproduction of the model's behavior. Thus, although the arousal of emotion may in part determine what the observer actually does, the emotional responses themselves are not, according to this hypothesis, necessarily essential links in the chain of responses involved in observational learning.

The foregoing considerations do not, however, imply that empathetic experiences are unimportant as determinants of behavior. Aronfreed (1966) has distinguished vicarious from empathetic experiences on the grounds that observers of a model may respond to two different sets of cues, the stimulus events impinging on the model and the responses of the model that reflect his affective state. Aronfreed defines the observer's affective experience as vicarious insofar as he responds to the first class of cues and as empathetic in respect to his responses to the second class of cues. He correctly notes that vicarious and empathetic experiences, so defined, may occur simultaneously, since both classes of cues are usually present.

Transmission of emotional responses has been demonstrated in a number of laboratory studies in which animal and human subjects have served as Ss (*e.g.*, Berger, 1962; Church, 1959; Haner & Whitney, 1960; Lazarus, Speisman, Mordkoff, & Davison, 1962; Miller, 1961; Miller, Banks, & Ogawa, 1962, 1963; Miller, Murphy, & Mirsky, 1959). Moreover, anecdotal accounts and field-study descriptions clearly indicate the influence of the transmission of emotion during times of crisis, often leading to disorganized panic behavior (*e.g.*, Cantril, Gaudet, & Hertzog, 1940). Nevertheless, observation of the administration of punishment to real-life or symbolic models is unlikely to arouse strong emotional responses in the observer unless he has already engaged in the punished behavior or possesses the characteristics for which the model is being punished, and consequently anticipates that he, too, will shortly experience the same consequences as the model. If the observer has not already deviated, his emotional reaction is likely to be minimal or at least secondary to an anticipation that he himself will deviate, and under these circumstances, the cognitive components of his responses to the situation are undoubtedly the crucial factors in determining its outcome. One can, in fact, conceive of many situations in which observation of punishment to another person does not prevent the observer from carrying out the punished act. In particular, the observer may have learned to regard himself as a privileged person on account of characteristics that he possesses but the model does not; a favored child in a family or a favored group in a society may respond in precisely this manner.

Because of the forms that reasoning may take, it is clearly impossible to make a simple summary of its effects. The majority of findings nevertheless suggest that most forms of reasoning are effective means of socializing children. Unlike other forms of discipline, reasoning is commonly used when the parent anticipates a deviation; some of its effectiveness may thus arise from its occurring early in a response sequence (Bandura & Walters, 1963b). Probably far more important, however, is the clarity with which the nature or the anticipated deviation and its possible consequences are presented and, for older children, the appeal that can be made to general rules. If a child has learned that an incipient activity falls in a class of previously disciplined activities, he may more readily refrain from carrying it out than if the activity is not so labeled. Generalization of this kind has been noted by Burton (1963).

VI. Consistency

Consistency of discipline is a complex concept that has been used in various ways. Sears *et al.* (1957) defined consistency in terms of the extent to which mothers followed through on their threats of punishment. Other investigators (*e.g.*, Bandura, 1960; Bandura & Walters, 1959) have utilized parental agreement concerning when and how punishment should be administered as an index of consistency. Consistency may also refer to the extent to which a single parent treats misdemeanors in the same manner each time they occur, to the similarity between the treatment that a child receives from his mother and his father, or to the similarity of the nature of the consequences a child experiences on the different occasions on which he exhibits a particular kind of disapproved behavior.

Although the popular child-training literature lays great emphasis on the importance of consistency of discipline, research findings, even from field studies, are meager. Sears *et al.* (1953) suggested that when reward and nonreward or punishment were associated with a single response system, the resultant conflict between expectancy of reward and expectancy of nonreward or punishment conferred motivational properties on the inconsistently disciplined class of responses. In support of this hypotheses, Sears *et al.* sought to demonstrate curvilinear relationships between children's aggressive, dependent, and identification responses, on the one hand, and maternal frustration and punishment, on the other, in the expectation that children who were moderately frustrated and punished would show a greater incidence of the frustrated and punished behavior than would children who had received either little or a great deal of frustration and punishment. The findings presented by Sears *et al.* in support of their hypothesis are open to alternative explanations, and they certainly fail to provide convincing evidence in favor of the conflict-drive hypothesis in the form that they state it (Walters & Parke, 1964a).

Evidence that parental inconsistency of discipline is associated with aggressive responses in childhood was provided by Glueck and Glueck (1950), who found that parents of delinquent boys were more "erratic" in their disciplinary practices than were parents of nondeliquent boys. A similar finding has emerged from other studies of delinquency and crime (*e.g.,* Andry, 1960; McCord, McCord, & Howard, 1961; McCord, McCord, & Zola, 1959). Bandura and Walters (1959) obtained some evidence that parental disagreement concerning disciplinary practices was greater within families of aggressive boys than within families of nonaggressive boys, and Bandura (1960) subsequently reported the existence of interparental disagreement in families of both aggressive and inhibited boys. In these field studies of delinquency and aggression, inconsistency has not received a sufficiently uniform definition and, in some cases, has been too imprecisely defined to permit a confident evaluation of the findings.

The majority of parents probably punish dependent behavior only when it becomes extremely burdensome (Bandura & Walters, 1959; Sears *et al.,* 1957); consequently, evidence that parents who punish dependency behavior are likely to have highly dependent children (Bandura, 1960; Sears *et al.,* 1957) could indicate that inconsistent parental handling of dependency behavior increases the dependency of children. It is probable, however, that a simple antecedent–consequent relationship is again not involved, since parents of persistently deviant children may desperately try one means after another of modifying the undesirable behavior.

Relevant laboratory studies of children's social behavior are extremely scarce. In fact, a study by Fisher (1955), in which pups served as subjects, probably provides the closest laboratory analogue to inconsistent discipline in a home situation. During half-hour sessions, conducted five times a week for thirteen weeks, half the pups were consistently rewarded by petting and fondling each time they approached the experimeter. The remaining pups received similar training, but in addition were each week given five additional sessions during which they were handled roughly and sometimes shocked for making approach responses. Tests conducted toward the end of, and following, the training showed that pups that had received both reward and punishment training exhibited greater dependency in the form of remaining close to the experimenter than did the pups in the 100% reward group.

A combination of reward and punishment was used by Fried and Banks (1965), who continuously reinforced children for making correct responses on two games that were presented in alternation. While playing one of the games, all Ss were forced to suck a cotton swab soaked in a mixture of water and powdered citric acid following six of their correct responses. One group was rewarded with a poker chip on 20 trials in each game, a second group was rewarded on 35 trials, and a third on 50 trials. After the intermittent-punishment treatment, the Ss were continuously punished for correct responses. The intermittent-punishment effect was calculated by subtracting the number of punished responses a S made on the game that had not been associated with punishment during training from the number of responses he made to the previously punished game. As the number of positive reinforcements during training increased from 20 to 50, scores changed from negative to positive values. The outcome suggested that behavior that has been frequently rewarded and infrequently punished shows considerable persistence in the face of consistently administered punishment. Unfortunately, Fried and Banks did not include a condition under which children received no punishment during the training session; a baseline for assessing the effects of the various reward-punishment combinations is therefore lacking.

Inconsistent discipline may also take the form of a partial reinforcement procedure in which a class of responses is sometimes rewarded and sometimes not rewarded but no aversive stimulus is presented. This kind of procedure has already been discussed in the section on withdrawal of rewards.

The outcome of a change in a disciplinary maneuver is probably highly dependent on the sequence in which the reinforcers occur. Support for the hypothesis is provided in two laboratory studies by Virginia Crandall and her associates, who demonstrated that "active nonreward" may have differing effects, depending on whether the nonrewarded response was previously rewarded or punished. In the first of these studies (Crandall, 1963), children were given the task of matching angles with a set of "standards" over a series of twelve trials. The responses of one group of Ss were verbally approved by the E on nine of the trials; Ss in a second group were told on nine trials that their responses were wrong; while for a third group of Ss, the E remained silent while testing. All Ss were given a second set of trials, during which the E made no response. A measure of each child's expectancy of success was secured at the onset of the session and again after each of the two series of trials. Nonreward following reward functioned analogously to negative reinforcement, whereas nonreward that followed punishment functioned analogously to a positive reinforcer. The second study (Crandall, Good, & Crandall, 1964) included a condition under which the E was removed from the room during the second series of trials in order to differentiate the effects of adult nonresponsiveness from those of extinction. The results obtained in the first study were supported and, in addition, the changes produced by nonreaction were significantly greater than those produced by extinction. The authors concluded that adult nonreaction acquires active, contrasting reinforcement value of the sign opposite to that of the adult's preceding verbal reinforcements.

In child-training situations, the effects of parental nonreaction are probably highly dependent on the interpretation a child places, as a result of his past experiences, on this kind of parental behavior. Walters, Parke, and Cane (1965) showed a group of children a film sequence in which a child broke a prohibition; the sequence ended with the mother's entering the room and standing beside the child in an impassive manner. After observing the film, the Ss, on whom a prohibition similar to that occurring in the film had been placed, were given a resistance-to-deviation test. A postexperimental interview revealed that while some of the Ss saw the mother's nonreaction as punitive, others interpreted the behavior as permissive or even rewarding. The former Ss exhibited significantly greater resistance to deviation than the latter Ss. It seems reasonable to believe that the differing interpretations were attributable to the Ss' prior home experiences. Most parents who employ nonreaction as a disciplinary measure deliberately or unwittingly provide emotional-intensity cues signifying their disapproval. It is therefore not surprising that nearly three-quarters of the Ss who were exposed to the nonreacting film mother interpreted her nonresponsiveness as punitive.

Little attention has been given in the child literature to the effects of repeatedly administering reward-punishment or punishment-reward sequences for a particular class of responses. Probably the latter kind of sequence is more usual and may be very frequent in families in which a parent tends to become emotionally upset after punishing a child and consequently tries to win back the child's love by a demonstration of affection. Under such circumstances, one might expect the punishment to acquire secondary reinforcing properties and to lose its potentiality for inhibiting undesirable behavior. Similarly, one might expect parental responses that are, for most children, positively reinforcing to lose this property if they are frequently followed by punitive parental reactions. Although there is no direct evidence in favor of these hypotheses, experiments with animals in which reward and punishment are associated with same goal response provide them with some indirect support (Martin, 1963).

The effects of inconsistency of discipline are, like those of reasoning, difficult to assess, partly because "inconsistency" can refer to a multitude of different combinations and orderings of parental responses to children's behavior (Becker, 1964), partly because no investigator has yet carried out a systematically designed series of related experiments aimed at determining the effects of different types of inconsistent treatment of a specific class of responses.

VII. Concluding Remarks

Although precise knowledge of the outcome of most of the disciplinary techniques reviewed in this paper is quite evidently lacking, it is possible to draw a few tentative conclusions concerning their efficacy.

Beliefs that punishment in the form of aversive stimulation is both ineffective for changing behavior and likely to produce harmful side effects have been largely based on Thorndike's (1932, 1935) later presentations of the law of effect, Estes' (1944) classic monograph on punishment, reports of experimentally induced neurosis (Maier, 1949; Masserman, 1943), and presentations of individual case histories. Both these beliefs may be challenged.

The studies reviewed in this paper, as well as the animal studies covered by Church (1963) and Solomon (1964), suggest that consistent and intense aversive stimulation can effectively suppress undesirable behavior, especially if it is judiciously timed. By itself, however, this kind of punishment is obviously highly ineffective for teaching a child what are correct and permissible patterns of behavior. Although Skinner (1953) has probably underplayed the importance of punishment in the socialization process, he is nevertheless indubitably correct in stressing the value of positive reinforcement for the shaping of social behavior. In fact, in real-life situations the suppressive effect of punishment is usually only of value if alternative prosocial responses are elicited and strengthened while the undesirable behavior is held in check. The primary practical value of studies of parameters that influence the efficacy of punishment is therefore to determine the conditions under which suppression will most readily occur.

Considerable emphasis has been placed in the child-training and clinical literature on the incidental socially harmful effects of punitive methods of discipline. Bandura (1962a, pp. 299–300), in criticizing a punitive method of behavior modification described by Boardman (1962), pointed out several possible side effects of aversive stimulation: it can produce conditioned anxiety that motivates undesirable patterns of behavior, including avoidance of the punishing agents, who are thus rendered ineffective; it can provide the recipient with aggressive models, whom he is likely to imitate; and it can increase the frequency and amplitude of aggressive behavior. Granted that objections of this kind are, under some circumstances, valid, there is nevertheless considerable evidence that the suppressive effect of punishment may be sufficiently powerful to permit ample time for the initiation of a program for strengthening alternative prosocial patterns of behavior. The initiation of such a program may well forestall the occurrence of the undesirable side effects.

Moreover, in real-life situations, these undesirable effects may be rarer than experimental outcomes might lead one to believe. In his interactions with parents and other socialization agents a child displays many behavior patterns, not all of which are unacceptable to them. Consequently, although the socialization agent may punish, even quite severely, certain classes of responses, he may concurrently reward, both materially and psychologically, a much larger proportion of the child's behavior. Under these circumstances, aversive stimulation delivered for specific classes of responses is not likely to lead to avoidance of the agent of punishment and, in addition, the punishment may be maximally effective on account of a generally positive relationship between the child and the disciplinary agent. Studies of atypical children (Bandura, 1960; Bandura & Walters, 1959; Boardman, 1962; Glueck & Glueck, 1950) do not contradict this point of view; generally speaking, the parents of such children tend to be either indiscriminatively punitive or to employ patterns of reward and punishment that are particularly conducive to the occurrence of undesirable side effects, for example, aggressive orientations manifested outside the home.

One conclusion to which this review of the literature thus leads is that aversive stimulation, if well timed, consistent, and sufficiently intense, may create conditions that accelerate the socialization process, provided that the socialization agents also provide information concerning alternative prosocial behavior and positively reinforce any such behavior that occurs.

There is considerable evidence that such factors as the timing, intensity, and frequency of aversive physical stimulation and the timing and severity of aversive verbal stimulation can influence their effectiveness as disciplinary procedures. In the case of techniques involving withholding and withdrawal of rewards, the outcome depends to a considerable extent on the timing and completeness of the deprivation, and the extent to which the denied goal has acquired value through its prior association with rewarding experiences. The manner in which a disciplinary technique is applied may, in fact, be more important than the form that it takes. For example, the effectiveness of any disciplinary technique may be enhanced when its termination is made contingent on a child's complying with the demands of the socialization agent (Bandura & Walters, 1963b). Both contingent termination of an aversive stimulus (Lövaas *et al.*, 1965b) and contingent reinstatement of a rewarding experience (Baer, 1962a) appear to be highly effective in changing behavior in directions desired by the experimenter. As Hill (1960) has suggested, physical punishment and deprivation of privileges would probably be as effective as "love-oriented" techniques in establishing self-control if their termination were as frequently made contingent on the child's compliance with socialization demands. Moreover, Aronfreed's (1964) research indicates that the acquisition of self-critical responses, which undoubtedly play a large part in fostering self-control, is facilitated if termination of punishment is contingent on their utterance. In addition, his most recent studies (Aronfreed, 1965) suggest that the close association of analogues of parental reasoning with deprivation tactics can facilitate response inhibition.

The importance of the relationship between the agent and recipient of punishment in the socialization process should not be minimized. Although Aronfreed's (Aronfreed, 1964; Aronfreed *et al.*, 1963) research suggests that this relationship is of little importance for the acquisition of self-critical responses, most of the available evidence indicates that the existence of a close affectional relationship between the agent and recipient of punishment enhances the effectiveness of various kinds of disciplinary procedures for producing social compliance.

Prior analyses of disciplinary techniques in social-learning terms (*e.g.*, Bandura & Walters, 1959; Hill, 1960) have exphasized the need to distinguish between component elements that involve the presentation of noxious stimuli and the withholding or withdrawal of positive reinforcers, respectively. While such analyses can assist in assessing the outcome of disciplinary practices, they have, generally speaking, given too little weight to perceptual cognitive factors. In varying degrees, each disciplinary maneuver is capable of eliciting both emotional and cognitive responses, and its outcome may depend, to a very large extent, upon the relative weight of these two classes of mediating events. Future laboratory investigations might well aim at more direct manipulations of perceptual-cognitive factors than have been customary up to the present. Although an admirable start in this direction has been made by Aronfreed (*e.g.*, 1963, 1965, 1966), it is probable that he still places too much weight on the role of the production and reduction of anxiety in the socialization process.

The success of a number of laboratory operations in promoting social control was attributed to cognitive factors. In fact, anticipation of punishment, with very little accompanying emotion, may frequently be capable of preventing deviant responses. Moreover, once the socialization process is well advanced, a child's behavior can be to a large extent controlled by identifying a particular response as an instance of a general class of for-bidden activities, thereby eliciting efforts to maintain already adopted standards of behavior. In addition, some of the inhibitory techniques discussed in the section on reasoning rely heavily on inducing cognitive, rather than emotional, change. Finally, in some instances the emotional response that a disciplinary act evokes may be contingent on its effective-ness for bringing about a perceptual-cognitive change.

Several specific examples of the manner in which perceptual-cognitive processes may function were noted in previous sections. For example, devaluation of a forbidden goal resulting from a mild threat of punishment may help to maintain response inhibition when punishment is no longer anticipated. The observation of punishment received by a model may serve as a cue to observers that the model's behavior is socially inappropriate. The relative ineffectiveness of delayed punishment may be due to a weaken-ing of the association between the perceptual-cognitive cues that are present when a deviant act is committed and the disciplinary agent's punitive response; this latter phenomenon may in fact, be only a special case of the superiority of contingent, as opposed to noncontingent, reinforcement, resulting from the clearer identification of the desirable or undesirable response that contingent reinforcement provides.

An example of the important role played by cognitive factors in inducing social conformity is provided in a recent study of imitation by Walters and Amoroso (1967), who demonstrated that physiological arousal contingent on, or associated with, information that the subjects' behavior was inappro-priate increased the probability of behavioral change in the direction specified by the model but that physiological arousal that was not associated with such information was relatively ineffective for producing behavioral change. Moreover, a study by Bandura and Rosenthal (1966) demonstrated that imitative behavior was a positive function of psychological stress, but that a negative relationship occurred when, in addition to psychological stress, subjects experienced increasing physiologically induced arousal. This study, also, seems to indicate that social conformity is not facilitated by arousal per se but only by emotional responses that are associated with, or are contingent on, certain kinds of cognitive structuring.

Undoubtedly, there are differences among individuals in respect to the extent to which their behavior is guided by cognitive, rather than emotional, factors. It may be tentatively suggested, however, that cognitive factors are likely to predominate when conformity to a rule, presented in forms ranging from relatively abstract general principles of behavior to the relative concrete provision of social models, does not conflict with conformity to a similar rule or debar the agent from demonstrating "competence" in White's (1959) sense of the term. It is interesting to note, for example, that the opposite of predicted results concerning the relation of child-training variables to children's resistance to deviation were obtained when not resisting involved a failure to achieve (Burton et al., 1961, 1966). Possibly, the child-training practices classified as reasoning tend primarily to bring a child's behavior under the control of cognitive factors; a dilemma may thus be created if failure to meet one set of standards, for example, "high achievement," conflicts with adherance to another set, for example, "moral conformity." In such cases, although emotional responses usually accompany the resolution of the choice, the decision that is reached may nevertheless be guided and largely determined by cognitive factors. Since such dilemmas are the exception rather than the rule in most societies, the frequently demonstrated relationship between parental reasoning and children's moral conformity may not represent a direct antecedent – consequent effect. When parental standards conflict with those adopted by the society in which the parents live, a preference for discipline through reasoning may, in fact, incline the parents' offspring to become social deviates. Instances of this kind of outcome are apparent in many biographies, autobiographies, and everyday observations.

Some of the inadequacy of learning-theory analyses of the effects of disciplinary techniques may arise from the covert or overt assumption that these techniques acquire their effectiveness through association with the occurrence of physical pain. This assumption is explicitly made, for example, by Dollard and Miller (1950) and is implicit in many other influential commentaries on the socialization process (e.g., Sears et al., 1957; Whiting & Child, 1953). Evidence assembled by Kessen and Mandler (1961) indicates that infants respond with distress reactions to many stimulus conditions that are not physically painful; that certain kinds of self-initiated and parental behavior, particularly those involving rhythmic stimulation, are congenital inhibitors of distress; and that the removal of such inhibitors may serve to disinhibit distress.

If this supposition is correct, much of the traditional thinking concerning the socialization process may have to be somewhat revised. The majority of stimulus events that inhibit distress are mediated by caretakers, and withdrawal of a caretaker's attention or affectional responses may thus have a disinhibitory effect. The efficacy of "withdrawal-of-love" techniques may consequently reside in their capacity to elicit very primitive distress reactions, which are dispelled as soon as affection or attention is reinstated (Walters & Parke, 1965). If this is the case, there is no reason to suppose that withdrawal of affection or attention primarily achieves its effect through a prior association of the presence of the caretaker with the reduction of physical pain caused by hunger, cold, or similar physically

RICHARD H. WALTERS AND ROSS D. PARKE

painful states, as some psychologists have assumed (*e.g.*, Dollard & Miller, 1950; Sears *et al.*, 1957). Moreover, there is evidence that such reduction of pain is not even the primary source of the formation of the first specific attachments of infants. Indeed, these attachments appear to be much more dependent on the occurrence of general sensory stimulation, including stimulation through the distance receptors (Walters & Parke, 1965). Since such stimulation, for all except deaf-blind children, is probably the primary basis of cognitive development, the foregoing considerations may provide basis for an enlarged understanding of the roles played by both emotional and cognitive factors in the socialization process. Unfortunately, controlled research on infant social behavior is as yet too little advanced to permit the formation of more specific hypotheses concerning the origins and early development of children's responses to the disciplinary techniques of socialization agents.

References

Allyon, T., & Michael, J. The psychiatric nurse as a behavioral engineer. *J. exp. anal. Behav.*, 1959, **2**, 323–334.

Andry, R. G. *Delinquency and parental pathology*. London: Methuen, 1960.

Aronfreed, J. The nature, variety, and social patterning of moral responses to transgression. *J. abnorm. soc. Psychol.*, 1961, **63**, 223–240.

Aronfreed, J. The effect of experimental socialization paradigms upon two moral responses to transgression. *J. abnorm. soc. Psychol.*, 1963, **66**, 437–448.

Aronfreed, J. The origins of self-criticism. *Psychol. Rev.*, 1964, **71**, 193–218.

Aronfreed, J. Punishment learning and internalization: Some parameters of reinforcement and cognition. Paper presented at Biennial Meeting Soc. Res. Child Develpm., Minneapolis, March, 1965.

Aronfreed, J. Conscience and conduct: A natural history of the internalization of values. Unpublished manuscript, Univer. of Pennsylvania, 1966.

Aronfreed, J., & Leff, R. The effects of intensity of punishment and complexity of discrimination upon the learning of an internalized inhibition. Unpublished manuscript, Univer. of Pennsylvania, 1963.

Aronfreed, J., & Reber, A. Internalized behavioral suppression and the timing of social punishment. *J. Pers. soc. Psychol.*, 1965, **1**, 3–16.

Aronfreed, J., Cutlick, R. A., & Fagen, S. A. Cognitive structure, punishment, and nurturance in the experimental induction of self-criticism. *Child Develpm.*, 1963, **34**, 281–294.

Aronson, E., & Carlsmith, J. M. Effect of the severity of threat on the devaluation of forbidden behavior, *J. abnorm. soc. Psychol.*, 1963, **66**, 584–588.

Baer, D. M. Escape and avoidance response of pre-school children to two schedules of reinforcement withdrawal. *J. exp. anal. Behav.*, 1960, **3**, 155–160.

Baer, D. M. Effect of withdrawal of positive reinforcement on an extinguishing response in young children. *Child Develpm.*, 1961, **32**, 67–74.

Baer, D. M. Laboratory control of thumbsucking by withdrawal and representation of reinforcement. *J. exp. anal. Behav.*, 1962, **5**, 525–528. (a)

Baer, D. M. A technique of social reinforcement for the study of child behavior: Behavior avoiding reinforcement withdrawal. *Child Develpm*, 1962, **33**, 847–858. (b)

Bandura, A. Relationship of family patterns to child behavior disorders. Progress Report, Grant M–1734. Stanford Univer., 1960.

Bandura, A. Psychotherapy as a learning process. *Psychol. Bull.*, 1961, 58, 143–159.

Bandura, A. Punishment revisited. *J. consult. Psychol.*, 1962, 26, 298–301. (a)

Bandura, A. Social learning through imitation. In M. R. Jones (Ed.), *Nebraska symposium on motivation.* Lincoln, Nebr.: Univer. of Nebraska Press, 1962. Pp. 211–269. (b)

Bandura, A. Influence of models' reinforcement contingencies on the acquisition of imitative responses. *J. Pers. soc. Psychol.*, 1965, 1, 589–595.

Bandura, A. Vicarious processes: A case of no-trial learning. In L. Berkowitz (Ed.), *Advances in experimental social psychology.* Vol. 2. New York: Academic Press, 1966. Pp. 1–55.

Bandura, A., & Huston, Aletha C. Identification as a process of incidental learning. *J. abnorm. soc. Psychol.*, 1961, 63, 311–318.

Bandura, A., & Rosenthal, T. L. Vicarious classical conditioning as a function of arousal level. *J. Pers. soc. Psychol.*, 1966, 3, 54–62.

Bandura, A., & Walters, R. H. *Adolescent aggression.* New York: Ronald Press, 1959.

Bandura, A., & Walters, R. H. Aggression. In *Child psychology: The sixty-second yearbook of the National Society for the Study of Education.* Part 1. Chicago: Nat. Soc. Stud. Educ., 1963. Pp. 364–415. (a)

Bandura, A., & Walters, R. H. *Social learning and personality development.* New York: Holt, Rinehart & Winston, 1963. (b)

Bandura, A., Ross, Dorothea, & Ross, Shiela A. Vicarious reinforcement and imitative learning. *J. abnorm. soc. Psychol.*, 1963, 67, 601–607.

Banks, R. K., & Vogel-Sprott, M. D. The effect of delayed punishment on an immediately rewarded response in humans. *J. exp. Psychol.*, 1965, 70, 357–359.

Becker, W. C. Consequences of different kinds of parental discipline. In M. L. Hoffman and Lois W. Hoffman (Eds.), *Review of child development research*, Vol. 1. New York: Russell Sage Foundation, 1964, Pp. 169–208.

Becker, W. C., Peterson, D. R., Hellmer, L. A., Shoemaker, D. J., & Quay, H. C. Factors in parental behavior and personality as related to problem behavior in children. *J. consult. Psychol.*, 1962, 33, 509–535.

Berger, S. M. Conditioning through vicarious instigation. *Psychol. Rev.*, 1962, 69, 450–466.

Birnbrauer, J. S., Wolf, M. M., Kidder, J. D., & Tague, Cecilia E. Classroom behavior of retarded pupils with token reinforcement. *J. exp. Child Psychol.*, 1965, 2, 219–235.

Boardman, W. K. Rusty: A brief behavior disorder. *J. consult. Psychol.*, 1962, 26, 293–297.

Brackbill, Yvonne. Extinction of the smiling response in infants as a function of reinforcement schedules. *Child Develpm.*, 1958, 29, 115–124.

Brackbill, Yvonne, & O'Hara, J. The relative effectiveness of reward and punishment for discrimination learning in children. *J. comp. physiol. Psychol.*, 1958, 6, 747–751.

Brown, P., & Elliott, R. Control of aggression in a nursery school class. *J. exp. Child Psychol.*, 1965, 2, 103–107.

Bruner, J. S., Matter, Jean, & Papanek, Miriam L. Breadth of learning as a function of drive level and mechanization. *Psychol. Rev.*, 1955, 62, 1–10.

Burton, R. V. Generality for honesty reconsidered. *Psychol. Rev.*, 1963, 70, 481–499.

Burton, R. V., Maccoby, Eleanor E., & Allinsmith, W. Antecedents of resistance to temptation in four-year-old children. *Child Develpm.*, 1961, 32, 689–710.

Burton, R. V., Allinsmith, W., & Maccoby, Eleanor E. Resistance to temptation in relation to sex of child, sex of experimenter, and withdrawal of attention. *J. Pers. soc. Psychol.*, 1966, 3, 253–258.

Cantril, H., Gaudet, Hazel, & Hertzog, Herta. *The invasion from Mars.* Princeton: Princeton Univer. Press, 1940.

Castaneda, A. Reaction time and response amplitude as a function of anxiety and stimulus intensity. *J. abnorm. soc. Psychol.*, 1956, **53**, 225–228.

Cheyne, J. A., & Walters, R. H. Timing and intensity of punishment and cognitive structuring as determinants of response inhibition. Unpublished manuscript, Univer. of Waterloo, 1967.

Chittenden, Gertrude E. An experimental study in measuring and modifying assertive behavior in young children. *Mongor. Soc. Res. Child Develpm.*, 1942, **7**, No. 1 (Whole No. 31).

Church, R. M. Emotional reactions of rats to the pain of others. *J. comp. physiol. Psychol.*, 1959, **52**, 132–134.

Church, R. M. The varied effects of punishment on behavior. *Psychol. Rev.*, 1963, **70**, 369–402.

Crandall, V. J. Achievement. In *Child psychology: The sixty-second yearbook of the National Society for the Study of Education*. Part 1. Chicago: Nat. Soc. Stud. Educ., 1963. Pp. 416–459.

Crandall, Virginia C. Reinforcement effects of adult reactions and nonreactions on children's achievement expectations. *Child Develpm.*, 1963, **34**, 335–354.

Crandall, Virginia C., Good, Suzanne, & Crandall, V. J. The reinforcement effects of adult reactions and nonreactions on children's achievement expectations: A replication study. *Child Develpm.*, 1964, **35**, 485–497.

Davitz, J. R. The effects of previous training on postfrustrative behavior. *J. abnorm. soc. Psychol.*, 1952, **47**, 309–315.

Dollard, J., & Miller, N. E. *Personality and psychotherapy*. New York: McGraw-Hill, 1950.

Dorwart, W., Ezerman, R., Lewis, M., & Rosenhan, D. The effects of brief social deprivation on social and nonsocial reinforcement. *J. Pers. soc. Psychol.*, 1965, **2**, 111–115.

Easterbrook, J. A. The effect of emotion on cue utilization and the organization of behavior. *Psychol. Rev.*, 1959, **66**, 183–201.

Eron, L. D., Banta, T. J., Walder, L. O., & Laulicht, J. H. Comparison of data obtained from mothers and fathers on child aggression. *Child Develpm.*, 1961, **32**, 457–472.

Eron, L. D., Walder, L. O., Toigo, R., & Lefkowitz, M. M. Social class, parental punishment for aggression, and child aggression. *Child Develpm.*, 1963, **34**, 849–867.

Estes, W. K. An experimental study of punishment. *Psychol. Monogr.*, 1944, **57**, No. 3 (Whole No. 263).

Eysenck, H. J. (Ed.) *Behaviour therapy and the neuroses*. New York: Pergamon Press, 1960.

Festinger, L. *A theory of cognitive dissonance*. Evanston, Ill.: Row, Peterson, 1957.

Fisher, A. E. The effects of differential early treatment on the social and exploratory behavior of puppies. Unpublished doctoral dissertation, Pennsylvania State Univer., 1955.

Freedman, D. G. Constitutional and environmental interactions in rearing of four breeds of dogs. *Science*, 1958, **127**, 585–586.

Freedman, J. L. Long-term behavioral effects of cognitive dissonance. *J. exp. soc. Psychol.*, 1965, **1**, 145–155.

Freud, S. Mourning and melancholia. In E. Jones (Ed.), *Collected papers*. Vol. IV. London: Hogarth Press, 1925. Pp. 152–170.

Fried, P. A. A methodological note on a punishing stimulus for children. *Psychonom. Sci.*, 1965, **3**, 62.

Fried, P. A., & Banks, R. K. Resistance to continuous punishment as a function of reinforced trials during intermittent punishment training under within-subjects conditions. Unpublished manuscript, Univer. of Waterloo, Ontario, 1965.

Gewirtz, J. L. Three determinants of attention seeking in young children. *Monogr. Soc. Res. Child Develpm.*, 1954, **19**, No. 2 (Whole No. 59).

Gewirtz, J. L., & Baer, D. M. The effects of brief social deprivation on behaviors for a social reinforcer. *J. abnorm. soc. Psychol.*, 1958, **56**, 49–56. (a)

Gewirtz, J. L., & Baer, D. M. Deprivation and satiation of social reinforcers as drive conditions. *J. abnorm. soc. Psychol.*, 1958, **57**, 165–172. (b)

Glueck, S., & Glueck, Eleanor. *Unraveling juvenile delinquency.* Cambridge, Mass.: Harvard Univer. Press, 1950.

Haner, C. F., & Brown, Patricia A. Clarification of the instigation to aggression concept in the frustration-aggression hypothesis. *J. abnorm. soc. Psychol.*, 1955, **51**, 204–206.

Haner, C. F., & Whitney, E. R. Empathic conditioning and its relation to anxiety level. *Amer. Psychologist*, 1960, **15**, 493. (Abstract)

Hartup, W. W. Nurturance and nurturance-withdrawal in relation to the dependency behavior of preschool children. *Child Develpm.*, 1958, **29**, 191–201.

Hartup, W. W., & Himeno, Yayoi. Social isolation *vs.* interaction with adults in relation to aggression in preschool children. *J. abnorm. soc. Psychol.*, 1959, **59**, 17–22.

Hill, W. F. Learning theory and the acquisition of values. *Psychol. Rev.*, 1960, **67**, 317–331.

Hoffman, M. L., & Saltzstein, H. D. Parent practices and the child's moral orientation. Paper read at Amer. Psychol. Ass. Annual Meeting, Chicago, September, 1960.

Hollenberg, Eleanor, & Sperry, Margaret. Some antecedents of aggression and effects of frustration in doll play. *Personality*, 1951, **1**, 32–43.

Holton, Ruth B. Amplitude of an instrumental response following the withdrawal of reward. *Child Develpm.*, 1961, **32**, 107–116.

Karsh, Eileen B., & Williams, Joanna P. Punishment and reward in children's instrumental learning. *Psychonom. Sci.*, 1964, **1**, 359–360.

Kausler, D. H., & Trapp, E. P. Motivation and cue utilization in intentional and incidental learning. *Psychol. Rev.*, 1960, **67**, 373–379.

Kessen, W., & Mandler, G. Anxiety, pain, and inhibition of distress. *Psychol. Rev.*, 1961, **68**, 396–404.

Krasner, L., & Ullmann, L. P. *Research in behavior modification: New developments and implications.* New York: Holt, Rinehart & Winston, 1965.

Lazarus, R. S., Speisman, J. C., Mordkoff, A. M., & Davison, L. A. A laboratory study of psychological stress produced by a motion picture film. *Psychol. Monogr.*, 1962, **76**, No. 34. (Whole No. 553).

Lefkowitz, M. M., Walder, L. O., & Eron, L. D. Punishment, identification, and aggression. *Merrill-Palmer Quart. Behav. Develpm.*, 1963, **9**, 159–174.

Leitenberg, H. Is time-out from positive reinforcement an aversive event?: A review of the experimental evidence. *Psychol. Bull.*, 1965, **64**, 428–441.

Levin, H., & Wardwell, Eleanor. The research uses of doll play. *Psychol. Bull.*, 1962, **59**, 27–56.

LeVine, Barbara B. Punishment techniques and the development of conscience. Unpublished doctoral dissertation, Northwestern Univer., 1961.

Lewis, M. Social isolation: A parametric study of its effect on social reinforcement. *J. exp. Child Psychol.*, 1965, **2**, 205–218.

Lewis, M., & Richman, Shanna. Social encounters and their effect on subsequent social reinforcement. *J. abnorm. soc. Psychol.*, 1964, **69**, 253–257.

Lövaas, O. I., Freitag, G., Gold, Vivian J., & Kassorla, Irene C. Experimental studies in childhood schizophrenia: Analysis of self-destructive behavior. *J. exp. Child Psychol.*, 1965, **2**, 67–84. (a).

Lövaas, O. I., Schaeffer, B., & Simmons, J. Q. Building social behavior in autistic children by the use of electric shock. *J. exp. Res. Pers.*, 1965, **1**, 99–109. (b)

Longstreth, L. E. The relationship between expectations and frustration in children. *Child Develpm.*, 1960, **31**, 667–671.

McCord, W., McCord, Joan, & Zola, I. K. *Origins of crime.* New York: Columbia Univer. Press, 1959.

McCord, W., McCord, Joan, & Howard, A. Familial correlates of aggression in nondelinquent male children. *J. abnorm. soc. Psychol.*, 1961, **62**, 79–93.

Maier, N. R. F. *Frustration: The study of behavior without a goal.* New York: McGraw-Hill, 1949.

Martin, B. Reward and punishment associated with the same goal response: A factor in the learning of motives. *Psychol. Bull.*, 1963, **60**, 441–451.

Masserman, J. H. *Behavior and neurosis.* Chicago: Univer. of Chicago Press, 1943.

Meyer, W. J., & Offenbach, S. I. Effectiveness of reward and punishment as a function of task complexity. *J. comp. physiol. Psychol.*, 1962, **55**, 532–534.

Meyer, W. J., & Seidman, S. B. Age differences in the effectiveness of different reinforcement combinations on the acquisition and extinction of a simple concept learning problem. *Child Develpm.*, 1960, **31**, 419–429.

Meyer, W. J., & Seidman, S. B. Relative effectiveness of different reinforcement combinations on concept learning of children at two developmental levels. *Child Develpm.*, 1961, **32**, 117–127.

Miller, N. Acquisition of avoidance dispositions by social learning. *J. abnorm. soc. Psychol.*, 1961, **63**, 12–19.

Miller, R. E., Murphy, J. V., & Mirsky, I. A. Nonverbal communication of affect. *J. clin. Psychol.*, 1959, **15**, 155–158.

Miller, R. E., Banks, J. H., Jr., & Ogawa, N. Communication of affect in "cooperative conditioning" of rhesus monkeys. *J. abnorm. soc. Psychol.*, 1962, **64**, 343–348.

Miller, R. E., Banks, J. H., Jr., & Ogawa, N. Role of facial expression in "cooperative-avoidance conditioning in monkeys". *J. abnorm. soc. Psychol.*, 1963, **67**, 24–30.

Mischel, W., & Grusec, Joan E. The model's characteristics as determinants of social learning. *J. Pers. soc. Psychol.*, 1966, **4**, 211–215.

Mowrer, O. H. *Learning theory and behavior.* New York: Wiley, 1960. (a)

Mowrer, O. H. *Learning theory and the symbolic processes.* New York: Wiley, 1960. (b)

Nelsen, E. A. The effects of reward and punishment of dependency on subsequent dependency Unpublished manuscript, Stanford Univer., 1960.

Nelson, F. B., Reid, I. E., & Travers, R. M. W. Effect of electric shock as a reinforcer of the behavior of children. *Psychol. Rep.*, 1965, **16**, 123–126.

Olds, J. The influence of practice on the strength of secondary approach drives. *J. exp. Psychol.*, 1953, **46**, 232–236.

Parke, R. D. Nurturance, nurturance-withdrawal, and resistance to deviation. *Child Develpm.*, 1967, in press.

Parke, R. D., & Walters, R. H. Some variables influencing the effectiveness of punishment for producing response inhibition. *Monogr. Soc. Res. Child Develpm.*, 1967, **32**, (Whole No. 109).

Patterson, G. R. Parents as dispensers of aversive stimuli. *J. Pers. soc. Psychol.*, 1965, **2**, 844–851.

Patterson, G. R., & Anderson, D. Peers as social reinforcers. *Child Develpm.*, 1964, **35**, 951–960.

Patterson, G. R., Littman, R., & Hinsey, C. Parental effectiveness as reinforcers in the laboratory and its relation to child-rearing practices and child adjustment in the classroom. *J. Pers.*, 1964, **32**, 180–199.

Peck, R. F. Family patterns correlated with adolescent personality structure. *J. abnorm. soc. Psychol.*, 1958, **57**, 347–350.

Penney, R. K. The effects of nonreinforcement on response strength as a function of number of previous reinforcements. *Canad. J. Psychol.*, 1960, **14**, 206–215.

Penney, R. K., & Kirwin, P. M. Differential adaptation of anxious and nonanxious children in instrumental escape conditioning. *J. exp. Psychol.*, 1965, **70**, 539–541.

Penney, R. K., & Lupton, A. A. Children's discrimination learning as a function of reward and punishment. *J. comp. physiol Psychol.*, 1961, **54**, 449–451.

Penney, R. K., & McCann, B. The instrumental escape conditioning of anxious and non-anxious children. *J. abnorm. soc. Psychol.*, 1962, **65**, 351–354.

Robinson, Nancy M., & Robinson, H. B. A method for the study of instrumental avoidance conditioning with young children. *J. comp. physiol. Psychol.*, 1961, **54**, 20–23.

Rosenblith, Judy F. Learning by imitation in kindergarten children. *Child Develpm.*, 1959, **30**, 69–80.

Rosenblith, Judy F. Imitative color choices in kindergarten children. *Child Develpm.*, 1961, **32**, 211–223.

Screven, C. G. The effects of interference on response strength. *J. comp. physiol. Psychol.*, 1954, **47**, 140–144.

Sears, R. R. Relation of early socialization experiences to aggression in middle childhood. *J. abnorm. soc, Psychol.*, 1961, **63**, 466–492.

Sears, R. R., Whiting, J. W. M., Nowlis, V., & Sears, Pauline S. Some child-rearing antecedents of aggression and dependency in young children. *Genet. Psychol. Monogr.*, 1953, **47**, 135–234.

Sears, R. R., Maccoby, Eleanor E., & Levin, H. *Patterns of child rearing.* Evanson, Ill.: Row, Peterson, 1957.

Setterington, R. G., & Walters, R. H. Effects of concurrent delays of material rewards and punishments on problem-solving in children. *Child Develpm.*, 1964, **35**, 275–280.

Skinner, B. F. *Science and human behavior.* New York: Macmillan, 1953.

Solomon, R. L. Punishment. *Amer. Psychologist*, 1964, **19**, 239–253.

Thorndike, E. L. *The fundamentals of learning.* New York: Teacher's College, 1932.

Thorndike, E. L. *The psychology of wants, interests, and attitudes.* New York: Appleton–Century-Crofts, 1935.

Turner, Elizabeth A., & Wright, J. C. Effects of severity of threat and perceived availability on the attractiveness of objects. *J. Pers. soc. Psychol.*, 1965, **2**, 128–132.

Ullmann, L. P., & Krasner, L. *Case studies in behavior modification.* New York: Holt, Rinehart & Winston, 1965.

Vogel-Sprott, M. D., & Banks, R. K. The effect of delayed punishment on an immediately rewarded response in alcoholics and nonalcoholics, *Behav. Res. Ther.*, 1965, **3**, 69–73.

Walters, R. H. Delay-of-reinforcement effects in children's learning. *Psychonom. Sci.*, 1964, **1**, 307–308. (a)

Walters, R. H. On the high-magnitude theory of aggression. *Child Develpm.*, 1964, **35**, 303–304. (b)

Walters, R. H. Implications of laboratory studies of aggression for the regulation and control of violence. *Ann. Acad. polit. soc. Sci.*, 1966, **364**, 60–72.

Walters, R. H., & Amoroso, D. M. Cognitive and motivational determinants of imitative behavior. *Brit. J. soc. clin. Psychol.*, 1967, in press.

Walters, R. H., & Brown, M. Studies of reinforcement of aggression: III. Transfer of responses to an interpersonal situation. *Child Develpm.*, 1963, **34**, 563–572.

Walters, R. H., & Brown, M. A test of the high-magnitude theory of aggression. *J. exp. Child Psychol.*, 1964, **1**, 376–387.

Walters, R. H., & Demkow, Lillian. Timing of punishment as a determinant of response inhibition. *Child Develpm.*, 1963, **34**, 207–214.

Walters, R. H., & Karal, Pearl. Social deprivation and verbal behavior, *J. Pers.*, 1960, **28**, 89–107.

Walters, R. H., & Parke, R. D. Social motivation, dependency, and susceptibility to social influence. In L. Berkowitz (Ed.), *Advances in experimental social psychology*. Vol. 1. New York: Academic Press, 1964. Pp. 231–276. (a)

Walters, R. H., & Parke, R. D. Influence of response consequences to a social model on resistance to deviation. *J. exp. Child Psychol.*, 1964, **1**, 269–280. (b)

Walters, R. H., & Parke, R. D. Emotional arousal, isolation, and discrimination learning in children. *J. exp. Child Psychol.*, 1964, **1**, 163–173. (c)

Walters, R. H., & Parke, R. D. The role of the distance receptors in the development of social responsiveness. In L. P. Lipsitt and C. C. Spiker (Eds.), *Advances in child development and behavior*. Vol. 2. New York: Academic Press, 1965. Pp. 59–96.

Walters, R. H., & Ray, E. Anxiety, social isolation, and reinforcer effectiveness. *J. Pers.*, 1960, **28**, 358–367.

Walters, R. H., Marshall, W. E., & Shooter, J. R. Anxiety, social isolation, and susceptibility to social influence. *J. Pers.*, 1960, **28**, 518–529.

Walters, R. H., Leat, Marion, & Mezei, L. Inhibition and disinhibition of responses through empathetic learning. *Canad. J. Psychol.*, 1963, **17**, 235–243.

Walters, R. H., Parke, R. D., & Cane, Valerie A. Timing of punishment and the observation of consequences to others as determinants of response inhibition. *J. exp. Child Psychol.*, 1965, **2**, 10–30.

Watson, J. B., & Raynor, Rosalie. Conditioned emotional reactions. *J. exp. Psychol.*, 1920, **3**, 1–14.

Weingold, H. P., & Webster, R. L. The effects of punishment on a cooperative behavior in children. *Child Develpm.*, 1964, **35**, 1211–1216.

White, R. W. Motivation reconsidered: The concept of competence. *Psychol. Rev.*, 1959, **66**, 297–333.

Whiting, J. W. M. The research program of the Laboratory of Human Development: The development of self-control. Unpublished manuscript, Harvard Univer., 1954.

Whiting, J. W. M., & Child, I. L. *Child training and personality*. New Haven: Yale Univer. Press, 1953.

Williams, C. D. The elimination of tantrum behavior by extinction procedures. *J. abnorm. soc. Psychol.*, 1959, **59**, 269.

Zipse, Deanna K. Effects of aggressive modeling and delay of reward on children's aggression. Unpublished paper, Univer. of Illinois, 1965.

POWER AS A PERSONALITY CONSTRUCT[1]

Henry L. Minton[2]

DEPARTMENT OF PSYCHOLOGY, STATE UNIVERSITY OF NEW YORK,
ALBANY, NEW YORK

POWER AS A PERSONALITY CONSTRUCT[1]

Henry L. Minton[2]

DEPARTMENT OF PSYCHOLOGY, STATE UNIVERSITY OF NEW YORK,
ALBANY, NEW YORK

POWER AS A PERSONALITY CONSTRUCT[1]

POWER AS A PERSONALITY CONSTRUCT[1]

Henry L. Minton[2]

DEPARTMENT OF PSYCHOLOGY, STATE UNIVERSITY OF NEW YORK,
ALBANY, NEW YORK

I. Latent and Manifest Power

Power as a psychological concept can be defined as the ability to cause environmental change so as to obtain an intended effect. This definition is in close agreement with Heider's (1958) discussion of the meaning of power, as well as with Bertrand Russell's (1938) definition of power as the production of intended effects. The term has more typically been used in the context of social relations, but it would seem to be equally appropriate in terms of the interaction between organism and physical environment.

Power can be conceived as a phenomenon occurring at two levels—manifest and latent. The production and implementation of power as exemplified by effectiveness, influence, power strategies, and attempts to gain or use power are at the level of manifest power, whereas expressed feelings of individual power and readiness to apply manifest power represent

[1] The original research reported was carried out while the author was at California State College at Los Angeles. The author thanks William Buchanan, Robert Smith, and John Stich for their assistance in data collection. A preliminary version of this paper was read by Professors Julian B. Rotter, John Schopler, and John Thibaut; their comments and suggestions are gratefully acknowledged.

[2] Present address: Department of Psychology, Miami University Oxford, Ohio.

latent power. Since this paper is concerned with an organismic analysis, only latent power is brought into focus. An extensive review of manifest power is provided by Schopler (1965).

Specifically, latent power would be an example of what Campbell (1963) refers to as an "acquired behavioral disposition." This is a generic term for such concepts as attitude, expectancy, set, and habit. Two characteristics of acquired behavioral dispositions are the effects of past events upon the behavior of organisms and the coordination of behavior in environments. Thus, latent power can be regarded as a disposition that has been acquired through past experiences in instrumental situations and that functions as a coordinator of behavior in such situations. As a disposition, it can further be conceived as varying along a dimension of powerlessness-powerfulness.

To clarify power as a construct it is necessary to discuss several concepts that approximate the meaning of power, but do not clearly specify it as a reflection of individual differences.

Autonomy has been discussed by several theorists. Angyal (1941) uses autonomy as a central concept in his theory of personality, defining it as a tendency toward self-determination, toward mastering oneself and the environment. Rank (1945), Fromm (1941), and Erikson (1950) also emphasize the theme of autonomy or individuality. Autonomy is viewed by all of these as a developing characteristic of the individual that can come into conflict with environmental restraints. The degree of one's autonomy reflects how successfully one has been able to come to terms with environmental demands while maintaining individuality. Angyal and Erikson do not present a clear differential dimension. Rank and Fromm do offer dimensions of individual differences, but in the form of a typology rather than a continuum. As Guilford (1959) points out, there are difficulties in supporting typological categories.empirically.

Another related concept is competence, which White (1959) defines as the individual's capacity to interact effectively with his environment. The motivating state underlying activities in the service of competence is labeled "effectance," and produces an accompanying experience termed a "feeling of efficacy." Efficacy is described as a feeling of being active, of doing something, of having an influence on something. This is essentially equivalent to the meaning of latent power. Piaget (1954) also uses the term efficacy, describing it as a dim sense or awareness that feelings of effort, of longing in one's actions, are somehow responsible for external events. Efficacy takes place during the sensorimotor period of development and serves as the basis for the development of feelings of psychological causality. However, both White and Piaget tend to view efficacy more as a general developmental characteristic than a differential one.

The various analyses of psychological causality[3] (Heider, 1958; Piaget, 1932; Werner, 1957) are also relevant. Psychological causality is a dimension of cognitive development in which the locus of causality for a personal act progresses from an external to an internal source. Ascribing responsibility for an act only on the basis of intentionality, and perceiving oneself rather than others as responsible for a personally intended act are reflections of an internal locus of causality. This type of internalization is inherent in feelings of powerfulness. The concept of causality, however, has not been clearly related to personality, although Witkin and his associates (Witkin, Lewis, Hertzman, Machover, Meissner, & Wapner, 1954; Witkin, Dyk, Faterson, Goodenough, & Karp, 1962) have investigated a dimension of individual differences, field dependence-independence, that reflects the degree of reliance on external versus internal cues of perception.

Thus, although autonomy, efficacy, and psychological causality are all close in meaning to latent power, there is some ambiguity in using them as personality constructs. There is also one construct, alienation, that bears an inverse relation to power. Seeman (1959) points out that one of the meanings of alienation is a feeling of powerlessness, and that this is distinct from four other meanings of the term alienation isolation, normlessness or anomie, self-estrangement, and meaninglessness.

The present paper will survey theoretical approaches and consequent attempts at measuring and manipulating the dimension of latent power. Variables that appear to be related to latent power will also be discussed. Following the review an evaluation of the literature will be made along with suggestions for an integrative analysis of power at both the manifest and latent levels. Extensive discussion of the relation of power to psychopathology or the interaction of power and social structure will be beyond the scope of this paper. However, implications for these areas will be raised.

II. Theories and Studies of Latent Power

The most direct approaches to the concept of latent power are those of Heider, Thibaut and Kelley, and Rotter. First, however, a brief survey will be made of several earlier approaches that had some influence on the theorists just mentioned.

A. EARLY APPROACHES

There has generally been more emphasis in the literature on manifest power, although the attempts at dealing with power as an attitude date back some years. Several psychoanalytic theorists wrote about power as

[3] Psychological causality should be distinguished from phenomenal causality. The former refers to person perception, the latter to thing perception. Michotte (1963) has conducted a systematic investigation of phenomenal causality.

an attitudinal characteristic of the individual. The first specifically to refer to power was Adler (1927) with his concept of the "will to power" in which power is equated with masculinity. It was postulated that although this striving for power is especially marked in women, it is found in all individuals when they feel inferior. Hence, according to Adler, if one has feelings of powerlessness, one attempts to compensate for this by striving for masculinity as a symbol of power. In his later writings Adler (1930) spoke of striving for superiority or perfection, which appears to be more commensurate with a broader conception of power as the general interaction of the individual with his environment.

Similar to Adler's view of power striving as a compensation for felt inferiority is Horney's (1942) discussion of the neurotic need for power. Such a need stems from anxiety and feelings of inferiority, and is sought as a means of protecting oneself from these feelings. Horney does distinguish neurotic power strivings from feelings of power based on personal attributes such as physical strength or ability.

Two other early conceptions of power as an attitude are provided by Sullivan and Rank. Their emphasis is not on power as primarily a compensatory mechanism for feelings of powerlessness, but rather as a general attitude of the developing individual. In Sullivan's (1947) system the "power motive" is the impulse to obtain and maintain a feeling of ability. Emphasis is placed on the ability to obtain security in interpersonal relations. Rank (1945) deals with power as an attitude in his concept of "will." The implication is that the individual can become an initiating power interacting with the environment. He states that " ... the inner world, taken in from the outside by means of identification, has become in the course of time an independent power, which in its turn by way of projection so influences and seeks to alter the external, that its correspondence to the inner is even more close" (Rank, 1945, p. 111, footnote). This conceptualization appears to be close to Bertrand Russell's idea of power as the ability to produce intended effects.

All these psychoanalytic approaches tend to be rather vague about how power feelings develop and how varying degrees of powerfulness are maintained, consistently other than by assuming that an innate feeling of inferiority must produce compensatory power strivings. This is especially true of Adler and Horney.

Another relatively early view of power was presented by Lewin (1936) as part of his field theory. The Lewinian emphasis is on the situational analysis of the individual's interaction with the restraining forces of the environment. Although this approach is in marked contrast to the psychoanalytic approach of innate needs and long-term strivings, there is an interesting similarity to the Rankian view of the individual's interaction with environmental forces. The Lewinian equivalent of power is space of free movement, which consists of those regions within an individual's life space that are accessible to one's abilities. The space of free movement is limited by two types of environmental forces: quasi-physical barriers, representing that which is beyond a person's abilities; and quasi-social barriers, representing that which is forbidden to the person. Lewin (1941) further points out that the space of free movement usually increases during development, although it can decrease as a result of regression. Power at both the latent and manifest levels can be represented by the space of free movement.

B. Heider's Concept of Power

Heider's (1958) exposition of power is presented within the context of a naive analysis of action. Action outcome is a function of the effective forces of the person and the environment. The effective personal force is composed of a motivational factor, labeled "trying," and a power factor. Heider points out that in a naive psychology a person trying to do something is significantly different from a person having the power or ability to accomplish something. It is therefore necessary to regroup "... the constituents of action in such a way that the power factor and the effective environmental force are combined into the concept 'can,' leaving the motivational factor clearly separate and distinct" (Heider, 1958, pp. 84, 85). The concept of can thus refers to a relatively stable relationship between the person and the environment, or more specifically between the power of the person and the strength of the environmental forces. Can, in other words, seems to be equivalent to Lewin's space of free movement. Power as a component of can represents the nonmotivational factors contributed by the person in effecting environmental change.

Power as an attitude is reflected by the attribution of can. Heider defines attribution as the linking of an event with its underlying conditions. In the case of can, a connection is formed between the success or failure of an action outcome and one of the two components of can—the person or environment. "If the success 'belongs' to the person, then the person is felt to be responsible for it; if it belongs to the environment, then the environment is held accountable" (Heider, 1958, p. 89). Thus, an attitude of powerfulness or high power is consistent with an action outcome of success ascribed to the person; and attitude of powerlessness or low power is consistent with success ascribed to the environment. In an action outcome of failure the foregoing relationship would be reversed. Heider's analysis of the attribution of can is relevant to both self- and other-perceptions of action.

Several conditions determining attribution to one or the other source are discussed. Task difficulty represents an invariable property of the environment. In the successful outcome of an easy task, causal attribution is assigned to the task. If the task is difficult, causal attribution is assigned to the person. The variable environmental factors of opportunity and luck also contribute to attribution. When the success of an act is connected with luck or opportunity, the environment rather than the person is seen as primarily responsible. Under a situation of luck environmental conditions are seen as a product of luck. Heider points out two conditions leading to the cognition of luck: an action outcome that is improbable or non-predictory and an action outcome that is contradictory to expectations.

Personal characteristics represent another set of determinants contributing to the cognition of can. The causal attribution of an act is connected with the person when the person is characterized by ability, knowledge, intelligence, strength, or an attitude of self-confidence. Variable personal factors such as fatigue and mood also tend to point to the person rather than the environment as the causal source of an act.

There are other factors underlying attribution that are not so clearly attached to one or the other source. Heider points out that social and legal status may at times be seen as belonging to the environment, and at other times as a personal characteristic. The distinction between ascribed and achieved status would seem to be relevant here, so that the person with achieved status would be more often connected with an act than the person with ascribed status. Possessions, needs, opinion, and suggestion are other factors mentioned that variably contribute to the placement of attribution.

In summary, Heider points out several variables that contribute to the development of a power attitude in a given situation. The power attitude is dimensionalized on a continuum extending from an environmental or external source to a personal or internal source of action.

Heider's conceptualization of power also refers to the development of a consistent attitude across situations. He states: "There also appear to be individual differences in the tendency to attribute the cause of events to the self or to outside sources . . . people differ in their propensity for heteronomous (external) versus autonomous (internal) attribution" (Heider, 1958, pp. 168, 169). Heider does not specifically point out how these consistent attitudes develop, although the inference is that they represent the cumulative effect of the various determinants of attribution.

C. THIBAUT AND KELLEY'S CONCEPT OF POWER

Thibaut and Kelley (1959), like Heider, conceive of power as a product of the person–environment interaction. Of direct relevance to the present concern is the relationship they postulate between power and "comparison level" (CL). The CL represents a zero or neutral point on a scale of out-comes. Any event or relationship that produces outcomes above the CL is a source of satisfaction to the individual; any event or relationship that produces outcomes below the CL is a source of dissatisfaction. This concept is very similar to Helson's (1948) adaptation level.

The neutral point of outcomes or comparison level is dependent on the outcomes that are salient at a given time. The CL thus tends to shift or adapt according to the outcomes being experienced. On this basis a general-ized expectation of what is satisfying and dissatisfying is built up. In other words, depending on the consistent level of salient outcomes across situa-tions, a person's CL represents his general level of expectation of outcomes. Thus, an individual with a generalized high CL will tend to emphasize rewards and deemphasize costs, whereas an individual with a generalized low CL will tend to emphasize costs and deemphasize rewards. The high-CL person is characterized by attitudes of powerfulness and optimism; the low-CL person by powerlessness and pessimism. Latent power therefore appears to be coincident with level of CL.

Consistent with Heider's discussion of the attribution of can, Thibaut and Kelley point out that the more powerful person will assign causality for success to his own range of control, while the less confident person will assign causality for success to external agents such as fate and good luck. In turn, the person who feels he is in control of the situation will attend more to environmental feedback, since this feedback is seen as the result of the person's actions rather than the environmental forces. Thus, in a given situation of positive feedback, the high-CL person will anticipate continued success, whereas the low-CL person will expect failure after having been successful.

Thibaut and Kelley also discuss manifest power. They conceive of two types of manifest power—fate control and behavior control. The differentia-tion of these is "...on the basis of whether or not B can, without exercising counter-power, attenuate the variations in his outcomes caused by A" (Thibaut & Kelley, 1959, p. 124). In fate control A can affect B's outcomes regardless of what B does; in behavior control A can affect B's outcomes only if he can make it desirable for B to vary his behavior too. Thus, in behavior control B's outcomes are a function of the interaction of his own behavioral choices with those of A.

There has been no direct empirical test of Thibaut and Kelley's approach to power attitudes; however, there have been several studies of the percep-tion of power in others that provide results consistent with their approach. Thibaut and Riecken (1955) demonstrated that causal attribution for a compliant act is dependent on A's perception of B's power. The perceived power was based upon an experimental confederate's status and competence.

When B was perceived as powerful, his compliance to A was seen as internally caused or spontaneous; when B was perceived as having little power, his compliance was seen as externally caused or coerced. With a low-power person, A saw himself as the causal locus for B's compliance. Heider (1958), commenting on the results of this study, points out: "...a person of power is more apt to be seen as commanding his own will than is a weak person. Conversely, the more ineffectual person is more apt to be seen as being pushed into things than is the person with a strong will" (p. 250).

In an interesting extension of the Thibaut and Riecken study Schopler and Matthews (1965) investigated the perception had by a powerful person of individuals dependent on him. In a problem-solving situation with a simulated partnership of "directors" and "associates" it was found that the director, or powerful person, gave more help to a partner whose dependence was perceived as being involuntary and the result of external factors rather than as voluntary and internally induced. It is pointed out that voluntary dependence is inversely related to the evocation of a social responsibility norm. A study by Jones and DeCharms (1958) gives similar results. In a problem-solving situation in which the perceiver was deprived of a reward because of the failure of another person, internal causality for the failure due to the other person's lack of effort was rated less favorably than external causality where the other person was perceived as being unable to solve the problem even if he tried.

D. ROTTER'S CONCEPT OF INTERNAL-EXTERNAL CONTROL

Rotter has developed a concept from his social learning theory (cf. Rotter, 1954, 1955, 1960) which reflects a continuum of latent power. In defining internal versus external control of reinforcement Rotter, Seeman, and Liverant (1962) state: " ... not only can situations vary in the degree to which people perceive that their own behavior rather than the behavior of others is the determiner of the reinforcement—but individuals themselves can vary in the degree to which the same event in the same situation is perceived as a function of their own characteristics versus the characteristics of others.—To include the notion of chance versus skill, own characteristics versus characteristics of others, own potential to control the enviroment versus influence of others, we have adopted the general term internal versus external control of reinforcement" (p. 474).

In other words, external control represents the attribution of causality to environmental forces; internal control represents the attribution of causality to personal forces. Although Rotter does not use the term power, his conceptualization of internal-external control appears to be highly consistent with the concept of power as used herein, and as used by Heider and Thibaut and Kelley. It should be pointed out that Seeman (1959) uses the term powerlessness as an equivalent of external control. It is thus assumed that the dimension of internal-external control reflects the latent power continuum.

Comprehensive reviews of the work relevant to the study of internal-external control have been presented elsewhere (cf. Lefcourt, 1966; Rotter, 1966). It will be sufficient here to refer to representative studies, as well as to report results that have been obtained by the present author.

Rotter's (1966) conception of the development of attitudes of internal-external control is quite similar to both Thibaut and Kelley's adaptation rationale for the development of power attitudes and Heider's situational analysis of causal attribution. According to Rotter a generalized expectation of one's causal relationship with events is developed on the basis of the perceived source of reinforcement. When the reinforcement is seen as not contingent upon the individual's behavior, it will have little salience in determining future outcome expectancies. Conversely, when the reinforcement is seen as internally caused by the individual, it will be highly salient in determining future outcome expectancies. Depending on one's reinforcement history, a consistent attitude will develop regarding the source of reinforcement as tending toward an internal or external locus.

1. Situational Comparisons

In a given situation the individual is disposed to interpret the locus of causality according to the generalized attitude of internal-external control that has been developed across situations. However, as Rotter points out, the nature of the situation and the degree to which it is structured will also determine the individual's causal attribution. Thus, the more uniform a situation is and the more clearly it is structured, the less one's generalized expectancy will contribute toward causal attribution. To analyze the role of situational determinants Rotter has hypothesized that perceived causal relations will be dependent on whether the task is structured as one of skill or one of chance. Consistent with Heider's hypothesis of environmental determinants of power, Rotter predicts that skill conditions lead to internal causality and chance conditions to external causality. Thus, in a skill situation one's expectancies of future outcomes will be more contingent upon past reinforcement than in a chance situation.

To test this hypothesis Rotter and his associates have conducted several studies comparing verbal expectancies in skill and chance learning tasks. Most of these studies (cf. Rotter, 1966) have used an ambiguous task that has been defined by the E as one of either skill or chance. The general results of these studies demonstrate that reinforcements under skill conditions have a significantly greater effect on shifting expectancies in the direction of past reinforcements. Under chance conditions there is a strong trend toward unusual shifts, that is, an increase in expectancies after failure and a decrease after success. This is often referred to as the "gambler's fallacy" (cf. Cohen, 1960).

Also reflecting of the general finding that reinforcements under skill are more salient in determining expectancies are the results regarding the rate of extinction of verbal expectancies. The criterion for extinction in these studies is defined as a stated expectancy of 1 or 0 on a scale of 10 for three consecutive trials. In one study, by James and Rotter (1958), 50% and 100% reinforcement schedules were each used in skill and chance conditions with an ESP-type task (a card-guessing problem). Among the skill groups there was a trend toward greater resistance to extinction under 100% reinforcement; among the chance groups there was significantly greater resistance under 50% reinforcement. In comparisons between skill and chance, the number of trials to extinction under 50% reinforcement was significantly greater for chance than skill, whereas the number of trials to extinction under 100% reinforcement was significantly greater for skill than chance. These findings indicate that under continuous (100%) reinforcement skill instructions are more consistent with the reinforcement schedule, and hence make it more difficult for the subject to accept the change in reinforcement during extinction as reflected by the greater number of trials to extinction. The S who is exposed to chance instructions under continuous reinforcement would seem to be more sensitive to the change in reinforcement during extinction since he is oriented to expect environmental variability beyond his control. The conditions during partial (50%) reinforcement are reversed so that chance instructions serve as the condition more consistent with the reinforcement schedule. What is perhaps most interesting about these results is that the person who is oriented toward internal causality is more greatly influenced by past reinforcements, so that he finds it more difficult to adapt to extinction after continuous reinforcement. As Rotter (1966) points out, this is a reversal of the partial reinforcement effect of greater resistance to extinction.

Rotter (1966) reports several other studies that are consistent with the findings of James and Rotter. However, in an unpublished study by Minton, Buchanan, and Stich using the same ESP-type task as in the foregoing studies, somewhat different results were obtained. Under continuous 100% reinforcement during acquisition the extinction of verbal expectancies was compared for skill, chance, and ambiguous instructions. In addition to the E, a scorekeeper was present to increase the saliency of reported feedback to the S about his performance. The scorekeeper reported the S's score at the end of each trial and sat in a position in which neither the E nor S could view the scoresheet. The results indicated no significant difference in trials to extinction under the three sets of instructions, although, consistent with the previous findings, the skill group did have the largest mean number of trials and the chance group the smallest. The results were reanalyzed by subtracting the number of unusual shifts during extinction from trials to extinction, as this appeared by inspection to be a confounding factor. These results showed a more marked trend in the predicted direction (skill group having the largest mean), but still failed to reach statistical significance. It appears that the presence of a scorekeeper tends to mitigate the effect of instructions of chance or skill. Interestingly, this is in the direction of greater internal control, since the means of the groups in this study are higher than the corresponding means of previous studies. If the scorekeeper was perceived as a confederate of the E (thus representing a situation of external control), then more rapid extinction would have been expected. The effects of chance and skill instructions in other than two-person situations need further investigation.

Rotter (1966) also reports on the results of several studies that indicate the conditions affecting perceptions of chance versus skill. Some of the conditions that account for a sequence of reinforcement as *not* being chance controlled are significant deviations from a 50% reinforcement schedule in a right-wrong situation, reinforcements that have a definite pattern, and minimal variability of performance in tasks where a scoring continuum is provided. Heider (1958), in his discussion of situational determinants of causal attribution, points to similar factors.

The situational comparisons of behavior under skill and chance conditions consistently indicate that the person who is confronted with external causality is less influenced by past reinforcements or past experience than the person who is confronted with internal causality. As Rotter points out, the person exposed to external causality may learn less, which raises interesting questions for learning theory, since such theory is often based on situations of external causality in the form of experimenter control. It might also be added that the amount of control the S perceives would also differentiate types of learning, such as in classical versus operant conditioning.

2. Individual Differences

Since the late 1950's a number of attempts have been made by Rotter and his associates to develop a measure of individual differences in attitudes of internal-external control. The first scale, developed by Phares and James (cf. Rotter, 1966), utilized separate Likert-type items for external and internal attitudes. Subsequently, forced-choice items were developed, providing a direct comparison of external and internal attitudes. The items were developed from a set of logical content areas, as exemplified by external control items representing attitudes of change, fate, or external control reinforcements. An item analysis of the original set of forced-choice items revealed high intercorrelation among specific content areas, and no further attempts were made to develop scales of subareas of internal-external control. Further revisions were made to control for social desirability and low item validity. The final version of the scale, which is referred to as the Internal-External Control (I-E) Scale, consists of 23 critical items and 6 filler items. The complete scale thus consists of 29 forced-choice items and is scored in the external direction. The item statements are in the form of expectancies rather than behavioral preferences, which is consistent with an attitudinal variable.

The psychometric data for the I-E scale are generally encouraging. Rotter (1966) reports moderate and consistent biserial item correlations with total score (ranging from .109 to .480). Both internal consistency and test-retest estimates of reliability are moderately high, with correlations generally in the .70's. Factor analyses of the I-E scale have indicated that much of the variance is included in a general factor. Additional factors involving only a few items have not been sufficiently reliable to suggest subscales. Evidence of good discriminant validity is indicated by low correlations with measures of social desirability and intelligence. Multimethod measurement shows significant agreement with the I-E scale by a story-completion test of internal-external control involving situations of moral transgression and a semistructured interview measure of internal-external control.

Normative data for the I-E scale show good agreement among several college samples.[4] Sex differences among these samples tend to be minimal, although in one case (University of Connecticut) females were significantly more external. Rotter (1966) points out that one difference between this sample and the others was the large size of the class ($n = 303$) from which all the Ss were drawn. A study by Wolfe (1966) using adult samples drawn from several communities found that females tended to be more external on the I-E scale and this difference reached significance at the .01 level when the samples were combined. There is thus the suggestion that sex differences on internal-external control may be more characteristic of noncollege than of college samples.

Other measures similar to the I-E scale have been developed. Dean (1961) constructed the Powerlessness Scale, consisting of nine Likert scale items, as a measure of one of Seeman's (1959) dimensions of alienation. Lefcourt (1963) reports a significant correlation of .39 ($p < .01$) between the I-E and powerlessness scales for a sample of 60 Negro Ss, but points out that since mean scores on both scales were higher in general for Negroes than for

[4]The author, in a group administration of the I-E scale at California State College at Los Angeles, obtained a mean of 8.35 and SD of 3.74 for a combined male-female sample of 148. This closely corresponds to the norms reported by Rotter. Also generally consistent was the close agreement in scores between males and females.

whites, a much higher relationship would have been obtained if a wider range of scores were used. Another related scale is Strodtbeck's (1958) V-scale. It consists of eight items, some with a high factor loading on "Mastery" and others with a high factor loading on "Independence of Family." The three mastery items deal with an individual's concern for demonstrating personal control of the environment. A significant relationship between the I-E scale and the full-length Strodtbeck scale ($r = -.26$, $p < .01$) is reported by Liberty, Burnstein, and Moulton (1966) for a sample of 106 United States Air Force basic airmen. A higher relationship ($r = -.33$) was found between the I-E scale and the three mastery items. There have also been three measures developed for assessing internal-external control with children. Bialer (1961) constructed a 23-item questionnaire that was adapted from some of the earlier forms of the I-E scale. Unlike other I-E adapted scales it is scored in the internal direction. Crandall, Katkovsky, and Preston (1962) developed a questionnaire of "self-responsibility" in achievement situations, which is titled the Intellectual Achievement Responsibility (IAR) Scale. A projective-type test that is similar to the Rosenzweig picture frustration measure has been developed by Battle and Rotter (1962). They (Battle and Rotter, 1963) report a significant correlation of $-.42$ ($p < .01$) between their measure and the Bialer measure.

The I-E scale has been correlated with other personality measures. In a comparison with the achievement scale from the Personality Research Form (cf. Jackson, 1965), unpublished data obtained by the present author, using a sample of 87 males and 61 females from California State College at Los Angeles, yielded significant negative correlations of $-.44$ ($p < .01$) and $-.25$ ($p < .05$), respectively. These results are consistent with Odell's (1959) finding of a significant negative relationship between achievement and externality ($r = -.25, p < .05$) for a sample of 74 males, and Lichtman and Julian's (1964) finding of a negative, although statistically insignificant, relationship between the same two variables ($r = -.27$) for a sample of 28 females. Odell used a TAT-like measure of achievement, while Lichtman and Julian used the story-completion method developed by French (1958). Thus, although different techniques were used, an inverse relationship between need achievement and external control has been consistently found. In the data reported by the author this relationship was more marked for males.

In other unpublished data of the author, using part of the sample referred to in the preceding paragraph (for the males, 21 of the original sample of 87 did not take the Role Concept Repertory (REP) Test), correlations were obtained between the I-E scale and Bieri's (1955) measure of cognitive complexity adapted from Kelley's REP test. A low but significant inverse relationship between external control and cognitive complexity scores was obtained for males, with correlations of $-.24$ ($p < .05$) for both the number of differences minus similarities among individuals and the total number of constructs. For females the results were reversed, with a positive coefficient of .24 between external control and the number of differences minus similarities, which was just below the significance level. The other complexity score was related in the same direction but considerably below the significance level. No relationship for either males or females was found between internal-external control and another test of cognitive complexity—a forced-choice form of the Barron-Welsh Art Judgment Test. [This test measures a preference for complex versus simple figures, whereas the REP test measures complexity in making social judgments. Sechrest and Jackson (1961) report low intercorrelations between the tests, and this was also replicated by the author in the foregoing study.] The results of the correlations of the I-E scale with both achievement and cognitive complexity as measured by the REP test indicate sex differences and suggest the relevance of considering the relationship of sex role identification to the development of power attitudes.

Other I-E correlations with personality measures are reported by Rotter *et al.* (1962) and Charde (1966). Based on an earlier Likert-type form of the I-E scale Rotter *et al.* report a significant relationship between external control and authoritarianism as measured by the California F scale. Internal control was related to level of aspiration while dependency, as measured by an incomplete sentences test, had a curvilinear relationship to the I-E scale. Charde (1966), using the Jackson-Minton Adjective Preference Scale (1963), found significant low correlations between internal control and the adjective scales of perceptive, assertive, and active for a college sample of females. She found no relationship between the I-E scale and the autonomy scale from the Personality Research Form (cf. Jackson, 1965). This is interesting since the term autonomy often is equated with power or mastery. However, autonomy can also imply an asocial tendency of being afraid to be influenced by others. This is consistent with what Sofer (1956) reports in her study as one type of "inner-directed" individual (cf. Riesman, 1954). Rotter (1966) points out that "Riesman has been concerned with whether the individual is controlled from within or from without" (p. 8), which differs from whether or not the individual believes he is in control of his environment.

The I-E scale has also been correlated with measures of anxiety. Butterfield (1964), using both the Child and Waterhouse (1953) Frustration-Reaction Inventory and the Alpert-Haber Facilitating-Debilitating Test Anxiety Questionnaire (1960) with a sample of 47, found that external control was related to nonconstructive problem-solving responses ($r = .57$, $p < .01$) and debilitating anxiety ($r = .61$, $p < .01$). Conversely, external control was negatively related to constructive problem-solving responses

($r = -.86$, $p < .01$) and facilitative anxiety ($r = -.82$, $p < .01$). Another comparison between the Alpert-Haber measure and the I-E scale was made by Watson (in press) with a sample of 648 college students. A correlation of .25 ($p < .01$) was found between I-E and debilitating anxiety, while a correlation of $-.08$ ($p < .05$) was found between I-E and facilitating anxiety. The results reported by Watson provide a more meaningful indication of the degree of relationship than those reported by Butterfield because of the much larger sample size. In a comparison between the I-E scale and the Mandler-Sarason Test Anxiety Questionnaire (1952) Liberty et al. (1966) report a correlation of .44 ($p < .01$) for a sample of 106 airmen. The relationship between test anxiety and external control seems consistent with the findings of an inverse relationship between external control and need achievement, suggesting that individuals who are external tend to be low on achievement orientation because of test anxiety or fear of failure. In comparisons between the I-E scale and the Taylor Manifest Anxiety Scale (1953) the results are not as conclusive as with test anxiety. Rotter (1966) reports one correlation of .24 ($n = 111, p < .05$) and another of .00 ($n = 114$). However, with a much larger sample Watson (in press) reports a correlation of .36 ($n = 648$, $p < .01$).

Another form of anxiety that has been compared with the control dimension is anomie or normlessness. Wolfe (1966) reports significant correlations ($p < .01$) of .42, .48, and .49 between a modification of the Srole (1956) anomia scale and the I-E scale for three adult samples drawn from separate communities. Consistent with this finding is Dean's (1961) report of a correlation of .48 ($p < .01$) between his scales of powerlessness and normlessness. Both of these scales were developed as measures of two of Seeman's (1959) dimensions of alienation.

Studies by Pervin (1963) and Cromwell, Rosenthal, Shakow, and Zahn (1961) provide data that are consistent with the general finding of a relationship between external control and anxiety. In the Pervin study, control was situationally manipulated in a condition of threat by varying the degree to which the S, as opposed to the E, could control the application of electric shock that the S would receive. S control of shock was found to be less anxiety arousing than, and preferable to, E control. In other words, a greater degree of anxiety is aroused in response to threat under a situationally induced condition of external control than one of internal control. This parallels the findings that a generalized expectancy of external control is associated with greater feelings of debilitation anxiety than an expectancy of internal control. In their study, Cromwell et al. (1961) compared a group of schizophrenics with a group of normals. It was found that schizophrenics were significantly more external on each of three measures of the control dimension. These measures included the original Likert-type scale, an early form of the forced-choice I-E scale, and the Bialer-Cromwell children's locus of control scale. In addition to the control scales, reaction time was measured under a sequence of four conditions, which differed according to the degree of control imposed by the E. As predicted, normals had a lower reaction time in the autonomous or internal conditions, whereas schizophrenics had a lower reaction time in the external control conditions. Since anxiety mediates schizophrenic behavior, it would be expected that a group of schizophrenics as compared to normals would feel more externally controlled and would perform better under conditions of external control.

Several studies indicate that internal-external control is generally independent of attitudes on social issues and political affiliation. Charde (1966) found no relationship with a social distance scale toward Negroes. Rotter (1966) reports a study in which mean scores on the I-E scale failed to differentiate college students who identified themselves as Democrats, Republicans, or independents. Unpublished data by the author yielded similar results with a sample of 136 students from California State College at Los Angeles, although some differences were seen between males and females. For the male group of 69, internal-external control was unrelated to the following measures: a 7-point scale of political liberalism–conservatism; Tomkins' (1963) measure of "left" versus "right" ideology; and Levinson's (1957) scale of attitudes on international relations. For the female group of 67, however, low but significant correlations were found between external control and conservatism ($r = .26, p < .05$), and between external control and an attitude of chauvinistic nationalism regarding international relations ($r = .28, p < .05$). These sex differences may reflect a more simplistic conceptualization of political issues on the part of females, especially as exemplified in the relationship of external control and chauvinistic nationalism. It is possible that the I-E scale might differentiate between individuals with extreme political affiliations and more moderate political groups.

Social class differences in internal-external control have been reported in several studies using noncollege populations. Battle and Rotter (1963) found a general relationship between higher social class and internal control in comparing Negro and white sixth- and eighth-grade children. A projectice-type test was used as a measure of internal-external control, and the general social class effect was obtained with race and intellectual level controlled. Specifically, it was found that lower-class Negroes were significantly more external than middle-class Negroes and lower-class or middle-class whites. Similar findings were obtained in a study by Lefcourt and Ladwig (1965a) of Negro and white prisoners. With most of the prisoners categorized in the lower socioeconomic class, Negroes were more external than whites as reflected by both the I-E scale and Dean's (1961) Powerlessness scale. Social class differences in the related attitude of "mastery" are reported by Strodtbeck (1958), who found middle-class and upper-class Jews higher on this variable than lower-class Italians. A study by Graves and Jessor (cf. Lefcourt, 1966) of a tri-ethnic community showed whites to be the most internal, followed by Spanish-Americans, with Indians being the most external.

3. Validity Studies

Rotter (1966) reports four types of criterion situations in which the I-E scale has been used as a predictor: performance in controlled laboratory tasks; attempts to control the environment; achievement situations; and reactions to social influence.

Individual prediction of performance in the ESP-type tasks has been only partially successful. The generally consistent prediction has been the tendency of externals to manifest the gambler's fallacy of unusual shifts. In the previously cited experimental study by Minton, Buchanan, and Stich a covariance design did not yield significant regressions of the I-E scale on the experimental measures.

Several investigations reported by Rotter have supported the hypothesis that individuals who are more internal will demonstrate more initiative and effort in controlling their environment. As an example, Seeman (Seeman and Evans, 1962; Seeman, 1963) has found that internals learn more about their environmental setting than externals. In the first study, using a scale adapted from an earlier form of the I-E scale, the investigators found that internals sought out and acquired more information in a hospital setting, and this was independent of occupational status, education, and ward placement. In a study with reformatory inmates in which level of intelligence was controlled Seeman (1963) found that internals knew more about their institution, the parole system, and long-range factors that could affect them after leaving the reformatory. Other studies have investigated the relationship between the control dimension and social action behavior. Gore and Rotter (1963), in a study with students at a southern Negro college, found a relationship between internal control and paper-and-pencil commitment to various civil rights activities. Consistent with these results, Strickland (1965) found that activists in a Negro civil rights movement were significantly more internal than nonactive Negroes who were matched for education and social economic status. However, in a study by Charde (1966), which investigated the relationship between internality and congruence between verbal attitude and overt action, the I-E scale independent of the degree of social distance did not predict actual volunteers for activities sponsored by an operating civil rights group. The study included a sample of both Negro and white students at California State College at Los Angeles, and the I-E scale failed to predict volunteers from either group. Although the Gore and Rotter study did not involve any follow-up of commitment, the difference in results may be due to the differences in the type of civil rights activities called for. The Charde study called for an individual and anonymous type of participation, such as tutoring or being a day camp counselor, whereas the other study called for organized group demonstrations. Only the latter type of activity seems to offer high reinforcement value for the college student. In addition, in both the Gore and Rotter study and the Strickland study there was high reinforcement value for the Negro subjects in being called upon to participate in activities aimed at a breakdown of segregation. Thus, it seems that internality will predict social action behavior only when such behavior has a high reinforcement value. It would also seem that internality is related to verbal attitude–overt action congruency when high reinforcement value is intrinsic to overt action. However, this relationship has not as yet been investigated.

Rotter hypothesizes a positive relationship between internal control and need for achievement, but points out that the strength of covariation is limited by the use of competition on the part of some externals as a defense against failure. The previously cited correlational data in which moderate relationships were obtained seem supportive of Rotter's hypothesis. The finding by the author that this relationship is more marked with college males than females is somewhat consistent with the findings of sex differences in early grade school children reported by Crandall et al. (1962). Using the IAR scale, they found it related to free-play achievement behavior and achievement test scores for boys but not girls. It was also found, however, that girls were more prone to assign responsibility to themselves for feedback of success or failure. This is in contrast to the finding by Wolfe (1966) with an adult sample that females were more external.

Rotter reports that studies investigating the effects of social influence as related to internal-external control have shown that internals are more resistive to subtle attempts that are not to their benefit. However, if given a conscious choice, the internal may conform. These results were obtained in studies using verbal conditioning and in an Asch-type yielding situation. The relationship of the control dimension to effectiveness in influencing others was investigated by Phares (1965). He found that internals were significantly more successful than externals in their attempt to change the attitudes of others. In addition, externals did not differ in the amount of change achieved from a control group who were not exposed to any influence situation.

A relevant issue for the validity of the control dimension is that of altering expectancies. The only available evidence is a study by Lefcourt and Ladwig (1965b) with Negro subjects who were inmates in a correctional institution. By imposing a reference group identification as jazz musicians they found that Negroes who were previously characterized as highly external acted with an internal orientation of competition against a white opponent in a game situation. The competitive mode was maintained even though the subjects were exposed to continuous losses. This persistance was not present in two control groups where there was an absence of the reference group identification. The control subjects manifested a failure-avoidance pattern which is consistent with an external orientation.

E. RELATED VARIABLES

There are several other variables that appear to be closely related to latent power or internal-external control. These include skill-chance preference, Machiavellianism, need for control, subjective probability, and attributed power.

1. Skill-Chance Preference

Personality differences in preference for skill- or chance-determined outcomes were investigated by Bortner (1964), who studied a group of males at a VA domiciliary. He used the Skill-Chance Preference (SC) Scale, which was adapted from a method developed by Shuford, Jones, and Bock (1960). The SC scale provides the subject with a choice between a skill-determined outcome and a chance-determined outcome. Although the odds for each choice vary across the ten trials and most subjects shift their preferences accordingly, it was found that some subjects maintained consistent choices. A group with highly consistent chance preferences was compared with a group with highly consistent skill preferences on the Id-Ego-Superego (IES) Test (cf. Dombrose and Slobin, 1958) and two measures of field dependence. The results indicated that chance subjects avoided situations in which their capacities might be tested, while skill subjects showed greater ego-control. The skill subjects also showed greater field independence as measured by the Machover criterion for the draw-a-person test (cf. Witkin et al., (1954), although no differences were found on the Thurstone modification of the Gottschaldt figures.

The SC scale appears to be similar to the I-E scale, although it measures task preferences rather than expectancies and identifies individuals only at the extreme ends of a dimension rather than along a continuum. It is quite possible that the SC scale might be more limited in eliciting extreme preferences with noninstitutionalized populations. It would seem that there is a close relationship between task preference and expectancy, but this needs to be investigated.

2. Machiavellianism

Christie (1964) has developed several forms of a scale consisting of items adapted from statements in Machiavelli's *The Prince* and *Discourses*. Individuals who score high on the Mach scale endorse items indicative of a cynical outlook, interpersonal detachment, and manipulativeness. An earlier form of the Mach scale had high negative correlations (ranging from $-.35$ to $-.75$) with measures of social desirability; however, Christie (1964) reports that the most recent form of the scale (Mach V), a forced-choice technique, is not substantially correlated with social desirability.

Several studies have compared scores on the Mach scale with laboratory situations of social manipulation. Exline, Thibaut, Brannon, and Gumpert (1961) induced subjects to cheat and found, contrary to prediction, that low scorers tended to cheat more frequently. However, it was found that when questioned about cheating by the E high scorers looked their interrogator in the eye significantly longer while maintaining their innocence. An unpublished study by Geis, Christie, and Nelson (cf. Jones, 1964) found that high scorers could more easily perform a deceptive and manipulative role with a peer. Geis and Christie (1965) report other studies that have indicated a relationship between high Mach scores and social manipulation. Consistent with interpersonal detachment, Jones, Gergen, and Davis (1962), in a study with female college students, found that those who scored higher on the Mach scale were more unresponsive to evaluative feedback from others. Other findings with the Mach scale have been reported by Singer (1964), who found a significant correlation between Machiavellianism and grade-point average with abilities held constant for males but not females.

There are some suggestions of a relationship between external control and Machiavellianism. Geis and Christie (1965) point out that high Machs appear to be fairly accurate in their perception of others, but this accuracy is based on indiscriminate cynicism and suspicion rather than on sensitivity. Insensitivity to feedback tends to be consistent with external control (cf. Sections II, D, 1; and II, D, 3). Another finding that is suggestive of a relationship between externality and Machiavellianism is Christie's (1964) citing of a positive correlation between a modified version of Srole's (1956) anomia scale and the Mach scale.[5] A positive relationship was also found when the I-E scale was compared with another modified version of the Srole scale (cf. Section II, D, 2).

3. Need for Control

Control or power in the sense of a goal has been discussed and assessed by Veroff (1957) and Schutz (1958). Veroff developed a TAT-like measure of

---

[5] W. S. Wahlin (personal communication) reports the following correlation coefficients between the combined Mach IV and V scales and the anomia scale: males ($r = .47, p < .01$, $N = 144$), females ($r = .53$, $p < .01$, $N = 124$); data were collected at the University of Rochester.

need for power similar to the measures of achievement and affiliation that had been developed by the McClelland and Atkinson group (cf. Atkinson, 1958). Five pictures are used as the stimuli and the stories are scored according to the system developed for the achievement and affiliation motives. Power motivation is defined as "... that disposition directing behavior toward satisfactions contingent upon the control of the means of influencing another person(s)" (Veroff, 1957, p. 1). Dominance strivings are considered as one means of control.

In an attempt to validate his projective measure of power motivation, Veroff (1957) compared two groups of students, one of which was assumed to have been aroused by power cues since they were candidates for student office. It was found that the power-aroused subjects had a greater degree of power imagery in their stories than the nonaroused group. Within the nonaroused group it was found that high scorers as opposed to low scorers had stronger interests in the job satisfaction of being a leader and in obtaining recognition from peers, as well as in being rated significantly higher by their instructors on frequency of argumentation and frequency of trying to convince others of their points of view in the classroom. Another interesting finding was that the achievement and power measures correlated at .27 ($p < .05$). Veroff does point out that the results could also be interpreted as recognition motivation. It may be that the need for control or power is itself a means toward achieving recognition or acceptance. This is consistent with the Adlerian view of power as a compensatory mechanism. It remains for future investigation to see if the need for power can be differentiated from the need for recognition.

Schutz (1958) considers control one of three interpersonal needs, the others being inclusion and affection. Control is defined as "... the need to establish and maintain a satisfactory relation with people with respect to control and power" (Schutz, 1958, p. 18). Schutz distinguishes between two dimensions of control: one is a dimension of feelings toward others ranging from a desire for complete control to noncontrol, the other a dimension of self-perception ranging from a feeling of being competent or responsible to a feeling of being incompetent or irresponsible. It would seem that the former dimension is synonomous with Veroff's need for power, while the latter is coincident with internal-external control or the self-perception of power. Herein lies the conceptual distinction between power drive and latent power. Schutz (1958), however, has developed measures only of the power drive or need for control. This is part of his FIRO-B (Fundamental Interpersonal Relations Orientations, form B). The control measures are expressed behavior, in the sense of "I control people," and wanted behavior, in the sense of "I want people to control me." These two measures are relatively differentiated from one another as evidenced by the low although significant correlation of .25 ($p < .05$). It would be expected that there is high agreement between Veroff's projective measure of the need for power and Schutz's measure of expressed control.

There is no evidence on the relationship between need for control and internal-external control. It is hypothesized that need for control should covary with external control, the rationale being that the need to control other people or things is a compensatory drive to reduce feelings of being externally controlled. Such a relationship is clearly reflected in analyses of the Negro American personality (Clark, 1965a, Pettigrew, 1964; Silberman, 1964), where the desire for power is a goal directed at reducing the pervasive feeling of powerlessness that has been continually reinforced by objective conditions.

Another interesting speculation is the relationship between Machiavellianism and need for control. As it has been pointed out that each of these dimensions should covary with external control, it would follow that Machiavellianism and need for control are related. However, such a relationship may be rather minimal, since Machiavellianism is seen as a covert and disguised way of manipulating others, while need for control is an overt and open expression of the desire to control others. In summary, it would appear that there are some externals who tend to be Machiavellian, some who tend to express a desire for control, and most likely some whose attitudes are primarily passive regarding any wish to manipulate others. The internal, on the other hand, feels that he can control his environment when called upon to do so; hence, he should be neither Machiavellian, power driven, nor passive.

4. Subjective Probability

There have been several analyses of goal-directed behavior as a joint function of the value of a goal and the subjective probability of success in achieving it. The earliest expression of this, by Lewin, Dembo, Festinger and Sears (1944), hypothesized "force" as a joint product of subjective probability and valence. Similar analyses have been presented by Edwards (1954), Tolman (1955), Atkinson (1957), Feather (1959), and the theorists discussed previously—Heider (1958), Thibaut and Kelley (1959), and Rotter (1954). It would seem that subjective probability represents an expectancy of how much power one has over his environment and thus is another way of measuring latent power.

Feather (1959) points out that theorists such as Rotter and Edwards assume that utilities, values, or valences are independent of subjective probability. He states, however, that such independence cannot always be assumed. The variable of wishful choice versus choice leading to commitment was found to be one that interacts with subjective probability. Feather

(1961) also found an interaction between the comparative strength of need achievement versus test anxiety and subjective probability. When the situation was presented as one of skill (high initial probability of success), subjects whose achievement need exceeded anxiety were more persistent in a task, whereas the reverse was true in tasks of low probability. In a further comparison (Feather, 1965) achievement and initial probability of success as expressed by the S rather than the E were significantly related in a task of moderate difficulty but not in an easy task.

A study by Watt (1965), which was generated from Rotter's theory, investigated the effects of earlier public commitment on changes in verbalized expectancies. The commitment situation, however, was unlike the one used by Feather (1959) in that subjects did not have to act on their commitments. It was hypothesized that there would be an inverse relationship between degree of previous commitment and the amount of change in expectancies following feedback. This was found to be true in the failure situation; however, high commitment raised expectancies after success more than low commitment. Watt interprets the latter finding as being the result of an achievement situation. It might also be pointed out that the lower degree of change in expectancies found in the experimental study of the author in which a scorekeeper was present as compared to other studies where only the experimenter was present may be consistent with the finding in the failure situation.

Another relevant study by Moulton (1965), which was generated from Atkinson's model, found that individuals high in fear of failure and low in need for achievement raised their level of aspiration following failure and lowered aspiration after success. These results are consistent with Rotter's (1966) report of the relationship between unusual shifts in expectancies and external control. The results of a study by Horwitz (1958) are also consistent in that subjects who had nonveridical attitudes regarding their own success or failure scored lower on need achievement than subjects who had veridical attitudes.

Interpersonal expectancies have been investigated by Harvey and Clapp (1965). They found that subjects who expected higher ratings reacted more positively than subjects with lower expectancies to unexpectedly favorable feedback, whereas subjects with lower expectancies reacted more adversely to unexpectedly unfavorable ratings.

The theoretical models and studies of subjective probability point to the importance of considering the interaction between expectancy and motive. Two variables that appear to be particularly related to such an expectancy as internal-external control or power over one's environment are the achievement motive and the degree of commitment one has to make in the situation.

5. Attributed Power

A variable that would seem to be related to the attitudes one has with respect to his own power is the power one attributes to others. Studies on attributed power that are related to Thibaut and Kelley's approach have already been discussed (cf. Jones and DeCharms, 1958; Scholper and Matthews, 1965; Thibaut and Riecken, 1955). The major finding in these studies is that individuals who are presented as being powerful are seen as being responsible for their own actions or in other words as being internally controlled. An extension of this is Pepitone's (1958) finding that the interpersonal attractiveness of a person ". . . varies with the degree of his responsibility for given positive or negative acts" (p. 260).

There are several other studies that have investigated attributed power that give some suggestion as to its relation to self-perception of power. Lippitt, Polansky, and Rosen (1952) in a study with summer camp boys found that self-perception of power within a group tended to be consistent with the power attributed by other members. In addition, a close correspondence between attribution and behavior was seen in that recipients of attributed power made more frequent attempts to influence others and were more often the models for spontaneous imitation. Meister (1956) similarly found a close correspondence between the type of behaviors observed and the perception of social relations. Studying children from age 8 through 18, he obtained evidence in support of Piaget's (1932) hypothesis that behavior at 11–13 shows a transition from relatively autocratic to democratic patterns, and that the congruency between observed behavior and perception parallels this transition. Another investigation related to the Lippitt *et al.* study is one in which college students were used by Heilbrun and Hall (1964). They report a significant relationship between the degree of power attributed to the mother and the amount of maternal identification by daughters. A trend in this direction was found for sons and maternal identification.

An experimental manipulation of the self-perception of power in a dyadic decision-making situation was investigated by Levinger (1959). Subjects were given varying initial perceptions of their own power resources relative to those of their partner. The partner who was an experimental confederate varied the extent to which he accepted or rejected the naive *S*'s attempts to influence him. It was found the *S*'s perception of his own power was affected by both the initial information of his relative power and the degree to which he was able to influence his partner.

Individual differences in response to power cues were studied by Wilkins and DeCharms (1962), using an impression-information task. They found that high-authoritarian subjects, as measured by the California F-scale, used more external power cues, such as position and possession of material objects, and less internal power cues, such as personal mannerisms and traits, than low-authoritarian subjects.

III. Toward A More Comprehensive Analysis of Power

From the foregoing review, the theories of Heider, Thibaut and Kelley, and Rotter appear to be in close agreement. Latent power is seen as both a situational and dispositional variable. Heuristically, Rotter's approach has been the most successful in that both an experimental schema and a differential scale have been developed and subjected to considerable empirical investigation. Studies of skill-chance preference, subjective probability, and attributed power have generated results that are consistent with the approaches of Heider, Thibaut and Kelly, and Rotter. Machiavellianism and need for control are two dimensions that appear to be conceptually differentiated from latent power, with the suggestion that each covaries with external control. The Adlerian view of power as a compensatory drive for an innate inferiority seems to be generally consistent with the three contemporary analyses of latent power in the sense of representing a continuing struggle by the individual to control or master his environment. Machiavellianism and need for control can be seen as compensatory mechanisms for feelings of powerlessness.

Work dealing with power as a personality construct, however, is still only at a formative stage. This is no doubt due to the general neglect of the concept by psychology. That this neglect exists is clearly pointed out by Clark (1965b); there are also lacunae in the investigations conducted to date. Perhaps the most basic unresolved issue is the generality of latent power across situations. It may well be that in addition to individuals who have highly generalized expectations of power there are those who may have strong feelings of power attached only to a limited range of situations or activities. Some suggestion of this is provided by Lefcourt and Ladwig's (1965b) study in which the use of a reference group identification markedly induced feelings of internal control. The variable of reinforcement value or incentive and its relationship to latent power or expectancy of success has not been dealt with generally in situational analyses. The theories and studies regarding subjective probability suggest the importance of considering the interaction of these two variables. Charde (1966) also points to the importance of considering the kinds of social situations that are relevant instigators of a generalized power expectancy. Other issues include sex differences, interaction between situational and dispositional factors, unidimensionality of the latent power construct, and empirical data on the relationships among latent power, Machiavellianism, and need for control.

There are also the questions of the objective sources from which power feelings derive and the developmental antecedents of generalized power expectancies. These two issues have not been systematically dealt with in the context of latent power. Rotter (1966) points out that little work has been done in studying antecedent conditions. There are, however, some suggestions in the literature as to the sources and developmental aspects of latent power. These will be discussed in an attempt to arrive at a more comprehensive analysis of power.

A. SOURCES OF POWER

In studying power as an attitudinal variable attention must be given to the objective sources that contribute to the individual's subjective feelings of power. Following the suggestion of Max Wertheimer,[6] power sources can be categorized as interpersonal, organismic, or institutional. Another categorization is provided by French and Raven (1959), who designate five sources of power: reward, coercive, referent, legitimate, and expert. Raven (1965) clarifies the preceding categories by distinguishing between public-dependent and private-dependent sources of influence. Expertness, reference, and legitimacy are seen as private dependent in that continuous surveillance in interacting with others is not necessary. Raven also adds the category of informational influence, which is an independent source of influence in that the communication content rather than the influencing agent is involved. Informational influence is thus not relevant as a personal basis of power. It might be well to point out that Raven uses the term power to refer to potential influence, whereas influence refers to kinetic or manifest power.

It is possible to match the Wertheimer and French and Raven categories as indicated in Table 1. In addition, Kelman's (1961) three types of social influence—compliance, identification, and internalization—which partly correspond to the Wertheimer-French and Raven classification are also included in Table 1.

Sources of power will be discussed under the headings of interpersonal, organismic, and institutional power. Following this, there will be a discussion about differences between levels of latent and manifest power as related to power sources. It should be noted that Raven and Kelman focus their analyses on social influence situations involving an influencing agent and a target. The emphasis here will be on how the influence situation can contribute to an individual's feelings of power.

[6] In the concluding remarks to M. Wertheimer's 1941 seminar on power conducted at the New School for Social Research; these notes, made available to the author by A. S. Luchins, are to be published in a forthcoming volume on Wertheimer's lectures on social psychology edited by A. S. Luchins.

TABLE I

SOURCES OF POWER[a]

Interpersonal power (W)	
Coercive power (F & R) ⎫	Compliance (K)
Reward power (F & R) ⎬	
Referent power (F & R)	Identification (K)
Organismic power (W)	
Expert power (F & R)	Internalization (K)
Institutional power (W)	
Legitimate power (F & R)	

[a] Key: W, Wertheimer; F & R, French and Raven; K, Kelman.

1. Interpersonal Power

Interpersonal power derives from an individual's interactions with others and includes three types of power sources: coercive, reward, and referent. Coercive power arises out of an influencing agent's ability to mediate punishment for the influencee, while reward power stems from the agent's ability to mediate rewards. For both of these power interactions the influencing agent must maintain continuous surveillance, which exemplifies Raven's (1965) public-dependent influence and Kelman's (1961) compliance. The third type of interpersonal power, referent, occurs when a person tries to match his behavior to that of another person or group. This process is referred to by Kelman as identification. The influencing agent does not have to maintain surveillance nor necessarily initiate the influence process.

Although many data have been gathered on the effectiveness of these power modes (cf. Schopler, 1965), there is no indication of how they affect power attitudes. It would seem that an influencing agent's possession of referent power would provide a greater feeling of internal power than either coercion or reward, because surveillance and, at times, initiation are not necessary. It would also follow that the influencee would have a lesser feeling of external power when exposed to or in search of referent influence. In comparing coercive and reward power there is some suggestion from a study by Zipf (1960) that reward power would provide the greater feeling of internal control. Zipf confirmed the hypothesis that reward power produces less resistance than coercive power.

2. Organismic Power

Organismic power stems from intrinsic characteristics and abilities of the individual. It includes Raven's (1965) category of expert power and Kelman's (1961) generally equivalent social influence process of internalization. However, the discussions of expert power and internalization are limited to social influence situations in which the source of power is based on the attribution of superior skills or knowledge to the influencing agent. The intrinsic characteristics of the influencing agent or expert become internalized by the influencee. Organismic power need not be limited only to social influence situations, for it can serve as a power source in any interaction the individual has with his environment.

Part of Lasswell and Kaplan's (1950) list of power sources provides an example of the particular attributes that can be categorized under organismic power. These would include skill or intelligence, enlightenment or education, physical power, and ability to provide affection. Feelings of internal power as related to organismic power would generally be dependent on the possession of these attributes. Heider (1958) suggests such a relationship in his discussion of the attribution of can. Additionally, in some cases, feelings of powerlessness over the lack of a particular organismic power source may be compensated for by the possession or acquiring of another organismic source. However, there will also be many cases in which the possession of personal power characteristics will not necessarily lead to feelings of powerfulness or competence. One's generalized power expectancy of internal-external control may be at variance with one's intrinsic power characteristics because of deficiencies in interpersonal power, legitimate power, or the developmental antecedents that should produce congruent power attitudes.

Feelings of power on the part of a person who is exposed to an influencing agent with expert power will tend toward external control. However, as Thibaut and Kelley (1959) point out, it is possible for the influencee in an extended relationship with an expert to acquire the knowledge or skills of the expert. Consequently, he may internalize the feelings of power that he had originally ascribed to the expert.

3. Institutional Power

Institutional power is based on sources that are extrinsic to the individual and reside in the individual's social environment. It includes Raven's (1965) category of legitimate power, which refers to a situation where an influencing agent is permitted or obliged to prescribe behaviors to an influencee who is required to accept such influence. The basis of legitimacy essentially resides in the legal or social structure. A term that would seem to be equivalent to legitimate power is "authority." Although Raven focuses on a dyadic social influence situation, institutional or legitimate power can involve interactions between groups or between an individual and a group.

As with organismic power, Lasswell and Kaplan's (1950) list of sources provides an example of institutionally based attributes of power. These would include status, moral standing, and wealth. On the basis of legal establishment and social norms, role prescriptions are attached to different levels of institutional attributes providing a source for what is considered to be legitimate.

Power feelings of internal control in relation to such characteristics as status, moral standing, and wealth would generally covary according to hierarchical position. However, there are other factors that would interact with position. For example, the distinction between ascribed versus achieved status or wealth would suggest that greater feelings of internal power would be attached to that which is achieved rather than ascribed. The way legitimate power or authority is utilized interpersonally would also affect power attitudes. The use or receipt of referent power as opposed to reward or coercion should provide the greatest degree of internal control, whereas coercive power should provide the least degree of internal control.

The inverse relation of feelings of external control or powerlessness to the social status hierarchy is well documented in a number of analyses of minority groups, including Negroes by Clark (1965a), Pettigrew (1964), and Silberman (1964) and Catholics and Jews by Baltzell (1964). Other evidence for such a relationship is provided by Lefcourt (1966) and Rotter (1966) in their review of studies comparing Negro and white subjects and lower-class and middle-class subjects. The position of minority groups in the social structure tends to produce divergent norms regarding legitimacy. The establishment tends to regard its power as legitimate while minority group members tend to regard their own lack of power as illegitimate. Such a divergency would seem to be a basic source of intergroup hostility. The extent of the difference in norms of legitimate power may be greatest when the social barriers of the establishment conflict with either the utilization of organismic power or the motivation to increase organismic power on the part of minority group members.

4. Latent versus Manifest Power

The foregoing discussion on sources of power suggests that feelings and manifestations of power are not necessarily equivalent. The manifestation of an individual's power generally follows from the objective source or power stimulus to which he exposes himself or is exposed. However, the individual's accompanying attitudes or feelings about his power may be quite divergent from the degree of his effectiveness or influence in a given situation. This is essentially because the individual possesses a generalized expectancy regarding his sense of personal power that has been developed from his record of success and failure in previous situations. It may be that the expectancy evoked in a given situation is a broad one in the sense of having been generalized over many different types of situations, or the expectancy may be one that is limited only to previous encounters in highly similar situations.

It is also possible that manifest power itself may be somewhat divergent from its source. An example would be an individual who is in a position of authority but either chooses not to use his power or is unable to use his power. Here power feelings of internal control would go along with the situation of choosing not to utilize one's power, which in itself is power through negativism.

A dimension of pathology with respect to power feelings also seems relevant. It is possible that an individual's feelings of personal power may be consistently divergent from his manifestation of power or the power sources with which he interacts, or both. Extensive belief systems, such as delusions of grandiosity or persecution, can be considered respectively as extreme forms of internal and external control, which in turn are markedly divergent from reality conditions.

In summary, the relationship between latent and manifest power needs to be systematically investigated. Such investigations might best proceed by using the various categories of power sources as a conceptual guideline.

B. DEVELOPMENTAL ANTECEDENTS

The developmental antecedents of a power attitude represent a cumulative sum of reactions to power sources or stimuli. Antecedents can be best considered within the contexts of cognitive development and social learning or socialization.

1. Cognitive Development

Discussions of cognitive development tend to focus on the progression of structural properties such as differentation and integration. Zajonc (1960) and Scott (1963) refer to the additional structure of unity or relatedness and include within this a specific property of dependence or determinance. It would seem that power could be considered as an example of such a property.

Differentiation, however, has been the only structural property to receive systematic investigation and measurement. There are several suggestions of a relationship between progressive differentiation and progressive power. Lewin (1936) points out that increasing knowledge brings greater control or power. White (1959) indicates that the degree of competence is a function of the amount of interaction with the environment. Harvey, Hunt, and Schroder (1961) hypothesize that there is a progression from external to internal control with increasing conceptual development.

The analyses of psychological causality by Piaget (1932), Werner (1957), and Heider (1958), previously referred to, all point out a developmental progression from external to internal causality. A study by Shaw and Sulzer (1964) provides partial support for Piaget's (1932) and Heider's (1958) hypothesis that children are less differentiated than adults with respect to attribution of personal and environmental responsibility. Studies by Nass (1956, 1964) indicate that factors other than chronological age, such as personality adjustment and familiarity with casual agents, also contribute to children's conceptions about causality. Muuss (1960) also found a relationship between causality and personality adjustment in children.

Another aspect of cognitive development relevant to power feelings is level of intelligence. Intelligence was referred to as one source of organismic power. Evidence of a relationship between intellectual differences and power feelings is provided by Bialer (1961) in a study with retarded and normal children. In comparing the relationship between an oral questionnaire of internal-external control and the Peabody Picture Vocabulary Test it was found that internal control significantly covaried with mental age even when chronological age was held constant. No relationship between locus of control and chronological age was found when mental age was partialed out. However, intellectual level as related to power feelings does not appear in groups with a more restricted range of intelligence, as evidenced by Rotter's (1966) report of negligible correlations between intelligence measures and the I-E scale for both college students and prison inmates.

In studies of individual differences in approach to cognitive tasks with adults, there is also the suggestion of a relationship between power feelings and dimensions of conceptual functioning. Wolfe (1965), in a study of VA domiciliary residents, found that conceptually concrete subjects as measured by the Situational Interpretation Experiment (cf. Harvey et al., 1961) were significantly more external on the I-E scale than conceptually abstract subjects. Other relevant findings are indicated by the author's previously cited report (cf. Section II, D, 2) of a significant relationship for males between internal control and measures of cognitive complexity, and Bortner's (1964) report that individuals with a preference for skill tasks were more field independent. Rotter (1966), however, found no relationship between an individual measure of internal-external control and field dependence-independence as measured by the Gottschalk Figures Test.

More investigations are needed to clarify what appears to be a relationship between certain aspects of the degree of cognitive development and latent power. It will be important to identify the particular cognitive dimensions that are relevant. Reflective of the problem of dimensionality in this area is Vannoy's (1965) factor analytic study of several measures of cognitive complexity, which was not supportive of unidimensionality.

As to the antecedents for a relationship between organismic cognitive dimensions and latent power, White's (1959) general hypothesis that the degree of competence is a function of the amount of interaction with the environment suggests that latent power and other cognitive structures each covary according to the degree of environmental enrichment to which the individual is exposed. The degree of enrichment to which the individual is exposed is basically a function of the socialization process, although his inherent level of abilities serves as a limiting factor.

2. Socialization.

Several writers (Maccoby, 1959; Mussen and Distler, 1959; Parsons, 1955) have proposed that social power, or the ability of a person to influence others, is a primary factor in determining identification. Support for this is seen in the previously cited study by Heilbrun and Hall (1964) and the finding by Bandura, Ross, and Ross (1963) that children primarily imitated a model who possessed rewarding power rather than one who was a competitor for rewards.

In addition to the degree of parental power utilized and its effects on identification, there is the suggestion that the type of parental power utilized may be particularly relevant to the development of latent power. Several theorists (Mowrer, 1950; Mussen and Distler, 1959; Slater, 1961) refer to a distinction between threat-based and support-based parental identification, which seems to parallel French and Raven's (1959) distinction of reward versus coercive power. Ausubel (1952) also makes such a distinction on a developmental basis with his concept of "satellization," which refers to the acceptance of parental values on the basis of personal loyalty to supportive parents. Ausubel indicates that there are personality differences between children who have experienced a period of satellization and those who have not.

It would seem that parental identification based on support may be considered as a developmental antecedent to a generalized power expectancy. Such a relationship is suggested by Harvey et al. (1961) in their theory of the levels of conceptual development. They point out that an individual who is arrested at an early stage is one who has been continually exposed to training agents who exercise complete or nearly complete control. The recipient of such training conditions tends to develop a marked dependence on external authority and external sources of causality. This is contrasted with the highly conceptually developed individual who has been the recipient of training conditions that emphasize rewards for exploration and initiative. Such an individual is one who develops internal sources of control and causality. It might also be pointed out that this approach provides for a consideration of the interaction of cognitive and social learning. Primarily supportive as opposed to primarily threatening social agents provide the recipient with greater opportunities for environmental enrichment.

Thibaut and Kelley's (1959) distinction of fate and behavior control presented in the context of social influence situations appears to be quite similar to the discussion of differences in training conditions of Harvey *et al.* Rotter's dimension of internal-external control also seems to be conceptually consistent with both of the foregoing, for it could be hypothesized that an internally controlled individual is one who has been primarily exposed to training conditions of behavior control, whereas an externally controlled individual is one who has been primarily exposed to training conditions of fate control.

There is empirical support of a relationship between parental training methods and power orientation in the area of socially prohibited behavior. Sears, Maccoby, and Levin (1957), Bandura and Walters (1959), Allinsmith (1960), and Aronfreed (1961) all found a relationship between the internal versus external orientation of parental discipline and parallel differences of orientation in children's responses to social transgression. In addition, Aronfreed (1961) found support for his hypothesis that high status or power within the social structure would provide greater reinforcement for internal control, in that middle-class children and boys showed more of an orientation toward internal monitors than working-class children or girls. This is consistent with the general finding (cf. Section III, A, 3) that individuals who are low on the social structure tend to have feelings of external control.

More investigations are needed in both identificaion and social influence situations to clarify the relationship between socialization variables and latent power. The analysis of sex and status differences in these situations should also be considered.

IV. Conclusion

Power as a personality construct has been typically thought of as a drive; however, a review of recent theoretical and empirical approaches would seem to indicate that power should be conceptualized as an attitude or expectancy. Psychoanalytic theorists such as Adler and Horney have tended to assume that each individual has an inherent feeling of powerlessness which instigates compensatory strivings toward power goals. It has been shown that power both in terms of its determinants and as a predictor operates in a more complex manner. However, there are situations in which the desire for power or control can serve as a compensatory mechanism for feelings of powerlessness.

Many issues still require clarification. Latent power is a product of both situational and dispositional determinants; however, there has been little investigation of the interaction of these factors or attempts to control one set while varying the other. The generality of power feelings across situations needs clarification. Further construct validation is needed with respect to both convergent validity among several methods measuring one trait and discriminant validity among measures of different traits. In particular, latent power must be distinguished from the related dimension of achievement. Evidence is also needed on the relationship of power feelings and aggression. Some suggestion of a relationship is provided by Berkowitz (1962), who reports several studies indicating that individuals who describe themselves as incompetent have a stronger predisposition to hostility.

The consideration of latent power as a personality dimension leads to some interesting implications. Several writers (Brayfield, 1965; Heider, 1958; Mowrer, 1960; Shoben, 1961; Wishner, 1962) have referred to power in terms of effectiveness and individual responsibility as a criterion of mental health. Thus, there is the suggestion of the relevance of the construct of power to the study of behavior pathology and behavior modification. The relationship of latent power to manifest power needs to be investigated and should serve to further our understanding of manifest power. Finally, Clark (1965b) points to the need for a unifying theory of power in order to understand social change. Perhaps the most important implication is, as Clark suggests, that a theory of power can serve as an integrative principle within psychology and for social science as a whole.

References

Adler, A. *Understanding human nature.* New York: Greenberg, 1927.
Adler, A. Individual psychology. In C. Murchison (Ed.), *Psychologies of 1930.* Worcester, Mass.: Clark Univer. Press, 1930. Pp. 395–405.
Allinsmith, W. The learning of moral standards. In D. R. Miller & G. E. Swanson (Eds.), *Inner conflict and defense.* New York: Holt, Rinehart, & Winston, 1960. Pp.141–176.
Alpert, R., & Haber, R. N. Anxiety in academic achievement situations. *J. abnorm. soc. Psychol.*, 1960, **61**, 207–215.
Angyal, A. *Foundations for a science of personality.* New York: Commonwealth Fund, 1941.
Aronfreed, J. The nature, variety, and social patterning of moral responses to transgression. *J. abnorm. soc. Psychol.*, 1961, **63**, 223–240.
Atkinson, J. W. Motivational determinants of risk-taking behavior. *Psychol. Rev.*, 1957, **64**, 359–372.
Atkinson, J. W. (Ed.) *Motives in fantasy, action, and society.* New York: Van Nostrand, 1958.
Ausubel, D. P. *Ego development and the personality disorders.* New York: Grune & Stratton, 1952.
Baltzell, E. D. *The protestant establishment: Aristocracy and caste in America.* New York: Random House, 1964.
Bandura, A., & Walters, R. H. *Adolescent aggression.* New York: Ronald Press, 1959.
Bandura, A., Ross, Dorothea, & Ross, Sheila. A comparative test of the status envy, social power and secondary reinforcement theories of identificatory learning. *J. abnorm. soc. Psychol.*, 1963, **67**, 527–534.

Battle, Esther S., & Rotter, J. B. Children's feelings of personal control as related to social class and ethnic group. *J. Pers.*, 1963, **31**, 482–490.

Berkowitz, L. *Aggression: A social psychological analysis.* New York: McGraw-Hill, 1962.

Bialer, I. Conceptualization of success and failure in mentally retarded and normal children. *J. Pers.*, 1961, **29**, 303–320.

Bieri, J. Cognitive complexity-simplicity and predictive behavior. *J. abnorm. soc. Psychol.*, 1955, **51**, 263–268.

Bortner, R. W. Personality differences in preference for skill or chance determined outcomes. *Percept. mot. Skills*, 1964, **18**, 765–772.

Brayfield, A. Human effectiveness. *Amer. Psychologist*, 1965, **20**, 645–651.

Butterfield, E. C. Locus of control, test anxiety, reactions to frustration, and achievement attitudes. *J. Pers.*, 1964, **32**, 298–311.

Campbell, D. T. Social attitudes and other acquired behavioral dispositions. In S. Koch (Ed.), *Psychology: A Study of science.* Vol. 6. New York: McGraw-Hill, 1963. Pp. 94–122.

Charde, Patricia M. Personality orientation, verbal attitude, and overt behavior. Unpublished master's thesis, California State College at Los Angeles, 1966.

Child, I. L., & Waterhouse, I. K. Frustration and the quality of performance: III. An experimental study. *J. Pers.*, 1953, **21**, 298–311.

Christie, R. The prevalence of Machiavellian orientations. Paper read at Amer. Psychol. Ass. Los Angeles, 1964.

Clark, K. B. *Dark ghetto: Dilemmas of social power.* New York: Harper & Row, 1965. (a)

Clark, K. B. Problems of power and social change: toward a relevant social psychology. *J. soc. Issues*, 1965, **21**, 4–20. (b)

Cohen, J. *Chance, skill and luck.* Baltimore: Penguin Books, 1960.

Crandall, V. J., Katkovsky, W., & Preston, Anne. Motivational and ability determinants of young children's intellectual achievement behaviors. *Child Developm.*, 1962, **33**, 643–661.

Cromwell, R., Rosenthal, D., Shakow, D., & Zahn, L. Reaction time, locus of control, choice behavior and descriptions of parental behavior in schizophrenic and normal subjects. *J. Pers.*, 1961, **29**, 363–379.

Dean, D. G. Alienation: Its meaning and measurement. *Amer. sociol. Rev.*, 1961, **26**, 753–758.

Dombrose, L. A., & Slobin, M. S. The IES test. *Percept. mot. Skills*, 1958, **8**, Monogr. Suppl. 3, 347–389.

Edwards, W. The theory of decision making. *Psychol. Bull.*, 1954, **51**, 380–417.

Erikson, E. H. *Childhood and society.* New York: Norton, 1950.

Exline, R., Thibaut, J., Brannon, C., & Gumpert, P. Visual interaction in relation to Machiavellianism and an unethical act. *Amer. Psychologist*, 1961, **16**, 396. (Abstract)

Feather, N. T. Subjective probability and decision under uncertainty. *Psychol. Rev.*, 1959, **66**, 150–164.

Feather, N. T. The relationship of persistence at a task to expectation of success and achievement related motives. *J. abnorm. soc. Psychol.*, 1961, **63**, 552–561.

Feather, N. T. The relationship of expectation of success to need achievement and test anxiety. *J. Pers. soc. Psychol.*, 1965, **1**, 118–126.

French, Elizabeth. Development of a measure of complex motivation. In J. W. Atkinson (Ed.), *Motives in fantasy, action and society.* New York: Van Nostrand, 1958. Pp. 242–248.

French, J. R. P., Jr., & Raven, B. H. The bases of social power. In D. Cartwright (Ed.), *Studies in social power.* Ann Arbor: Univer. of Michigan Press, 1959. Pp. 150–167.

Fromm, E. *Escape from freedom.* New York: Holt, Rinehart & Winston, 1941.

Geis, Florence, & Christie, R. Machiavellianism and the tactics of manipulation. Paper read at Amer. Psychol. Ass., Chicago, 1965.

Gore, Pearl Mayo, & Rotter, J. B. A personality correlate of social action. *J. Pers.*, 1963, **31**, 58–64.

Guilford, J. P. *Personality.* New York: McGraw-Hill, 1959.

Harvey, O. J., & Clapp. W. F. Hope, expectancy, and reactions to the unexpected. *J. Pers. soc. Psychol.*, 1965, **2**, 45–52.

Harvey, O. J., Hunt, D. E. & Schroder, H. M. *Conceptual systems and personality organization.* New York: Wiley, 1961.

Heider, F. *The psychology of interpersonal relations.* New York: Wiley, 1958.

Heilbrun, A. B., & Hall, C. L. Resource mediation in childhood and identification. *J. Child Psychol. Psychiat.*, 1964, **5**, 139–149.

Helson, H. Adaptation-Level as a basis for a quantitative theory of frames of reference. *Psychol. Rev.*, 1948, **55**, 297–313.

Horney, Karen. *Self-analysis.* New York: Norton, 1942.

Horwitz, M. The veridicality of liking and disliking. In R. Tagiuri and L. Petrullo (Eds.), *Person perception and interpersonal behavior.* Stanford: Stanford Univer. Press, 1958. Pp. 191–209.

Jackson, D. N. The development and evaluation of the Personality Research Form. Unpublished manuscript, Univer. of Western Ontario, 1965.

Jackson, D. N., & Minton, H. L. A forced-choice adjective preference scale for personality assessment. *Psychol. Rep.* 1963, **12**, 515–520.

James, W. H., & Rotter, J. B. Partial and 100% reinforcement under chance and skill conditions. *J. exp. Psychol.*, 1958, **55**, 397–403.

Jones, E. E. *Ingratiation: a social psychological analysis.* New York: Appleton-Century-Crofts, 1964.

Jones, E. E., & DeCharms, R. The organizing function of interaction roles in person perception. *J. abnorm. soc. Psychol.*, 1958, **57**, 155–164.

Jones, E. E., Gergen, K. J., & Davis, K. E. Some determinants of reactions to being approved or disapproved as a person. *Psychol. Monogr.*, 1962, **76**, No. 2 (Whole No. 521).

Kelman, H. C. Processes of opinion change. *Publ. Opin. Quart.*, 1961, **25**, 57–78.

Lasswell, H., & Kaplan, A. *Power and personality.* New Haven: Yale Univer. Press, 1950.

Lefcourt, H. M. Some empirical correlates of Negro identity. Unpublished doctoral dissertation, Ohio State Univer., 1963.

Lefcourt, H. M. Internal versus external control: A review. *Psychol. Bull.*, 1966, **65**, 206–220.

Lefcourt, H. M. & Ladwig, G. W. The American Negro: A problem in expectancies. *J. Pers. soc. Psychol.*, 1965, **1**. 377–380. (a)

Lefcourt, H. M., & Ladwig, G. W. The effect of reference group upon Negroes task persistence in a biracial competitive game. *J. Pers. soc. Psychol.*, 1965, **1**, 668–671. (b)

Levinger, G. The development of perceptions and behavior in newly formed social power relationships. In D. Cartwright (Ed.), *Studies in social power.* Ann Arbor: Univer. of Michigan Press, 1959. Pp. 83–98.

Levinson, D. J. Authoritarian personality and foreign policy. *Conflict Resolution*, 1957, **1**, 37–47.

Lewin, K. *Principles of toplogical psychology.* New York: McGraw-Hill, 1936.

Lewin, K. Regression, retrogression, and development. *Univer. Iowa Stud. Child Welf.*, 1941, **18** (1), 1–43.

Lewin, K., Dembo, Tamara, Festinger, L., & Sears, Pauline, S. Level of aspiration. In J. McV. Hunt (Ed.), *Personality and the behavior disorders.* Vol. 1. New York: Ronald Press, 1944. Pp. 333–378.

Liberty, P. G., Jr., Burnstein, E., & Moulton, R. W. Concern with mastery and occupational attraction. *J. Pers.*, 1966, **34**, 105–117.

Lichtman, C. M., & Julian, J. W. Internal vs. external control of reinforcement as a determinant of preferred strategy on a behavioral task. Paper read at Midwest. Psychol. Ass., St. Louis, 1964.

Lippitt, R., Polansky, N., & Rosen, S. The dynamics of power. *Human Relat.*, 1952, **5**, 37–64.

Maccoby, Eleanor E. Role-taking in childhood and its consequences for social learning. *Child Develpm.*, 1959, **30**, 239–252.

Mandler, G., & Sarason, S. B. A study of anxiety and learning. *J. abnorm. soc. Psychol.*, 1952, **47**, 166–173.

Meister, A. Perception and acceptance of power relations in children. *Group Psychother.*, 1956, **9**, 153–163.

Michotte, A. *The perception of causality.* New York: Basic Books, 1963.

Moulton, R. W. Effects of success and failure on level of aspiration as related to achievement motives. *J. Pers. soc. Psychol.*, 1965, **1**, 399–406.

Mowrer, O. H. *Learning theory and personality dynamics.* New York: Ronald Press, 1950.

Mowrer, O. H. "Sin": The lesser of two evils. *Amer. Psychologist*, 1960, **15**, 301–304.

Mussen, P. H., & Distler, L. Masculinity, identification, and father-son relationships. *J. abnorm. soc. Psychol.* 1959, **59**, 350–356.

Muuss, R. E. The relationship between "causal" orientation, anxiety, and insecurity in elementary school children. *J. Educ. Psychol.*, 1960, **51**, 122–129.

Nass, M. L. The effects of three variables on children's concepts of physical causality. *J. abnorm. soc. Psychol.* 1956, **53**, 191–196.

Nass, M. L. The deaf child's conception of physical causality. *J. abnorm. soc. Psychol.* 1964, **69**, 669–673.

Odell, Miriam E. Personality correlates of independence and conformity. Unpublished master's thesis, Ohio State Univer. 1959.

Parsons, T. Family structure and the socialization of the child. In T. Parsons & R. F. Bales (Eds.), *Family, socializations, and interaction processes.* Glencoe, Ill.: Free Press, 1955. Pp. 35–131.

Pepitone, A. Attributions of causality, social attitudes, and cognitive matching processes. In R. Tagiuri & L. Petrullo (Eds.), *Person perception and interpersonal behavior.* Stanford, Calif.: Stanford Univer. Press, 1958. Pp. 258–276.

Pervin, L. A. The need to predict and control under conditions of threat. *J. Pers.*, 1963, **31**, 570–587.

Pettigrew, T. F. *A profile of the Negro American.* Princeton, N. J.: Van Nostrand, 1964.

Phares, E. J. Internal-external control as a determinant of amount of social influence exerted. *J. Pers. soc. Psychol.*, 1965, **2**, 642–647.

Piaget, J. *The moral judgment of the child.* New York: Harcourt Brace, 1932.

Piaget, J. *The construction of reality in the child.* New York: Basic Books, 1954.

Rank, O. *Will therapy and truth and reality.* New York: Knopf, 1945.

Raven, B. H. Social influence and power. In I. D. Steiner & M. Fishbein (Eds.), *Current studies in social psychology.* New York: Holt, Rinehart & Winston, 1965. Pp. 371–382.

Riesman, D. *Individualism reconsidered.* Glencoe, Ill.: Free Press, 1954.

Rotter, J. B. *Social learning and clinical psychology.* Englewood Cliffs, N. J.: Prentice-Hall, 1954.

Rotter, J. B. The role of the psychological situation in determining the direction of human behavior. In M. R. Jones (Ed.), *Nebraska symposium on motivation.* Lincoln: Univer. of Nebraska Press, 1955. Pp. 245–268.

Rotter, J. B. Some implications of a social learning theory for the prediction of goal directed behavior from testing procedures. *Psychol. Review*, 1960, **67**, 301–316.

Rotter, J. B. Generalized expectancies for internal versus external control of reinforcement. *Psychol. Monogr.*, 1966, **80**, No. 1 (Whole No. 609).

Rotter, J. B., Seeman, M., & Liverant, S. Internal versus external control of reinforcement: A major variable in behavior theory. In. N. F. Washburne (Ed.), *Decisions, values, and groups.* Vol. 2. London: Pergamon Press, 1962. Pp. 473–516.

Russell, B. *Power, a new social analysis.* New York: Norton, 1938.

Schopler, J. Social power. In L. Berkowitz (Ed.), *Advances in experimental social psychology.* Vol. 2. New York: Academic Press, 1965. Pp. 177–218.

Schopler, J., & Matthews, M. W. The influence of the perceived causal locus of partner's dependence on the use of interpersonal power. *J. Pers. soc. Psychol.,* 1965, **2**, 609–612.

Schutz, W. C. *FIRO: A three-dimensional theory of interpersonal behavior.* New York: Holt, Rinehart & Winston, 1958.

Scott, W. A. Conceptualizing and measuring structural properties of cognition. In O. J. Harvey (Ed.), *Motivation and social interaction.* New York: Ronald Press, 1963, Pp. 266–288.

Sears, R. R., Maccoby Eleanor E., & Levin, H. *Patterns of child rearing.* Evanston, Ill.: Row, Peterson, 1957.

Sechrest, L., & Jackson, D. N. Social intelligence and accuracy of interpersonal predictions. *J. Pers.,* 1961, **29**, 167–182.

Seeman, M. On the meaning of alienation. *Amer. sociol. Rev.,* 1959, **24**, 783–791.

Seeman, M. Alienation and social learning in a reformatory. *Amer. J. Sociol.,* 1963, **69**, 270–284.

Seeman, M., & Evans, J. W. Alienation and learning in a hospital setting. *Amer. sociol. Rev.,* 1962, **27**, 772–782.

Shaw, M. E., & Sulzer, J. L. An empirical test of Heider's levels in attribution of responsibility *J. abnorm. soc. Psychol.,* 1964, **69**, 39–46.

Shoben, E. J., Jr. Personal responsibilities, determinism and the burden of understanding. *Antioch Rev.,* Winter, 1961.

Shuford, E. H., Jones, L. V., & Bock, R. D. A rational origin obtained by the method of contingent paired comparison. *Psychometrika,* 1960, **25**, 343–356.

Silberman, C. E. *Crisis in black and white.* New York: Random House, 1964.

Singer, J. E. The use of manipulative strategies: Machiavellianism and attractiveness. *Sociometry,* 1964, **27**, 128–150.

Slater, P. E. Toward a dualistic theory of identification. *Merrill-Palmer Quart.,* 1961, **7**, 113–126

Sofer, Elaine G. Inner-direction, other-direction, autonomy: A study of college students. In S. Lipset & L. Lowenthal (Eds.), *Culture and social character, the work of David Riesman.* New York: McGraw-Hill, 1956. Pp. 316–348.

Srole, L. Social integration and certain corollaries. *Amer. sociol. Rev.,* 1956, **21**, 709–716.

Strickland, Bonnie R. The prediction of social action from a dimension of internal-external control. *J. soc. Psychol.,* 1965, **66**, 353–358.

Strodtbeck, F. L. Family interaction, values and achievement. In D. McClelland (Ed.), *Talent and society.* New York: Van Nostrand, 1958. Pp. 138–195.

Sullivan, H. S. *Conceptions of modern psychiatry.* Washington: William Alanson White Psychiatric Foundation, 1947.

Taylor, Janet. A personality scale of manifest anxiety, *J. abnorm. soc. Psychol.,* 1953, **48**, 285–290.

Thibaut, J. W., & Kelley, H. H. *The social psychology of groups.* New York: Wiley, 1959.

Thibaut, J. W., & Riecken, H. W. Some determinants and consequences of the perception of social causality. *J. Pers.,* 1955, **24**, 113–133.

Tolman, E. C. Principles of performance. *Psychol. Rev.,* 1955, **62**, 315–326.

Tomkins, S. Left and right: A basic dimension of ideology and personality. In R. W. White (Ed.), *The study of lives.* New York: Atherton Press, 1963. Pp. 388–411.

Vannoy, J. E. Generality of cognitive complexity-simplicity as a personality construct. *J. Pers. soc. Psychol.* 1965, **2**, 385–396.

Veroff, J. Development and validation of a projective measure of power motivation. *J. abnorm. soc. Psychol.*, 1957, **54**, 1–8.

Watson, D. The relationship between locus of control and anxiety. *J. Pers. soc. Psychol.*, in press.

Watt, N. F. Public committment, delay after committment, and change in verbalized expectancies. *J. Pers.*, 1965, **33**, 284–299.

Werner, H. *Comparative psychology of mental development*. (Rev. ed.) New York: International Universities Press, 1957.

White, R. W. Motivation reconsidered: The concept of competence. *Psychol. Rev.*, 1959, **66**, 297–333.

Wilkins, E. J., & DeCharms, R. Authoritarianism and the response to power cues. *J. Pers.*, 1962, **30**, 439–457.

Wishner, J. Efficiency: Concept and measurement. *Personality research. Proc. XIV int. congr. appl. psychology*. Vol. II. Copenhagen: Munksgaard, 1962, Pp. 161–187.

Witkin, H. A., Lewis Helen B., Hertzman M., Machover, Karen, Meissner, Pearl B., & Wapner. S. *Personality through perception*. New York: Harper, 1954.

Witkin, H. A., Dyk, Ruth B., Faterson, Hanna F., Goodenough, D. R., & Karp, S. A. *Psychological differentiation*. New York: Wiley, 1962.

Wolfe, R. N. Two views of anomie and the nature of normlessness. Paper read at East. Psychol. Ass., Atlantic City, 1965.

Wolfe, R. N. Situational determinants of anomie and powerlessness. Paper read at East. Psychol. Ass., New York, 1966.

Zajonc, R. B. The process of cognitive tuning in communication. *J. abnorm. soc. Psychol.*, 1960, **61**, 159–167.

Zipf, Sheila G. Resistance and conformity under reward and punishment. *J. abnorm. soc. Psychol.* 1960, **61**, 102–109.

A THEORY OF RESPONSE INTERFERENCE IN SCHIZOPHRENIA[1]

William E. Broen, Jr., and Lowell H. Storms.

DEPARTMENT OF PSYCHOLOGY, UNIVERSITY OF CALIFORNIA, LOS ANGELES, CALIFORNIA
AND NEUROPSYCHIATRIC INSTITUTE, UNIVERSITY OF CALIFORNIA CENTER FOR THE
HEALTH SCIENCES, LOS ANGELES, CALIFORNIA.

I. The Importance and Nature of Response Interference in Schizophrenia

Is response interference a major characteristic of schizophrenia? The theory of response interference that we shall present does seem to fit and organize the results of many recent experiments on schizophrenia. But when a theory is judged only by its accord with experiments, there is a danger that both theory and experiments miss that which is fundamental in the behavior they are trying to understand. The response posibilities in most experiments are so restrictive that there may be a legitimate concern regarding whether a theory is useful only to organize the particular data that current research biases generate. Thus, before discussing the theory and recent experiments, let us first consider what is central in schizophrenia.

There does seem to be some uniformity in the examples that clinical observers and researchers have used to illustrate what they see as central in schizophrenia. Cameron (1938) used the following interchange to illustrate one of three major aspects of schizophrenic thinking. A schizophrenic explained that wind blows "due to velocity . . . due to loss of air, evaporation of water." When asked, "What gives it the velocity?" he replied, "The

[1]Partially supported by USPHS Grant No. 3-RO1-MH-12373-01.

contact of trees, of air in the trees" (p. 16). Cameron (1938) used other examples to illustrate that, "First of all, our material shows surprisingly little irrelevance. It is evident that even when dealing with hypothetical and very abstract matters in problems imposed from without, our schizophrenic patients show for the most part a prevailing tendency to stick to the subject. While their attempts do not satisfactorily dispose of the problem, their content hovers around it" (p. 17). Their problem is that "Competing terms cannot be completely discarded, there is a spurious equivalence given to several terms in a given cluster, and the product remains a more or less unorganized conglomerate" (p. 18). Bleuler (1950) put it in another way: "It looks as though ideas of a certain category . . . were thrown into one pot, mixed, and subsequently picked out at random . . . " (p. 16).

Quotes from schizophrenics reflect the same thing. Here are different schizophrenics' descriptions of the difficulties they sometimes experience (all from McGhie and Chapman, 1961). "My thoughts get all jumbled up. I start thinking or talking about something but I never get there. Instead I wander off in the wrong direction and get caught up in all sorts of different things that may be connected with the things I want to say but in a way I can't explain. People listening to me get more lost than I do" (p. 108). Another schizophrenic says, "My trouble is that I've got too many thoughts. You might think about something, let's say that ashtray and just think, Oh! yes, that's for putting my cigarette in, but I would think of it and then I would think of a dozen different things connected with it at the same time" (p. 108). And a description from a third schizophrenic, "I just can't concentrate on anything. There's too much in my head and I can't sort it out. My thoughts wander round in circles without getting anywhere. I try to read even a paragraph in a book but it takes me ages because each bit I read starts me thinking in ten different directions at once" (p. 109). And another: "I wish I could think without interruption—not from others, but from inside myself" (p. 109). The central factor seems to be that thinking is disorganized by interference from competing associations, sometimes a number of them simultaneously.

Susceptibility to intrusion of competing associations also seems to characterize the substitution of ideas that is so particularly schizophrenic. Bleuler (1950) illustrated this aspect of schizophrenia with the following question to a schizophrenic and his reply: "'Is something weighing heavily on your mind?'—'Yes, iron is heavy'" (p. 19). In similar vein, Arieti (1955) considers schizophrenic thinking to be implicit in the reply "White House," to the question, "Who was the first president of the United States?" (p. 4). This substitution of associated responses is what Cameron (1938) considers to be the second characteristic of schizophrenic thinking. Substitution of associated words in a context of disorganized variation among related ideas is shown in a schizophrenic's explanation of why he is alive: "Because you really live physically because you have menu three times a day; that's the physical." He was then asked, "What else is there besides the physical?" and replied, "Then you are alive mostly to serve work from the standpoint of methodical business" (Cameron, 1938, p. 21.)

Each of these examples reflects the same major characteristics. Words, questions, or thoughts evoke a number of associations which the schizophrenic is unable to organize appropriately. The different associations seem abnormally equivalent and thinking is characterized by disorganized shifting among the family of associates.

Of course normals also have many associations. The difference seems to lie in the ability of normals to keep appropriate associations clearly dominant. Discussing associations to the idea of water to illustrate differences between schizophrenic and normal thinking, Bleuler (1950) said, "Naturally, even the most limited idea of water is composed of various concepts such as fluid, evaporable, cold, colorless, etc. But in the normal mind only those part concepts dominate the picture that belong to a given frame of reference. The others exist only potentially, or at least retreat into the background so that we cannot even demonstrate their influence" (p. 17).

There are many ways to conceptualize the abnormal equivalence that concurrent associations seem to have for schizophrenics. As in our previous discussion (Broen & Storms, 1966), we view equivalence in terms of strength of competing response tendencies. The probability that one particular response will occur is seen as an increasing function of the strength of that response relative to the strengths of competing tendencies. Normal, appropriate responding means that the strengths of competing response tendencies are hierarchically ordered, with appropriate responses clearly dominant and therefore having high probability. Competing response tendencies are evoked in normals, but because their strengths are relatively low, these associated, but deviant, responses will rarely intrude. The central difference in schizophrenia is seen as a partial collapse of response hierarchies. The strengths of competing responses are more equivalent, resulting in the fragmentation of dominant chains of thought by the intrusion of competing associates. The result is the tendency toward randomized choice among a family of loosely related ideas that Bleuler sees as characteristic of schizophrenia, and the schizophrenic's inability to discard competing ideas with the " . . . spurious equivalence given to several terms in a given cluster . . . " that Cameron (1938, p. 18) emphasizes.

Of course, not all response tendencies that compete with each other are associations to single stimuli. When multiple stimuli are present, the response tendencies evoked by these stimuli also compete, and if schizophrenics are basically deficient in ability to organize competing response tendencies hierarchically, this deficiency should also apply to competition from different stimuli. Thus, if a schizophrenic is preoccupied with certain ideas and is asked an unrelated question, his response should take the form of abnormal interpenetration of associates to both his preoccupation and the question. This interpenetration of themes is the final kind of schizophrenic disturbance that Cameron (1938) emphasized. An example is provided by the response of a schizophrenic woman with severe thought disorganization. She had a number of bizarre preoccupations, including religious preoccupation, with predominant concern about her body and injuries to it, such as having her back broken. Her answer to a question about how fish can live in water was, "Because it's learned to swim." When then asked, "What if it couldn't swim?" she replied, "Not naturally, he couldn't. Why do certain gods have effect on the seas like that? What does the earth have such an effect to break their backs? The fishes near home come to the surface and break?" She was then asked "Why?" and replied, "I think it it is due to bodies that people lose. A body becomes adapted to the air. Think thoughts and break the fishes" (Cameron, 1938 p. 25).

As we have seen, the nature of schizophrenic behavior seen in free-response speech samples suggests that schizophrenic deficit involves increased susceptibility to interference from competing responses, which we view specifically as a partial collapse of response hierarchies. Fortunately this response-interference description of schizophrenic deficit is also the picture that emerges from recent experimental literature. After an extensive review of laboratory studies of schizophrenia over the past two decades, Lang and Buss (1965) concluded: "In brief, interference theory, as a broad explanation of schizophrenic deficit, has clearly been supported by research findings and appears to be the only theory comprehensive enough to account for what is known." They continued later, "The disturbance that appears in all studies of deficit concerns the initiation of responses to selected stimuli and the inhibition of inappropriate responses. All intelligent behavior represents a compromise between the demands of the immediate environment and a previously established set of the organism, but the schizophrenic makes a uniquely poor bargain. External stimuli, associational and biological 'noise' routinely suppressed by normal subjects, intrude, and responses to appropriate stimuli are not made" (pp. 97, 98). Thus, the trend of the evidence from research investigations that have good controls, although often characterized by some degree of artificiality and narrowed observation, leads to the same emphasis as do clinical observations and free-response studies.

Since both clinical and research observations suggest that response interference is central to schizophrenia, we shall focus on the factors that influence this response interference. First, we shall discuss factors that affect response competition and lead to response interference in normals, emphasizing those influences that we believe might aid in the understanding of schizophrenia. This will lead into a presentation of our previously proposed theory predicting partial collapse of response hierarchies in normals under certain conditions, and some experimental tests of the theory. With an additional hypothesis, the theory will be extended to account for the greater interference and apparently more easily collapsed hierarchies in schizophrenics. A number of important implications of this theory will be compared with a broad range of research evidence regarding schizophrenic behavior.

II. Factors Affecting Response Interference in Normals

A. SUGGESTIONS FROM PRIOR THEORY AND RESEARCH

Because interference from competing responses is prominent in schizophrenics, factors that affect differences in strength between dominant and competing responses should be important in determining schizophrenic behavior. What are some of these factors? Theory and research about response competition in normals provide several suggestions. Let us discuss first a group of paired-associate learning studies done within the framework of Hull-Spence theory. The theory used in these studies has features in common with our discussion thus far. Degree of response interference is viewed as an inverse function of differences in strengths between simultaneously evoked response tendencies. These response strengths (RS) are in turn a joint function of level of habit strength (H) and drive (D) level $(D \times H = RS)$. Response strength may also be inhibited by nonreinforced occurrence. The habit strength of a response reflects learning history. When in past learning a stimulus has been appropriately associated with more than one response, the stimulus will evoke a hierarchy of habit strengths that are arranged in accordance with past association frequencies. Because of conventions of language usage and shared experiences in our culture, an individual's hierarchy of habit strengths tends to reflect cultural norms. Commonly used associations tend to be dominant, with more remote associates at relatively low strength. Drive level also affects the hierarchy of response strengths. Because of its multiplicative effect, drive increases the response strength of dominant responses more than it increases competing response strengths. Thus, increased drive, such as an increase in emotional excitation, should increase the probability of dominant associates.

In one test of the theory (Spence, Farber, & McFann, 1956a), an anxiety scale was used to select Ss who varied in level of emotional response. It was predicted that, because D (emotionality) energizes dominant responses more than competing responses, high anxiety Ss should be superior to low anxiety Ss in paired-associates learning where the associative connections between the paired words were strong at the beginning of learning and competing associations were weak. This prediction was confirmed. High anxious Ss performed better throughout the learning trials. Under such conditions, anxiety does seem to increase the probability of dominant responses.

The results of a second experiment reported in the same article were not as straightforward. In this second experiment two sets of word pairs were to be learned. For one set the correct response was relatively strong at the beginning of learning. In the other set the correct associative connections were relatively weak. For both sets of word pairs, competing (incorrect) associates were stronger than had been the case in the first experiment. Let us first discuss the pairs where the correct associations were relatively weak at the beginning of learning. If anxiety facilitates stronger—in this case incorrect—associates, then at the beginning of learning, high anxious Ss should do worse then low anxious Ss. This is what occurred. At the end of learning, however, as correct associates become dominant, high anxious Ss should be the superior group. This did not happen. The high anxious Ss performed more poorly throughout. Thus, high anxious Ss do not always show facilitation of dominant responses.

Note the condition where this facilitation of dominant responses by high drive did not occur: toward the end of training, and in an experiment where competing associates were stronger. To see the reliability of the effect of these two conditions we turn to the other set of word pairs, where correct associative connections were relatively strong at the beginning of learning. Here the high anxious Ss were the superior group in the early trials, but their superiority in giving dominant responses did not continue to the end of training. On later trials they did worse than low anxious Ss. This crossover—high drive Ss giving more dominant responses than low drive Ss at the beginning of learning, and less at the end of learning—has been replicated in three other experiments where competing associates had significant strength (Lövaas, 1960; Ramond, 1953; Spence, Taylor, & Ketchel, 1956b). High drive does not seem to facilitate dominant responses at the end of training. In other words, the facilitating effect does not hold when habit strength is high.

B. A Theory of Response Interference in Normals

In an earlier article (Broen & Storms, 1961) we suggested that these and other results of this type could be interpreted by including in the theory a response-strength ceiling that is lower than maximum $D \times H$. Thus early in training, when dominant response habit strength (H_D) is low, the full multiplicative effect of drive may occur, but later in training, when H_D is high, the ceiling restricts the full increase in the strength of the dominant response. Thus late in training, and especially when the habit strength of competing responses (H_c) is high, the multiplicative effect of high drive may increase RS_c more than RS_D, thus reducing the difference between strengths of dominant and competing responses (reduce $RS_D - RS_C$). If higher D reduces $RS_D - RS_C$, this would decrease the probability of the dominant (correct) response and high D Ss would do worse than low D Ss. Table I provides a theoretical illustration of this effect.

TABLE I

THEORETICAL ILLUSTRATION OF THE DIFFERENT EFFECTS OF DRIVE AT THE BEGINNING AND LATER STAGES OF LEARNING[a]

| | | Response strength (RS ceiling = 6) | |
| | | Low D Ss (D = 5) | High D Ss (D = 10) |
Stage	H		
Beginning			
Correct R	.5	2.5	5.0
Incorrect R	.4	2.0	4.0
$RS_D - RS_C$		.5	1.0
Later			
Correct R	1.0	5.0	6.0
Incorrect R	.4	2.0	4.0
$RS_D - RS_C$		3.0	2.0

[a]Adapted from Broen and Storms (1961). Inhibition of competing responses was not taken into account in these calculations, but would only increase the crossover effect, since competing responses would be inhibited more rapidly in the low drive group because of their greater frequency in this group early in learning.

It should be noted that the specific theoretical relationship between $\%R_D$ and $RS_D - RS_C$ that we shall use follows that used in Hull's (1952) computing practices. The relationship is monotonic, but not linear. When $RS_D - RS_C$ is large, decreasing the difference a specific amount will cause a lesser reduction in $\%R_D$ than if $RS_D - RS_C$ were initially smaller. This specific relationship is not important in our discussion thus far, but will be used later.

When the effects of response-strength ceiling are considered, it can be seen that an increase in drive will affect response interference differently depending on the initial drive level. Figure 1 illustrates how, beginning at low drive levels, at first increased drive should increase the difference between dominant and competing responses (distance B), while additional

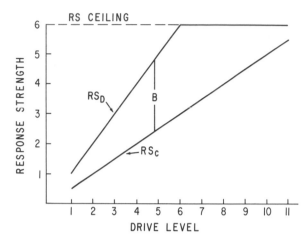

FIG. 1.   How RS ceiling and the multiplicative effect of D combine to make $RS_D - RS_C$ an inverted U-shaped function of D.

drive is expected to reduce this difference. Because the probability of the dominant response ($\%R_D$) is an increasing function of distance B, an inverted U-shaped relationship between drive level and $\%R_D$ is implied. Note also that increased drive is not seen as ever reducing RS_D. Decrement in $\%R_D$ occurs because $RS_D - RS_C$ is reduced, not because RS_D itself is reduced. In this conception, performance decrement under increased drive must depend on the presence of competing responses that have sufficient habit strength to be significantly facilitated by drive, while the dominant response is restricted by response-stength ceiling.

Thus far four factors, H_D, H_C, drive level, and response-strength ceiling, have been mentioned as affecting interference from competing responses. Let us now turn to some research on normal subjects that has been done in our laboratories at the University of California, Los Angeles, to test implications from the theoretical interrelationships between these factors.

C. RESEARCH TO TEST THE THEORY

To us, the most intuitively improbable prediction from the theory was that increased drive would be more likely to cause a decrement in dominant response when H_D is stronger. The opposite outcome, that strong responses are less likely to be interfered with when drive is increased, is suggested by common sense. At least this is what would usually be expected if the drive condition were a stress situation and its major effect were thought to be to bring new interfering responses into the situation. Such new interfering tendencies should compete more effectively when appropriate responses are weak.

With the collaboration of Herbert Schenck, we tested our theory's prediction in a pilot study. Response hierarchies that had different levels of H_D were tested under low and high drive. We could not predict that specific levels of H_D and drive would produce ceiling effects, but from the verbal-learning results we felt that with fairly extensive training, drive need not be extreme to produce these effects and that we should be able to obtain ceiling effects by using moderate shock as a drive. Female introductory psychology students were trained in a two-response lever-pressing task, where one response was made dominant and specified levels of H_D and H_C were arranged by forcing specific numbers of responses. Learning began with one response given 90% reinforcement and the other 60% reinforcement. When S was within five responses of the number of training responses desired for either lever, the forced responding began. Counters were placed above each lever and, as S had been instructed previously, she was to press each lever the number of times indicated on the counter. She could choose how to pattern her responding, and was to continue to try to be correct as often as possible. During the forced trials, reinforcement continued as before. This procedure was used to train three groups of Ss, each with a different response hierarchy as described later. Each S learned one hierarchy on one pair of levers and her response frequencies were then tested for 30 trials without shock. Then, on another pair of levers, she learned the same hierarchy, and responding was tested for 30 trials while S experienced electric shock at a level below what she had stated she could take during an earlier demonstration. Responses were not reinforced during the test trials. In order to select Ss with adequate attention and motivation, training criteria were used. These criteria were more than 50% responding to the dominant lever by the end of the free response training, and during the no-shock test condition. Thirty of 47 preliminary Ss met these criteria, leaving 10 Ss for each hierarchy.

The three response hierarchies had different H_D and H_C, but we attempted to keep $H_D - H_C$ about the same for each hierarchy by using Spence's (1956) formula for H to compute the number of responses to be given in training in order to get equal $H_D - H_C$. Whether or not this method would yield hierarchies that were roughly equivalent in degree of competition could be tested later. In the highest H_D hierarchy, R_D was given 101 times in training. The two other dominant responses were given 35 and 20 times. The respective competing responses were given 59, 27, and 15 times.

The results were as follows: The three response hierarchies did appear to be roughly equivalent in $H_D - H_C$ in that, in an analysis of variance, the number of R_D during the no-shock trials were not significantly different. The major result was that, in accordance with the hypothesis, an analysis of variance trend test showed a significant ($p < .05$)[2] relationship between level of H_D and the change in R_D frequency from low to high drive. The average R_D changes from low to high drive were: 2.3 for the low H_D hierarchy; $-.70$ for the middle H_D hierarchy; and -3.6 for the hierarchy with highest H_D.

Note that the results do no seem to be explainable in terms of distraction under increased stress. Any form of distraction should affect dominant responses in the same way, usually making responses more random, thus decreasing dominant responses. However, here the direction of effects on dominant responses was different for low and high H. The probability of dominant responses with low H tended to increase while the probability of high H responses tended to decrease.

The response hierarchies in the study just described varied primarily in H_D. In each hierarchy there was considerable response competition. Now we turn to a study where the level of response competition was varied so as to enable study of the role of strength of a competing response in determining susceptibility to decrement under high drive. The theory states that R_D decrements under increased drive are a joint function of high H_D and high H_C. When competing responses are stronger, the multiplicative effects of increased drive will increase their strength more, and will cause more decrement when a high H dominant response is restricted by response-strength ceiling. To test this, Broen, Storms, and Schenck (1961) did the following experiment. A response hierarchy with a high strength dominant response and a high strength competing response (HH hierarchy) was used. The tendency of this hierarchy to collapse under increased drive was compared to that of two other response hierarchies: one that also had a high strength dominant response but a low strength competing response (HL hierarchy); and another with somewhat lower strength dominant and competing responses (LL hierarchy).

The task was a lever-pressing task. Introductory psychology students were instructed to choose one of two levers to press on each trial. RS level was varied by varying reinforcement probability. Those Ss who were to learn the HH hierarchy were given reinforcement for .9 of their presses on the dominant lever and .6 of their presses on the other lever. The reinforcement probabilities for dominant and competing responses for the groups learning the HL and LL hierarchies were .9, .3 and .6, .3, respectively. The same lever was always dominant and training was extensive—300 trials. Only reinforcement probabilities differed among the groups. A formula for predicting asymptotic performance from reinforcement probabilities (Estes, 1954) was used as a learning criterion to select the final S groups. For these Ss, the response intended to be dominant had become clearly dominant.

---

[2] In this chapter the word significant will only be used to describe results with p equal to or less than .05.

Also, comparison of $\%R_D$ for the last 50 and next to last 50 training trials showed no difference, indicating that training had indeed been continued to asymptotic levels.

With reinforcement continuing as in training, each group was then tested for which of the two possible responses they would choose, with highly aversive white noise (121 db) used as the stress (drive) condition. The prediction from the theory was that the HH group would have the largest decrease in frequency of dominant responses from the last 50 training trials to the 50 test trials. The results were that only this high H_D-high H_C group showed a significant decrease in number of dominant responses. Their average change of -10.0 dominant responses was significantly different from an average increase of 1.4 in the HL group. This is important because both hierarchies had high strength dominant responses that had been carried to asymptotic response levels, with the same high (.9) reinforcement probabilities. This is what was expected from the theory. R_D decrement under increased stress is not only a function of H_D strength but is also greater with stronger H_C. The average change for the LL group was a nonsignificant -4.1. Although, as expected, the LL decrement was less than the decrement for the HH group, decrements for the two groups were not significantly different. It is possible that this lack of significance was due to insufficient differences in habit strength between the two groups. Clearer difference might have been found if there had been reduced response frequency as well as reduced reinforcement for the group that was intended to have low response strength. In spite of this interpretive difficulty, the weight of the evidence is clearly in support of the theory. In different response hierarchies, increased drive did lead to different changes in interference from competing responses. The only significant R_D decrement was where it would be expected from the theory, in the hierarchy with both dominant and competing responses possessing high habit strength.

Another study on normals is of special interest because it applies the theory to another kind of behavior that has been thought to occur in schizophrenia—regression to a response that had been appropriate earlier. Levin (1965) trained introductory psychology students in a paired-associates task where different numbers were associated with different colors. After an S-R pair had been learned to a criterion of four consecutive correct responses, the correct response to that stimulus was changed. Test trials were then interspersed with subsequent learning trials. Testing was done under different drive levels. The drive variable was muscular tension induced by gripping a hand dynamometer. Four different groups were tested under four levels of grip pressure. This procedure was chosen as the drive variable because it is experimentally manipulable and its variation produces the same kind of behavior changes that occur when drive is varied by selecting S

groups who differ on the Taylor Manifest Anxiety Scale (Lövaas, 1960).

During the test trials, the regressive response, the response that had previously been correct, was a well-trained response that was the strongest of several possible incorrect responses. Careful consideration of the theory will show that when incorrect responses are considered alone, the inverted U-shaped relationship predicted for drive and $\%R_D$ should also hold for the dominant error. This is because when errors alone are considered, the multiplicative effect of increased drive should favor the dominant error to the point where this error reaches ceiling strength. If drive is increased beyond this point, it can only increase the relative strength of other errors, thus decreasing the proportion of dominant errors. This inverted U-shaped relationship for the dominant error is most likely when this error is a strong, well-trained response, as was the case for regressive errors in the Levin study. Levin did find this inverted U-shaped relationship. The proportion of errors that were regressive responses increased from zero to low to medium tension, and then decreased under high tension.

To summarize, we have looked at research on normals in order to learn of factors that are related to partial collapse of response hierarchies—reduction in dominant responses because of increased interference from competing responses. Our reason was that this response-interference phenomenon seems to be important in schizophrenia and, unless behavioral processes are quite different in normals and schizophrenics, studying normals should help to focus our attention on relevant variables.

We have discussed three such variables: strength of dominant responses, strength of competing responses, and drive (anxiety, stress, tension) level. These variables were included in a theory of response interference that was tested and received some support in experiments with normal subjects. We now look at the theory as applied to schizophrenia.

III. Response Interference in Schizophrenia

A. THE THEORY AS APPLIED TO SCHIZOPHRENIA

In an earlier discussion of schizophrenia (Broen & Storms, 1966) we made two changes in the theory, which will also be used here. The first change represents an attempt to move toward a better definition of the response-energizing variable we have called drive. We will change to using the term arousal (A) to denote the response-energizing variable. Thus, $A \times H = RS$. Arousal implies the state of relatively diffuse excitation or activation we have implied by the term drive, but in addition, current usage of the term arousal indicates a state that may be measured by changes in peripheral physiological indicants such as heart rate, blood pressure, and respiration rate. Thus, this variable in the theory would seem to be defined better by this change. The studies we will cite when discussing the effects of arousal variation used independent variables that were similar to variables that have been shown to lead to the general physiological changes indicative of arousal. Induced muscular tension seems to be a particularly good example of such a variable in that induced muscular tension apparently has an increasing monotonic relationship to physiological measures of arousal (Pinneo, 1961). Another example is white noise (see evidence cited in Berlyne, Borsa, Hamacher, & Koenig, 1966).

The second and more important change is an addition to the theory, and refers to a major difference between normals and schizophrenics. Groups of schizophrenics are assumed to have a lower average response-strength ceiling than normals. Thus, the response hierarchies of some schizophrenics should begin to collapse under lower levels of arousal than would be required for similar effects in normals. Figure 2 illustrates the interrelationships of level of ceiling, arousal level, and differences in strength between dominant and competing responses.

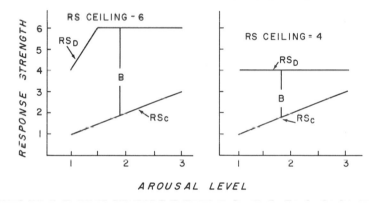

FIG. 2.   Arousal has different relationships to $RS_D - RS_C$ in normals (left) and schizophrenics (right).

The left and right halves of Fig. 2 illustrate the different effects of arousal on response hierarchies expected for normals and schizophrenics, respectively. Note that at all except minimal levels of arousal, schizophrenics are seen as having less difference between strengths of dominant and competing responses (distance B). This is the partial collapse of response hierarchies that seems to underlie much schizophrenic behavior. The cause of this partial collapse may be a low ceiling or increased arousal, or both. On the *average*, groups of schizophrenics are assumed to have higher arousal than normals, as well as a lower average ceiling.

In order to generate specific predictions concerning differences between schizophrenics and normals, some additional comments are needed. First, response strength is assumed to be increasingly inhibited over trials with response-contingent punishment, and inhibited to a lesser extent by non-reinforced occurrences. Second, let us consider the definition of habit strength. Habit strength is assumed to be an increasing function of number S-R occurrences and is also assumed to vary inversely with the amount a stimulus differs from a training stimulus. In experiments that use common stimuli and responses, such as associations to familiar words, we will assume that the strength of the dominant response is at its maximum, and the average habit strength of a competing response in schizophrenics is an increasing function of the relative frequency of that response as observed in normals. Thus schizophrenics' response hierarchies are not assumed to differ from normals' response hierarchies either in content or in rank order of response strengths. Differences between normals and schizophrenics are predicted primarily from expecting schizophrenic response hierarchies to be more collapsed. Unless special procedures have been used to lower arousal level, or if competing responses are not evoked, these differences should always be observed in standard experiments where familiar (high strength) responses are tested. This is because the theory states that schizophrenic behavior reflects response-strength ceiling effects. Thus those people who exhibit schizophrenic behavior in their usual environment should also show ceiling effects under the stress of standard experimental situations.

As we begin discussing research with schizophrenic subjects it must be remembered that the diagnosis of schizophrenia is applied to people who differ considerably, so it may be that the process we are discussing is not important in more than a subgroup of schizophrenics. Later we shall make a few tentative statements about some differences among schizophrenics, but still, there has not been enough research on homogeneous subgroups to be able to specify exactly which subtypes of schizophrenics seem to be disturbed by the process we call response disorganization or partial collapse of hierarchies. Actually, relating this process to the usual schizophrenic subcategories is not our goal. If response disorganization is an important process in schizophrenia, then the best way to reduce the heterogeneity that now exists would be to develop measures that specifically tap the changed behavior expected from this process and use these measures to define subgroups. Before this is done, however, there should be better understanding of the nature of the process. Fortunately some advance can be made through research with relatively heterogeneous groups of subjects. If partial collapse of response hierarchies occurs in many schizophrenics, and if the process works as has been hypothesized here, then average differences between schizophrenics and normals should be in accord with predictions from the theory. So we shall compare theoretical implications with average group data, and shall discuss "schizophrenics" while recognizing the underlying heterogeneity. The hope is that the knowledge gained will enable later and better differentiation based directly on better knowledge of underlying process.

B. RELEVANT RESEARCH

1. Schizophrenia Involves a Partial Collapse of Normal Response Hierarchies

One very important aspect of the theory is the expected similarity between the behavior of groups of schizophrenics and normals. In schizophrenics, low RS ceilings or high arousal, or both, are seen as having led to partially collapsed response hierarchies, but these variables should not change the content of response hierarchies. These variables should also tend to leave the rank order of responses unchanged in schizophrenics, although the greater equalization of response strengths may result in some minor rank changes being observed in any particular data sample. Again, in speaking of the similarities we are speaking of average data. Among individuals, normals as well as schizophrenics, there is considerable variation in the content of response hierarchies, especially in the nondominant associates that reflect unique or infrequent experiences. Hence, if response hierarchies are partially collapsed in schizophrenia, the competing responses that intrude more often will, at times, reflect idiosyncratic experience. However, this does not change the predictions regarding average data.

A study by Gottesman and Chapman (1960) provides evidence about average response hierarchies in normals and schizophrenics. Thirty normals and 30 fairly regressed chronic schizophrenics, matched with the normals on estimates of premorbid intelligence, took a multiple-choice syllogistic reasoning test. There were five possible responses to each syllogism: the four possible forms of conclusions to syllogisms (e.g., "All pots are black" form A; "No pots are black" form E; "Some pots are black" form I; and "Some pots are not black" form D) and the fifth alternative, "None of these conclusions is proved." Actually, each of the 26 experimental syllogisms did not validly prove any one of the four conclusions, so the answer "none proved" was always correct. However, many errors were made by both normals and schizophrenics. There were items where each of the possible types of invalid conclusion was the preferred error in normals, thus giving a chance to see whether or not schizophrenics' response hierarchies vary in accord with normals' response hierarchies. The results are shown in Fig. 3.

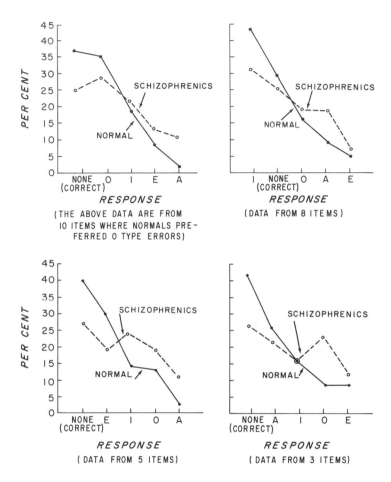

FIG. 3. Normal and schizophrenic response hierarchies by type of error preferred by normals [from data in Gottesman & Chapman (1960)].

Schizophrenics made significantly more errors than normals but, as can be seen in Fig. 3, they did not seem to stick to any specific type of reasoning error. Instead, their response hierarchies tended to be like that of normals. The main difference seemed to be that the percentages of the alternate responses were closer together for schizophrenics—their response hierarchies were partially collapsed.[3]

An alternate interpretation of the data just presented is that some schizophrenics respond like normals, while the rest, because of factors such as inattention to the task requirements, scatter their response choices among all the available alternates. While it is likely that some schizophrenics showed much more complete randomization than others, the important point is the explanation of this randomization. In the theory, randomization is expected in severely disturbed schizophrenics as a number of response tendencies approach ceiling. But in the theory, this randomization, unlike that due to inattention, should occur only among those response tendencies that have significant strength for normals. In accord with this expectation, there is considerable research, especially by Chapman (e.g., 1958, 1961), showing that the important factor in schizophrenics' errors is a specific increase in the frequency of those particular tendencies that are present but non-dominant in normals' response hierarchies. These particular responses increase more than is due to any tendency toward randomization among all the possible response alternates. This could not be demonstrated in the Gottesman and Chapman study just discussed because each of the several error possibilities seemed to have significant strength in normals' hierarchies. Even with five possible responses, the least frequent response tended to occur about 5% of the time in normals. In the next study we will look at, there are only three response possibilities, two being incorrect. Of the two possible errors, one is very weak in normals—occuring only in about one of each 300 trials. Thus we can see whether schizophrenics tend to use randomly all response possibilities, or if they only show an increase in those specific error tendencies that occur significantly in normals' hierarchies.

In this study (Chapman, 1958), chronic schizophrenics and normals who did not differ in educational level did a card-sorting task. On each trial, a sorting card with a word on it was to be put with a response card that had a word in the same conceptual class (could be called by the same name). In addition to the correct card there were two other response cards. One of these cards showed a word with an associative but incorrect connection to the word to be sorted (e.g., "head" when the word "hat" should have been sorted with "dress," or "shoe" as the associative distractor when "mule" should have been sorted with the word "horse"). The other response card bore an irrelevant word. Correct responses were dominant for both groups, but schizophrenics made significantly more errors than normals. Normals had a nondominant tendency to respond to the associated distractor, with negligible tendency to respond to the irrelevant world. So schizophrenics' choices of these two words are relevant to the question of the nature of

---

[2]In another syllogistic reasoning study, Williams (1964) did not find differences between schizophrenics and normals. Unlike Gottesman and Chapman who matched groups on estimates of premorbid intelligence, Williams matched on current verbal intelligence. Williams chose this variable because it has been shown to have a substantial correlation with syllogistic reasoning ability. The fact that groups were essentially matched on current reasoning ability (actually schizophrenics were nonsignificantly higher) may be the reason that schizophrenics were not inferior in reasoning ability.

TABLE II

MEAN ERROR CHOICES OF HIGHLY ASSOCIATED AND IRRELEVANT WORDS[a]

Association basis[b]	Normals		Schizophrenics		Difference between groups	
	Assoc.	Irrel.	Assoc.	Irrel.	Assoc.	Irrel.
Contiguity of objects	2.03	.09	6.75	.31	4.72	.22
Contiguity of words	1.03	.09	5.03	.62	4.00	.53
Rhyme	.38	.12	1.91	.81	1.53	.69

[a] Adapted from Chapman (1958).

[b] Chapman used three different bases of association for the associated response cards. The data are divided according to items using these different association bases. There were 30 items of each type.

response randomization in schizophrenia. Table II gives the relevant data.

These data show clearly that most schizophrenic errors and the major differences between normals and schizophrenics were due to an exacerbation of the specific error tendencies that occur significantly in normals' response hierarchies. The major difference is not due to schizophrenics' random use of the possibilities the task presents, in that schizophrenics showed relatively little exacerbation of the response tendency that was negligible in normals' response hierarchies. In his discussion of these results, Chapman also noted that "Similarly, in each of three previous studies [Chapman, 1956a,b; Chapman & Taylor, 1957], the specific kind of error which accounted primarily for the difference between schizophrenics and normals tended consistently to be committed more often by normals than other types of errors which had an equal opportunity to occur by chance" (Chapman, 1958, p. 278). Fey's (1951) study of schizophrenics and normals on the Wisconsin Card Sorting Test also shows that those errors that most differentiated schizophrenics and normals occur often in normals.

The final study (Gottesman, 1964) we will discuss in this section meets the theoretical boundary conditions especially well. Schizophrenics and normals were given a forced-choice paper-and-pencil word-association test of 51 items. Each stimulus word was from the Kent-Rosanoff test, and there were three possible responses: the dominant normal adult association; the association usually given by children; and an irrelevant word. The dominant responses for normals were thus high strength responses, and judging from their frequency of occurrence in normals, the child-preferred associations were very strong competing responses. Thus, with high H_D and H_C, and because as in all these studies there were no special attempts to reduce experimental stress, schizophrenics should show a clear collapse of normals' response hierarchies. Normals chose the dominant adult association an average of 31.75 times and the child association 18.56 times. The schizophrenics chose the child association significantly more than normals, and had an almost equal tendency to respond with the normally dominant and the strong competing association, averaging 23.44 and 25.00 choices, respectively. Thus, schizophrenics' tendency toward equalization of the two responses that were strong in normals' hierarchies is clear. It is also clear that this randomization within the response tendencies that are fairly strong in normals was not due to a broader tendency to ignore task stimuli or requirements. The tendency to choose the irrelevant word was weak in normals (chosen an average of 1.31 times) and the irrelevant word was chosen only a little more by schizophrenics—an average of 1.88 times. Thus, schizophrenic disorganization does seem specifically to reflect a reduction in the difference in strength between normals' dominant responses and those competing responses that also have significant strength in normals.

2. Stability and Commonality of Associations

If response hierarchies are partially collapsed in schizophrenia, the alternate responses will be more equal in strength, and therefore in probability. If trials are repeated, there will be more switching from one response to another than if a single response were clearly dominant. Also, to the extent that normal behavior means sharing dominant responses with other persons, increased intrusion of responses that are usually lower in response hierarchies means that behavior should be more unusual, that is, show less commonality with norms. Third, because partial collapse of response hierarchies affects both commonality and stability, these variables should be correlated.

In one study that is relevant to these implications from the theory, Sommer, Dewar, and Osmond (1960) tested the associations of normals, chronic schizophrenics, and acute schizophrenics to the 100 words in the Kent-Rosanoff list. The testing was repeated a week later. Response stability was measured by counting the number of responses that were identical in the two sessions. The mean stability scores were 52 for the normals and 44 for the schizophrenics—a statistically significant difference.

Response commonality was measured in several ways: first, by giving each response a score equal to the number of persons in the Kent-Rosanoff sample (1000 normals) who had given that response. Schizophrenics responses tended to have lower commonality. Median commonality scores were most frequently in the 50–99 range for normals and the 0–49 range for both acute and chronic schizophrenics. Commonality was also measured by measuring responses against each group's own norms. The average percentage of persons giving their own group's dominant response was 35 for normals and 28 for schizophrenics. Thus, schizophrenics differed from each other more than normals did, indicating that low commonality in schizophrenics is not due to schizophrenics learning to respond in abnormal but shared ways. As Sommer *et al.* put it, there is not a "schizophrenic language." As an inverse measure of commonality, Sommer *et al.* also counted the number of associations that had not been given by anyone in the Kent-Rosanoff sample of normals. The median number of private associations was 9 for the normals, 11 for acute schizophrenics, and 13.5 for chronic schizophrenics. Thus, even though normative commonality is less in schizophrenics, it should be noted that the proportion of responses schizophrenics make that are not strong enough in normal response hierarchies to occur in normative data is quite low and is not much higher than in normals. The main point, though, is that Sommer *et al.* did find that response commonality and stability are both lower in schizophrenics than in normals. Because both are reduced, some disintegration of response hierarchies seems a more likely explanation than any kind of explanation involving a stable shift to specific deviant responses.

We (Storms & Broen, 1964) also studied stability and commonality in schizophrenics, using the theoretical account to arrange conditions that should cause these measures to vary. Normals, neurotics, and recently hospitalized schizophrenics gave four responses to each of 16 words on each of two successive days. For example, subjects were given the word "birds" and were instructed to "give four examples of that kind of thing." The stimulus words were divided into two equal groups according to whether or not clinical psychologists judged the words to be anxiety producing (e.g., "countries" was judged as not producing anxiety, "diseases" as anxiety producing). In addition, one half the subjects responded under time pressure and one half under instructions to relax. Both anxiety and time pressure were assumed to be drive conditions. As our later shift from drive to arousal suggests, we now would prefer conditions that are more clearly shown to be relevant to the theory by demonstrating arousal effects on peripheral physiological measures.

The basic drive prediction was that drive should decrease stability and commonality in schizophrenics and that this effect would be greater in schizophrenics than in the other groups. The reason for this prediction can be seen in Fig. 2 (Section III, A). (Neurotics were not assumed to differ from normals in level of RS ceiling, and were expected to be less affected by ceiling effects than schizophrenics.) Because of schizophrenics' lower ceilings, increased drive (arousal) should cause more collapse in schizophrenics' response hierarchies. In spite of *post hoc* dissatisfaction with the drive conditions, it seems worthwhile to look at the results. The study is certainly relevant to the questions posed at the beginning of this section, and the additional information on anxiety and time pressure is at least suggestive.

The stability measure was the number of first-day responses given on the second day. An overall test of group differences was significant, with normals being most stable and schizophrenics least, although specific tests showed only the normals differing significantly from the other two groups. Also, as expected from the theory, schizophrenics were more unstable on responses to anxiety categories than the nonanxiety categories. This increase in instability under higher anxiety was significantly greater for schizophrenics than for the other groups. The only significant effect of time pressure was to increase instability more in schizophrenics than in neurotics, who became more stable under time pressure.

Commonality was measured by using the Cohen, Bousfield, and Whitmarsh (1957) norms. A response was given a score of 1 if it was one of the four most common normative responses, 2 if it was in the next four, and so on. As expected, schizophrenics' responses were significantly less common than the responses given by the other groups. However, there were no significant groups by drive interactions.

To summarize the results of this experiment: as predicted, schizophrenics tended to have lower response stability and commonality. Also, the drive conditions tended to reduce response stability more in schizophrenics than in the other groups, although the same effect did not occur on the commonality measure. The expected positive correlation between commonality and stability was also found: $r = .32$ for neurotics, .36 for schizophrenics, and .56 for normals, although the size of the correlations suggests that even if the common variance in these measures is due to common effect of degree of organization of response hierarchies, each measure is also substantially influenced by other factors. In general, the results of this study support the basic view of partial collapse of response hierarchies in schizophrenics and the expected effects of this process on associative stability and commonality. The prediction that drive (arousal) would exacerbate this process more in schizophrenics than in other groups was supported for stability but not commonality. In a later section, we shall discuss further the role of arousal in schizophrenics, using somewhat better operational definitions of this variable.

Dokecki, Polidoro, and Cromwell (1965) have provided more data on associative stability and commonality in schizophrenics. The Kent-Rosanoff association test was given twice, with a 48-hour interval separating the testing sessions, to a group of schizophrenics with good premorbid adjustment [Phillips (1953) scale scores of 15 or below]; a group of schizophrenics with poor premorbid adjustment (Phillips scores of 16 and over), and to a group of hospitalized tuberculosis patients. The poor premorbid schizophrenics acted as expected from the theory, giving lower commonality associations and having less stable associations than the TB patients. The predicted relationship between stability and commonality was also found in that, in all three subject groups, those subjects who tended to give associations with lower commonality had lower stability scores. However, the good premorbid schizophrenics did not differ from the TB patients in associative commonality or stability. It would be tempting to conclude that this latter result occurred because Phillips scale scores are related to degree of collapse of response hierarchies in schizophrenics, with only poor premorbid schizophrenics experiencing partial collapse of response hierarchies. However, in the Storms and Broen (1964) study, unlike the Dokecki *et al.* results, neither commonality or stability were significantly correlated with Phillips scores. The difference in results may lie in the length of time since hospitalization. In the Storms and Broen study, all schizophrenics were tested within four days of hospitalization, while in that by Dokecki *et al.* there was an average of 3.78 years current hospitalization for the good premorbids and 6.56 years for the poor premorbids. It may be that both good and poor premorbid patients are experiencing collapse of response hierarchies at the time of hospitalization, but in good premorbid patients this process is reduced more rapidly during the course of hospitalization. This speculative hypothesis is in accord with considering collapse of response hierarchies as being a major contributor to schizophrenic deficit, together with evidence indicating that schizophrenics with good premorbid adjustment have a better prognosis for recovery than poor premorbids (Farina, Garmezy, & Barry, 1963).

3. The Differen: Effects of Increased Arousal

One of the reasons why lowered stability and commonality were predicted for schizophrenics was that the responses being tested were familiar, high strength associates to the stimuli. If dominant responses have low habit strength, it is less likely that response-strength ceilings will restrict response strength and cause partial collapse of response hierarchies. This relationship between habit strength of dominant responses and amount of collapse of response hierarchies is quite specific, and as noted before, the usual expectation is the opposite—that strong dominant responses should be more resistant to the effects of factors that increase response interference. Earlier we discussed a pilot study that tested the effects of one variable that should increase interference (electric shock) on response hierarchies with different dominant response strengths. As predicted, there was more reduction in dominant response frequency where dominant response strength was higher. However, the prediction is important enough to require additional confirmation. There are also questions about generalizing to abnormal populations from the normal Ss used in the pilot study, and using methods of varying response strength that are different from those used in that study. These considerations led to the following study.

Broen, Storms, and Goldberg (1963) tested the effects of arousal on different response hierarchies, using stimulus generalization to vary the strength of the dominant responses. The theoretical points that were tested can be best understood by looking at Fig. 4. Figure 4 illustrates a situation where different responses—left and right lever presses—are learned to training stimuli (S_{TL} and S_{TR}) at the ends of a stimulus continuum. The solid line represents the strength of the left response tendency as generalized from its training stimulus to other stimuli. The dashed line represents the strength of the tendency to press to the right. The theoretical effect of increased arousal can be realized by considering what should happen if arousal is doubled. The strength of all response tendencies should be doubled. This doubling will increase distance A, thus increasing the pro-

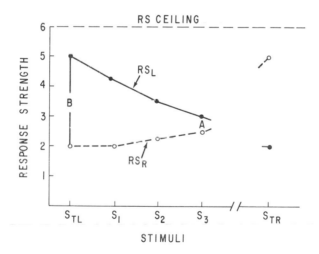

FIG. 4. Hypothetical generalization of response strength for left and right lever presses that have been trained to stimuli at the opposite ends of a continuum.

bability of the dominant response to S_3. However, at the training stimuli, dominant response strength will be restricted by the ceiling. With the strength of the competing response being doubled, distance B will decrease from 3 to 2; and the probability of the dominant response will decrease. By using Hullian procedures (Hull, 1952, p. 26) for computing response probability from differences in response strength (e.g., distances A and B), the specific theoretical effects of doubling arousal can be computed. Figure

5 shows the computed probabilities for the dominant response in the situation illustrated in Fig. 4 and for that situation when arousal is doubled. This figure shows one half of the stimuli in the symmetrical theoretical situation in Fig. 4. Figure 5 was used by Broen *et al.* (1963) to generate experimental predictions.

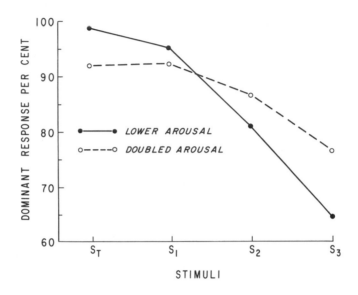

FIG. 5. Hypothetical gradients of stimulus generalization for the situation illustrated in Fig. 4 and for the same situation when arousal is doubled [adapted from Broen *et al.* (1963)].

The experimental situation was as follows. Subjects first learned to press a lever to the left in response to a small gray square (S_{TL}) and to the right to a large gray square (S_{TR}). A green light indicated correct responses. Ss were given 48 trials to learn the task to a criterion of 14 correct responses in the last 16 trials. Three of 20 initial Ss did not meet this criterion. Then the final Ss were told that they would see some more squares, that they should continue to press either to the left or right on each trial, but that the green light would not always come on when they were correct. In these test trials the stimuli were the two training stimuli together with six different gray squares whose sizes varied between the sizes of the training stimuli. Correct responses to the training stimuli continued to be reinforced; other responses were not. Each S took these test trials under three levels of arousal, the lowest of which was the same as in training. Arousal was varied by inducing different levels of muscular tension by having Ss squeeze a hand dynamometer at zero pressure or at one-quarter or one-half of their maximum grip. The experimental treatment was symmetrical, left and right responses being trained and tested under the same conditions, so the data from the two halves of the stimulus continuum were combined to yield a continuum with four stimuli as was illustrated in Fig. 5.

The Ss were college-student psychiatric outpatients. No formal diagnosis had been made, but from tentative diagnoses and MMPI profiles, the majority of the subjects seemed to have some degree of schizophrenic reaction. With the possibility of some diagnostic heterogeneity, and because we did not know, *a priori*, the level of training needed for ceiling effects with these new responses, we did not feel that decrement would necessarily occur under the first increase in arousal. We did think it very likely that the range of arousal we were using would produce decrement at some level. However, the decrement prediction was only that increased arousal could cause a decrement in dominant responses, and if it did, this decrement would occur first at S_T. It was also predicted that the arousal level where this decrement first occurred would continue to facilitate R_D at S_3 (the third stimulus from S_T, which, with six intermediate stimuli, is the farthest generalization stimulus at which the response that is dominant at S_T should still be dominant). The result should be a significantly flatter generalization gradient, as was illustrated in Fig. 5. Note that this flattening cannot be the result of influences that act to randomize response choice, such as inattention or distraction. The same response that is dominant at S_T is dominant (should be above 50%) at S_3, so randomization of the two response choices would lower the gradient toward 50% at all stimuli, instead of increasing the probability of the dominant response at S_3. If this facilitation does occur at S_3, it would help to define the major effect of induced muscular tension as being response energizing, as is expected of increased arousal.

Let us turn to the results, which are presented in Table III. During testing there were 12 presentations of each type of stimulus under each arousal level. Thus, as can be seen from the arousal ($A = 0$) column of Table III, the responses that were dominant at S_T were also dominant (over 50%) through S_3. Thus, in this important respect the experimental situation was appropriate for the predictions. Compared to the lowest arousal condition, the medium arousal condition (one-quarter grip; $A = \frac{1}{4}$) yielded a non-significant increase in dominant response frequency at S_T with significant facilitation of dominant response frequency at S_3. The highest arousal level caused a significant decrement in frequency of dominant responses at S_T and, as predicted, this arousal level still increased dominant response frequency at S_3. The result was a significantly flatter generalization gradient. Thus, as expected, increasing arousal first led to a dominant response decrement where that response was strong—at the training stimulus. At generalization stimuli, where ceiling effects were not expected because response strength

TABLE III

MEAN TRAINED RESPONSES FOR A = O AND MEAN RESPONSE DIFFERENCES
WHEN AROUSAL IS INCREASED TO A = ¼ AND A = ½[a]

Stimulus	Responses for A = 0	(A = ¼) − (A = 0)		(A = ½) − (A = 0)	
		Difference	SD	Difference[b]	SD
S_T	11.44	.15	.08	−.35[c]	.16
S_1	11.35	−.20	.29	−.09	.29
S_2	10.44	−.15	.29	.24	.36
S_3	6.47	.74[c]	.31	.88[c]	.18

[a] Data from Broen et al. (1963).
[b] Significant linear trend, $p < .05$.
[c] Significant difference, $p < .05$.

was lower, dominant response frequency continued to be facilitated.

Because we had not predicted the specific level at which decrement at S_T would occur, the occurrence of this decrement has less weight than confirming the more specific prediction regarding continued facilitation of $\%R_D$ at S_3. Also, although the decrement at S_T was significant, its absolute value was quite small. So a second experiment (also reported in Broen et al., 1963) was designed that would necessitate predicting a decrement in a dominant response under a specific level of arousal. We also wanted to arrange conditions that would make the decrement larger, so conditions were designed to be more theoretically favorable to decrement.

Ss again learned to press a lever either to the left or right in response to training stimuli that were similar but discriminable. The training stimuli were silhouettes of a house beside a tree, and differed only in the angle of the lowest tree branch. Other changes were guided by the theory's statement that dominant response decrement is more likely with higher strength dominant and competing responses, lower ceilings, and higher arousal. In order to increase H_D and especially to increase H_C, there were more training trials (75 for each S_T) and reinforcement was probabilistic (.9 of correct Rs and .5 of incorrect Rs were reinforced by a green light). The Ss were hospitalized schizophrenics (lower ceilings). The arousal levels during testing were the zero grip that was used during training and the one-half maximum grip level, where decrement occurred in the last experiment.

As expected from increased response competition, this task was difficult. Twenty of 42 initial Ss did not meet a criterion, namely, 22 correct responses in the final 36 training trials, that was used to insure dominance of correct responses. The final Ss were tested under conditions that, except for arousal variation, were the same as training conditions. Only training stimuli were presented, with each S_T presented 18 times under each arousal condition to each S.

The prediction was that the higher arousal condition (one-half grip) would lead to decrements in dominant responses to both training stimuli. The prediction was confirmed. The mean change from low to high arousal for left responses at their training stimulus was -1.25 ($p < .05$). There was also significant right response decrement at S_{TR} (mean change $= -1.93, p < .05$). The combined mean change was thus -3.18 ($p < .05$).

Taken together, these last two experiments support the prediction that increased arousal can increase the frequency of weak dominant responses, while reducing the frequency of the same responses when they are stronger and are therefore more likely to be restricted by ceiling.

The theory also predicts that increased arousal will have different effects in schizophrenics and normals. As can be seen in Fig. 2 (Section III, A), when initial arousal level is low and dominant response frequency is equivalent in schizophrenics and normals, an increase in arousal should decrease the probability of dominant responses more in schizophrenics than in normals. This prediction was tested in a third experiment (Broen & Storms, 1964) in this series on the effects of arousal.

Normals and schizophrenics were tested on a task very similar to that used in the last experiment. Both normals and schizophrenics were hospitalized, the normals being ambulatory general medical and surgical patients. In order to make it easier to obtain equivalent performance for the groups in the conditions intended as low arousal trials, care had been taken to make the basic task a relatively low stress situation for schizophrenics as well as normals. The responses were nonverbal, reinforcement was impersonal (green light), and there was no comment on incorrect responses. Also, the stimuli to be discriminated were neutral. They were the silhouettes with different branch angles used in the last experiment. These stimuli were used here because they were similar to the stimuli that, in a study by Dunn (1954), were discriminated as well by schizophrenics as by normals. Using the same probabilistic reinforcement as in the last experiment, Ss were given 120 trials to learn to press a lever to the left in response to S_{TL} and to the right for S_{TR}. Each S was then tested under both low (zero grip) and high (grip $=$ one-half maximum) arousal conditions with other conditions the same as during training. In test trials, each S_T was presented 20 times in each arousal condition. Because the prediction asks that both groups have correct responses dominant and have similar performance under the low arousal test condition, a performance criterion was applied to the low arousal test condition. A criterion of at least 13 correct responses in the 20 trials was used separately for S_{TR} and S_{TL}. For S_{TR}, 30 of 45 initial schizophrenic Ss met the criterion, and 24 of 32 normals. For S_{TL}, 25 schizophrenics and 23 normals met the criterion.

Specific tests of the number of dominant responses showed that the final schizophrenic and normal Ss were not different in performance at S_{TL} or S_{TR} under low arousal. However, as predicted, the high arousal condition led to greater dominant response decrement in the schizophrenics than the normals. At S_{TR} the mean change in the dominant (right) response from low to high arousal was $-.33$ for normals and -1.90 for schizophrenics. The between-groups difference in decrements was statistically significant. At S_{TL} the respective changes in the left response were $-.22$ and -2.68 with the schizophrenics' decrement again being significantly larger.

Because the greater schizophrenic decrement could have been caused by selecting schizophrenics whose low arousal performance was temporarily raised by chance factors and comparing them with normals whose low arousal performance was not spuriously high, a control analysis was done. Schizophrenics and normals were compared for changes from the final learning trials to the low arousal test trials. The between-groups difference did not approach significance at either S_{TL} or S_{TR}.

The results of this series of experiments support the theoretical position that when initial arousal is low and performance is similar for schizophrenics and normals, increased arousal interacting with schizophrenics' lower ceilings will tend to collapse response hierarchies more in schizophrenics. Also, when arousal is sufficient to lead to partial collapse of response hierarchies, the decrement occurs specifically where it is expected from ceiling effects—where response strength is greatest. Of course one important aspect of each of these studies was that there was response competition. The foregoing results are not expected when response competition is absent. It should be noted that in the first study, where the amount of dominant response decrement under increased arousal was quite small, competition, as indicated by the high frequency of dominant responses, was relatively low (see Table III, this section). One of the things we did to obtain greater arousal decrements was to use probabilistic reinforcement and increase the number of training trials to make competing responses stronger.

4. Strength of Competing Responses as a Determinant of Amount of Schizophrenic Deficit

The strength of competing responses should not only be important for the amount of deficit schizophrenics will experience when arousal is increased, it should also be an important determiner of the difference between schizophrenics' and normals' performance. Earlier (Section III, B, 1) we discussed the role of competing responses in determining the *characteristics* of schizophrenic deficit—the same competing responses tend to be evoked in schizophrenics and normals, and schizophrenics specifically make more of those errors that normals also make. In this and the following section the focus will be on the *amount* of schizophrenic deficit. The theory predicts that if familiar appropriate responses are tested, schizophrenic deficit, relative to normal performance, will be greater on tasks where competing responses are stronger.

Because we shall focus on this prediction, its rationale must be clear. In the theory some schizophrenics are assumed to have near-normal ceilings, with abnormal arousal that is more than sufficient to raise appropriate responses to ceiling. The multiplicative effect of their abnormal arousal causes stronger competing responses to increase more than weak competing responses. With appropriate responses limited at ceiling, the result is a performance deficit that will be greater in situations where competing responses are stronger.

A deficit resulting from lower ceilings will also be greater in situations that evoke stronger competing responses. Remember that the specific theoretical relationship between $RS_D - RS_C$ and $\%R_D$ is not linear. When $RS_D - RS_C$ is small, reducing this difference a specific amount reduces $\%R_D$ more than when $RS_D - RS_C$ is initially larger. Lower ceilings in schizophrenics means that for familiar responses $RS_D - RS_C$ is usually smaller than in normals. So if response competition (RS_C) is increased by a specific amount, $\%R_D$ will be reduced more in schizophrenics than in normals.

It should be noted that this prediction holds only if competing responses remain below ceiling, so that an increase in stronger competing responses is not restricted relative to the increase in weaker responses. To demonstrate that competing responses are below ceiling, situations where the prediction is tested should show clear dominance of correct over competing responses in schizophrenics.

It should also be clear that the theory does not suggest the converse of the foregoing prediction—that on tasks where competing responses are negligible, the higher average arousal in schizophrenics should cause them to have correct responses of higher strength, and therefore they should perform better than normals. Lower average ceilings in schizophrenics should limit response strength, at least when responses are familiar. Thus, schizophrenics are not necessarily expected to perform better than normals on simple tasks. The prediction is only that, when appropriate responses have high strength, schizophrenic deficit will be greater on tasks where competing responses are stronger.

Before we consider some recent data concerning this prediction, we should note that degree of response competition should not be defined by how many responses an experimenter counts. "Simple" reaction-time (RT) tasks, where the only data are the speed of a single response, are not free from competing responses. As we noted early in this chapter, competing responses are not only alternate responses to a single stimulus, but also come from other stimuli, such as a subject's own preoccupations or irrelevant external stimuli. Some of these competing responses can be fairly strong in "single-response" tasks. Schizophrenic exacerbation of competing responses to irrelevant stimuli should cause decrement in timed tasks, such as "simple" RT tasks, which require a specific speedy reaction to a change in a specific stimulus.

Tasks that are simple in the sense that the theory would predict little schizophrenic decrement can, however, be arranged. One method would be to present a stimulus, and to count only the correct (normally dominant) response and a limited number of incorrect responses to that stimulus, with the data being in terms of response occurrence rather than speed of the correct response. Other responses will occur—especially in schizophrenics— but will tend to affect the data much less. This method allows better control of the strengh of those competing responses that do affect the data. On tasks where the competing responses that are counted have negligible strength in normals, exacerbation of these responses in schizophrenics should be minimal. On tasks where competing responses are stronger in normals, the probability of these responses should be even higher in schizophrenics, resulting in larger differences between schizophrenics and normals.

A study of this type was done by Chapman (1961). Normals and chronic schizophrenics who did not differ in educational level took a concept-sorting test where names of familiar objects were sorted according to whether or not the objects belonged to a specified conceptual class. Two kinds of objects could be incorrectly included in a specified class: objects that were similar (e.g., vegetables when the class was fruit) or dissimilar (e.g., items of sports equipment). There were equal numbers of both these kinds of objects. For both similar and dissimilar objects the clearly dominant response was to correctly sort the objects as not belonging to the specified class. For normals, however, the objects were different in the number of competing inclusion responses they evoked. Overinclusion responses were rarely evoked by dissimilar objects, with response competition being stronger for similar objects. Thus, according to the theory, schizophrenic deficit relative to normals should be greatest in sorting the similar objects. Table IV shows that this is what occurred. The table is divided into two kinds of concepts Chapman used—narrow and broad concepts. The results are in accord with the prediction for both.

Another way to test the prediction that schizophrenic deficit will be greater when response competition is stronger is to use learning tasks where old responses provide different degrees of competition for the new responses that are to be learned.

However, the prediction was based on considering ceiling effects on

TABLE IV

MEAN OVERINCLUSIVE ERROR SCORES FOR OBJECTS THAT WERE SIMILAR
AND DISSIMILAR TO THE INSTRUCTED CONCEPT[a]

Type of object	Normal	Schizophrenic	Difference between groups
Narrow concepts			
Similar	2.06	9.39	7.33
Dissimilar	.06	1.18	1.12
Broad concepts			
Similar	.33	5.56	5.23
Dissimilar	.09	1.29	1.20

Adapted from Chapman (1961).

correct, dominant responses, but learning tasks often begin with weak correct responses, and learning may not be continued to the point where ceiling effects are possible. Schizophrenic deficit may not occur at all. It would seem possible to get around this problem by reasoning backward; by finding those studies where there was a schizophrenic deficit and then reasoning that the deficit should be greater where response competition was greater. This type of prediction would conform fairly well to the research literature (e.g., Kausler, Lair, & Matsumoto, 1964; Lang & Luoto, 1962). It would also be compatible with the theory, but it would not necessarily show anything about ceiling effects. Schizophrenic deficit may occur without ceiling effects if incorrect responses are dominant and weak, as is possible early in learning. In such cases the incorrect dominant responses may be below ceiling and may be stronger in schizophrenics than in normals because of schizophrenics' higher average arousal. This may be part of the explanation for a schizophrenic deficit that has occurred when measures such as number of correct responses in the first few learning trials are used (Lang & Luoto, 1962).

A measure of learning ability such as the number of trials needed to reach a criterion is more likely to reflect ceiling effects, because it is more influenced by the total course of learning. The more rigorous the criterion, the more this measure will be weighted by the later stages of learning, where ceiling effects are expected. Also, if schizophrenics can meet this criterion, it shows that competing responses are below ceiling, thus meeting the boundary condition discussed earlier.

In addition to measuring correct responses on early trials, Lang and Luoto (1962) also used a fairly rigorous trials-to-criterion measure in a learning task where response competition was varied. Schizophrenics did reach the rigorous criterion, but they tended to take longer to reach it than normals. Thus, this study may be relevant to our predictions concerning response competition and ceiling effects. We will examine this study to answer two questions: (1) Was the schizophrenic deficit greatest where response competition was greatest? and (2) Was this deficit due to ceiling effects?

Lang and Luoto (1962) first gave hospitalized normals and chronic schizophrenics the Kent-Rosanoff word-association test. Then the Ss learned a list of 10 S-R pairs, where the stimuli were nonsense syllables and each response was one of the stimulus words from the Kent-Rosanoff list. When an S-R pair was learned to a criterion of 4 successive correct trials, it was dropped from the list. Because the nonsense syllables did not have strong prior associated responses that would compete with correct responses, normals and schizophrenics would not be expected to differ greatly in ability to learn this first list. Then the Ss learned a second 10-pair list to the same criterion. In list II the stimulus terms were the same as in list I. Each S's own association to the list I response formed one half of the responses for list II. For these pairs, the specific list I response would interfere with correct list II responses, but these incorrect responses also should mediate correct responses, thus partially offsetting the response interference. S-R pairs of this type will be called *mediating pairs*. On the other five pairs, the stimuli from list I were paired with unrelated words. Thus the responses learned in list I would only interfere with learning. These pairs will be called *competing pairs*. Thus the competing responses were stronger on list II than on list I, and should interfere especially on the competing pairs. According to the theory, the schizophrenic deficit relative to normals should vary directly with the degree of response competition. Table V shows that this was the case. Schizophrenic deficit tended to be greater on list II and especially on the competing pairs.

TABLE V

SCHIZOPHRENIC DEFICIT FROM NORMAL PERFORMANCE IN MEAN TRIALS REQUIRED TO ACHIEVE CRITERION FOR MEDIATING PAIRS, COMPETING PAIRS, AND TOTAL LIST[a,b]

List	Mediating	Competing	Total
I	.08	−.58	−.25
II	1.97	3.40	2.72

[a] Data from Lang and Luoto (1962).
[b] For comparison with list II, list I pairs are also divided into mediating and competing pairs, according to what type of pair the stimulus term was in on list II.

Although, as is expected from ceiling effects in the theory, schizophrenic deficit did vary in accordance with strength of response competition, it must still be shown that this was not due to a deficit in the first few trials, which would not require an explanation in terms of ceiling effects. What is needed is a closer examination of where the deficit occurred in list II. Ceiling effects would lead to the decrement being greater later in learning. The number of trials required to learn successive pairs is relevant here. Remember that when an S-R pair was learned to criterion, it was dropped from the list. Hence, pairs where response competition was low enough so that correct responses could become clearly dominant in only a few trials were dropped first. For these pairs where correct responses achieved only moderate strength, ceiling effects should be minimal and schizophrenic deficit should be minimal. The pairs that remained longer were those that required more trials in order for correct responses to become dominant over stronger competing responses. On these pairs, correct responses achieved high strength, and it is in exactly this kind of situation, with a strong dominant response and strong competing response, that ceiling effects should lead to most schizophrenic deficit. Thus, if the deficit is due to ceiling effects, schizophrenics should do worse relative to normals on the pairs that it took longer to learn. Figure 6 shows that this is what happened.

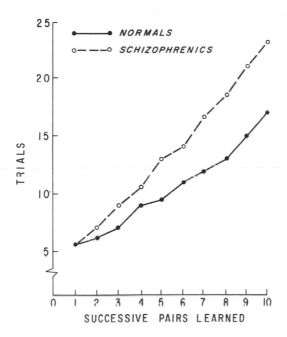

FIG. 6.   Mean number of trials required to learn successive pairs from list II [adapted from Lang & Luoto (1962)].

Lang and Luoto (1962) noted that, by itself, the hypothesis that schizophrenics have higher drive (arousal), which would lead to deficit by strengthening incorrect responses when they are dominant, "... suggests that differences should appear early rather than late in learning. The picture of increasing deviation with successive pairs implies the effects of a second variable" (p. 118). It seems that response-strength ceiling may be this needed variable.

5. Reducing Competing Responses Should Enable Schizophrenics to Perform More like Normals

If, as the theory and the research just discussed suggest, schizophrenic deficit is greater when response competition is greater, then reducing competing responses should help schizophrenics more than normals. In a similar vein Blaufarb noted that Lothrop (1961) had reasoned that "... some of the present tasks of conceptual thinking, in terms of their ambiguous structure encourage the production of irrelevant responses" (Blaufarb, 1962, p. 471). Blaufarb thought that "if one accepts the notion that the abstracting ability of schizophrenics is itself unimpaired, it could be expected that a more precise and amplified structuring of a task stimulus would lead to improved abstracting performance" (p. 471). Blaufarb (1962) tested this hypothesis by comparing interpretation of proverbs by normals and chronic schizophrenics when the proverbs were presented alone, and when the proverbs were given in sets of three with each proverb in a set having the same meaning. The schizophrenics were significantly worse than the normals in interpreting the proverbs in the more ambiguous single-proverb condition. When ambiguity was reduced through using the sets of proverbs, however, the schizophrenics improved significantly and their performance did not differ from that of the normals. Thus, reducing competition from alternate interpretations decreased the difference between schizophrenics and normals.

Hamlin, Haywood, and Folsom (1965) used Blaufarb's tasks to test a wider range of subjects: a mixed group composed of nonschizophrenic patients and nonpsychiatric patients, and three groups of schizophrenics divided according to hospital status into discharged, open-ward, or closed-ward groups. The interpretations made by the open-ward and discharged "schizophrenics" improved significantly from the ambiguous to less ambiguous methods of presentation, but the nonschizophrenics' interpretations did not. So reducing competition from alternate interpretations was again more beneficial to schizophrenics. Unlike the other two groups of schizophrenics, however, the closed-ward schizophrenics did not benefit significantly from the reduced competition made possible by additional information.

We shall comment later on this inability of some schizophrenics to use additional information. For now, we only look ahead to note that it is likely that the more withdrawn, long-term schizophrenics seem able to use only a limited amount of information. Additional information is likely to be used by these individuals only when it is intense, more obvious, or made more important for the individual. If this is the case, then one very good method for reducing schizophrenic deficit would be to use intense or personally important stimulation in a way that would reduce competing response tendencies. Aversive stimulation which is used to punish incorrect responses is one such method which should then enable schizophrenics to perform more like normals.

The problem is that intense aversive stimulation should also increase arousal, and the theory then leads us to expect an opposing effect, namely, that intense aversive stimulation should collapse response hierarchies more in schizophrenics than normals. However, remember that the theory states that the special effect of arousal in schizophrenics is due to the facilitation of competing responses while dominant responses are restricted by schizophrenics' lower average ceilings. The negative effect of arousal is only in strengthening the competing response tendencies that are present. If competing tendencies are reduced, the negative effect of arousal should be reduced. Thus the opposing effects of aversive stimulation that is used to punish competing response tendencies should appear in sequence. When the stimulation is first used, competing tendencies should still be strong. Because of schizophrenics' lower average ceiling, the multiplicative effect of arousal on competing responses will collapse schizophrenics' response hierarchies more, and schizophrenic deficit should be increased. But later, as competing tendencies are reduced, schizophrenics should do better and better relative to normal performance, ending with less deficit than they had initially, because of the eventual reduction in competing response tendencies.

The results of an experiment by Pascal and Swensen (1952) support these implications from the theory. Schizophrenics and normals were tested on a complex reaction-time task where, following a ready signal, left or right switches were to be pulled, depending on the pattern of stimulus lights. At the end of a training period the schizophrenics' performance was significantly poorer than that of normals. Then, on subsequent trials aversive (116-db) white noise was turned on with the ready signal, and the schizophrenics were told that it would not go off until the correct response was made. Thus, the aversive noise was extended when any kind of interfering response was made. This punishment should eventually tend to suppress such responses. In accord with the theory, however, the initial effect was to make schizophrenics' performance worse and to increase schizophrenics' deficit relative to normals. Then, as punishment of competing responses continued, the schizophrenics improved until their performance was not significantly different from that of the normals.

It seems reasonable to interpret the effect of the white noise in Pascal and Swensen's study as first having a net facilitating effect on competing responses in schizophrenics, due to the arousal component, with a long-term effect that reduces competing responses and thereby reduces schizophrenic deficit, due to its punishment aspect. However, contrary to our hypothesis that the decreased deficit was due to reduced response competition, it is possible that a continued elevation in arousal is itself sufficient to reduce schizophrenic deficit.

This possibility was studied by Karras (1962). In this study, after about 40 practice trials, one group of chronic schizophrenics performed a two-choice reaction-time task with an aversive level of white noise used as in the Pascal and Swensen study. In another group, after the practice trials the white noise was on throughout the task, regardless of the quality of the performance, and so was not specifically tied to the occurrence of inter-fering responses and could not act to suppress them. These conditions should differentiate the effects of reducing competing responses from the effects of continuing a higher level of arousal. Compared to a control group of chronic schizophrenics who experienced no noise, the condition where noise should decrease competing responses led to significantly faster reaction times. This improvement was negligible in the first block of trials. It became notable only later, as would be expected if the punishing effects required time to overcome arousal effects. In contrast, in the pure arousal condition, reaction times were significantly slower, and this slower perfor-ance appeared in the first block of trials and was maintained.

The one puzzling aspect of this study was that in yet another group, when moderate white noise was on continuously it led to even greater deficit than higher, aversive level. However, this does not change the major conclusion that, by itself, continued higher arousal leads to poorer per-formance in schizophrenics. Both continuous arousal groups did significantly worse than the control group. In accordance with the theory, aversive noise improved schizophrenic performance only when it was arranged so that it would punish competing responses and after several trials, which made it possible for this effect to occur.

6. Reward versus Punishment

It is still possible that the major effect of the response-contingent noise in the Pascal and Swensen and Karras studies was to reinforce relevant responses instead of punishment competing responses. This would not be expected from the theory, because schizophrenic deficit is seen as due in part to the restriction of relevant responses at ceiling strength. Thus, for well-practiced responses—and the task was practiced prior to the noise condition in both these experiments—rewarding correct responses should have little effect. According to the theory, punishing competing responses should be a more effective procedure for reducing schizophrenic deficit than rewarding correct responses.

Cavanaugh, Cohen, and Lang (1960) studied the effects of punishment versus reward in chronic schizophrenics in another two-choice reaction-time task. After practice trials, one group of schizophrenics was censured ("That was bad—too slow") if their performance on any trial was slower than a predetermined time. A second group was rewarded for fast trials with "That was good—very fast." A control group of schizophrenics received no additional information. Trials were continued past the trials on which the reward or punishment information was given. The results are shown in Fig. 7.

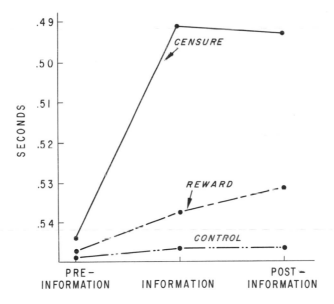

FIG. 7. Mean reaction time for control, reward, and punishment conditions [adapted from Cavanaugh *et al.* (1960)].

The group that was reinforced for good performance did not do significantly better than the control group in either the information or postinformation trials. However, the schizophrenics whose poorer trials had been punished were significantly better than both the reward and control groups in both information and postinformation trials. Thus it seems likely that the schizophrenics' improvement in the Pascal and Swensen and Karras studies, which involved similar tasks, was due to punishing competing responses rather than reinforcing correct responses.

The relative effects of reward and punishment should be somewhat different for normals. The theory states that normals differ from schizophrenics in having higher average ceilings and lower average arousal. This implies that in normals: (*a*) there is more ceiling room for the beneficial effect of reinforcement, and (*b*) competing responses will not intrude as much, so punishing these responses should be less useful than in schizophrenics. Since reduction of competing responses is more beneficial to schizophrenics, punishing competing responses should be more effective than reward for decreasing the difference between schizophrenic and normal performance. However, the design of an experiment that tests this hypothesis must be such that all incorrect responses are punished. Otherwise punishment may only serve to increase the frequency of "safe" incorrect responses, and these incorrect responses will be exacerbated in schizophrenics.

In an experiment relevant to the hypothesis, Rita Atkinson (Atkinson & Robinson, 1961) either verbally rewarded each correct response or verbally punished each incorrect response, and compared the effectiveness of these conditions in schizophrenics and normals. The task was to learn lists of 15 pairs of fairly similar adjectives to a criterion of one errorless trial. The data were changes in this trials-to-criterion measure from a practice list to a list learned under the experimental conditions. With the pairs being similar adjectives, which should have fairly high associative strength initially, and with learning measured by trials to criterion, the data should reflect ceiling effects. Thus the theoretical implications discussed in the last paragraph should apply. As expected from the theory, the results showed that the benefit from suppressing competing responses, relative to rewarding correct responses, was significantly greater in schizophrenics than in normals. Schizophrenics reached the criterion faster when incorrect responses were punished than when correct responses were rewarded. The reverse was true for normals. For them, learning was faster when correct responses were rewarded.

C. Response Disorganization and Narrowed Observation

The major theme of the discussion has been that, compared to normals, many schizophrenics' response hierarchies are partially collapsed, at least under certain conditions. But this must in turn affect schizophrenics in other ways. They should react to their own behavior and be affected by others' reactions to their behavior. The quotes from schizophrenics at the beginning of this chapter indicated that acute schizophrenics recognized that their own responses were disorganized and were disturbed by it.

What can they do about it? If disorganization is due to the simultaneous occurrence of alternate response tendencies, this means that reducing the number of these response tendencies would make schizophrenics feel less disorganized.

We said earlier that competing response tendencies may come from multiple reactions to a single stimulus or from multiple stimuli. The multiple-stimulus source of competing responses can certainly be reduced. One early schizophrenic described his reaction to multiple stimulation as follows: "My concentration is very poor. I jump from one thing to another. If I am talking to someone they need only to cross their legs or scratch their head and I am distracted and forget what I am saying. I think I could concentrate better with my eyes shut" (McGhie & Chapman, 1961, p. 104). The reaction of another early schizophrenic was much the same. "I don't like moving fast. I feel there would be a breakup if I went too quick. I can only stand that a short time and then I have to stop. If I carried on I wouldn't be aware of things as they really are. I would just be aware of the sound and the noise and the movements. Everything would be a jumbled mass. I have found I can stop this happening by going completely still and motionless. When I do that, things are easier to take in" (McGhie & Chapman, 1961, p. 106). Both of these schizophrenics seem to have been beginning to learn that their response disorganization can be reduced by narrowing the range of stimuli they observe. Most of the descriptions of their own experience by early schizophrenics compiled by McGhie and Chapman (1961) reflect recognition of disorganization without thoughts about how to handle it. However, as Broen (1966) has suggested, it is likely that many long-term schizophrenics eventually learn to narrow their breadth of observation in an attempt to cope with their inability to handle multiple stimulation.

Breadth of observation should be near normal in acute schizophrenics and reduced in chronics because it would take time to learn to reduce breadth of observation habitually. Reduced observation would be most likely in those chronics who most need reduced response interference and who would be more comfortable with reduced vigilance. There is some evidence that suggests that paranoid schizophrenics may have less response disorganization than other schizophrenics (Lester, 1960), and we would also expect that paranoids would not be as comfortable with reduced vigilance. Therefore, we would expect reduced observation primarily in chronic non-paranoid schizophrenics. Of course, reduced observation will only reduce, not eliminate, interference from multiple stimulation, and it will not reduce the interference from alternate responses to central stimuli that our research discussion has emphasized.

Which stimuli are observed and which are not observed should not be a random matter. We have said that dominant responses tend to be the same for normals and schizophrenics. Observation habits should follow the same laws as other responses. Thus reduced observation should follow these lines: The chronic's initial observing response in new situations will usually be to observe those stimuli that also evoke the dominant observing responses in normals. But, having learned that observing many stimuli often leads to response interference, the chronic will not proceed much further. His observation of those stimuli that evoke the secondary and tertiary observing responses in normals will be reduced. Thus, stimuli that do not evoke the dominant observing responses—e.g., stimuli that have lesser intensity or are peripheral in a stimulus display—should be observed less by chronics than by normals. The same should hold true for internal stimulation. When multiple stimuli that are relevant to performing a task are held in memory, the chronic schizophrenic should tend to stop scanning his memory after the stronger, more recent events have been scanned. It should also occur in performance that requires scanning internal lists of meanings of a symbol. Chronics should tend to stop scanning after considering the first meanings that occur to them.

Observation that is abnormally narrowed to a subset of available information should contribute to deficit in chronic schizophrenia. This is the cost of learning to reduce one of the sources of response interference. Information is reduced but feelings of confusion are probably less.

There is quite a bit of recent evidence that suggests that chronic schizophrenics do have narrowed observation which follows the lines discussed in the foregoing. We will not review this evidence in detail because different aspects of this narrowing have been so well covered by others and our major purpose here is only to point to the possible relationship between this process and the response-interference process we have focused on. Venables (1964) has reviewed a fairly extensive body of literature indicating that chronic nonparanoid schizophrenics tend to narrow their observation to central stimuli, ignoring peripheral information, and that this narrowing tends not to occur in acute schizophrenics. Zahn, Rosenthal, and Shakow (1963) presented data showing that, in reaction-time tasks with irregular preparatory intervals (PIs), chronic schizophrenics are overinfluenced by the length of the most recent PI. The explanation given by Zahn et al. is quite similar to the lines of our discussion. "In the present experiment it might be speculated that the patients, being unable to handle the information provided by the series of varied PI's, simplify the task by [basing] their pattern of preparation disproportionately on the information provided by the immediately preceding trial" (p. 51). Chapman, Chapman, and Miller (1964) have given a stimulating discussion of what we see as another aspect of this same process—chronic schizophrenics' narrowed utilization

of different meanings of multimeaning words. Chapman et al. suggest that
"... schizophrenics do not weigh simultaneously the several different
aspects of meaning in order to answer appropriately the question at hand,
but instead answer by using a more limited number of aspects of the meaning.
Moreover, the aspects of meaning which schizophrenics use to excess appear
to be those which are prominent for normal persons" (p. 51). Chapman et al.
(1964) then discussed a number of experiments comparing the performance
of normals and chronic schizophrenics that supported this hypothesis.

Thus, chronic schizophrenics do tend to narrow their observation. This
is a specific method of meeting the environment that should reduce response
interference, and it has been found in chronics but does not seem to
characterize early schizophrenics. Thus, it does seem likely that narrowed
observation is learned over time as a method of reducing the effects of the
basic disturbance, response interference. Relevant longitudinal studies are
certainly needed.

IV. Summary

All of us, normals as well as schizophrenics, live in a world where
the richness and variety of stimulation, while often delightful, can make
it difficult to focus on any single line of thought or action. Yet efficient
behavior requires this focusing, and in spite of the presence of competing
response tendencies, normals are usually efficient. Their response tendencies
are arranged hierarchically, with appropriate responses clearly dominant,
and competing responses rarely intrude.

In contrast, schizophrenic behavior seems to be characterized by
response interference—disorganized fluctuations among appropriate and
competing responses. Thus, in order to understand schizophrenia, it is
important to learn about the process underlying response interference.

The theory presented here specifies the nature of response interference,
the variables that determine response interference, and how and when
normals and schizophrenics should differ in response interference.

According to the theory, the type of response interference that is
important in schizophrenia results from a partial collapse of response
hierarchies. Dominant and competing responses have the same hierarchical
order as in normals, but the strengths of the different response tendencies
are closer together. The result is that response probabilities are closer
together in schizophrenics, and the remote associates, the interfering attention responses, and other error tendencies that occasionally occur in
normals are exacerbated in schizophrenics. The research we have discussed
indicates that this is the nature of response interference in schizophrenia.

In the theory, response hierarchies collapse when the strength of
dominant responses is restricted by lower average response-strength ceiling

in schizophrenics. The collapse will be exacerbated by increased arousal which, with dominant responses at ceiling, acts only to multiply the strengths of competing responses. This theory implies that the conditions that favor a collapse of response hierarchies due to the ceiling effect are high strength dominant and competing responses and increased arousal. As we have seen, recent experiments suggest that these are the conditions under which competing responses intrude more and schizophrenic deficit is increased.

Although response interference may be a fundamental characteristic of schizophrenia, all schizophrenic behavior would not be expected to reflect the basic aspects of this process. The experiencing of pervasive response interference must influence a person's attitudes about himself, lower his expectancies of success in complex situations and willingness to take part in them, and increase his feeling of being at the mercy of interfering stimulation, unable to control his own thoughts and actions.

There should also be attempts to cope with response interference that become habitual over time. One way that competing responses can be reduced is by narrowing breadth of observation. If, when meeting a complex situation, a person scans fewer stimuli, then the number of competing responses should be reduced. There is considerable recent evidence that many chronic schizophrenics do habitually reduce their breadth of observation. This means that information is lost, and incomplete or less important aspects of situations may be overemphasized. But the offsetting benefit should be some reduction in the schizophrenic's feeling of being at the mercy of a distracting, disorganizing, confusing environment.

References

Arieti, S. *Interpretation of schizophrenia*. New York: Brunner, 1955.

Atkinson, Rita L., & Robinson, Nancy M. Paired-associate learning by schizophrenic and normal subjects under conditions of personal and impersonal reward and punishment. *J. abnorm. soc. Psychol.*, 1961, **62**, 322–326.

Berlyne, D. E., Borsa, Donna M., Hamacher, Jane H., & Koenig, Isolde D. V. Paired-associate learning and the timing of arousal. *J. exp. Psychol.*, 1966, **72**, 1–6.

Blaufarb, H. A demonstration of verbal abstracting ability in chronic schizophrenics under enriched stimulus and instructional conditions. *J. consult. Psychol.*, 1962, **26**, 471–475.

Bleuler, E. *Dementia praecox or the group of schizophrenias*. New York: International Universities Press, 1950.

Broen, W. E., Jr. Response disorganization and breadth of observation in schizophrenia. *Psychol. Rev.,* 1966, **73**, 579–585.

Broen, W. E., Jr., & Storms, L. H. A reaction potential ceiling and response decrements in complex situations. *Psychol. Rev.*, 1961, **68**, 405–415.

Broen, W. E., Jr., & Storms, L. H. The differential effect of induced muscular tension (drive) on discrimination in schizophrenics and normals. *J. abnorm. soc. Psychol.*, 1964, **68**, 349–353.

Broen, W. E., Jr., & Storms, L. H. Lawful disorganization: The process underlying a schizophrenic syndrome. *Psychol. Rev.*, 1966, **73**, 265–279.

Broen, W. E., Jr., Storms, L. H., & Schenck, H. U., Jr. Inappropriate behavior as a function of the energizing effect of drive. *J. Pers.*, 1961, **29**, 489–498.

Broen, W. E., Jr., Storms, L. H., & Goldberg, D. H. Decreased discrimination as a function of increased drive. *J. abnorm. soc. Psychol.*, 1963, **67**, 266–273.

Cameron, N. Reasoning, regression and communication in schizophrenics. *Psychol. Monogr.*, 1938, **50**, No. 1 (Whole No. 221).

Cavanaugh, D. K., Cohen, W., & Lang, P. J. The effect of "social censure" and "social approval" on the psychomotor performance of schizophrenics. *J. abnorm. soc. Psychol.*, 1960, **60**, 213–218.

Chapman, L. J. Distractibility in the conceptual performance of schizophrenia. *J. abnorm. soc. Psychol.*, 1956, **53**, 286–291. (a)

Chapman, L. J. The role of type of distracter in the "concrete" conceptual performance of schizophrenics. *J. Pers.*, 1956, **25**, 130–141. (b)

Chapman, L. J. Intrusion of associative responses into schizophrenic conceptual performance. *J. abnorm. soc. Psychol.*, 1958, **56**, 374–379.

Chapman, L. J. A reinterpretation of some pathological disturbances in conceptual breadth. *J. abnorm. soc. Psychol.*, 1961, **62**, 514–519.

Chapman, L. J., & Taylor, Janet A. Breadth of deviant concepts used by schizophrenics. *J. abnorm. soc. Psychol.*, 1957, **54**, 118–123.

Chapman, L. J., Chapman, Jean P., & Miller, G. A. A theory of verbal behavior in schizophrenia. In B. A. Maher (Ed.), *Progress in experimental personality research.* Vol. 1. New York: Academic Press, 1964. Pp. 49–77.

Cohen, B. H., Bousfield, W. A., & Whitmarsh, G. A. *Cultural norms for verbal items in 43 categories.* Univer. of Connecticut Stud. Mediation verbal Behav., Tech. Rep. No. 22, 1957.

Dokecki, P. R., Polidoro, L. G., & Cromwell, R. L. Commonality and stability of word association responses in good and poor premorbid schizophrenics. *J. abnorm. Psychol.*, 1965, **70**, 312–316.

Dunn, W. L. Visual discrimination of schizophrenic subjects as a function of stimulus meaning. *J. Pers.*, 1954, **23**, 48–64.

Estes, W. K. Individual behavior in uncertain situations: An interpretation in terms of statistical association theory. In R. M. Thrall, C. H. Coombs, & R. L. Davis (Eds.), *Decision processes.* New York: Wiley, 1954. Pp. 127–138.

Farina, A., Garmezy N., & Barry, H. Relationship of marital status to incidence and prognosis of schizophrenia. *J. abnorm. soc. Psychol.*, 1963, **67**, 624–630.

Fey, Elizabeth T. The performance of young schizophrenics and young normals on the Wisconsin Card Sorting Test. *J. consult. Psychol.*, 1951, **15**, 311–319.

Gottesman, L. E. Forced-choice word associations in schizophrenia. *J. abnorm. soc. Psychol.*, 1964, **69**, 673–675.

Gottesman, L. E., & Chapman, L. J. Syllogistic reasoning errors in schizophrenia. *J. consult. Psychol.*, 1960, **24**, 250–255.

Hamlin, R. M., Haywood, H. C., & Folsom, Angela. Effect of enriched input on schizophrenic abstraction. *J. abnorm. soc. Psychol.*, 1965, **70**, 390–394.

Hull, C. L. *A behavior system.* New Haven: Yale Univer. Press, 1952.

Karras, A. The effects of reinforcement and arousal on the psychomotor performance of chronic schizophrenics. *J. abnorm. soc. Psychol.*, 1962, **65**, 104–111.

Kausler, D. H., Lair, C. V., & Matsumoto, R. Interference transfer paradigms and the performance of schizophrenics and controls. *J. abnorm. soc. Psychol.*, 1964, **69**, 584–587.

Lang, P. J., & Buss, A. H. Psychological deficit in schizophrenia: II. Interference and activation. *J. abnorm. Psychol.*, 1965, **70**, 77–106.

Lang, P. J., & Luoto, K. Mediation and associative facilitation in neurotic, psychotic, and normal subjects. *J. abnorm. soc. Psychol.*, 1962, **64**, 113–120.

Lester, J. R. Production of associative sequences in schizophrenia and chronic brain syndrome. *J. abnorm. soc. Psychol.*, 1960, **60**, 225–233.

Levin, I. P. Induced muscle tension and response shift in paired-associate learning. Unpublished doctoral dissertation, Univer. of Calif., Los Angeles, 1965.

Lothrop, W. W. A critical review of research on the conceptual thinking of schizophrenics. *J. nerv. ment. Dis.*, 1961, **132**, 118–126.

Lovaas, O. I. Supplementary report: The relationship of induced muscular tension to manifest anxiety in learning. *J. exp. Psychol.*, 1960, **59**, 205–206.

McGhie, A., & Chapman, J. S. Disorders of attention and perception in early schizophrenia. *Brit. J. med. Psychol.*, 1961, **34**, 103–116.

Pascal, G. R., & Swensen, C. Learning in mentally ill patients under conditions of unusual motivation. *J. Pers.*, 1952, **21**, 240–249.

Phillips, L. Case history data and prognosis in schizophrenia. *J. nerv. ment. Dis.*, 1953, **117**, 515–525.

Pinneo, L. R. The effects of increased muscle tension during tracking on level of activation and performance. *J. exp. Psychol.*, 1961, **62**, 523–531.

Ramond, C. K. Anxiety and task as determiners of verbal performance. *J. exp. Psychol.*, 1953, **46**, 120–124.

Sommer, R., Dewar, R., & Osmond, H. Is there a schizophrenic language? *Arch. gen. Psychiat.*, 1960, **3**, 665–673.

Spence, K. W. *Behavior theory and conditioning.* New Haven: Yale Univer. Press, 1956.

Spence, K. W., Farber, I. E., & McFann, H. H. The relation of anxiety (drive) level to performance in competitional and non-competitional paired associate learning. *J. exp. Psychol.*, 1956, **52**, 296–305. (a)

Spence, K. W., Taylor, Janet, & Ketchel, Rhoda. Anxiety (drive) level and degree of competition in paired-associate learning. *J. exp. Psychol.*, 1956, **52**, 306–310. (b)

Storms, L. H., & Broen, W. E., Jr. Verbal associative stability and appropriateness in schizophrenics, neurotics, and normals as a function of time pressure. *Amer. Psychologist*, 1964, **19**, 460. (Abstract)

Venables, P. H. Input dysfunction in schizophrenia. In B. A. Maher (Ed.), *Progress in experimental personality research.* Vol. 1. New York: Academic Press, 1964. Pp 1–47.

Williams, E. B. Deductive reasoning in schizophrenia. *J. abnorm. soc. Psychol.*, 1964, **69**, 47–61.

Zahn, T. P., Rosenthal, D., & Shakow, D. Effects of irregular preparatory intervals on reaction time in schizophrenia. *J. abnorm. soc. Psychol.*, 1963, **67**, 44–52.

Author Index

SUBJECT INDEX

A

Achievement
  intellectual, 241
  need for, 251
Aggression, 184
Alienation, 231
*Alpert-Haber Facilitating-Debilitating
  Test Anxiety Questionnaire*, 242
Anhedonia, 79
Anomie, 231
Anxiety
  approach-avoidance conflict, 4–7
  arousal, 32–40
  avoidance conditioning, 52–54
  defenses, 50–54
  developmental aspects, 70–76
  fear, differentiated from, 32–40
    inhibition of, 7–19
    ratings, 19–22
  generalization, 40–50
  GSR, 6–7, 12–16
  Manifest Anxiety Scale (MAS), 244
  perceptual defense, 8–9
  personality types, 29–31
  physiological measures, 22–30
  power, and, 242–244
  primary *vs.* "signal," 35–36
  psychopathology, 76–82
  psychotherapy, 82–85
  response interference, 273–274
  sport parachuting, 3–32
  TAT, 9–10
  test, 242
  theory, 1–89
Approach-avoidance conflict, *see* Conflict
Arousal
  anhedonia, 79
  anxiety, 32–40
  basis of motivation, 34–38
  combat, 34, 35, 39, 42–43, 52
  directed *vs.* undirected, 38–40
  EEG, 37
  fear, differentiated from, 32–40
  GSR, 63–65
  "law of excitatory modulation," 47, 66–
    67
  panic, 35

Pavlovian concepts, 36, 43–47
  physiological indices, 37–38
  schizophrenia, 280–283, 290–296
  surprise, 62–63
Authoritarianism, 242
Autistic children, treatment of, 180–181
Autonomy, 230–242

B

Barron-Welsh Art Judgment Test, 242
Behavior
  punished in model, 209–213
  self-defeating, 166–169
  sexual, 185
  social, children, 179–228

C

California F Scale, 242
Children, perception of power, 252
  social behavior, 179–228
Civil rights, participation, 246
Coercive power, 255
Cognitive complexity, 241–242, 259
College students, I-E Test norms, 240
Combat, 34, 35, 39, 42–43, 52
Competence, motive, 230
Concept formation, schizophrenia, 285–
  286, 298
Conditioning, avoidance, 52–54
Conflict
  approach-avoidance, 4–7, 102–103
  competing response hypothesis, 98–99
  definition, 91
  delay of gratification, 129–130
  description, 91–92
  discrimination, 97
  dissonance, 94–95
  double approach-avoidance, 102–103
  dynamogenic hypothesis, 99–102
  experimental neurosis, 93–94, 217
  exposure to, 91–125, 147–150
  generalization of, 96–105
    patient populations, 104–105
    personally relevant material, 105–109
  homosexuality, 118–119
  induction, methods, 97–98
  intensity, 119–121